AUTHORSHIP IN FILM ADAPTATION

AUTHORSHIP IN FILM ADAPTATION

////////////////////////////////////

Edited and with an Introduction by Jack Boozer

University of Texas Press   Austin

Copyright © 2008 by the University of Texas Press
All rights reserved
Printed in the United States of America
First edition, 2008

Requests for permission to reproduce material from this work should be sent to:
   Permissions
   University of Texas Press
   P.O. Box 7819
   Austin, TX 78713-7819
   www.utexas.edu/utpress/about/bpermission.html

♾ The paper used in this book meets the minimum requirements of ANSI/NISO Z39.48-1992 (R1997) (Permanence of Paper).

LIBRARY OF CONGRESS CATALOGING-IN-PUBLICATION DATA

Authorship in film adaptation / edited by Jack Boozer.
   p.   cm.
   Includes bibliographical references and index.
   ISBN 978-0-292-70285-1 (cloth : alk. paper) — ISBN 978-0-292-71853-1 (pbk. : alk. paper)
   1. Film adaptations.   2. Motion picture authorship.   I. Boozer, Jack, 1944–
   PN1997.85.A92   2008
   808.2′3—dc22
                                          2007049228

This book is dedicated to the memory of my mother, Ruth, who died October 24, 2006, at the age of eighty-nine. She gave me a love for literature and the arts, and confidence in the search for that particular kind of truth.

CONTENTS
///////////

Acknowledgments ix

Introduction: The Screenplay and Authorship in Adaptation 1
JACK BOOZER

PART I
HOLLYWOOD'S "ACTIVIST" PRODUCERS AND MAJOR AUTEURS DRIVE THE SCRIPT 31

1   *Mildred Pierce:* A Troublesome Property to Script 35
    ALBERT J. LAVALLEY

2   Hitchcock and His Writers: Authorship and Authority in Adaptation 63
    THOMAS LEITCH

3   From *Traumnovelle* (1927) to Script to Screen—*Eyes Wide Shut* (1999) 85
    JACK BOOZER

PART II
SCREENPLAY ADAPTED AND DIRECTED BY 107

4   Private Knowledge, Public Space: Investigation and Navigation in *Devil in a Blue Dress* 111
    MARK L. BERRETTINI

5   "Strange and New...": Subjectivity and the Ineffable in *The Sweet Hereafter* 131
    ERNESTO R. ACEVEDO-MUÑOZ

PART III
WRITER AND DIRECTOR COLLABORATIONS: ADDRESSING GENRE, HISTORY, AND REMAKES 157

6 *Adaptation* as Adaptation: From Susan Orlean's *The Orchid Thief* to Charlie (and "Donald") Kaufman's Screenplay to Spike Jonze's Film   161
FRANK P. TOMASULO

7 From Obtrusive Narration to Crosscutting: Adapting the Doubleness of John Fowles's *The French Lieutenant's Woman*   179
R. BARTON PALMER

8 The Three Faces of *Lolita*, or How I Learned to Stop Worrying and Love the Adaptation   203
REBECCA BELL-METEREAU

9 *Traffic/Traffik*: Race, Globalization, and Family in Soderbergh's Remake   229
MARK GALLAGHER

PART IV
VARIATIONS IN SCREENWRITER AND DIRECTOR COLLABORATIONS   253

10 Adapting Nick Hornby's *High Fidelity*: Process and Sexual Politics   257
CYNTHIA LUCIA

11 Adaptable Bridget: Generic Intertextuality and Postfeminism in *Bridget Jones's Diary*   281
SHELLEY COBB

12 "Who's Your Favorite Indian?" The Politics of Representation in Sherman Alexie's Short Stories and Screenplay   305
ELAINE ROTH

Notes on Contributors   325

Name and Title Index   329

ACKNOWLEDGMENTS

//

I want to recognize in particular my colleagues whose work appears in these pages. Their devotion to the task and sustained goodwill have made the completion of this book a challenging and pleasurable campaign. This also applies to editor Jim Burr and the fine staff at the University of Texas Press, and to scholars Arthur M. Eckstein, Martha Nochimson, and Kelly Hankin. I was further aided by two excellent graduate assistants, Harper Cossar, who has just completed his doctoral degree in film in our Moving Image Studies program at Georgia State University and Kristopher Cannon.

The publisher and I would also like to gratefully acknowledge the permission granted to reproduce the following copyrighted material in this book:

Chapter 1: Albert J. LaValley, "A Troublesome Property to Script." Introduction to *Mildred Pierce* in the Wisconsin/Warner Brothers Screenplay Series. Copyright © 1980. Reprinted by permission of The University of Wisconsin Press. (This chapter does not include the final three sections of the original article.)

Chapter 4: "Private Knowledge, Public Space: Investigation and Navigation in *Devil in a Blue Dress*," by Mark Berrettini, from *Cinema Journal* 39:1, pp. 74–89. Copyright © 1999 by the University of Texas Press. All rights reserved.

AUTHORSHIP IN FILM ADAPTATION
/////////////////////////////////

INTRODUCTION: THE SCREENPLAY AND AUTHORSHIP IN ADAPTATION

////////////////////////////////////

Jack Boozer

THIS COLLECTION OF ESSAYS ORIGINATED IN THE OBSERVATION that the study of literature-to-film adaptation has generally overlooked the actual process through which a source text is transformed into a motion picture. This process includes in particular the central role of the screenplay. The increasing attention to intertextual and intermedial influences in adaptation over the last two decades provides an opportunity to highlight the most consistent and crucial example of intertextuality at work, namely, the writing of the transmedial screenplay. Literature-to-film adaptation involves the textual transposition of a single-track medium of published writing into a document that embraces the scenic structure and dramatic codes of the multitrack medium of film. The composition of the screenplay illuminates the evolution of ideas that will determine the film production's relationship to its source text. In this introduction I describe the multiple roles and significance of the adapted screenplay and its history, as well as its centrality to the collaborative authorship that is at the heart of film adaptation. Focusing on the screenplay in adaptation necessarily foregrounds issues of authorship in a theoretical environment that has been weighted toward semiotics, poststructuralism, and broadly conceived influences of cultural intertextuality. The fragile status of authorship in the shifting landscape of adaptation theory is specifically addressed in the final section of this introduction.

The two previously published essays and ten original ones in this collection each emphasize some aspect of the process of film adaptation as it can be traced from the source text and adapted screenplay through the film's production, exhibition, and reception. The four parts of the book are organized around the three dominant arrangements for adaptive screenwriters in English-language cinema:

1. The screenwriter in service to an activist producer or established auteur;
2. The screenwriter and director as one and the same individual; or
3. The screenwriter and director in a variety of other collaborative relationships.

Although not all the chapters place major emphasis on the screenplay in adaptation, all do consider some aspect of the adaptive process as such. The case studies chosen for discussion also represent both cultural diversity and diversity in critical approaches to adaptation. A focus on authorship, however, remains a touchstone throughout the collection.

Historically, the adapted screenplay has been viewed only as an interim step in the binary focus on the source literature (usually the novel) and on the film. The script has been deemed merely a skeletal blueprint for the adapted film and thus unworthy of serious consideration in its own right. There are several reasons for this binary critical emphasis, beginning with the essential point that a work of fiction or drama typically has a single author and a readily consumable existence in published form, just as an adapted film can be recognized as a finished entity on screen. The adapted screenplay, however, has had no comparable existence as a finished artifact for public consumption (with the exception of published transcripts). Interest in the adapted screenplay mainly follows from an initial critical or public interest in the adapted film. But whereas the audience of an adapted film might rush to purchase copies of the source text (underscoring an adapted film's direct value to publishers), a much smaller readership will seek the film transcript, and only a tiny group will seek a late screenplay draft or shooting script, assuming such is even available. Other reasons for disregarding the screenplay in adaptation study include the multiple revisions a script undergoes during development (at times by different hands), Hollywood's traditional low regard for the screenwriter generally, and a resistance to any sort of transposition of esteemed canonic literature (the "hallowed word") to another medium, especially one that has been associated with mass entertainment.

In respect to this last issue, the adaptation of high-profile best-sellers to the screen can prove as controversial as the adaptation of literary classics. In the recent adaptation of Dan Brown's best-selling mystery thriller, *The Da Vinci Code*, the film version was criticized for softening the book's main thematic thrust, namely, that since antiquity, conservatives within the Catholic Church have suppressed the role of women, including the role of Mary Magdalene, with whom Jesus may have sired children to produce a still extant lineage. Did film director Ron Howard (who at an early point worked with other producers and the screenwriter) already commit to deemphasizing that theme to stem possible boycotts and thus increase ticket sales? Often overlooked but also notable in this regard is that modern writers and directors tied to studio support are frequently asked to work with studio promotional departments to consider a film's marketing in relation to its final story construction.[1] The who and why surrounding the process of adaptation at the screenwriting stage, then, can begin to answer these kinds of preproduction questions and issues. Meanwhile, the closed fixation only on literary source and finished film both in journalistic reviews and scholarly study has often shown an indifference to the evolving intentions of producers, writers, and directors and their shifting levels of input and authority.

In scholarly and trade publications, several articles and a few chapters in collections over the years have given some attention to specific cases of adapted screenplays (see especially *Literature/Film Quarterly*, in publication since 1973), although the script per se has received little extended treatment as the key step in the process of adaptation. Excluding the numerous how-to texts on screenwriting and marketing and at least two recent manuals on writing adaptations, only a handful of publications on the subject of screenwriting and screenwriters have mentioned adaptation even casually.[2] Adaptation study as a whole has, however, received considerable academic focus, with no fewer than eleven books on the subject appearing since 1996,[3] and three more from Robert Stam in 2005 alone.[4] Kamilla Elliott, in her introduction to the collection *Rethinking the Novel/Film Debate* (2003), notes that "recent critics rightly protest novel and film studies' neglect of ... screenplays" (6). Overall, then, the growing interest in the theory and critical assessment of adaptation supports the need for a closer look at the screenplay/screenwriter and writer-director collaboration in the genesis of adaptation.

For the moviegoing public in general, the screenplay has largely remained no more visible than a category on film credits or on film awards lists. In awards ceremonies that include recognition of the screenplay, the scriptwriter stands in for a document that few ever see or read. Those who have tracked down the screenplay have usually had to locate specialty libraries, vendors, or Internet sources, only then to have to rely either on an uncertain script draft dating or on a film's verbatim transcript, which is the version typically published when a feature screenplay is offered as a book. Such transcripts imitate the finished film in standard or nonstandard script form on the page and hence reveal little of the process of adaptation. To uncover that process requires comparing the completed film with the last script draft prior to shooting. Also helpful in understanding the process of adaptation are interviews with or commentaries from the principal figures responsible for a film—producers, writers, directors, and actors. Although such commentaries are often largely anecdotal, their increasing availability through publications, the Internet, DVD supplementary material, and television commentary has made investigating the adaptation process and the centerpiece screenplay more than ever viable.

It is the screenplay, not the source text, that is the most direct foundation and fulcrum for any adapted film. As the film's narrative springboard, it guides the screen choices for story structure, characterization, motifs, themes, and genre. It indicates what will or will not be used from the source, including what is to be altered or invented, and in what settings and tonal register. Because the modern adapted screenplay at the point of input from the director includes so many key decisions relative to the source, it remains the essential conceptual and creative bible for the film's construction. The writing births the overriding narrative that all the filmmaking participants serve during production. Unlike the original source text, which can be read at the reader's pace, the screenplay is the directive for the film performance in a designated time frame. Whatever alterations are made during shooting and editing, the adapted screenplay as it exists just before production starts is the most prescriptive guide to the film in the mind's eye of writer and director.

An adapted screenplay that is recognizable for its quality increases the likelihood that a successful film might be made. This belief is associated with the Hollywood truism that you can make a bad film from a good script but you can't make a good film from a bad script. A director may have the benefit of the screenplay *and* the source text for consideration in production, but script quality, irrespective of the quality of the source text, remains essential for production. In adaptive film projects, the lack of a relatively complete screenplay when production begins can cause great anxiety on the set and hurt the quality of the finished product.[5] Since modern directors work out the transmediation of their source text in the screenplay (usually in conjunction with the adaptive scriptwriter), their interpretation of the literary property and its presentation is already largely decided on. Virtually all of Alfred Hitchcock's films were rather loose adaptations, but he was known for adhering closely during shooting to his finished scripts. Other auteur directors, such as John Ford and Robert Altman, have a reputation for improvising even adapted scripts on the set, although the script remains the jumping-off point for innovation, thus necessitating script rewrites after the fact to accommodate changes made along the way.[6]

The basic format of narrative film scripts conveys their practical specificity. Their goal is to portray drama through concrete descriptive passages and character dialogue within individual scenes, which are designated as either interior or exterior locations. Scenes form the building blocks of sequences and story or character arcs that make up the larger sections or "acts" of the narrative. Because Hollywood scripts are usually written to fit within exhibitors' preferred two-hour maximum running time (120 script pages), as well as to appeal to mass audiences, efficiency and clarity in story and characterization have been standard practice. The adapted screenplay usually pares down dialogue and avoids metaphorical style in description. All of this is intended to set a mood and tone, as well as tell a story in the eventual service of an audiovisual design. The expressive language of fiction in paragraph and chapter form describes circumstances, attitudes, and feelings that readers are left to invoke ("imagine") directly for themselves, while the screenplay is structured to work in the service of a narrative that is read in the moving scenic terms of imaging for the camera. The screenplay must organize and telegraph audiovisual codes to directors, actors, and technicians for the sake of production. The script format thus appears intrusive to a reader, and its written style is less intimate and rich than fiction. It points to the potential specificity and power of fully realized, framed, and mobile iconic imagery ready for editing. The page layout and story elements of the adapted script demonstrate its media-transformational function for the performance of film narrative.

Unlike the solitary, imaginative origin of most fiction (however informed by a cultural milieu), the composition of an adapted screenplay takes place not only under the shadow of myriad narrative expectations but in a complex environment of business, industrial, and artistic considerations. Some version of a screenplay must answer in preproduction to a producer and director. It is usually required by a producer not only to generate specific project funding but also to initiate the attachment to the production of other above-the-line personnel, including the director, director of photography, and stars. Screenplays determine specific production budgets and can also leverage immediate capital from speculative investors, from upfront theatrical distribution deals, and from potential DVD sales for a film, including possible ancillary product contracts. The director, meanwhile, mandates the script required for performance and editing needs. This script presumes its eventual technical and aesthetic performance in an audiovisual space of specific time, pacing, and place. As the central narrative cog in all three stages of film production, the screenplay determines the contributions of the hundreds of individuals who typically work on any given project.[7]

Given its many functions, then, there tend to be at least two main versions of a script. In the preproduction stage, there is first the one that helps bring together budget resources and key personnel, and then the one that is coordinated by the director for production. In modern film development, William Goldman observes,

> There are two entirely different versions of any screenplay. There is stuff that is written before the film is a go project, and there is what's written once the movie is actually going to be shot. And sometimes they have very little to do with each other. The purpose of the earlier version is to make it happen. The purpose of the latter version or versions is to be as supportive to your director as you can.[8]

Goldman's last sentence also points up the service role that the Hollywood screenwriter plays in relation to the producer and director. Once the director approves the final draft, that screenplay is arranged into a shooting script for production, and notations on this script during shooting become the continuity script.[9]

In one case, Stanley Kubrick, who wanted to work through his own extended visual conception for the adaptation of Arthur Clarke's *The Sentinel*, first composed a 40,000-word descriptive prose piece with Clarke in preparation for their writing the initial screenplay for what became *2001*.[10] Kubrick sought to fully develop the visual details that would be indicative of an atmosphere and mood for his largely style-driven narrative. This circumstance also highlights how some later auteurs, who often locate and purchase their own source material, already have some connection to the source material and some intention in relation to it, which they continue to develop throughout the scriptwriting stage. Directors use the screenwriting stage of development in collaboration with the writer to invent and refine their story and image conceptions.[11] The scripting process may even suggest a whole new unity of narrative emphasis and meaning, or at least may encourage a director to see further possibilities for cinematic forms of storytelling. How a critical analyst interprets the information provided by a late script draft can therefore make all the difference not only in assigning specific authorship to the quantity and degree of intended source alterations but also to recognizing how the initial screenplay conception may have been altered by performative and technical factors in the production and postproduction stages. A critic's familiarity with a late script can enhance awareness of where the subsequent production soared beyond its original scripted intent, became waylaid, or simply changed direction.

The scholarly study of the screenplay in Hollywood studio cinema has already helped shed light on some well-known examples of scriptwriting confusion. For instance, a famous controversy has surrounded what transpired in the writing of the original script for *Citizen Kane*. Although not technically an adaptation, since the life of William Randolph Hearst had not been published in a biography used directly in the writing of the screenplay, the film nevertheless played fast and loose with the life story of a living person (and the producers had to negotiate screenplay changes because of it, owing to the threat of a lawsuit). Long a matter of contention among film critics over screenplay authorship between Herman Mankiewicz and Orson Welles, the puzzle seems largely now to be laid to rest. As Tom Stempel writes in *Framework*:

> While Mankiewicz had the energy and the early enthusiasm to whip out a lengthy first draft (the two written on his own at 250 and then at 325 pages that provide the basic structure for the eventual film), he did not necessarily have the dedication to do the fine-tuning any script required. Welles, on the other hand, did not necessarily have the patience to do all the creative work required on a first draft, but was brilliant as an editor/rewrite man. As a screenwriting collaboration, they were well matched.[12]

Another factor that is obvious in this historic if nonsimultaneous "collaboration" is the assumption during the writing by both Mankiewicz and Welles that Orson would play the main role. It may be assumed that Welles's script editing in particular was oriented not only to story conflation but to the fine-tuning of the dialogue that he and his colleagues among the Mercury Theatre cast would deliver.

Specific challenges for adaptive writers and filmmakers usually include ways to visualize the fiction narrator's exposition, metaphors, and interior character observations and their thought processes, all of which help to convey story tone as well as character psychology. The determination of filmic equivalents for some or all of these fictional devices is part of the craft and art of the adaptation process. Ruth Prawer Jhabvala, the constant screenwriter on the Ismael Merchant and James Ivory producer-director team, wrote several publicly successful and close adaptations of heritage literature (particularly by Henry James and E. M. Forster). She has observed that she sometimes changes and also typically cuts even the dialogue in novels down to about one-fourth, noting that "dialogue in a novel is always full of artifice" and is therefore often unwieldy in the mouths of actors on the screen.[13] The exchange or alteration of certain literary for filmic devices in adaptation is thus a given, and the screenwriter and director must make choices in this regard either to enhance cinematic drama or to address unforeseen production issues.

These issues frequently involve casting and performance, which can change a screenplay in all three stages of production. Casting actors, of course, is not determined by the screenwriter unless the writer also happens to have a producer or director role in the film.[14] American cinema offers numerous examples of adapted scripts that have been written and produced with certain performers in mind. It is also true that best-sellers have been written with a movie version and a film star in mind, as in the case of John Grisham's novel *The Pelican Brief*. The author projected Julia Roberts for the lead role in the inevitable film adaptation, and the screen rights were also purchased before the novel was actually written. Furthermore, of course, the attachment of "bankable" stars to a production after the adapted script is completed can push certain roles in certain directions on the set to the point that character and story directions are significantly changed.

Adaptations also typically have more limited options in the casting of lead characters because of the expectations of audiences relative to the given character profiles in the source text. Close matching can bring success, as attested to by the definitive performances of leads Anthony Hopkins and Jodie Foster in *The Silence of the Lambs* (1991, Jonathan Demme), who mirror the physiognomy of their characters and convincingly project their traits just as described in the novel. Certain actors may have the look of a fictional character but lack the affect, while others may not look the part detailed in the source but may nevertheless succeed in capturing the inner life of the character in the film role. An example of the latter is the full-figured version of Renee Zellweger as Ruby in *Cold Mountain* (2003, Anthony Minghella), who was critically praised for her energetic portrayal in this supporting role. The character Ruby, however, is described in Charles Frazier's novel as "broad-nosed," "frail chested," and "corded through the neck and arms." Another example is that of Denzel Washington, whom writer-director Carl Franklin brought in for the role of detective Easy Rawlins in his adaptation of *Devil in a Blue Dress* (1995). The lead actor felt that his characterization of Rawlins should be more active and skilled than in the novel or in Franklin's initial screenplay, and the director agreed and made adjustments to script and film.[15] Whether an actor's performance is attuned to the adapted script or the script is adjusted to the actor depends finally on the director's intent in relation to the source text.

Adaptive screenplays and films face the inevitable question of their specific orientation to their source, and there is no simple answer about what is appropriate that could possibly satisfy all readers and audiences. In critical approaches, the direct matching of the content of a literary source with its film version may serve useful descriptive goals concerning transmediation, but it has also long encouraged an evaluative form of "fidelity criticism" that has necessarily privileged the original literary work, particularly literary classics, to the detriment of the cinematic "derivation." The versatility of the visual and sound palette available to screenwriters and filmmakers, however, can provide a wealth of alternative ways to convey the intricacies of the source text, and therefore disobliges a simplistic comparative cataloging across the two media. In this line of thought, critical writing on film adaptation has frequently suggested that the screenplay and film should mainly seek to capture "the essence" of the source text through audiovisual "equivalents." Because exact iconic images of fiction in film are impossible (owing to the variations of each fiction reader's particular imagination) and in any case are likely to fail dramatically (owing to film's need to establish its own "live" scenic rhythms as opposed to literary ones), it is essential to locate the goal that any particular adaptation sets for itself. To this end, the screenplay can reveal the transformational decisions that account for a change in medium, as well as the initial story and dialogue alterations that point to the conceptual goal of the film adaptation.

The issue of authorial intent, therefore, must be a part of any discussion of fidelity in adaptation. One way that critics and theorists of adaptation have repeatedly addressed this issue of allegiance has been to assign labels to what is usually presented as three levels of a film's distance from its source. Most of these labels, which have been used over the years,[16] offer some variation on the following terminology:

1. A literal or close reading (such as the Ishmael Merchant-James Ivory adaptation of *Howard's End*, with Ruth Prawer Jhabvala as writer);
2. A general correspondence (such as Anthony Minghella's highly sensitive screenwriter-director "reading" of Michael Ondaatje's poetic and lengthy novel *The English Patient*); or
3. A distant referencing (as in the Coen brothers' tacit borrowing from Homer's *The Odyssey* for *O Brother, Where Art Thou?*).

Although such descriptive categories can be used to help readers and viewers appreciate the film adaptation's intention and its right to go its own way, any preoccupation with fidelity to the literary original and its presumed superiority also tends to constrain the discussion of each film's immersion in its own particular cultural and historical moment. Part of the comedic point in the Coen brothers' Depression-era comedy (released in 2000) is that mundane and narrow-minded facts of life surrounding antiheroes in the twentieth century can unsettle the gravity of ancient heroic epics such as *The Odyssey*. In contrast, serious costume dramas, including *Howard's End* and *The English Patient*, can succeed in speaking to the present through the sheer realistic credibility of the characters and issues represented in their particular historical circumstances.[17]

All three recent adaptations—*Howard's End*, *The English Patient*, and *O Brother*—were critically and commercially successful films despite differing degrees of closeness to and different relationships with their literary source. Interestingly, all three also show an extremely tight association between writer and director in each project's conception (especially in the case of Minghella, who assumed both roles). Each writer was closely allied with each director's intention and in addition had a thorough grounding in film tradition. The Coen brothers took their title, historical moment, and tone for their film from writer-director Preston Sturges's *Sullivan's Travels* (1942), in which the line "O brother, where art thou?" occurs. Certainly, the quality and success of many adapted films have been rooted in a strong writer-director team approach, such as that between Martin Ritt and Irving Ravetch/Harriett Frank, Jr., or Alfred Hitchcock and John Michael Hayes. The recognition of the potential power of cinema is also observable among those who have a particularly strong personal devotion to rendering a literary source. Some examples are actress Emma Thompson's script for *Sense and Sensibility* (1995, Ang Lee) and Christopher Hampton's screenplay rendition of his already adapted stage version of *Dangerous Liaisons* (1988, Stephen Frears) from the period novel by Choderlos de Laclos. Furthermore, because all of the adaptations mentioned above were well received by critics and audiences, very few negative criticisms regarding lack of fidelity to source resulted. On the contrary, a renewed appreciation of, or at least attention to, the source material was the typical consequence. The film adaptation's tendency to create or reenergize public interest in the literary source, and through this renewed interest to spark a wider discussion of the aesthetic force and cultural meanings of the page and screen texts and their temporal contexts, reinforces the intermedial as well as historiographic dimensions of adaptation study.

CLASSICAL HOLLYWOOD AND THE ADAPTED SCREENPLAY

The major studios of classical Hollywood had story departments with a stable of writers who were usually assigned to adaptation projects according to their genre experience. Robert Wise observed, "In my time, all the major studios had story departments to cover all the established and upcoming books. They provided directors with all the information they needed, like synopses."[18] Studio directors didn't have to actually read their sources for adaptation, especially in the rush to produce the many films demanded by the studios' exhibitors prior to 1948. Furthermore, the formulation of and final say on a script seldom began and ended with the story department, which answered to the studio head or to the production manager in the studio system. As independent-minded director Frank Capra wrote in a letter to the *New York Times* in 1939, "about six producers today pass upon ninety percent of the scripts and cut and edit about ninety percent of the pictures."[19]

Thomas Schatz points out that David Selznick, while at MGM with Irving Thalberg, closely oversaw and proved the viability of filming classics as major productions in the 1930s, and he successfully produced several while there.[20] Even in cases where a studio sought out a specific writing talent to adapt a literary work, studios continued to rule the process. At Columbia, noted screenwriter Budd Schulberg explained why he did not write the final script used to adapt his own 1947 novel, *The Harder They Fall*.

> I had a fight with Harry Cohn about that, not the first or last. I had done the book on my farm in Bucks County, and I had also done the screen adaptation there. He insisted that if I did the screenplay, I must do it at the studio.... I really had left Hollywood because I couldn't stand that routine. It just did not fit my method of work. I said I would do the screenplay at the farm and then come out for conferences.... One thing I couldn't stand about that system was that there was a secretarial Pool that typed up the pages, about four or five a day, as you wrote. They would send those pages right up to the front office. The writer could not look at the work and turn it in when it was ready. The front office was more or less looking over your shoulder every step of the way. That's counterproductive to any real creativity. I refused to work under that system, so I didn't get to do the script.[21]

Schulberg had a reputation for doing extensive and intensive hands-on research for his screenplays because he felt compelled by the sociopolitical realities of the American experience. His realist scenario for *On the Waterfront* (1954) was based partly on Malcolm Johnson's Pulitzer prize–winning articles on crime on the New York waterfront, but also on months of Schulberg's own research, which included attending longshoremen union meetings and anti-crime commission hearings. He also insisted that the film's director, Elia Kazan, and actor Marlon Brando join him in spending extended time on the docks with the longshoremen before shooting started. It was as if Schulberg were preparing a nonfiction exposé on the subject while simultaneously building a script. All of this explains why his Academy Award for *On the Waterfront* was in the category of Story and Screenplay rather than Original Screenplay. In his study of screenplay documents, Tom Stempel further discovered that the film's legendary taxicab scene, reputed to have been improvised by Marlon Brando and Rod Steiger, appeared in an early Schulberg draft, "closer to its final form in the film than almost any other scene."[22] Stempel also observes the irony related to this Schulberg and Kazan film: "the best screenplay to come out of the HUAC investigations was written by a screenwriter [and a director] who had testified."[23] Schulberg's leftist ideological bent, in any case, did not make him an easy fit with Hollywood's producer-driven and studio image-driven system of the time.

George Bluestone's landmark academic study, *Novels into Film: The Metamorphosis of Fiction into Cinema* (1957), considers two adaptations from popular sources and three from classic literature, including *The Grapes of Wrath*. He points out that whatever the cultural status of the source, cinema can find its own methods for creating quality and significance. However, in noting how linguistic metaphors can be accomplished in film only when "they arise naturally from the setting," he also shows limitations in his recognition of film's rhetorical arsenal. Nevertheless, his observations are generally wide-ranging and informative of collaborative, industrial, and political realities in Hollywood adaptation. He remarks on the way director John Ford and his cinematographer Gregg Toland created objective details for *The Grapes of Wrath* (1940) that were not in the novel (or the screenplay) in order to heighten character and story in the film. But he notes also that the strongest sociopolitical commentary in Steinbeck's novel is missing from the film, and that Darryl Zanuck at Fox was so concerned about investor resistance to the production of *The Grapes of Wrath* that he announced it under another title, *Highway 66*.[24] Bluestone also makes several references to the film's screenwriter, Nunnally Johnson, and his many contributions, including structural changes that provided a stronger story line, better pacing, and a greater unity for the film. Writer Johnson said, for example, that he moved Ma's speech and "chose it for his curtain line because he considered it the 'real' spirit of Steinbeck's book,"[25] and in fact the novelist had no public qualms with the filmmakers' results.[26] As for director Ford, he glibly claimed not to have read the novel at all,[27] which, if true, means that his visual interpretations were based almost entirely on his feel of the story from the script. Bluestone's book is not inclined to theory, but its practical realization of the industrial and creative process that is cinema, including his willingness to add the screenwriter's name alongside the director's, does recognize the screenplay's significance.[28]

Adaptations of both classic and popular literature have consistently dominated the world of Hollywood's award-winning films. Historically, the great majority of Academy Award–winning films have been adaptations. But the Motion Picture Academy did not consistently distinguish two categories of adapted versus original writing, partly owing to a tendency also to award the best story (not necessarily from a literary source). The Academy had had separate awards for Best Writing: Adaptation and Best Original Story since 1931, but those categories were ambiguous as to whether the person responsible for an original story might have also helped on the screenplay, and whether a winning screenplay in this category was necessarily also adapted. The titles for the three writing awards in 1942 were Best Original Motion Picture Story, Best Original Screenplay, and Best Screenplay (Adaptation). The category of Best Motion Picture Story was finally discarded in 1957, which marked the clear modern distinction between either an original or an adapted screenwriting award category. The distinction between the two awards concerns whether or not a screenplay is based on previously published material.[29] In copyright law, an adaptation is defined as a "derivation that recasts, transforms or adapts a previous work," which already suggests the varied forms that adaptation may take. In any case, the adapted screenplay finally gained a clear award status, whether it originated from published news reports, popular fiction, or classic literary sources. The dominance of popular material for adaptations is reflected in the number of chapters in this book that are concerned with such sources.[30]

Of greatest overall significance here is that the Academy Award for an adaptation is given to a screenplay and not to a film—there is no Oscar category for Best Adapted Motion Picture. This recognizes the distinct nature of the art of adaptive writing versus original scriptwriting, as well as the importance of the screenplay-writing stage in the adaptation process. Whether the predominance of film adaptations that win Best Film awards suggests more about the advantage of films based on already familiar stories and characters in Academy voters' minds or about the willingness of producers to back, and major directors to shoot, "presold" material is unclear. The focus on the screenplay in the competition involving adapted films, however, is a salient point, for the screenplay has always been a crucial aspect of motion picture adaptation, whether it has been recognized as such or not. In fact, one of the reasons for considering Academy Awards in this discussion is the paucity of other forms of significant evidence regarding the viewing public's historical assessment of adapted screenplays.[31]

NEW WAVE AUTEURISM AND THE NEW HOLLYWOOD AFTERMATH

The French New Wave critics and filmmakers, who began work in the middle of the 1950s and continued on through the 1960s, considered film a kind of extension of creative literary authorship that used the camera instead of the pen. Canonic literature, as it was complacently adapted and filmed in France up until this time in what François Truffaut called the "tradition of quality," was to be replaced by original scripts and films, or at least by more creative, "auteurist" adaptations. André Bazin commented specifically on the adaptation of quality literature versus popular textual sources: "The more important and decisive the literary qualities of the work, the more the adaptation disturbs its equilibrium, the more it needs a creative talent to reconstruct it on a new equilibrium not indeed identical with, but the equivalent of, the old one."[32] This notion of equivalency in adaptation calls attention to cinema's particular need to do certain things differently in the transmediation from literature. Furthermore, the auteurists' central attack (mounted by Truffaut's 1954 essay *La politique des auteurs*) was not on adaptation in general so much as on its frequent tendency toward a complacent style and passive allegiance to literary sources. Several films by New Wave directors were in fact adaptations, including Truffaut's *Jules and Jim* (from the novel by Henri-Pierre Roche) and Jean-Luc Godard's *Masculine-Feminine* (from the story by Guy de Mauppasant). The New Wave challenge did succeed in shifting the emphasis in Western critical thinking from the literary source text and its dominant status in adaptation to the film work in the hands of a creative director—and particularly a writer-director—whose style and personal vision were of primary importance. The French auteur theory accented the director's inspiration through a personal approach that may or may not be borrowed in part from literature, and thus advanced the message of film modernism and its self-conscious experimentation with form as an ingredient of narrative and theme.

Because auteur theory touted the artistry of film as a medium that was culturally as significant as literature, New Wave critics created their own pantheon of great directors, and also called attention to hitherto underappreciated Hollywood film genres in which some of those directors worked. These genres included the film noir, the suspense thriller, the disenfranchised youth film, the thoughtful Western, and the comedy. One of the distinguishing features of so-called auteur directors, in fact, was their sole engagement with, or more frequently an active collaboration in, the composition of the screenplay, including those adapted from a previous source. Alfred Hitchcock, who virtually created the genre of the suspense thriller, not only depended on published sources for his films but also took a strong hand with his hired screenwriters in every one.[33] The French cineastes also noted that auteur directors, including Howard Hawks and Anthony Mann, among several others, asserted some degree of creative independence from mainstream Hollywood studio filmmaking even as they worked in and around it. The auteur theory was as much about originality and resistance to conservative standardization as it was about directorial inspiration and vision. This meant going further than simply creating a new artistic initiative, a romance of the great artist. There was an ideological leaning in the realist theory of Bazin and in the progressive and socially engaged writing and filmmaking of those such as Truffaut and particularly Jean Luc Godard. Their contributions to the academic and cultural appreciation of cinema as art, as something more than casual entertainment for the whole family, encouraged a more sophisticated film audience and greatly influenced public attitudes toward film. But the focus on the director's dominance in the 1960s, which followed the producer's dominance in the Hollywood studio era, still did not raise the status of the writer per se. New Wave directors emphasized the cinematic search for truth, whatever their story's origin.

One aspect of the eventual rejection of auteurism by American film critics such as Richard Corliss had to do with the overemphasis on the director at the expense of the screenwriter, for which Corliss makes a strong case in his book, *The Hollywood Screenwriters*. In part a challenge to Andrew Sarris's cataloguing of great directors, Corliss traces the extensive contributions of many writers during the studio era that repeatedly put their stamp on major Hollywood films, including adaptations. There were many screenwriters in this category, including Samson Raphaelson (who wrote for Ernst Lubitsch), Garson Kanin (who could be said to have written for Judy Holliday and the Tracy-Hepburn combo), Jules Furthman (who wrote for Howard Hawks), and Ben Hecht (who wrote for virtually everyone who was a someone). Considering the director's role, Corliss was inclined to observe that Hollywood directors were essentially "interpretive artists" *unless they also wrote their own films*. Nor did Corliss feel that auteur critics in France or Hollywood were really adhering to the notion that auteurism was mainly about style: "visual style is not auteur criticism's major interest. The auteurist is really writing about theme criticism. And themes—as expressed through plot, characterization and dialogue—belong primarily to the writer."[34] If Corliss was on shaky ground here, he did ultimately recognize that the best Hollywood films resulted "from the productive intersection of a strong writer and a strong director—and often a strong actor—exploring mutually sympathetic themes and moods."[35] But the efforts of Corliss to boost the recognition of screenwriters had little lasting effect, especially within the narrow rubric of writer versus director as auteur.

In addition to European influences,[36] which included the French New Wave, and the demise of the hegemonic studio system and the censorship codes that survived into the 1950s, perhaps the greatest impact on writers and directors and their cultural status was felt from the historical events of the late 1960s, which also awakened America's social and political consciousness. The assassinations of key national leaders and the growing terror of the Vietnam War, along with the civil rights movement and the women's movement, which gained momentum throughout that decade, all added up to what some called a counterculture revolution, and one that the quickly dubbed "New Hollywood" took an important part in. Its launch date is usually assigned to the 1967 release of director Arthur Penn's generic hybrid *Bonnie and Clyde*, for which writers David Newman and Robert Benton received a National Society of Film Critics' Award for Best Adaptation. Novelists and screenwriters continued to lack power in the production system, though Mario Puzo's novel *The Godfather* made him an obvious choice to work with writer-director Francis Ford Coppola on the adaptations that became the main Godfather films. *The Godfather* and *The Godfather: Part II* (1972 and 1974), garnered a Best Film and Best Adapted Screenplay award (alongside Coppola's award for Best Director in 1974), which recognized both their strong stylistic and storytelling achievements. These films also showed a new angle on the treatment of the violent mafia—the underbelly of capitalism based on "family" allegiances. The new appreciation for originality in American film style, content, and genre that had begun in the late 1960s encouraged yet more flexible and innovatively cinematic adaptations of challenging literary sources. Much of what has apparently attracted modern talent to adaptation, after all, has not been so much literary sophistication in the source, which can be an obstacle to visual treatment, but something in the narrative that has immediate, significant cultural relevancy.

In 1975, the Best Adapted Screenplay award went to Laurence Hauben and Bo Goldman for transforming Ken Kesey's novel and its follow-up Broadway play, *One Flew Over the Cuckoo's Nest*, to the big screen. The film's screenwriters and director Milos Forman take full advantage of opportunities to open the novel up and to convert its internal narrator's primary metaphor of the mythical "Combine"—systemic institutional oppression—into more realistic forms. Forman's earlier Czechoslovakian film *Fireman's Ball* (1967) presented a metaphor for a system of political oppression that had been internalized by an entire nation, which partly explains the choice of Foreman to direct *Cuckoo's Nest*. Beyond the latter film's political theme, Foreman and writers Goldman and Hauben also created a screen text that can be read for its time as a comment on individual inspiration and passion in filmmaking over and against the forces of timidity and middle-brow conventionalism that had dominated mainstream Hollywood productions up until the advent of the New Hollywood movement. The work of Michael Douglas as producer[37] on *Cuckoo's Nest* (and on some seventeen other films that followed), moreover, is a reminder of some of the major contributions of producers, whose unwavering belief in the cultural importance of certain projects made their realization possible.

A few producers should be recognized based on their track record relative to the New Wave guidelines of an original orchestration of talent that is determined to move beyond complacent commercial cinema. Saul Zaentz, for example, produced major film adaptations such as *Amadeus* (1984), *The Unbearable Lightness of Being* (1988), and *The English Patient* (1996). Producers, whether working inside or outside studios, are usually the ones who initiate the purchase of screen rights to published material, along with the hiring of writers and directors to create the screen adaptation. An alternative case, however, is when a screenwriter or a potential director develops a strong adaptation only to realize an unwillingness on the part of financial backers until the cultural moment seems right for such a project. For example, the script for *Brokeback Mountain* (adapted from E. Annie Proulx's short story) was shopped around by writers Larry McMurtry and Diana Ossana for four years until it was made and eventually won the Oscar for Best Film in 2005. Larry McMurtry was also credited as an executive producer.

There are always larger industrial and audience factors at work in the entertainment business, and these factors can have an impact on the kinds of adaptations that are green-lighted for production in Hollywood. The 1970s,

1980s, and 1990s saw exploding costs for films, a resulting drop in the output of big- and middle-budget films, and the financial necessity for big opening weekends across the cineplexes of America. The need for huge film openings also added to the gross inflation in film costs by requiring massive marketing campaigns that increasingly exceeded the production costs of the movie. The level of financial risk in a single major film could make or break studios and consequently put tremendous pressure on the few writers and directors who were finding their work to be commercially viable.[38] Adding to this was the fact that most of the Hollywood studios had become absorbed into huge conglomerates, which created further levels of administrative approval. Ironically, this situation may have helped the number of adaptations being considered for major backing, but it did not generally advance the quality of what was being produced. If film marketers felt a little safer with adaptations, the conservative strategy to increase the number of sequels and remakes left adaptive writers yet narrower options for creativity. More recently, conglomerates in the new millennium look particularly to adapted screenplays and films that may have strong potential for sequels (called "tent-pole" projects). Commercially, too, the exploding market in DVD sales of movies has enriched the media conglomerates while leaving directors and particularly writers, whose entire screenplay may be offered on a DVD, with small compensation. The lucrative post-theatrical market in DVDs now outgrosses most theatrical box office, and the designation of who receives these profits remains contentious, particularly for creative talent.

The contrast between adapted films that become commercial blockbusters and those that garner Best Adapted Screenplay awards is very revealing of the dimensions of the Hollywood world of adaptation projects. This has become even more pronounced in recent decades. Peter Benchley scripted his own best-seller *Jaws* (1975, Steven Spielberg) along with Carl Gottlieb, and the movie became the top box-office grosser of that year, while the Adapted Screenplay award winner was *One Flew Over the Cuckoo's Nest*. In 1986, the top box-office hit was based on an article written and then adapted by Ehud Yonay, Jim Cash, and Jack Epps for *Top Gun* (Tony Scott). The Best Adapted Script award that year went to Ruth Jhabvala for *A Room with a View* (James Ivory), based on E. M. Forster's novel. In 1993, Spielberg cowrote with Michael Crichton an adaptation of the novelist's best-seller, *Jurassic Park*, while the Best Adapted Screenplay award went to Steven Zaillian for his script for *Schindler's List* (Spielberg). In 2002, the top-grossing film was *Spider-Man* (Sam Raimi), based on the Marvel comic book series, while the Best Adapted Screenplay award went to Ranald Harwood for *The Pianist*

(Roman Polanski), based on the World War II Warsaw memoir by Wladyslaw Szpilman. These contrasting examples are not overly selective for any given year, and they show the continued prominence of adapted material in the industry and its power with viewers, whether for mass appeal or for films more likely to be associated with aesthetic quality and social insight as viewed by the Academy.

For those trying to become established as screenwriters, to write a non-contract script based on someone else's published work means having money to buy at least a timed "option" on a source "property," and possibly also the money to secure the full rights. This usually requires the kind of track record and financial risk most individuals outside the Hollywood money loop cannot afford. McGilligan reflects on this: "The niches for personal expression, as Walter Hill notes... have dwindled. Young writer-directors can find a sanctuary with smaller, independent films, but Hollywood writers, as always, have to trust in bigger financing, an empathetic producer, fortitude, and luck."[39] Add to this the sheer reduction in the number of theatrical films made in Hollywood, as well as the radical current decline in feature films made for network television, and any inclination toward risk and originality in adaptation seems to have been reduced for all but a few producer-writer-director stalwarts. They too must find sufficient inspiration in literary sources to devote significant chunks of their lives and perhaps their livelihood to the effort. The screenplay thus takes its place in a world of Hollywood cinema that remains predominantly a complex entertainment business in which only extraordinary efforts by gifted collaborators have succeeded on occasion in raising it to a level of artistic as well as cultural power.

THEORIES OF STRUCTURALISMS AND THE DISAPPEARING AUTHOR

The influence of the auteur theory began to wane with the academic rise of semiotics and structuralism. Semiotics declared the centrality of the sign and sign systems (the signifier and the signified) that could be applied to visual media as well as written language. The increased emphasis on referentiality and the problem with the notion of representation in visual communication, which Christian Metz partly formalized in the notion of the "imaginary signifier" in cinema, shifted attention from the "speaker" or writer and director to the act of language/sign usage in communication and its meaning. Interest turned also to structuralist approaches based in cultural anthropology. Structuralism accented narrative formulas and cultural constructions (often in Lévi-Straussian binary patterns of opposition) that worked both within language or signs and across audiovisual media. Structuralist theory tended to trace cultural influences and patterns in broad historical strokes. Writers and directors had not presumably invented so much as recontextualized what was already ingrained in cultural history. More relevant to adaptation, deconstructionist Jacques Derrida pushed structuralism to poststructuralist dimensions by observing not only that any sense of an original is impugned through a variety of cultural factors from the outset, but also that the original may be enhanced by a "copy" (or adaptation) through a fresh reading, which suggests a full circularity of influences. Roland Barthes attacked the status of authorship directly in his 1968 essay, "The Death of the Author." He also reified the work of critical interpretation in relation to the source under study, as if every literary source were only a reinterpretation of earlier sources, including critical ones. Michel Foucault's essay, "What is an Author?" (1969), further insisted on reduced attention to a singular "author-function" and raised additional "suspicions . . . concerning the . . . creative role of the subject." Julia Kristeva, borrowing from M. M. Bakhtin's universalist realm of direct and indirect discursive influences subsumed under the term dialogism, further developed the idea she named "intertextuality," which challenged the prestige of prior sources as opposed to the realm of discourse that circulates around them. Broad intertextual approaches increase the emphasis on the array of possible cultural and industrial influences on an author and text.[40] Taken as a whole, then, this multiple-front, evolving theory had the effect of leveling the playing field between any "high culture" presumptions of the literary source contrasted with the film adaptation that followed it. Further, however, the theoretical extreme led by Barthes and Derrida belittled the role of all authorship by reducing source novel writers, and screenwriters and directors by implication, to invisibility or mere "author-functions" in a galaxy full of textual influences and cultural signifiers.

Poststructuralism's challenge to the idea of the unified subject and the unified text remains current. Lacanian psychoanalytic theory as well as Bakhtin's reading of fiction and criticism further questioned the possibility of subject or author autonomy, and thus the discrete individuality of any author's narrative and style. Robert Stam explains further:

> The Bakhtinian "proto-structuralist" conception of the author as the orchestrator of pre-existing discourses, along with Foucault's downgrading of the author in favor of a "pervasive anonymity of discourse," opened the way to a non-originary approach to all arts. Bakhtin's attitude toward the literary author as inhabiting "inter-individual terri-

tory" suggested a devalorization of artistic "originality" . . . adaptation becomes simply another "zone" on a larger and more variegated map.[41]

In contradistinction to approaches emphasizing unity and originality, then, poststructuralism has emphasized rather the gaps and fissures that are a part of the "subject" and the artifact, and (along with "proto-structuralism") the multivocality of influences that shape both. In all of this Stam notes Bakhtin's modification of theoretical language that allows at least for "inter-individual territory,"[42] but where subjective authorship would seem to remain of modest consequence.

Literature and film as well as language translation theorists, however, have begun to raise questions about the total erasure of the individual creative voice. Issues of personal style continue to exist alongside issues of personal worldview within specific historical eras. In his essay, "The Unauthorized Auteur Today" (1993), Dudley Andrew challenged dogmatic theorizations of adaptation that slammed the door on all claims of authorship. He had already suggested in an earlier chapter on adaptation that "[i]t will no longer do to let theorists settle things with a priori arguments. We need to study the films themselves as acts of discourse. We need to be sensitive to that discourse and to the forces that motivate it."[43] The implied sense of a possible personal as well as cultural "motivation" in the process of adaptation resides here. Similarly, in Mireia Aragay's recent collection, *Books in Motion*, she observes that "a redefined notion of auteurism has become a central focus in recent writing on adaptation."[44] Intertextual study can reveal both the screenwriter's struggle for a creative take on preexisting literary materials and the collaborative process tied to the director who seeks to put his or her particular reading on the screen. An adapted film begins as a screenplay transformation of a source, and eventually becomes a film derivation from that screenplay. Recognizing this specificity of textual stages not only confirms adaptation's intertextual status but can also point more precisely to the contributions of key individuals and their most significant impact along the way. Tracing generic, institutional, ideological, and cultural influences need not entirely displace considerations of key creative decisions by individuals most directly responsible for a film. Those broader influences, if considered only in isolation, may miss the way they are finally filtered through the specific interpretations of producers, writers, and directors. Has the deterioration of the subject position in poststructuralism and postmodernity reached the point of total concession by all to a complete erasure of creative inspiration and dedicated conviction of purpose?

Having accepted the convincing theoretical case for a greater balance and more active intercourse between source and adapted texts, the tendency to highlight any variety of cultural influences while overlooking the stage of personal or interpersonal authorship remains troubling. Must we forget that in the end, it is always certain individuals who write a novel or a screenplay and who direct actors and films? And while the majority of their decisions may be recognized as resulting from larger historical and cultural contexts, and from certain guiding perspectives adapted from the source, that the primary talent in a given film adaptation can also serve as very specific individual antennae of interpretation that may be more than the sum of those larger influences? Whatever remains of the creative subject and individual inspiration and effort implies a particular voice, and not necessarily only a culturally mimetic one. Contemporary conditions of mass mediation have certainly altered the process of psychological and social development related to individual identity. Important recent adaptations such as *To Die For* (1995) and *Adaptation* (2002)[45] in fact take these very themes of the media-absorbed and degraded personal reality of the individual as their primary subject. If poststructuralism signals the death of the unified subject and text in a welter of cultural influences, and if postmodernism emphasizes reality's absorption into commercial and political mediations that leave the subject exteriorized and hollowed out, then neither theory would seem capable of doing more than reconfirming the power of larger forces already at work. What remains of the subject's "expressive voice" may be only the final resistant echoes of real cultural memory no longer able to make connections even with its own most personally and deeply felt experiences. Does this leave adaptation study with only so many cycles of textual borrowing and transference where no personal agency remains? Certainly, great cinema is not solely individual expression, but neither does it seem only a summary mirror of cultural forces.

There is a reason why so many case studies look to issues of authorship for understanding. The closer one gets to a work, the more the particulars of story treatment, visual style, performance, tone, pacing, scoring, editing, and themes become recognizable as a series of decisions attributable to individuals. And this applies equally to adaptation study. Just as an adapted film can change an entire cultural view of a source—such as Francis Ford Coppola's *Apocalypse Now* (1979) "updating" Joseph Conrad's *Heart of Darkness*—so too can special efforts by individuals such as Alfred Hitchcock or Stanley Kubrick change the way we look at the balance between literary source and adapted film. As we step back from the aesthetic particulars of a work, it is possible to see larger circumstances and trends affecting whole groups of films. Both macro- and microperspectives for critical interpretation are useful, and there is no reason to disparage one for the other. Hence, Foucault's ideas on author functions can be seen as his analytical distance from the daily reality and personal efforts of those caught up in the pressurized circus of adaptive screenwriting and film production, where certain decisions may breach as well as follow larger cultural norms. Significant theorists and writer-directors alike are usually reactive to culture in the sense that they can bring something unique to it and also, perchance, modify its direction. Certainly, the history of film includes its changing pantheon of theorists as well as filmmakers, however divergent their functions and methods.

In the Hollywood filmmaking contexts and constraints of rights and contracts, institutional structures of production and branding, and the assignment of screen credits, creative talent can ultimately choose either a lazy approach of audience exploitation through cultural clichés, spectacle, and commercial reification or look instead toward a careful cultural observation, uniqueness of expression, and cultural engagement. Surely it is individuals and their dedication of energy to something illuminative in film that makes the latter happen. Successful transformations such as *Million Dollar Baby* (2004, Clint Eastwood), which Paul Haggis adapted from an "F. X. Toole" short story (and just after the author's death), thematizes singular dedication to class mobility and a specific kind of fulfillment. This confirms a fundamental American myth, but one that is also placed by these authors against very specific gender, class, and racial stereotypes. The film was also made for $30 million and grossed $100.4 million within five months, figures suggesting that its particular message and aesthetic, as driven home by the personal commitment of its makers, have communicated something universal to audiences (not to mention the implication in its box-office success that art and commerce need not be mutually exclusive). Part of the significance of narrative film writing and production resides in its potential to reach millions worldwide, and thus to make a difference in ways and at levels that literature has been unable to achieve.

Nevertheless, the two narrative media share in what can be, as several theorists have already suggested, a largely beneficial synergy. And this synergy is often most in evidence through the intertextual script that links them. As I have attempted to demonstrate, the adapted screenplay asserts the main parameters and direction of authorial intention, whatever the final outcome on the big screen may be. Bazin wrote in 1948 that the public impact of films was greater than novels at myth-making, and he noted also the way film adaptations reinforce rather than eliminate the relevancy of drama and the novel.⁴⁶ There appears to be a longing for the audiovisual image in the descriptive suggestion of the word, and a longing for the word to describe the full immediacy of the film image. A critical approach to adaptation that recognizes authorial desire through the script intertext as well as the film can reveal—like the many sketches a sculptor might draw in preparation for completing a statue—the significant stages of smaller decisions that finally add up to the whole.

Beyond formalistic or poststructuralist cross-textual analyses, then, there should also be room in the equation for consideration of the adaptive writer's and director's orchestration of voice and desire in cinema short of an overly romanticized auteurism. Stam reinforces this view in his comments on authorship:

> Auteur studies now tend to see a director's work not as the expression of individual genius but rather as the site of encounter of a biography, an intertext, an institutional context, and a historical moment ... they [directors, and to this I would add screenwriters] "orchestrate" pre-existing voices, ideologies, and discourses, without losing an overall shaping role ... a director's work can be both personal *and* mediated by extrapersonal elements such as genre, technology, studios, and the linguistic procedures of the medium.⁴⁷

A revised contemporary sensitivity to adaptive film authorship would therefore also include the environments of all three texts—literary, script intertext, and film. All three can be sites of personal and cultural struggle and perhaps revelation. We look to locate and recognize both definitive individual voices and extrapersonal contexts when they show themselves across the developmental writing stages of adaptation, as well as on through the multitrack dimensionality and enunciating voice of the completed film. The chapters that follow, using a variety of methods in their engagements with specific examples, work to recognize and interpret what is most significant and meaningful in the many procedural stages and forms of adaptation represented here.

NOTES

1. The promotional factor was put to direct use, for example, in the ploy by the makers of the Hobbit book-to-film trilogy, who encouraged readers to post their

suggestions for the making of the film online as these projects were being developed and written. In this case the films' fidelity not only to the fantasy novels but to their readers' imagined realizations of them was encouraged as a form of audience pretesting. This approach clearly influenced the development of the adapted screenplay.

2. Among these are Tom Stempel's *Framework: A History of Screenwriting in the American Film* (1988), Linda Seger's and Edward Jay Whitmore's *From Script to Screen: The Collaborative Art of Filmmaking*, and Pat McGilligan's *Backstory* series of screenwriter interviews, including *Backstory 4: Interviews with Screenwriters of the '70s and '80s* (2006). Long the main text on the writing of adaptations is Linda Seger's *The Art of Adaptation* (1997), followed by Kenneth Portnoy's *Screen Adaptation: A Scriptwriting Handbook*, 2nd ed. (1998).

3. These include John M. Desmond and Peter Hawkes, *Adaptation: Studying Film & Literature* (2006); Mireia Aragay, ed., *Books in Motion: Adaptation, Intertextuality, Authorship* (2005); Kamilla Elliott, *Rethinking the Novel/Film Debate* (2003); Sarah Cardwell, *Adaptation Revisited: Television and the Classic Novel* (2002); Ginette Vincendeau, ed., *Film/Literature/Heritage: A Sight and Sound Reader* (2001); James Naremore, ed., *Film Adaptation* (2000); Robert Giddings and Erica Sheen, eds., *The Classic Novel: From Page to Screen* (2000); Timothy Corrigan, *Film and Literature: An Introduction and Reader* (1999); Deborah Cartmell and Imelda Whelehan, eds., *Adaptations: From Text to Screen, Screen to Text* (1999); John C. Tibbetts and James M. Welch, eds., *Novels into Film: The Encyclopedia of Movies Adapted from Books* (1999); and Brian McFarlane, *Novel to Film: An Introduction to the Theory of Adaptation* (1996).

4. The Robert Stam titles include *Literature Through Film* (2005) and two titles co-edited with Alessandra Raengo: *Literature and Film* (2005) and *A Companion to Literature and Film* (2005). These texts tend to cover the adaptation categories of literary history, theory, and international and other influences, respectively.

5. Robert Wise writes, for example:

> I absolutely believe in getting the script in order before starting to film. On one occasion, on *Star Trek: The Motion Picture*, we had only the first half of the script ready when we had to start shooting.... In the meantime, there were delays after delays. Finally I had to start shooting. The script rewrites kept on coming until the last day of shooting. That was not a satisfactory way to work and I think the film shows it.
>
> —From foreword in Tibbetts and Welch, eds., *Novels into Film*, viii–ix

6. See Arthur Eckstein's "Darkening Ethan: John Ford's *The Searchers* (1956): From Novel to Screenplay to Screen," *Cinema Journal* 38, no. 1 (1998): 3–24.

7. As a complex and expensive medium and industry, film encompasses, in addition to producers, writers, directors, and often storyboard artists, the contributions of CPAs and budget analysts, performers, art directors, and set builders, agents,

technicians, special effects departments, all descriptions of equipment, schedulers, composers, editors, promotion and advertising, distributors, and exhibitors, to name only some of the skills, technology, and jobs required.

8. Stempel, *Framework*, 184.

9. The shooting script is a special script alteration that more thoroughly addresses the technical requirements of production. The shooting script includes numbered scenes, expanded descriptive details for special effects, and so on. Shooting scripts may be used as the basis for storyboards, which are typically hand drawn (or created using computerized images) that lay out the approximate angle and "look" of each individual shot in the visual progression of scenes. Once production is under way, the shooting script will also carry notations by the "script girl" to indicate actual camera takes on the set that will be delivered to the film's editors as a continuity script to aid in cutting and identifying all the rough footage. See also William Horne's "See Shooting Script: Reflections on the Ontology of the Screenplay," *Literature/Film Quarterly* 20, no. 1 (1998): 52.

10. Selznick's famous battle with Hitchcock over the control of the script for "Selznick's" production of *Rebecca* is also apropos here. See the introduction to Part I of this book.

11. See Chapter 2, on Hitchcock's working methods, and the discussion in Chapter 3 of *Eyes Wide Shut* and screenwriter Fredric Rafael's *Eyes Wide Open*.

12. Stempel, *Framework*, 121. Herman Mankiewicz and Orson Welles also shared the Academy Award for Best Original Screenplay.

13. McGilligan, *Backstory 4*, 159. Jhabvala's comments on screenplay dialogue in these interviews are also supported in reverse by writer-director Robert Benton, who tells the story of convincing an actor for his film *Bad Company* to sound more like a Jimmy Stewart than a Montgomery Clift by having writer David Newman write lines for him "so that if Daffy Duck did the part he would sound like Jimmy Stewart." When the actor read them, he gave in (26).

14. See Chapter 10 by Cynthia Lucia on *High Fidelity*, a film that John Cusack starred in as well as co-wrote and co-produced. Another example is Emma Thompson's script adaptation of Jane Austen's *Sense and Sensibility* (1995, Ang Lee), in which she also played the lead role.

15. Interview of Carl Franklin in *Creative Screenwriting* 4, no. 1 (1997): 20.

16. Geoffrey Wagner divides what he calls "modes" of adaptation into three comparable categories of distance from the source: *transposition, commentary* and *analogy*, with analogy being the most distant. See his *The Novel and the Cinema* (Rutherford, NJ: Fairleigh Dickinson University Press, 1975), cited in Joy Gould Boyum's *Double Exposure: Fiction into Film* (New York: Plume, 1985), 69.

17. These three examples also suggest that quality in adaptation may be more closely associated with talent and conviction in story truth than in reliance on a big budget, even for historical films. The Merchant-Ivory British production was shot in 1992 for only $8 million; Minghella's sweeping project, also British, was shot in 1996

for only $31 million; and the Coen brothers' comedy was shot in the United States in 2000 for about $26 million.

18. Wise, foreword to Tibbetts and Welch, eds., *Novels into Film*, viii.

19. Richard Glatzer and John Raeburn, eds., *Frank Capra: The Man and His Films* (Ann Arbor: University of Michigan Press, 1975), 15.

20. Thomas Schatz, *Genius of the System* (New York: Metropolitan Books, 1996), 75. Similarly, Albert LaValley's description of Warner Bros. producer Jerry Wald's domination of the development of the script for the film *Mildred Pierce* (1946) in Chapter 2 provides yet another example of how this might work in relation to writers.

21. Gary Crowdus and Dan Georgakas, *Cineaste Interviews* (Chicago: Lake View Press, 2002), 365–366. *The Harder They Fall* (1957, Mark Robson) gave the screenplay credit to Philip Yordan.

22. Stempel, *Framework*, 165.

23. Ibid., 166. Both of them nevertheless went on to create highly regarded films, such as the next one they did together, *A Face in the Crowd* (1957, Elia Kazan, based on Schulberg's short story), which details the rise and fall of a countrified media huckster.

24. Bluestone, 159. "Working titles" are often assigned to films in production for a variety of reasons, but Zanuck specifically used "Highway" in his working title to prevent possible politically motivated interruptions and controversy while shooting of this controversial novel took place out on a public highway location.

25. Ibid., 167.

26. Johnson was graciously complimented on his script by Steinbeck himself, who recognized the difficulty of transforming his more than 500-page novel into what was "more dramatic in fewer words than my book." Johnson had completed a successful populist script of *Jesse James* for Zanuck the previous year, and he seemed the obvious choice to adapt Steinbeck's progressive novel (*Framework*, 83).

27. Bluestone, *Novels into Film*, 169.

28. Ibid., 64. Bluestone writes: "An art whose limits depend on a moving image, mass audience, and industrial production is bound to differ from an art whose limits depend on language, a limited audience and individual creation."

One special consequence of appealing to a mass audience in the studio era was the conservatively imposed system of film censorship, which was effectively instituted as a mandated Production Code in 1932. The Code exerted a great influence on the writing of all types of screenplays, which had to be cleared prior to production. By 1934, screenplays had to be pre-approved by the Joseph Breen office before shooting went forward, but it was adaptations such as *The Moon Is Blue* that began to break the Code's hold in 1953.

29. See "The Best Screenplay and Writing Academy Awards" for an extended historical breakdown of the writing award categories (http://www.filmsite.org/bestscreenplays.html).

30. In the American Film Institute's current list of 100 Best American Movies of all time, for example, thirty-one of the top fifty are adaptations, and of those only five or six could be considered literary classics ("America's 100 Greatest Movies," AFI.com). Best-selling stories and novels have far outnumbered quality literary works as sources for film, and the arena of popular sources is also larger because it includes nonfiction as well as fiction, including biographies, history, and current newspaper, magazine, and TV news stories, as well as comic books, film and TV documentaries, and TV programs.

31. The Writers Guild has been recognizing screen writers since 1953 with the Laurel Award for those who "advance the literature of the motion picture through the years, and have made outstanding contributions to the profession of the screenwriter." But this award is not for individual screenplays and generally recognizes contributions in adapted and original scripts.

32. André Bazin, *What Is Cinema?*, ed. and trans. Hugh Gray (Berkeley and Los Angeles: University of California Press, 1967), 56. This statement assumes, of course, that a writer and director actually seek "equivalency" in an adaptation.

33. See Thomas Leitch in Chapter 2, this volume, on Hitchcock.

34. Richard Corliss, ed., *The Hollywood Screenwriters* (New York: Avon Books, 1970), 11.

35. Ibid., 20.

36. Looking back on and arguing for the numerous examples of fine films that were adaptations in the European tradition generally is Andrew S. Horton and Joan Magretta's collection, *Modern European Filmmakers and the Art of Adaptation* (New York: Frederick Ungar, 1981).

37. Kirk Douglas had bought the rights to Kesey's novel with the idea of playing the Randall P. McMurphy role, but he had difficulty getting it developed until he allowed his son Michael to take over as producer. Michael promptly chose Jack Nicholson as McMurphy, Forman to direct, and the screenwriters mentioned.

38. As David Cook observed: "This condition has been seen as inhibiting the creative freedom of people working within the industry, especially since it has become common practice for producers, directors, writers and stars to receive a percentage of the net profits of their films as well as a smaller fixed salary, or fee-for-service." David Cook, *A History of Narrative Film* (New York: W. W. Norton, 1996), 935.

Consider also the fate of scriptwriters versus producers presented in Michael Tolkin's script adaptation of his own Hollywood insider novel, *The Player* (1992, Robert Altman, who also had a major hand in the script). Hollywood screenwriter Walter Hill further reports the yet darker comment by his writing colleague David Giler, who said that "your work is only read by the people who will destroy it" (*Backstory 4*, 148).

39. *Backstory 4*, 12. McGilligan's comment on young writer-directors also suggests the contradiction in the current situation, where adaptations have generally not been accessible territory for most young writers. In contrast, the expanded pub-

lic interest in the screenplay, which has continued to grow over the last thirty years, has created increased numbers of new writers who have been aided by the proliferation of screenplay competitions and grants, as well as academic courses and programs in screenwriting.

40. The essays by Roland Barthes and Michel Foucault are included in John Caughie, ed., *Theories of Authorship: A Reader* (London: Routledge and Kegan Paul, in association with the BFI, 1981).

41. Stam, *Literature and Film*, 9.

42. Ibid.

43. Dudley Andrew, "The Unauthorized Auteur Today," in *Film Theory Goes to the Movies*, ed. J. Collins et al. (New York: Routledge, 1993), 77–85. See also D. Andrew, *Concepts in Film Theory* (New York: Oxford University Press, 1984), 106.

44. See Mireia Aragay's "Introduction: Reflection to Refraction: Adaptation Studies Then and Now" in her *Books in Motion*, 28. On the same page, Aragay cites the analysis of a contributor, Margaret McCarthy, who found in German director Doris Dorrie's "auteurist identity a paradoxical blend of individual expression and adaptation to pre-existing conventions and constraints."

45. See Frank P. Tomasulo on *Adaptation*, Chapter 6 this volume. Regarding *To Die For*, see also my chapter, "Women and Murder in the Televirtuality Film," in *Killing Women: The Visual Culture of Gender and Violence*, ed. Annette Burfoot and Susan Lord (Ontario: Wilfrid Laurier University Press, 2006), 139–154.

46. André Bazin, "Adaptation or the Cinema as Digest," in Naremore, ed., *Film Adaptation*, 25–26.

47. Robert Stam and Toby Miller, *Film and Theory: An Anthology* (Malden, MA: Blackwell Publishers, 2000), 6.

REFERENCES

Aragay, Mireia, ed. *Books in Motion: Adaptation, Intertextuality, Authorship*. New York: Rodopi, 2005.

Bazin, André. *What Is Cinema?*, edited and translated by Hugh Gray. Berkeley and Los Angeles: University of California Press, 1967.

Behlmer, Rudy, ed. *Inside Warner Bros. (1935–1951)*. New York: Viking, 1985.

Bluestone, George. *Novels into Film*. Berkeley and Los Angeles: University of California Press, 1957.

Boozer, Jack. "Women and Murder in the Televirtuality Film." In *Killing Women: The Visual Culture of Gender and Violence*, edited by Annette Burfoot and Susan Lord, 139–154. Ontario: Wildred-Laurier University Press, 2006.

Bricknell, Timothy, ed. *Minghella on Minghella*. London: Faber & Faber, 2005.

Cardwell, Sarah. *Adaptation Revisited: Television and the Classic Novel*. New York: Manchester University Press, 2002.

Cartmell, Deborah, and Imelda Whelehan, eds. *Adaptations: From Text to Screen, Screen to Text*. New York: Routledge, 1999.

Caughie, John, ed. *Theories of Readership: A Reader*. London: Routledge and Kegan Paul, in association with BFI, 1981.

Corliss, Richard, ed. *The Hollywood Screenwriters*. New York: Aron Books, 1970.

Corrigan, Timothy. *Film and Literature: An Introduction and Reader*. Upper Saddle River, NJ: Prentice Hall, 1999.

Desmond, John M., and Peter Hawkes. *Adaptation: Studying Film & Literature*. New York: McGraw-Hill, 2006.

Elliott, Kamilla. *Rethinking the Novel/Film Debate*. Cambridge: Cambridge University Press, 2003.

Giddings, Robert, and Erica Sheen, eds. *The Classic Novel: From Page to Screen*. New York: Manchester University Press, 2000.

Glatzer, Richard, and John Raeburn, eds. *Frank Capra: The Man and His Films*. Ann Arbor: University of Michigan Press, 1975.

Literature/Film Quarterly, 1979–present.

McFarlane, Brian. *Novel to Film: An Introduction to the Theory of Adaptation*. New York: Oxford University Press, 1996.

McGilligan, Patrick. *Backstory 4: Interviews with Screenwriters of the '70s and '80s*. Berkeley and Los Angeles: University of California Press, 2006.

Naremore, James, ed. *Film Adaptation*. New Brunswick, NJ: Rutgers University Press, 2000.

Portnoy, Kenneth. *Screen Adaptation: A Scriptwriting Handbook*, 2nd ed. Boston: Focal Press, 1998.

Schatz, Thomas. *Genius of the System*. New York: Metropolitan Books, 1996.

Seger, Linda. *The Art of Adaptation: Turning Fact and Fiction into Film*. New York: Henry Holt, 1997.

Seger, Linda, and Edward Jay Whetmore. *From Script to Screen: The Collaborative Art of Filmmaking*. New York: Henry Holt, 1994.

Stam, Robert. *Literature Through Film*. Oxford: Blackwell, 2005.

Stam, Robert, and Alessandra Raengo, eds. *A Companion to Literature and Film*. Oxford: Blackwell, 2005

———, eds. *Literature and Film*. Oxford: Blackwell, 2005.

Stempel, Tom. *Framework: A History of Screenwriting in the American Film*. Syracuse, NY: Syracuse University Press, 1988.

Thompson, Emma. *The Sense and Sensibility Screenplay and Diaries*. New York: Newmarket Press, 1996

Tibbetts, John C., and James M. Welch, eds. *Novels into Film: The Encyclopedia of Movies Adapted from Books*. New York: Checkmark Books, 1999.

Vincendeau, Ginnette, ed. *Film/Literature/Heritage: A Sight and Sound Reader*. London: BFI, 2001.

PART I
//

HOLLYWOOD'S "ACTIVIST" PRODUCERS AND MAJOR AUTEURS DRIVE THE SCRIPT

> *There's basically an adversary relationship between writers and directors. Personally, I don't like directors; I think they're jealous, petty and frustrated. They'd like to be writers, only they can't do it.*
>
> —William Goldman (originally quoted from a *New Times* interview)

"Activist" producers and major auteurs of Hollywood cinema have often turned to already published sources for their projects. Their subsequent control over the adapted screenplay demonstrates a dominant pattern of authorship. This has sometimes resulted in their taking the screen credit listing "A Film by..." as opposed to simply "Produced by" or "Directed by" or even "Written and Directed by." In one famous 1940 case, then independent producer David Selznick listed his opening credit as "Selznick Studio / Presents its Production of Daphne du Maurier's Celebrated Novel / Rebecca." After listing the star players and then himself again as producer, he lists two writers' names under "Adapted by," and two other names in very small print underneath as "Screenplay by." Incidentally, Selznick received the Academy Award for Best Picture, while Hitchcock was nominated for but did not receive the Best Director award. Rebecca was also nominated for a Best Adapted Script for two writers who did not receive the award. Selznick's slavish attention to novelist Daphne du Maurier's approval of the adaptation was clearly asserted by him over and against the initial intention of newly arrived director Hitchcock to construct his own "interpretation" of the novel. Their contest of wills over script and shooting gave special meaning to the concept of collaboration in the studio era.

Another producer who was equally hands-on when configuring story detail was the former writer turned activist producer at Warner Bros Studio, Jerry Wald. An informed account of Wald's enforcement of his creative and marketing sense through the script adaptation of James M. Cain's novel Mildred Pierce is provided in Chapter 1 by Albert J. LaValley. He tracks Wald's story oversight through Wald's hiring of several writers to develop his intentions for a new film genre hybrid. Of the different writers who worked on the script, including William Faulkner, only Ranald MacDougall's name appears on the final screenplay credit. (As LaValley notes, more information on the construction of this script is available in Rudy Behlmer's book, Inside Warner Bros. (1935–1951), which holds that Wald had the idea for a flashback structure and murder well before he knew of Paramount's intentions with the making of Double Indemnity, released in 1944.)

Major auteurs, like activist producers, are also defined by the extent of their involvement in selecting and sometimes purchasing the sources for their projects, or at least in shaping the adapted screenplay and all phases of production. Auteurs have won their positions of creative control because of their consummate storytelling skills, notable style, and recognized success with audiences, including their direction of at least one or two cinema landmarks. Hence, when developing adaptations, these individuals usually overshadow both lesser known source material and the screenwriters who work with them, whether or not the directors also add their name to the screenwriter credit. How many filmgoers paid attention to the pulp novel by Robert Bloch or the script by Joseph Stefano when their work was credited on-screen for Psycho (1960)? As a matter of record, some directors have also been forceful in asserting script credit where it may not have been warranted. This situation eventually resulted in a Writers Guild ruling that requires directors or any writer to have composed at least 50 percent of an original screenplay and a third of an adapted script before adding their names to the writer credit on the screen.

Thomas Leitch in Chapter 2 provides an insightful view of Alfred Hitchcock's constant reliance on novels and short stories as the basis for his films, and the variety of writers whom he employed over time to adapt the works, which he usually located and purchased on his own. This survey of Hitchcock's working methods, which were surprisingly consistent during his American years, illuminates both the director's nose for material that could be developed into engagingly visual suspense thrillers and his feel for cinematic plot and casting. Leitch carefully unveils in project after project the way this master of suspense would either collaborate with or replace his hired scribes while developing the exact visual plotting that he wanted to storyboard and lock in for his films.

In Chapter 3, Jack Boozer offers a case study of Stanley Kubrick's last film, Eyes Wide Shut (1999). He looks to screenwriter Frederic Rafael's important book, Eyes Wide Open, for details of Kubrick's working method on this project. Kubrick showed an unforthcoming dependence on the writer to help him formulate the bulk of the actual script, if not, of course, the exact audiovisual style, which is also key to the film's final impact and meaning.

1

MILDRED PIERCE
A Troublesome Property to Script

//

Albert J. LaValley

THE FILM *MILDRED PIERCE* HAS ITS ORIGIN IN JAMES M. CAIN's novel of the same name. Published in 1941, it followed Cain's successful series of 1930s tough guy novels: *The Postman Always Rings Twice, Career in C Major, Double Indemnity,* and *Serenade.* Departing from their narrow framework, taut narratives, and first-person male protagonists,[1] Cain offered a female protagonist, both strong and weak, as his central character. Out of the ruins of her marriage and the Depression, Mildred builds a profitable enterprise in her chain of restaurants. Yet Mildred loses all: her restaurants, her daughter, and her husband. Her business drive is founded on the forbidden wish to control the love of her daughter Veda. What Joyce Carol Oates calls "the lure of the unconscious," symbolized by Veda's extraordinary beauty and her superb musical talents, leads Mildred to destruction. Mildred becomes a great success and a figure of power who controls all the men around her, yet Veda's love remains elusive. Veda's artistic success outstrips Mildred's financial one, and finally she betrays her mother by sleeping with Mildred's second husband, Monte.[2] At the novel's end, Mildred is ruined financially and degraded emotionally. She is back in the Glendale cottage with her first husband, Bert. Together, they contemplate starting over. "In Cain, life is a bungling process and in no way educational."[3]

The book and the film are similar in broad narrative outline, except that the film adds a murder and omits Veda's success in a musical career. The film departs strikingly from its source, however, by tying into different cinematic traditions: the women's movie, film noir, and murder mysteries. With the addition of glamourous sets, star treatment, and a contemporary setting, all made lavish by a big budget and producer Jerry Wald's desire for the grand treatment, *Mildred Pierce* (hereafter referred to as *MP*) struck a tone and style far removed from Cain's novel. Its highly glossy look and its somewhat lurid subject matter were to become a hallmark of Warners films of the late 1940s, particularly those produced by Wald after his great success with *MP*.

Ironically, before Wald decided to make *MP*, it was most likely the milieu of the novel and its struggling working-class heroine that made it an appropriate vehicle for Warner Brothers with its strong tradition of proletarian heroes and heroines and concern for social causes dating from the early 1930s. The positive aspects of Mildred probably prompted Warners to buy the book. Rough, resilient, lower-class and lower-middle-class women who made their way up in life had been portrayed at Warners by Bette Davis, Ginger Rogers, Joan Blondell, Glenda Farrell, Ann Sheridan, and Ida Lupino. The noble, self-sacrificial side of Mildred also easily allied itself with the later 1930s and early 1940s women's movies, such Bette Davis vehicles as *Dark Victory* (1939), *The Old Maid* (1939), and *Now, Voyager* (1942).

There was also a longstanding tradition of tough crime dramas at Warners, much of it concerned with gangsters, racketeers, and tough young men raised in street settings (*Little Caesar*, 1930; *The Public Enemy*, 1931; *They Made Me a Criminal*, 1939; *Angels with Dirty Faces*, 1938; and the Wald co-scripted *They Drive by Night*, 1940, and *The Roaring Twenties*, 1939). By the 1940s this tradition had taken a turn toward a more romantic, less sociological noir film, often with Bogart as the charismatic hero, doomed in *High Sierra* (1941) and *The Big Shot* (1942) but positive and victorious in *The Maltese Falcon* (1941), *Casablanca* (1943), and *The Big Sleep* (1946).[4] To Some extent the film *MP* adhered to these traditions. The great success of *Double Indemnity* (Paramount, 1944), adapted from Cain's 1937 novella, practically ensured that a crime would be added (although he had taken pains to avoid violence in *MP*). *Laura* (20th Century-Fox, 1944) was a striking example of how the women's movie could be combined with the whodunit.

Cain's name on the book and Veda's presence as a catalyst for Mildred's neurotic drives also pushed the film away from the Warners social dramas and women's movies of the thirties and toward the dark, brooding film noir of the forties with its stress on melodrama, the unconscious, and unsettling emotions.

MP is at once in touch with the oldest and strongest Warners traditions of the 1930s and early 1940s as it also heralds the more sour, disenchanted, and disturbing world of Warners postwar America. This division is evident both thematically and stylistically within the film itself. Its flashbacks are shot in a higher key, a brighter light than its murky film noir present-tense framework. Mildred as the noble sufferer aligns herself with the heroines of women's movies: Barbara Stanwyck's *Stella Dallas* (Goldwyn-UA, 1937) sac-

Jerry Wald was a successful screenwriter before becoming a producer at Warner Bros. in 1942. As producer, he oversaw and guided the adaptation of the novel Mildred Pierce *into a dark women's film with a flashback and murder.*

rificing herself for her daughter, Bette Davis's Charlotte Vale in *Now, Voyager* as she rises out of obscurity and oppression, and Rosalind Russell's Louise Randall in *Roughly Speaking* (Warners, 1945) as she suffers the trials of domestic life while shaping up her shiftless husband's business.

Yet these themes are much altered. Unlike Stella's daughter, Mildred's Veda is ungrateful and vicious. As a catalyst for Mildred's drive to power, Veda taints the film's central action. The aims of power become questionable. The American dream of greater success for one's children acquires a sour edge. In its path lie sexual excess, business corruption, and depersonalization. Even Mildred's nobility has overtones of masochism. While Mildred attempts to salvage basic familial values outside her oppressed housewife role, she jeopardizes those same values by her grim drive for power and her iron determination. Domestic relations in the film are fragmented and riddled with a mixture of sexuality, business calculation, and deceit. Bert is relegated to secondary status even before he leaves the house; Monte gives Mildred money partly as a sign of sexual attraction; her marriage with him later is purely one of convenience to get Veda back; her treatment of Veda suggests the role more of lover than mother; her use of her admirer Wally involves his recurrent dismissal in a sexual role and his increased subservience as a humiliated follower who finally seeks revenge.

Finally, the noir framework and Crawford's glacial performance emphasize a guilt-ridden Mildred, capable of trickery and lies. As the film begins, she coldly and mysteriously lures Wally to the beach house to plant him at the scene of the murder. Throughout the film we are never certain that she is not Monte's murderer. Even when she is cleared, she is not exculpated. She made Veda what she is, and Veda, in shooting Monte, did what Mildred in her anger wanted to do. It is Mildred who brings the gun to the beach house, presumably to kill Monte for betraying her in business. While the duplicity in love and marriage that she unexpectedly discovers at the house might have more logically pushed Mildred into a crime of passion, she falls instead into the role of the tragically wronged woman. It is Veda, suddenly rejected by Monte, who does the killing Mildred came to do. She acts out her mother's revenge and assumes her guilt.

This tangle of passions and duplicitous motives and the bitter views of marriage, family, and business distinguish *MP* from such noir films as the classic Warners detective stories, *The Maltese Falcon* and *The Big Sleep*, in which the detective provides a moral norm that counters the often cynical world view. *MP* is also distinguished from such romantic noir films as *Spellbound* (1945), *Laura*, and *The Dark Mirror* (1946), in which the narratives end with an affirmation of the couple. The strong disenchantment in *MP* and the somewhat despicable quality of all the characters point the way to what Paul Schrader calls the "second phase of film noir."[5] It is a phase marked by bitterness, dis-enchantment, turbulent emotions, and the failure of love. Though *MP* shares some aspects of the first phase of noir—studio filming and a stress on talk over action—it nowhere conveys a mood of romantic optimism covered by a layer of cynicism that characterizes such Warners films as *Casablanca, Passage to Marseille* (1944), and *To Have and Have Not* (1944). *MP* points to *Gilda* (1946) and *Fallen Angel* (1946) and at Warners to *The Strange Love of Martha Ivers* (1946), *The Unsuspected* (1947), *Dark Passage* (1947), *Flamingo Road* (1949), *Possessed* (1947), and *The Breaking Point* (1950), most of these involving the major talents of *MP*.

JAMES M. CAIN'S WORK AND THE NOIR TRADITION

Cain's novels of the late 1930s and early 1940s constitute one of the fundamental influences on film noir. Three of them—*The Postman Always Rings Twice* (1934), *Double Indemnity* (1936), and *MP* (1941)—made excellent noir films in 1946, 1943, and 1945 respectively. Other minor novels and stories came to the screen earlier; Warners had produced and adapted *The Embezzler* in 1940 under its original title, *Money and the Woman*. But in any event the books mirror the bleak world of shifting values and isolated individualism that was the Southern California of the 1930s and that became the movies' picture of it in the 1940s. In their urban setting, their tough guy knowingness, their mixture of strong realism and surrealistic detail and mood, their sense of universal treachery and futility, their reliance for narrative progression on the complications of passion, dream, and unconscious wishes, they antedate much of film noir's themes and methods. Like film noir, Cain's major books chronicle the lure of the American dream and brand it a falsity.

Ironically, Cain had turned to novel writing when one of his own American dreams had fizzled. Cain had come to Hollywood as one of the bright young journalists of the early 1930s, and when his career as a screenwriter seemed about to end, at the age of forty-two he wrote *The Postman Always Rings Twice*. It was an instant success, critically and popularly. It caused a minor scandal with its realistic treatment of sex and passion and was banned in Boston. Just as ironically, Cain's instant success as a novelist made him now much sought after as a screenwriter by the same studios that had previously fired him. Disenchantment and cynicism obviously came easily to him. Though Cain was not at Warners during the writing and filming of *MP*, he was later to become a writer there in the late forties, possibly as a result of the success of the film *MP*.

Like many young journalists and writers during the beginning of the period of sound films, Cain turned to Hollywood for its lucrative possibilities. Like many of these other New York writers, Cain held the movies in low esteem and saw himself as squandering his talents on them.

Before going west, he had enjoyed success in a variety of prestigious positions: as a professor at St. John's College in Maryland, as a reporter for the *Baltimore Sun* and the *New York World*, as a writer for *The Nation* and *The American Mercury*, and as managing editor for Harold Ross at *The New Yorker*. He was admired not only by Ross but also by H. L. Mencken and Walter Lippmann, for whom he had also written.

Cain was frank about his failure as a screenwriter. "My dislike of pictures went down to my guts and that's why I couldn't write them."[6] Though his list of credits is fairly lengthy in the American Film Institute's *Who Wrote the Movie?* most of the films he cites are adaptations, upon which he did not work, of his novels. He claims he was never asked to adapt his own novels into films, though Billy Wilder says he asked him to do *Double Indemnity* and turned to Chandler because Cain was busy. At the time of *MP* the film, Cain was writing one of his few original scripts, *Gypsy Wildcat*, for Jon Hall and Maria Montez. Most of the time Cain was a rewrite man, a script doctor, not an original scriptwriter.

As a novel, *MP* clearly represented a forcefully willed new direction for Cain, a deliberate avoidance of the taut, first-person tough guy form that had made *Postman* and *Double Indemnity* so successful. In *MP* Cain sought a broader perspective on Southern California. It contained no crime; it offered a wide range of detail. It was in conscious opposition to his usual books: female protagonist versus male, third person versus first, long and episodic versus short and fast-moving narrative, history versus the present, grand social scale versus the triangle.

Since most people think of *MP* the film when the title is mentioned, it may be useful to point out the most significant ways in which the novel differs from the film, before discussing the difficulties with the novel itself—difficulties that were to translate themselves into problems with the scriptwriting of *MP*. Briefly put, in the novel: (1) there is no murder, though Mildred in the penultimate chapter nearly strangles Veda when she discovers her in bed with Monte; (2) the narration is told without flashbacks in standard fashion, chronologically; (3) the period of time covered is longer, from the early

Depression to 1941 rather than from 1941 to 1945; (4) the narration is third person not first, though there is much close attention to Mildred's thoughts and feelings; (5) Veda achieves a successful career as a coloratura soprano with a climactic performance in the Hollywood Bowl; (6) the setting is much more tawdry and lower class—Mildred, though she has shapely legs and some sexual attractiveness, is no Joan Crawford and by the end of the book is fat on booze; and (7) the narrative is very episodic in structure with events linked loosely, much less dramatically.[7]

Cain's plan to expand on his tough guy novels with *MP* did not fully succeed. He broadened the action and perspective but at a cost. The fast-paced action for which he was known is absent; instead, the book plods along with journalistic detail frequently overwhelming the plot line. Toward its end, verisimilitude disappears entirely; swift changes in plot and character abound, and one climax follows rapidly upon another.

Veda's musical career undergoes the most distortion, causing havoc with the central plot of Mildred's love for her and straining the reader's credibility. It is easy to see why it had to disappear in the movie. Within a few chapters, Veda is a horrible failure in a piano audition for a maestro named Treviso and a glorious success as a coloratura soprano when he accidentally discovers her singing a tune in a parking lot. The book's resolution is particularly disturbing, offering both the satisfactions of melodramatic wish fulfillment and realistic domestic tragedy almost simultaneously. When Mildred discovers Veda in bed with Monte, she attacks and throttles her. Veda is nearly killed and loses her glorious voice. But Mildred's vindication is short-lived; Veda reveals that her injury was faked to get out of an unwanted contract and to elope with Monte. At the end Mildred is back with Bert, freer and wiser, but impoverished and disillusioned.

Such wild changes clearly promote melodrama and undermine the realism of the earlier chapters, a common critical complaint made against Cain and *MP* in particular. They suggest, as Oates has noted, that the source for such actions may lie in the unconscious, in Mildred's psyche—not in the dreary realistic details the book accumulates—a theme the movie amplifies by its film noir style.

Cain also seems uncomfortable in this third-person voice, which he here used extensively for the first time. Oates finds this the chief flaw of the novel: "*Mildred Pierce*, . . . over-long and shapeless, must surely owe its flaws to the third-person omniscient narration, which takes us too far from the victim and allows us more freedom than we want. To be successful, such narrowly-conceived art must blot out what landscape it cannot cover; hence the blurred surrealistic backgrounds of the successful Cain novels, *Postman* . . . and *Serenade*."[8]

The novel has a problem holding Mildred in clear perspective. Its detailed accounting of her world and close attention to her thoughts create a Mildred of determination and resilience. But when Cain takes a larger view or stresses the confused working of her unconscious wishes, Mildred becomes a victim. Often she is the stereotype of the lower-class Southern California housewife with aspirations beyond her status. Cain mocks her Spanish-style bungalow and the astrologically acquired names of her children, Veda and Moire (Ray), which she mispronounces. These moments resemble the satiric technique of Nathanael West.

At other times she is mercilessly victimized by a sexuality that she cannot control, despite all her noble ambitions and plans. Ultimately all she does must be judged in light of her wish to gain Veda's affection—in a sense, to be the Veda that she cannot be because of her background, class, appearance, and work.

From the perspective of the unconscious, Veda represents all that Mildred most desires: art, music, elegance, and sexual beauty. Veda is an intensification of Mildred's yearnings and ideals, and also of her darker unconscious impulses and energies. Mildred's money-making schemes, noble in purpose but corrupt in their original design to win Veda's love, are mirrored in Veda in a more distorted form: the ruthlessness of blackmail, marriage as a way to class and money. Further, Mildred's commitment to realize her wish exacts a repression of sexuality that takes revenge upon her. Despite her resistances, Mildred regularly falls victim to Wally's and Monte's sexual designs upon her. She prefers snuggling and cuddling with Veda to sleeping with Bert or Monte. When Veda announces her pregnancy, she is stricken with sexual jealousy. Given the projection of her sexuality onto Veda, it is not unreasonable that it is Veda who finally goes to bed with Monte. Sexual repression and the need to work, the demand to subordinate all concerns to winning Veda back, produce a Mildred who becomes tough on booze. At the end of the book Mildred is described as a plump, savage animal who flings herself at Veda in fury. Cain gives Mildred noble plans and ambitions but cynically undermines them by her constant failure to see the larger, overarching forces of society and sexuality that really direct her.

What Cain was attempting in *MP* is not always clear. He is on record as having said he tried to write a novel about a woman who uses men to gain her end, not the traditional *femme fatale* but a "victim of the Depression, a venal

American housewife who didn't know she was using men, but imagined herself quite noble."[9] He stresses Mildred's neurotic, compulsive behavior as she tries to gain Veda's love and respect. In the preface to *The Butterfly* (1946), he said, "I write of the wish that comes true . . . for some reason a terrifying concept, at least to my imagination. Of course, the wish must have terror in it. I think my stories have some quality of the opening of a forbidden box, and that it is this, rather than violence, sex, or any of the things usually cited by way of explanation, that gives them the drive so often noted."[10]

Still, this broader perspective on Mildred is not entirely successful in undermining her. Cain refuses to believe that she is simply typical; she has a "squint" in her eye that argues for shrewdness of character and a tough stance against adversity. Today, with the women's movement asking readers to reconsider and reevaluate women characters in fiction, Mildred's resilience and determination may seem more striking and positive than Cain intended them to be. His own interpretation of her seems misogynistic; he sees her as the realistic version of the more romantic crime novel's *femme fatale*.

JERRY WALD'S ROLE AS PRODUCER

As the producer of *MP*, Jerry Wald was its most important shaping force. Not only did he make all the major preproduction decisions—most importantly offering the role to Joan Crawford for her "comeback"—but he also oversaw the entire production. As the eight treatments and screenplays testify, Wald valued the screenplay as the most important component of the successful film. The many versions reveal not just the difficulty of scripting an unwieldy novel but also Wald's insistence on finding the right person to articulate on paper his conception of the film with the correct tone and the proper dramatic structure and theme. In print, Wald was modest about his role as producer. "I only block out the stories, the other fellow does the real work."[11] After the writer, Wald listed in order of importance the performers and the director. Last was "the producer who is coach on the sidelines cheering the team on and doing a general supervisory job." Yet, despite this insistence, *MP* bears many hallmarks of a strong and intransigent Wald, one who determined the basic directions and tone of the film. The difficulties behind scripting *MP* and the dizzying succession of scriptwriters point to Wald's determination to shape it his way, to go beyond domestic drama and the women's movie to a more lurid melodrama of murder and infidelity.

Yet if Wald was a strong producer and controlled his writers by forceful directives, he was also anchored in the Warners world and its studio traditions, both of genre and film production. He had no desire to break with them completely. By background Wald was a perfect part of Warners of the 1930s, an emigrant from the newspaper world to the scriptwriting department of the studio. Like Cain and many others, he moved from journalism to scriptwriting. During the 1930s and early 1940s Wald wrote sixty-five scripts, notably *The Roaring Twenties* (1939), *Torrid Zone* (1940), *They Drive by Night* (1940), and *Manpower* (1941). These propelled him into a producer's role where he became famous for World War II films: *Action in the North Atlantic* (1943), *Destination Tokyo* (1944), *Objective Burma* (1945), and *Pride of the Marines* (1945).

In *MP* Wald saw an appealing risk of moving away from war and action movies. While he had produced two Kaufman and Hart comedies (*The Man Who Came to Dinner* and *George Washington Slept Here*—both 1942) neither one achieved the success of the war films. His bent was not toward comedy. A women's movie with roots in realism and with some of the strong sexual elements of an original novel might prove an auspicious choice.

Wald loved risk and ambitious projects. While he regularly praised the movie code of censorship, he clearly enjoyed pushing it to its limits and making movies of subjects that were supposedly unfilmable. *MP* was the first in a long line of projects that moved between the lurid and the artsy, often combining both: *Flamingo Road*, *Johnny Belinda* (with its important rape scene), *Sons and Lovers* from the D. H. Lawrence novel, *Peyton Place* and its sequel from the scandalous best seller, steamy versions of Faulkner, *The Long Hot Summer*, and *The Sound and the Fury*. When he died unexpectedly at age fifty Wald was busy on a never-produced version of James Joyce's *Ulysses*, a perfect blend of high art and highly censorable material.

Just as *MP* was emerging from property to project in 1944, Paramount released *Double Indemnity* to great critical acclaim. With a screenplay by its director Billy Wilder and the noted mystery writer Raymond Chandler, *Double Indemnity* went further than previous noir films in depicting the meanness, venality, lust, and sordidness of its central characters. Its dark location photography, which departed from studio practice, won high acclaim for enhancing that realism. Its retrospective narration and bitter voice-over added to the mood of futility, disenchantment, and failure—especially since it was being told by a dying man.

Wald was much taken by that film and envisioned *MP* as similar—more a women's movie as its plot dictated, but one with *Double Indemnity*'s and Cain's reputation for murder and lurid sexuality. Much of *Double Indemnity* entered into the film *MP*—particularly the retrospective narration, the flashbacks and voice-over, and the murder as a climax—but Warners, as *MP* testifies, was still anchored in the studio system. Filmmaking was more a collaborative effort at Warners than at Paramount, and the movie did not have a pioneering talent like Wilder's behind it. Wald did not see himself as either writer or director. Unlike Wilder he was not ready to upset studio traditions. Instead, he saw himself as working within them, giving them a new direction, combining crime and the women's movie, and pushing the treatment up to big budget glamour.

Because of Wald's conception of his role within the studio and the novel's more traditional themes and manner, its lack of a murder and crime, and the affinity of the protagonist with earlier Warners genre pictures, *MP* was more of a traditional studio movie and less of a breakthrough film than *Double Indemnity*. Wald nowhere pressed to break the carefully controlled pattern of studio filming and to follow *Double Indemnity* into its pioneering on-location realistic camera work. Instead, studio lighting and camera work in *MP* were reinforced to highlight glamour, luxury, and Crawford's star status. Yet, with its sense of bitterness and duplicity in family life, love, and business, *MP* introduced an important note of disenchantment into the world of Warners films and heralded the new trend of blending crime and the women's movie.

Wald's kind of realism in the women's movie took it out of the idealistic and yearning tradition typified by *Now, Voyager*. "In retrospect," says David Thomson, "he turned Warners from crime to the women's picture."[12] Before leaving Warners in 1952, he was to produce four more Crawford pictures: *Humoresque, Possessed, Flamingo Road* (which reunited her with Zachary Scott), and *The Damned Don't Cry*. Later at Fox he produced a fifth, *The Best of Everything*.

His was not the traditional realism of character and detail; these he tended to purge from the novel and many of the scripts. Realism for Wald meant a kind of contemporary chic, an explicitness about sex and topics forbidden by the production code, a certain decadence that allowed a glimpse of the underside of life. He insisted on updating the film and taking it out of the dreary "realistic" thirties and the Depression. He stripped away Monte's faded playboy qualities and gave him a highly charged elegance, which nevertheless concealed corruption. Mildred's added glamour also removed her from the novel's tougher lower-class and far less beautiful depiction. Though he could not be as explicit as the novel about Mildred's sexual relations with Wally and Monte, he could go further than most films of the time and suggest a highly tangled web that finally seems more decadent than that in the novel, where the sexuality is often innocent and impulsive. Most importantly, it was Wald's decision to tell the story in flashback in the manner of *Double Indemnity* and to add the murder and Veda's failure as a singer to give the film dramatic impact that the episodic novel lacked. He steadfastly insisted on a movement toward a climactic murder, one that realistically oriented screenwriters, particularly the gifted Catherine Turney, found difficult to incorporate in their scripts.

Wald's newspaper background clearly put him into closer contact with the Warners crime tradition than its weepy one and he may have felt comfortable having a murder story as a framework. More likely he simply thought the combination would be potent box office, drawing different audiences. Wald's combined interests pushed Warners toward a special brand of women's movie, one with noirish overtones, crime, and rather lurid sexual suggestions. The combination proved extremely difficult to attain. As usual, Wald first called for a treatment and commissioned the best screenwriters he could find. But *MP* was to prove an extremely troublesome property to script. An already overly complicated novel was now further complicated by Wald's insistence on additions and new directions.

TURNEY'S SCRIPTS AND MALTZ'S COMMENTS

Mildred's rocky road to the screen involved at least eight treatments and screenplays, several of them unfinished, beginning with Thames Williamson's treatment dated January 21, 1944, a year before the movie was filmed, to Ranald MacDougall's revised final screenplay dated December 5, 1944, but incorporating many changes up through February 24, 1945, when the movie was nearing completion. Further changes occurred between the revised final and the shooting. Like *Casablanca*, much of *MP* was being put in final script form just a day or two ahead of the camera; some of it was probably written on the set, and some was improvised by the actors and Curtiz. The extreme difficulties of getting a workable script sprang from a basically unwieldy book that was made even more cumbersome by the superimposition of a crime story. The problem of condensing *MP* and giving it dramatic shape within standard running time and standard screenplay length was never satisfactorily resolved. Condensation brought odd juxtapositions and various inconsistencies. The movie is most opaque about the financial structure of Mildred's business. Elsewhere character motivations remain obscure, and key information is withheld.

The eight treatments and screenplays can be conveniently divided into two groups, the first clustered around two lengthy screenplays by Catherine

Turney, written in the spring and summer of 1944, and the second around two equally lengthy ones by Ranald MacDougall. In both cases, excellent first versions stop about two thirds of the way through because of length. Too much of the novel—the parts where different strands trailed into episodic and often melodramatic plots—remained to be treated in too few pages. How to give some unity and direction to this cluttered material was the obstacle that both Turney and MacDougall faced.

Constituting the first group are Williamson's treatment, Turney's two screenplays, and Albert Maltz's comments with detailed ideas for making characters, themes, and plot more believable and realistic. Much of *MP* as it appears on the screen was shaped by Turney's screenplays, somewhat abetted by Williamson's and Maltz's suggestions. The direction of these screenplays is toward realism, domestic drama, even soap opera, i.e., more toward the conventional Warners formulas and less toward the bitter, stylized, and theatrical world of film noir. These scripts underline Mildred's lower-middle-class origins and her struggle; they support her attempts to make her own way more fully than MacDougall's, and they rarely suggest anything duplicitous. There is no indication that they were written for Crawford since the trio of Crawford-Curtiz-Carson was not announced for the film until October 1944.

Williamson's treatment needs no detailed comment since he simply followed most of the incidents of the book in elaborate detail, easy enough to do in a 28-page treatment but impossible in a 175-page script. Williamson was a writer of textbooks on economics, sociology, and American democracy in the 1920s and a regional and ethnic novelist in the 1930s. Most of his finished screenplays were conventional westerns. He did not bring any perspicacity to *MP*, but in three important suggestions he shaped the scripts that followed: he shifted the time to the present, he used a flashback technique in which Mildred talks to the police, and he rehabilitated Bert to become a fit husband for Mildred. All three probably reflect Wald's directives rather than Williamson's originality.

Turney's two screenplays are certainly as strong as MacDougall's but differ in being more akin to domestic drama than film noir. They are delicate, carefully observed, realistic, and clear in their dramatic thrust. If MacDougall did not use their actual dialogue, he followed their general line of development. Turney's scripts follow the book closely, particularly in its clearer early parts, but it is she who determines which scenes are dramatized and which omitted, where the emphasis will fall, how the scenes should be dramatically linked, and what the overall structure should be. Most of her choices are followed in all the other scripts, even to reworking her original scenes, so it seems appropriate to call her a co-author of the screenplay, even though her name does not appear on the final credits.[13]

Had Catherine Turney received the co-credit that seems her due, *MP* would have been her first screenplay credit. A burgeoning playwright in the late 1930s, she came under contract to Warners from 1943 to 1948. After *MP*, she received credit for the writing of *My Reputation, Of Human Bondage, One More Tomorrow, A Stolen Life, The Man I Love,* and *Cry Wolf.*

Set in 1939 to the present, Turney's first screenplay moves nicely through the book's essential incidents, dramatizing them effectively with the central idea that Mildred is doing all this, wrongly but nobly, for Veda's sake. She begins, as the book does, with Mildred and Bert's quarrel and breakup, but she underlines Mildred's flaw as well as Bert's lack of work. "I want her [Veda] to have cake. Ray's like me—She'll eat bread and be glad to get it, but not Veda." Bert argues, "The moment she [Veda] was born, I might have been that picture on the wall." He warns Mildred that "when she's got all she wants from you, she'll walk out."

Following the book closely, she retains such minor characters as Bert's parents and Lucy Gessler, Mildred's neighbor, tough-minded confidante, and salty adviser. After Bert's departure, Turney shows Mildred's financial plight, her failed attempt to win Wally honorably, her decision to take a job, her agonizing hunt for work, and her finding the restaurant job. Later she acquires the pie concession, meets Monte in the restaurant, and has a key showdown with Veda when Veda discovers she is a waitress. Mildred saves face by telling her she is "learning the business to open her own." She presents the idea to Wally, gets a divorce from Bert, and goes to Arrowhead with Monte. When Ray dies from pneumonia after this trip, Mildred blames herself. With Veda now her only child, Mildred intensifies her drive for the restaurant with success. She begins an affair with Monte, though largely for Veda, and Veda begins an affair with Ted Randolph (later Ted Forrester). Things now take a turn for the worse. Mildred loans Monte money and Veda requires increasingly lavish spending. Mrs. Randolph threatens Mildred in her interview; the marriage of Veda and Ted is "settled" in the lawyer's office, and shortly afterward Mildred learns of Veda's role in blackmailing the Randolphs. Mildred rips the check up and throws Veda out of the house. Here Turney's screenplay ends at 147 pages and with a third of the book remaining.

The conclusion is in outline form. In a variation on Mildred's interview with Treviso in the book, Mildred realizes that she needs to lure Veda back. Seeing Veda in the nightclub, she must rescue her; she venally proposes marriage to Monte to get his Pasadena house. A party is planned to announce

Mildred's engagement to Monte; Veda has been reconciled to Mildred. But upstairs in a business conference Ida (a friend she met as a waitress) and Wally, acting for Mildred's creditors, take the restaurants away from her. Downstairs she discovers Veda in Monte's arms. There is no murder. Mildred simply walks out and returns to Glendale and Bert. "One morning you wake up and suddenly realize that you're free." Mildred and Bert join hands; "there will be a good basis between them for the rest of their lives."

I have stated these incidents at length because they form the spine of the later scripts and the film. Gone is much of the extraneous and episodic material. Veda's lengthy musical career is omitted. Such melodramatic scenes as the confusingly climactic visit of Mildred to denounce Monte on a rainy New Year's Eve—and her final indignity at having to be rescued by him from her flooded car—are toned down and merged with more realistic, similar scenes that strengthen the central plot. The importance of the blackmail and check-ripping scene is built up and preceded by an original scene with the lawyers. Mildred and Bert's private sleuthing and their hiring a detective to find Ted, who is on the run, are omitted. Presumably for the censor's sake, Veda is married secretly to Ted, and Mildred keeps her virtue at Arrowhead with Monte and earlier with Wally at dinner when he tries to court her. (In the book, she yields to an overpowering sexuality, particularly with Monte, which complicates her guilt about Ray's death.)

Turney's script shows some strong structural qualities. Three major confrontations occur between Mildred and Veda: after Mildred discovers Letty in the uniform Veda knows her mother wears to the restaurant, when Mildred discovers Veda's blackmail of Ted, and when she finds her in Monte's arms. There is also good use of a device wherein Veda's face is superimposed on Mildred's at crucial, critical moments, for example, when Monte offers to do things for Veda if Mildred will be more loving. Turney's script can be described as a realistic women's movie. It lacks both the extreme cynicism of Cain's book and its strong sexual subcurrents; unlike the film, it has few stylized noir overtones, and the accent is not on the mixture of duplicitous sexuality and business but on Mildred's struggle. It is a good domestic drama, more humanly believable than the book, but it is clearly not the movie that the more ambitious and "masculine" Wald wanted.

The problems of the script in length, structure, and tone led Wald to call in Albert Maltz for advice. Wald had worked with Maltz on *Destination Tokyo* and *Pride of the Marines*, both big hits. Maltz was also a highly successful playwright. With his friend George Sklar he had co-authored three of the 1930s' most important socially conscious left-wing plays, *Black Pit*, *Peace on Earth*, and *Merry-Go-Round*. He was asked not to write a script but to see how Turney as a novice scriptwriter could extricate herself from her difficulties and work along clearer lines. Wald may have also wanted a more trusted masculine voice to evaluate her script and to give it a tougher, more realistic tone. Maltz's sixty-two pages of comments on *MP* make the most interesting reading on the film and provide a behind-the-scenes picture of Wald's intentions and his creative force in shaping the movie. They also reveal the balancing act of bringing Turney's script into conformity with both his own social realism and Wald's more melodramatic basic theme: "A mother sacrifices a great deal for a child she loves. The child turns out to be empty of real talent and a bitch who betrays her mother."

Maltz praises both Wald's intent and Turney's first script. Turney has done "an admirable job in terms of selection, construction, and dialogue" but the script has two main flaws. It is still too episodic and biographic, appropriate for the novel but not for a movie that should be "mounting toward a payoff situation." And the Veda Turney has conceived is even more unbelievable than the one in the book. "Mildred becomes an utter idiot for not seeing through her." This problem is intensified by Turney's success with the other characters, whom she has made more human than those in the book; he regards Cain's as "neurotic to the point of freakishness."

His solution is to deepen the realism of the book by centering the plot on a more believable Veda who conceals her treachery under charm and who changes subtly throughout. To this end he suggests eliminating Ray and purging both Monte and Bert of any melodramatic qualities. Maltz argues for consistency and depth of character and through these to social implications. Bert and Monte must both be "attractive failures, weak men who get onto the skids once they lose the financial cushion upon which their security and personality graces depend." And Veda's breakup should not be rendered in an unconvincing melodramatic blackmail scene, but should be based upon her "spiritual breakup when the bubble of her talent bursts." Maltz is moving in the direction of social analysis through realistic psychology. His ideas for the script look back to his plays of the 1930s rather than to Cain's novel or a modern, more stylized equivalent that needed Wald's violent payoff of blackmail, murder, and extreme action. Only a few of Maltz's ideas were heeded even in Turney's rewritten version, and when she abandoned the script, the new writers went in even more divergent directions. Intent on something more extravagant than the social realism of the New York theater that Maltz provided, Wald did not get from Maltz the kind of realism he was after.

Maltz ultimately envisioned the film as a heroic drama of one of the millions of little people, limited and flawed, but struggling and courageous. It is very much the vision of the socially conscious playwright of the thirties. Familiar with Brecht in Hollywood left-wing circles, he may also have seen Mildred as analogous to Mother Courage, another figure crippled by her background and the system she is in, but tough and unbowed. He saw it as the story "of a courageous woman—and of a modern Job. Mildred Pierce is not a glamorous woman in the obvious sense; she is by no means perfect; she has all of the limitations of her lower-middle-class upbringing and environment. In addition, she is the victim of a fatal (but typical) flaw: She is blind to her children's real nature. Yet despite the successive tragedies of her life she remains unbowed. The film is to be called *Mildred Pierce* but it might be called *Courage*."

Turney's second script manages the complexities of the last part of the novel quite nicely. She keeps Ray as a character and still lets Mildred manipulate Monte into romance and marriage for Veda's sake. (Maltz had felt that Mildred remained too attached to Bert and that her handling of Monte made her seem villainous.) As though following Maltz's suggestions, she writes a socially conscious scene in which Monte's snobbish sister sneers at Mildred and the people from the restaurant. Harkening to Wald's idea about Veda's overturned musical ambitions, she supplies the original scene of Veda's singing in a sleazy nightclub. Without much conviction, she writes the obligatory scene in which Veda kills Monte and follows it with a scene where Veda seeks help from Mildred, who now at last realizes Veda is no good. There is also a scene where Mildred contemplates suicide on a bridge, which MacDougall was later to transpose to the Santa Monica Pier and highlight as the first view of Mildred in the film. In Turney's version, the dilemma is resolved when Mildred calls the police and frees herself from Veda: "It takes a long time to kill the way I felt toward you. Not quick—like you killed Monte. But you killed it."

Turney's second script was doomed before it was started. She was caught between the melodramatic scenario Wald demanded and the more realistic treatment she and Maltz felt the story should have. And between her own psychological and domestic realism and that of Maltz with its more leftist bent, there was still another gap. However good her second script is, it looks patched to meet Wald's demands, some of Maltz's urgings, and her own interests. It is a bad fusion of the women's movie and film noir. It is still basically—despite the murder of Monte—a sensitive, nonviolent, domestic drama to which the murder seems appended and unintegrated. The handling of Veda's musical career, particularly the rejection by Treviso, also seems awkward, without buildup and without clear aftereffects.

Whether Turney could have solved these problems with a third script or more rewriting is a moot point. Immediately after the mercurial Wald had seen *Double Indemnity* he called her and announced, "From now on, every picture I make will be done in flashback," but she had been opposed to the flashback idea from the start.[14] Turney then argued in conference with Wald that while she could go along with Mildred's murder of Monte as "the inevitable climax of a realistic drama," *MP* was not a murder mystery like *Double Indemnity* where murder was "the raison d'être for the story." "I did attempt, finally," Turney admits, "to try to develop it [the script] in flashback theme but at no time was I happy about it."

At this stage the script still had no director. Outside circumstances then forced Turney from the project; she had to honor a prior commitment to script *A Stolen Life* for Bette Davis, with the star acting as her own producer for the first time under a plan Warners had devised for its big stars to get a tax break. Davis had seen parts of *My Reputation* (released January 1946), Turney's first solo screenplay, and wanted her as a writer for *A Stolen Life*. Turney was assigned by Davis to be with the story from writing to preview. Any further participation in *MP* had to be indirect.

By this time, according to Turney, Michael Curtiz had entered the scene, liked the flashback idea, and had decided to push it further in the direction of a whodunit. Because *Mildred Pierce* seemed too dull to him, he had altered the title to *House on the Sand*. The story of Turney's tangential connection with the final scripts and more importantly her own removal from the credits of her name as co-writer is best told in her own words:

> [Curtiz] wanted a lot of rewriting and Wald tried but failed to have me assigned because Bette [Davis] was adamant in refusing to release her writer. I wouldn't have been happy about it either. Ranald MacDougall had been working for Wald who was high on him, and so Randy was assigned to work with Curtiz. Joan [Crawford] was most upset about the changes and the concept of Curtiz, but eventually accepted it. The new flashback sequences came through to me from the script department as I was still listed as the first credit on the script. A lot of footage seemed wasted to me and important characterization and development in the basic theme had to be cut. When the Final was delivered to me, the credits were reversed—I was second. It

seemed to me a fair arrangement inasmuch as Randy had been working closely with Curtiz while I was with *Stolen Life*. But I deplored the flashback style and my then agent thought I should remove my name. I had received nothing but solo credits and my agent objected to my being second banana, so to speak. As it turned out, it was a grievous mistake on his and my part, but in all fairness, it was not Jerry Wald's decision.[15] In fact, before I asked to be removed he told me many times, "You'll be protected with the credits—you broke the back of the story," etc. Despite this, several prints had gone out with my name still on the credit list—mostly in the South, I gather, because I got some fan mail from people who apparently liked my work.[16]

The Quigley publication *Year Book* for 1946 lists Turney as one of the box-office champions for that year for *MP*, hence the mention in several reference books of Turney as co-writer.

GRUEN'S AND FAULKNER'S SCREENPLAYS

With the next set of scripts Wald starts the project over. Turney's script provided a base upon which his own ideas for the film and the improvisations of other writers could be added. Since a faithful rendering of all the strands of the book had proved to be impossible, the new scripts depart more strikingly from it and condense and omit still more of the major incidents. To the domestic, realistic drama is added a new tone and stance; the accent is on the lurid, the extravagant, and the outrageous. The scripts become more bitter and neurotic.

Of the five later scripts, two are by Ranald MacDougall. His first is unfinished, for the same reasons of length as Turney's. It is preceded by Margaret Gruen's, a wildly baroque and extravagantly emotional version that departs from the book with an almost lunatic freedom, and followed by rewrites by William Faulkner and Louise Randall Pierson. Faulkner's rewrite gradually takes on enough independence to become an original script, as extravagant as Gruen's but much better written. Pierson sticks to rewriting special scenes and goes beyond MacDougall's script. She offers the major confrontation between Mildred and Veda, and she devises some scenes for the final part, notably Mildred's rejecting Monte in her office, which MacDougall later incorporated.

This flurry of activity by new writers, the movement in many new directions with frequent hasty rewrites, becomes more understandable when we realize that the film was nearing production without a suitable or complete script. By October Curtiz was assigned to direct Joan Crawford and Jack Carson in the movie, and production was slated to begin on December 6, with a sixty-day production schedule. Probably because of both script and casting delays, production seems to have been held up. *Motion Picture Herald* reported that shooting on the film began during the week of December 16, 1944, and stopped during the week of March 17, 1945, about thirty days over an already lengthy schedule. (By contrast, *The Big Sleep*, which was being shot just a bit before, had only a forty-two-day schedule.) Shooting may have been held up even further because several major members of the cast were not announced until late December or early January: Zachary Scott, Ann Blyth, and Eve Arden. The numerous inserts in the script with their dates stretching from December to late February also testify that a script was not ready. And when we see the number of changes from final script to film, it is clear that even at the time of filming much of the screenplay was in a state of flux. MacDougall was not exaggerating when he claimed that he wrote the final screenplay while the movie was being filmed.[17]

By October Wald knew he had to depart significantly from both the book and Turney's scripts, but the new versions, both MacDougall's three-part, present-tense framework with flashbacks (written between the end of October and the beginning of December) and Gruen's and Faulkner's more baroque elaborations, had problems of their own. Faulkner and Gruen not only left the book far behind but offered in its stead outlandish melodramatic actions that perhaps only a Douglas Sirk could have carried off with any credibility or style. MacDougall gave Wald the requisite flashback form and made it central, but he dawdled over the present, needlessly complicating its action and atmosphere. When he turned to the flashback there was little time for the story to develop. In his initial foray he also relied less on Turney's structure and more on the incidents of the book; soon he found himself entrapped with too many actions and climaxes.

For a moment we should look at the extravagant screenplays of Gruen and Faulkner, little of which reached the screen, but which nevertheless pointed to the lurid, strange, and disturbing version that did. Gruen's screenplay initiates these freer variations on the book in a wild and outrageous way. Of all the scripts, the writing here is the weakest and the characterizations the thinnest. Mildred is a simple-minded fool and Veda an open, conniving bitch; both characters are often ludicrous.

MacDougall's first draft followed, but Faulkner's screenplay, which started as inserts and reworkings of MacDougall's, was written at the same time and more appropriately belongs with Gruen's in its accent on the Gothic and outlandish. Faulkner's name on a screenplay compels our interest, though usually for reasons apart from his screenwriting. His writing is better than Gruen's but his version is equally bizarre. As with Gruen, it is difficult to tell whether he is seriously executing an assignment or simply giving himself up to lurid variations on a story. Faulkner was obviously unsuited by temperament to a story like *MP*. His best writing was done on a more personal basis for Howard Hawks (*To Have and Have Not* and *The Big Sleep* from this period at Warners), and he may have regarded this assignment with glum futility. Clearly, however, he has read the book and the other screenplays and has reflected on them. He reduces much of the action and character portrayals to Mildred's elaborate voice-over and focuses instead on off-center action. He is obsessed with the contractual arrangements behind the restaurant and is rightly puzzled by how Mildred could finance it. In the book Wally simply sells Mildred the old real estate office for her restaurant. It is the Depression, real estate is dead, and he needs to claim the tax loss. But in MacDougall's version, which Faulkner follows, she gets the old, run-down house from Monte Beragon. In MacDougall, Wally fast-talks Monte into signing over the deed to Mildred even though she plans to pay much later. Monte may not be as conned as Wally thinks he is; he is moved by Mildred's desperate plea and is attracted to her. His easy lifestyle allows him to indulge in a whim.

Faulkner wants something more financially sound and believable. He makes Wally, Mildred, and Monte partners from the start. Though late changes do something similar with the film, Monte's involvement in the business comes much later and is clearly marked out as an exchange for marriage to Mildred. Wally's involvement remains cloudy, a late insert to make his takeover at the end credible. Faulkner is no help in spelling out the terms of the partnership, nor does he elucidate the takeover at the end. Even Mildred says at one point that she cannot understand a thing that is happening. With its sleazy, underhanded business dealings and with Wally chewing on a fat cigar, Mildred's world seems more akin to the Snopeses of Faulkner's novels than it does to either the world of Cain or MacDougall. At times the script veers off into the Gothic. After Ray's death Veda sleepwalks in grief. There are huge rings under her eyes, but Mildred soon discovers they are the result of mascara. Quickly she suppresses her discovery. When Mildred marries Monte, Veda drinks a bit of poison, her aim being to disrupt the marriage night by claiming Monte for an attendant in her hospital room. There is even the suggestion that Veda caused Ray's death by insisting both stay in the water at Arrowhead long enough to show off her new bathing suit.

Faulkner also tries to work in Veda's singing career but he lets Veda subvert it herself. Mildred buys the critical world of Pasadena to attend Veda's recital, but Veda responds with a salacious song, a flimsy costume, and insults for the guests. Following Curtiz's symbolic retitling, Faulkner calls the film "House on the Sand," a phrase inspired by MacDougall's first draft where Mildred describes the sinking foundations of the Malibu house to Wally. The metaphor of family collapse runs through Faulkner's script.

Aside from the three-way partnership, which the film handles differently, Faulkner's only other significant contribution seems to be in casting Lottie, Mildred's maid, as a black woman. However, he did not envision Butterfly McQueen. His Lottie is more like Hattie McDaniel, a Dilsey type, who finally comforts a distraught Mildred after Ray's death by holding her and singing "Steal Away." "God damn! How's that for a scene?" Faulkner wrote in the margin.

MACDOUGALL'S SCRIPTS AND PIERSON'S REVISIONS

With MacDougall's first script, *MP* begins to resemble the film. The major innovation, a present-tense story that features a murder and puts the material of the book into flashback form, accorded with Wald's ideas from the start of the project. It gave the "masculine" and melodramatic point of view that he wanted and put the women's film in a strange new context, one of jealousy, treachery, and sexual confusion mixed with shady business dealings. Surrounding the flashbacks was a disturbing world of film noir conventions: police stations late at night, a frightened and suicidal woman on a fog-shrouded pier, a body in a huge and elegant beach house. This material subtly played over the flashbacks, giving them a different interpretation and lending them an element of neurosis and sexual excess. MacDougall gives us both a Mildred who can give Wally the chills with the way she makes love—a noir scene in the present—and a devoted matriarchal figure intent on success for herself and her family—women's movie scenes from the flashbacks. It is MacDougall who successfully solves the problem of fusing the women's movie with film noir.

One of the wunderkindern, along with Norman Corwin, Arch Oboler, and Orson Welles, who came to fame in radio in the late thirties and early forties, MacDougall authored the prestigious war broadcast series *The Man behind the Gun*. His first script at Warners for Wald was a war film, *Objective Burma*, co-written with Lester Cole. When Wald ran into snags with Turney's scripts, he turned to MacDougall for a fresh perspective. MacDougall brought to his perception of the book a cold, detailed, glittering style, and he imaginatively reworked its incidents and those in Turney's screenplays. He gave depth and body to Wald's idea of a present-tense framework with a murder—so much so, in fact, that his first draft contains almost as many pages of this material as it does of Mildred's flashback. MacDougall did not come from the socially conscious left-wing theater as many of Wald's writers did. He was from the newer medium of radio, with its emphasis on flashy effects, quick dramatic momentum, and an economical use of devices to catch and hold a listener and involve him. His appeal was ahistorical and apolitical, his focus more on myth than on naturalism and social context. Radio with its stress on attention-getting devices and its demands for clean, spare storytelling in a limited time was good training for subduing an episodic novel, now further complicated by a new story in the present tense.

With a keen dramatic sense MacDougall wisely shapes his first flashback around the possibilities of Bert's and Mildred's guilt and concludes its dovetailing back into the present at mid-movie with Bert's smashing the glass out of Monte's hand when the latter proposes a somewhat insulting toast. Within this flashback MacDougall solved a number of problems that had perplexed the other screenwriters.

He involves Monte in Mildred's business from the start, making him the owner of the White Elephant, which under a special arrangement with him Mildred will transform into a restaurant. By letting Wally seemingly fast-talk Monte into this and having Monte act magnanimously or out of romantic whim, he underscores the mixture of sexuality and business that permeates Mildred's relationship with these two double-dealing, weak, and often meretricious men. MacDougall wisely sets the acquisition scene in the Santa Monica house (Malibu in the script, but a number of references in the film suggest Santa Monica) where we first witness the present-tense murder of Monte. The glamourous set is seen under several lights, ranging from the enticingly romantic aura of this scene to the passionate swimming party and the chilling death of the opening and end. Mildred's entrance into the world of business dealing is also her entrance into a distorted passion. She moves from the simply garbed homemaker who doesn't drink to the powerful, stylishly dressed *femme fatale* who drinks her liquor straight. MacDougall powerfully uses his settings and basic actions to plot the dramatic curve of the script.

The Santa Monica beach house replaces the more rustic Arrowhead setting where all previous scripts had set the beginnings of their romance. This is not so much an idyll for Mildred as Arrowhead seemed, but the entrance into a more complex, entangled world. Santa Monica brought the murder into the proximity of the Los Angeles setting and probably suggested the pier as a place for a suicide attempt that Turney had placed elsewhere. The creation of Wally's Hawaiian cafe on the pier provides an inspired link to the Mildred-Monte story and foregrounds the distorted romantic triangle and its unfulfilled sexuality. Like the beach house, the nightclub repeats itself with a difference, though it never fully escapes its tawdry overtones; later we see Veda perform her act there. Both the beach house and the pier are more urban than Arrowhead and contribute a sinister note in place of the healthy release Arrowhead had suggested. Further, the problem of Mildred's staying overnight at Arrowhead (did she sleep with Monte, as in the book, or didn't she?) had proved insuperable; here the environment added enough suggestions of sex—a closetful of bathing suits all belonging to his "sister"—and Mildred could be whisked back to her house the same night, satisfying the viewer's desire and the censor's demands. MacDougall cleverly lets the children go to Arrowhead instead; it's a more innocent place and the water is cold enough to provide an occasion for Kay's contracting pneumonia.

Especially striking in MacDougall's first draft are the homages to *Citizen Kane*. Here the detective shows Mildred photos that appear as live action later in the film. In its circular movement and structure, its beginning with a death and its fatalistic movement forward until the missing shot has been supplied at the end (here no Rosebud, but Ann Blyth firing the gun) *MP* resembles Kane. As in Kane too, images open up and are deepened. A simple murder has layers of plot beneath it. The episode in the house with Wally resonates with incompleteness that bit by bit is filled in during the film. Mildred's peculiar punishment for him makes us wonder what he could have done to her to deserve so cruel a trick.

MacDougall's troubles start with his second flashback, which works less successfully than the first. Instead of following Turney, he succumbs to the book's elaborate plotting. With stress on Mildred's various losses the script becomes maudlin. Ending with Veda's exit from the house, his first draft ran to 163 pages. Condensation was in order.

MacDougall stopped his first draft on December 2, and *MP* was slated to begin shooting December 6. Inside this pressurized atmosphere MacDougall began to cut, condense, and rework scenes and devise the whole latter part of the script. He was aided by Louise Randall Pierson, who had been reworking his material and occasionally going ahead on her own, devising new scenes. Pierson had just adapted *Roughly Speaking*, her memoir in which a strong woman holds her family together, for a film directed by Curtiz. Her work on MacDougall's script suggests an attempt to humanize his dialogue, to give it a more domestic and realistic touch; MacDougall often had a tin ear. He incorporated little of her material in his final script but he did adopt her original scene of Mildred's dismissal of Monte in her office. This neatly condensed the complex and lingering relationship with Monte that forms a major plot thread of the latter half of the book. Using this scene, MacDougall avoided the sprawl of his earlier script. But no amount of screenwriting magic can disguise the odd conjunction in the film of Mildred's telling Wally she is in love with Monte and in the next minute telling Monte she no longer is in love with him.

It is impossible to tell how much of the finished script existed by the beginning of shooting, which seems to have been delayed until December 16. By December 5, MacDougall had reworked the first eighty-four pages—up through the children's departure to Arrowhead—mainly by cutting mercilessly, particularly in the dawdling scenes in Detective Peterson's office where in the first version much was made of his mixture of malevolence and kindness (it is still there in his insinuating tone). But even here, changes after December 5 and during shooting continued. Part Two carries no date, but large portions of it were also altered in the final script and still further during filming.

The final script goes further in condensing scenes and tying plots together by focusing more sharply on Mildred. She is made stronger than ever. Instead of stressing her sufferings, as in the first script, MacDougall foregrounds her entry into a world of business, power, and romance. By this time MacDougall knew Crawford was to be the star of the film, and this knowledge clearly altered his emphasis.

The two major male roles are built up. Wally and Monte are treated more fully and continuously than in the book and other screenplays, and both are seen in business as well as romantic lights. Wally's character is closest to Cain's conception of him, but his role is amplified. Jack Carson was first announced as Crawford's co-star, not Zachary Scott. Along with Ida and Lottie, Wally also provides some of the necessary comic relief, and he extends it thematically into the more bitter role of the rejected suitor and finally into that of disillusioned sexuality. "I hate all women," he tells Ida. "Thank God you're not one." The effect of introducing Monte earlier and in a business-romantic context also deepens his impact.

MacDougall also strengthens the women's roles that help to define Mildred. Ida is built up as a confidante to Mildred, filling the role that Lucy Gessler did in the book and earlier scripts. Her caustic wit is further amplified—and still further, possibly by Eve Arden herself, on the set—adding comedy and commentary on the distorted dimensions of Mildred's relationships with Veda, Monte, and Wally. Ida has no part in cheating Mildred out of her restaurants, as she did with Wally in the book and in several scripts. She is an ideal of sorts to Mildred, one suited to a business desk, someone she can count on for help and advice in her workaday world. Yet Mildred quickly rises to supplant her. When they meet, Ida is managing Mr. Chris's restaurant (in the film, though not in the script, he is cut and it appears that she may be the owner of the restaurant), but soon she is working for Mildred. Her asexuality and matter-of-fact wit keep her from sharing Mildred's more glamourous style and sense of power. Ida is all there at first glance. If she partly functions as an ideal to Mildred, she is also a warning. There is a slight lesbian edge to her personality and her relationship with Mildred. Yet Ida has surrendered her sexuality; as she tells Mildred in scene 254, she has never been married and men treat her as the big sister type. Her freedom from men gives her the perspective to judge them cynically and correctly; she knows just what Wally and Monte are angling for. Yet this same freedom limits her power. She knows it's a man's world and she has nothing to bargain with. Her insight and intelligence don't get her power. Mildred keeps her sexual power over men and with it secures her financial empire.

Veda stands in sharp contrast to Ida, who links her with the money parasites like Monte and Wally who hover around Mildred. Like Ida, however, she functions as an ideal for Mildred. She is everything Mildred strives for. Mildred wants her love and is willing to devote all her moneymaking schemes and energy to getting it. Mildred also wants Veda's social status, glamour, and elegance. At the same time, Veda is all that Mildred represses beneath her mask of control and dignified stoicism. As we have noted before, Veda is Mildred's unconscious in both its idealized and darker aspects.

It is Veda who has the ultimate romantic moment with Monte; her passion at the bar seems far more exciting than Mildred's more innocent fireside moment after the swim. It is she who activates a sexual relation with Monte after Mildred turns her marriage with him into a business proposition. Finally it is she who shoots Monte, with the gun that Mildred took from her office to use against him for his business double-dealing. Veda is part of Mildred in more ways than Mildred knows. Mildred walks a fine line between the sexual deficiency of Ida and the sexual excess of Veda; she may protect her power thereby, but it is short-lived. She projects a sense of control, a kind of mask abetted by Crawford's performance. It begins to crumble when the worlds of business and sexuality take their revenge upon her. If Mildred partly represents a new ideal for woman, a movement away from the home and into a career, much like what the war had spawned, she also represents the vulnerability of that role, its demands of control upon the sexual self and its subservience to the world of masculinity in business. Ultimately Mildred must be avenged and restored to her woman's role in the home. MacDougall's script both celebrates and condemns Mildred.

MacDougall hints that Mildred's attempt to reach her business success is out of harmony with the "correct" picture of the nuclear family—correct, that is, to a masculine writer and the times of 1944. In the first flashback Mildred hesitates over her statement about placing Veda and Kay above Bert: "Maybe that's right and maybe it's wrong." Perhaps, it is hinted, Bert may be justified in his affair with Maggie Biederhof. The result is unnatural and leads to Mildred's move away from pies and kitchens to the world of business with its harsh dealings and the elegant boudoir with its sexual excess, destruction, and death. MacDougall's script, like much of film noir, punishes the active, powerful, and aggressive woman with her fatalistic charms—in this case, both Mildred and Veda. The *femme fatale* side of Mildred, represented by Veda as an excess, is killed. Mildred is rehabilitated through her ordeal with the detective and her guilt. She is purged of the Veda in her, both the elegant yearnings for superior status and her more hard-edged, tough, masculine business dealings. Mother love is restored to its proper perspective within the "natural" rhythms of the family context. Bert takes Mildred back and they exit to dawn and the swell of religious music that suggests a heavenly sanctioned marriage bond.

Mildred Pierce received Academy Award nominations for best picture and best screenplay, and Crawford won for best actress. Thus established as a trusted writer, MacDougall wrote the screenplays for two more of her films, *Possessed* and *Queen Bee* (1955), directing her in the latter.

NOTES

1. Joyce Carol Oates, "Man under Sentence of Death: The Novels of James M. Cain," in *Tough Guy Writers of the Thirties*, ed. David Madden (Carbondale: Southern Illinois University Press, 1968), 116.

2. The name is spelled Monty in the novel, Monte in the script. For the sake of consistency in the introduction, I have adopted the spelling Monte.

3. Oates, "Man under Sentence of Death," 124.

4. Released in 1946 but actually shot before *MP*.

5. Schrader, "Notes on Film Noir," in *Awake in the Dark: An Anthology of American Film Criticism, 1915 to the Present*, ed. David Denby (New York: Vintage, 1977), 278–290.

6. Quoted in David Madden, *James M. Cain*, Twayne's United States Author's Series (New York: Twayne, 1970), 43.

7. Charles Higham reports that Cain wrote Wald a series of stinging letters objecting to these changes, particularly to Wald's dramatic idea of making Veda a washout musically and putting her in a tawdry nightclub (Warner Brothers [New York: Scribners, 1975], 184–185). Interestingly, Cain himself was the son of an opera singer, aspired to an operatic career, and made his last and most successful marriage with a coloratura soprano. Music plays a large and often learned role in many of his novels. As Oates has observed, music for Cain was a reservoir of the unconscious.

8. Oates, "Man under Sentence of Death," 112.

9. Madden, *James M. Cain*, 61.

10. Quoted in Madden, *James M. Cain*, 61.

11. Lowell E. Redelings, "The Hollywood Scene," *Hollywood Citizen News*, January 21, 1946.

12. David Thomson, *A Biographical Dictionary of Film* (New York: Morrow, 1976), 592.

13. Kingsley Canham lists her as co-author in his filmography on Curtiz in *The Hollywood Professionals*, vol. 1 (New York: A. S. Barnes, 1973), and Whitney Stine in *Mother Goddarn* (New York: Hawthorn, 1976) seems to believe she is the sole author of the screenplay (193).

14. Letter from Turney to LaValley, March 10, 1980.

15. This is in answer to my suggestion that Wald may have wanted a more masculine version of the script and that there may have been some antifeminism in her release from the project.

16. Letter from Turney to LaValley.

17. Interview in the *Los Angeles Times*, July 9, 1967.

2

HITCHCOCK AND HIS WRITERS
Authorship and Authority in Adaptation

//

Thomas Leitch

ALFRED HITCHCOCK ROSE TO FAME FIRST AS THE LEADING PRAC-
titioner of the suspense thriller, then as the quintessential Hollywood auteur, even though virtually all his films were adaptations of work by other hands.[1] His well-known aversion to classic novels such as *Crime and Punishment* as source material, his less widely remarked disinclination to return to the work of any single author, and his close identification with a single genre, the Hitchcock thriller, all helped establish his claim to be the primary creator of his films.[2] Although Hitchcock was never quick to share credit for his films with anyone else, he clearly regarded his collaborations with screenwriters as something special:

> The most enjoyable part of making a picture is in that little office, with the writer, when we are discussing the story-lines and what we're going to put on the screen. The big difference is that I do not let the writer go off on his own and just write a script that I will interpret. I stay involved with him and get him involved in the direction of the picture. So he becomes more than a writer; he becomes part maker of the picture.[3]

Stories of Hitchcock's all-day story conferences with his writers, sometimes extending for weeks before the screenplay was actually begun, are legion. Clearly, he enjoyed the company of writers and regarded them as collaborators rather than mere technicians like cinematographers, production designers, and actors. As Bill Krohn reports, Hitchcock tirelessly presented himself as "a control freak who pre-planned every shot of his films and was fond of saying that once the screenplay was finished, the actual making of the film bored him."[4]

Once he found a writer with whom he could comfortably work, Hitchcock took pains to maintain their working relationship. Eliot Stannard, who worked on all nine of Hitchcock's completed silent features (1925–1929), followed him from Gainsborough to British International for *The Ring* (1927) and remained for three more films.[5] After supplying the dramatic source for *Blackmail* (1929), Charles Bennett worked on five of Hitchcock's British films (1934–1937) and one of his first American films, *Foreign Correspondent* (1940). Although his constant shuffling among studios throughout the 1940s prevented Hitchcock from establishing close relations with any one writer, that pattern changed as soon as he became an independent producer. He engaged Hume Cronyn to work on the adaptations of *Rope* (1948) and *Under Capricorn* (1949). He hired Angus MacPhail, who had worked with him as story editor at Gaumont British during the 1930s, as a writer on *Bon Voyage* (1944), *Aventure Malgache* (1944), *Spellbound* (1945), *The Man Who Knew Too Much* (1956), *The Wrong Man* (1957), and *Vertigo* (1958). And he enjoyed perhaps the most fruitful of all his screenwriting collaborations with John Michael Hayes on *Rear Window* (1954), *To Catch a Thief* (1955), *The Trouble with Harry* (1955), and *The Man Who Knew Too Much*. Years after *Vertigo* and *North by Northwest* (1959), Hitchcock sought their principal writers, Samuel Taylor and Ernest Lehman, for *Topaz* (1969) and *Family Plot* (1976). Such a remarkably rich set of collaborations raises several overlapping questions about the process of film adaptation, the status of adapters, and the nature of cinematic authorship.

What properties or forces determine the economic value of a given literary property? Adaptation begins with acquisition. Hitchcock saw each acquisition as a challenge to spend as little money as possible, or even to turn a profit. Having purchased the rights to "Bulldog Drummond's Baby" for £250 from British International after producer John Maxwell vetoed the project that became *The Man Who Knew Too Much* (1934), he promptly sold them back to Michael Balcon, the head of Gaumont British, for twice that amount.[6] Twenty years later he sold the rights to David Dodge's novel *To Catch a Thief* (1952), which he had purchased in 1951 for $15,000 before publication, to Paramount for $105,000.[7] Hitchcock was equally frugal in acquiring adaptation rights himself, bidding through intermediaries in order to keep his name from inflating the value of his target properties. As a result, he spent only $7,500 for the rights to Patricia Highsmith's *Strangers on a Train* (1950), $11,000 for Jack Trevor Story's *The Trouble with Harry* (1949), and $9,000 for Robert Bloch's *Psycho* (1959).[8] Only the hunch that the anonymous bid must mean that "one of Hollywood's leading ladies was interested in playing Marnie" drove Winston Graham's price for the rights from the $25,000 Hitchcock originally offered to the $50,000 he ultimately paid.[9]

These deals have consistently been represented as disappointments for authors, who would have sought more money had they known that the filmmaker interested in their work was the Master of Suspense. Patricia Highsmith cannot have been mollified when Hitchcock told her, on meeting her years later, that "really she should pay him to make the film, it would mean so much to her in terms of later reputation and sales."[10] Jack Trevor Story claimed that he had received only $500 of the $11,000 paid his publisher, even though Hitchcock charged Paramount $78,000 for rights to *The Trouble with Harry*. In 1977, after Hitchcock's agents had asked Story to assign Hitchcock the renewal rights for the property in perpetuity for no additional fee, he told the *London Sunday Telegraph* tartly, "I have no intention of maintaining Alfred Hitchcock in his old age."[11]

It is tempting to agree with Hitchcock that these properties were worth more than the price for which they sold because of Hitchcock's interest in them. Because of their association with Hitchcock, the careers of both Highsmith and Bloch were undoubtedly boosted. Virtually any current novelist whose work Hitchcock adapted would get a financial boost, even if the particular film at hand, like *The Trouble with Harry*, lost money. Surely it does not follow, however, that novelists should make adaptation rights to their work available gratis. Any given property's economic value depends on the more general question of what makes valuable properties valuable. Is *Psycho* valuable because of its own qualities—a hair-raising story and a climactic surprise that provide an ideal armature for a successful horror film—or because it provides promising grist for the Hitchcock mill?

Nonpartisan observers might well suggest that a property's value depends both on its intrinsic aesthetic qualities and on the possibilities it may offer a brand-name filmmaker. But this compromise still leaves several problems unresolved. François Truffaut told Hitchcock that Pierre Boileau and Thomas Narcejac wrote *D'entre les morts* (1954) "especially . . . so that you might do a screen version of it. . . . When they found out that you had been interested in acquiring the rights to *Diabolique*, they went to work and wrote *D'entre les morts*, which Paramount bought for you."[12] Does the value of *D'entre les morts* as a Hollywood property depend on the story it tells or on its marketing from before its conception as a potential Hitchcock film? Is the primary author who creates this value the actual team who wrote the novel or the stipulative auteur for whom it may have been written? And if its value depends on a combination of the authors, the filmmaker, and the authors' calculation of the filmmaker's needs and tastes, then what role do the adapters, the writers who produce the treatment and each of several versions of the screenplay, play in helping create or augment this value? Is the value of a given property created mainly by its author or by someone else? Difficult as they are to answer, these questions usefully imply a broader series of problems.

Whose film is it? The credits in Hitchcock's early films, which frequently give the authors of their sources more prominence than the director, make it clear why Hitchcock came to covet authorship. *Juno and the Paycock* (1930) is "by Sean O'Casey, adapted and directed by Alfred Hitchcock." *The Skin Game* (1931) is "a talking picture by John Galsworthy." *Number Seventeen* (1932) is "by J. Jefferson Farjeon, from the play 'Number Seventeen' produced by Leon M. Lion." Most galling of all, the opening credit of *Rebecca* (1940) announces "David O. Selznick's production of Daphne du Maurier's celebrated novel," with Hitchcock's name withheld until the final credit. No wonder Hitchcock took such pride in displacing the writer or producer by having his own name listed above the title. And no wonder the first film in which he achieved this position of eminence was *Saboteur* (1942), a loanout from Selznick.

Although both Hitchcock and Selznick evidently conceived their films as having a single author each, all were collaborations among so many creators that the question of authorship became murky, especially in light of Hitchcock's typical relations with his writers. True, he had little use for the authors of the properties his films adapted. Of all his films, only *Dial M for Murder* (1954) was scripted by the author of the original property. But he was well-known for working closely with screenwriters, as his reference to "stay[ing] involved with [them] and get[ting them] involved in the direction of the picture" suggests. He especially enjoyed working with writers who could match him in tossing out brilliant episodes and images often tangential to the plot. In consequence, Steven DeRosa, reviewing Angus MacPhail's notes for the remake of *The Man Who Knew Too Much*, concludes: "Exactly how much of this material was the sole work of Angus MacPhail, or the combined work of MacPhail and Hitchcock, or the sole work of Hitchcock with MacPhail taking notes, is unknown."[13] Yet Hitchcock's remark that this intimate collaboration makes the adapter "more than a writer; he becomes part maker of the picture" because "I ... get him involved in the direction of the picture" defines writers as filmmakers only to the extent that they are thinking like directors rather than like writers.

In presenting himself to interviewers as the only begetter of his films, Hitchcock typically indicated that he storyboarded and precut every sequence of every film before shooting began, relying on screenwriters mainly to provide dialogue and continuity. But this claim has been contested by Hitchcock screenwriters from Charles Bennett to Evan Hunter, who have emphasized either their close collaborations with the director or their frequent independence of him. Following the customary line of his interviews, Hitchcock told *Oui* in February 1973 that "I always insist on sitting with the writer from the very beginning and creating about a 100-page outline of all the details from the first shot to the end. Then I let the writer go away and complete the dialogue and character."[14] As Steven DeRosa notes, however, Hitchcock did not work closely with John Michael Hayes in drafting the treatment for *Rear Window* because the director was busy planning the preproduction of *Dial M for Murder*.[15] And Samuel Taylor recalls that he added the character of Midge to *Vertigo* without any participation from Hitchcock: "I told him I was going to create a character. He said, 'Fine.' I went off and I created the character. It was as simple as that. He didn't know anything about Midge until he read the script and liked it."[16]

Frank Launder, the co-scenarist for *The Lady Vanishes* (1938), disputed even more sharply Hitchcock's account that he had hired Launder and Sidney Gilliat to adapt Ethel Lina White's novel *The Wheel Spins* (1936). According to Launder, he had asked to write the script with Gilliat for Gainsborough as far back as 1936. It was only after its original production fell through that Hitchcock read the script and asked to direct the film. Launder insisted that even though the film's characteristic mixture of suspense and humor made it Hitchcock's calling card in America, the director first assigned to the film for which Gilliat had written the treatment and the two had collaborated on the screenplay "was to be not Hitchcock at all but Roy William Neill."[17]

The problem of assigning the authorship of Hitchcock's films is deepened by the general difficulty of disentangling different writers' contributions to a given film. It is a commonplace of film history that the writing credits assigned most films represent only the tip of the iceberg. Some forty-five writers have been identified as contributing in some way to *Gone with the Wind* (1939), whose screenplay is credited solely to Sidney Howard. Three further complications magnify these problems in Hitchcock's credits. The director's preference for collaborating closely on the treatments for his films makes it hard to determine who contributed what to the finished product. His habit of working out an extended treatment in close collaboration with a single writer or group of writers before leaving the work of crafting dialogue and deepening character to others meant that his treatments were often written by different hands than his screenplays. And his increasingly imperious determination to maintain his own status as auteur made him delegate to trusted insiders whatever functions of authorship he could not retain himself.

These problems are often reflected in the writing credits on Hitchcock's films. His thrillers for Gaumont British, for example, list separate credits for the screenplay, continuity, and dialogue, and sometimes for additional dialogue as well. Do these credits correspond to work done at different phases of the project, work of different orders of importance, or makework designed to award credit or win a salary for some particularly favored collaborator? This last possibility is corroborated by Hitchcock's continuing support of Angus MacPhail. He won MacPhail an adaptation credit on *Spellbound* over Selznick's objections that Ben Hecht was more properly the sole screenwriter.[18] Ten years later, Hitchcock attempted unsuccessfully to get MacPhail, who collaborated with him on the treatment for the 1956 *The Man Who Knew Too Much*, credited on that finished film as well. John Michael Hayes successfully petitioned the Writers Guild of America to reject this later claim, leaving him as the sole credited screenwriter on all four of his collaborations with Hitchcock. Yet Steven DeRosa concludes that "as MacPhail's notes reveal, he contributed both to the structure and several key episodes that made it into the finished film."[19]

The crucial question here is what kinds of contributions to a film should be officially recognized on the screen as contributions. Even the most extensive credits cannot possibly list all a film's contributors. The best that can be done is to establish a hierarchy of contributors, placing some in smaller type and eliminating some from the official record entirely. The screenplay for *Suspicion* (1941) went through draft after draft at the hands of successive writers. Which hands are to count as having most decisively shaped the film? If the ingredients that make *The Lady Vanishes* a quintessentially Hitchcockian thriller were actually the work Launder and Gilliat prepared for Roy William Neill, the question is not simply how to parcel out the contributors' credits but whether and how it is possible to establish authorship of the entire film.

Hitchcock always maintained that the most important stage in writing was his initial collaboration on a detailed, scene-by-scene treatment to which dialogue could be added later, often by another writer. But Joseph Stefano, the screenwriter for *Psycho* (1960) who also wrote the first treatment for *Marnie*, is nowhere listed on the latter film's credits. In fact, his treatment, apparently in violation of WGA rules, was never shown to Evan Hunter, who inherited the project when Stefano, busy as producer of the television series *The Outer Limits*, declined to return to it.[20] Later, Hitchcock dismissed Hunter from the film when the writer submitted an alternative to the spousal rape scene the director had demanded. Hitchcock broke WGA rules again by not showing Hunter's successor, Jay Presson Allen, any of Stefano's or Hunter's material, or even telling her that they had worked on the film.[21]

Hitchcock's dalliances with celebrity screenwriters whose names might enhance his films' artistic cachet and box-office potential introduce a further complication. The pattern was set by Thornton Wilder, who worked on the treatment for *Shadow of a Doubt* (1943). Hitchcock was so taken with Wilder that, unsatisfied with Wilder's top billing among the film's three screenwriters, he requested a special credit "acknowledg[ing] the contribution of Mr. Thornton Wilder to the preparation of this production." Hitchcock pursued first Ernest Hemingway, then John Steinbeck, for *Lifeboat* (1944), his following film, but with less satisfactory results. Hemingway turned him down, and Steinbeck's treatment took the form of a novelette so highly colored by the subjectivity of the sailor from whose viewpoint its flashbacks are presented that Hitchcock deemed it unfilmable. Even so, Steinbeck, credited with the film's original story, was nominated for an Academy Award, engendering, according to Patrick McGilligan, "decades of misunderstanding" about what he brought to the film. Reviewing the claims of Steinbeck's admirers that he shaped the story's allegory or provided the focal idea of a lifeboat at sea, McGilligan contends that they are disproved by "incontrovertible evidence" in studio files.[22] In *Strangers on a Train* (1951), Raymond Chandler's top billing among the screenwriters conceals the fact that his collaboration with Hitchcock ended in an unprecedented scene of invective (by the writer) and stony silence (by the director). In an equally dramatic later scene for the benefit of Czenzi Ormonde, his new writer, Hitchcock "made a show of pinching his nose, then holding up Chandler's draft with his thumb and forefinger and dropping it into a wastebasket."[23] Apart from Hitchcock's wife, Alma Reville, who is listed as the adapter of Robert Hichens's 1933 novel, the sole screenwriter credited in *The Paradine Case* (1947) is David O. Selznick, the film's producer. Yet Patricia Hitchcock O'Connell reports that "in looking through my parents' papers, I discovered that both another uncredited writer and Hitch himself had been involved with the script. I never found a script by David O. Selznick."[24] Even screenwriters who are duly credited as writers may have shaky claims as the authors of the films to which they have ostensibly contributed.

If everyone wants to take the credit for a good film, who should get the blame when a film goes wrong? Veteran script doctors like Ben Hecht often work on projects with the contractual agreement that their names will not appear on the credits. Even primary writers occasionally reverse their normal tropism and try to get their names removed from the credits, as Raymond Chandler attempted to do with *Strangers on a Train*.[25] McGilligan adds an especially savory anecdote concerning *Torn Curtain* (1966), which had begun with Hitchcock's futile efforts to entice Vladimir Nabokov into the project. When Brian Moore, the novelist who had written the first draft of the screenplay, indicated reservations about it, Hitchcock called on the British team of Keith Waterhouse and Willis Hall to polish it. The writing credits he submitted for the film—"Story by Brian Moore, Screenplay by Brian Moore, and Keith Waterhouse & Willis Hall"—went to arbitration. Waterhouse later told McGilligan the story behind what turned out to be Moore's solo credit as writer:

> Hitchcock "campaigned valiantly" for [Waterhouse's] name and Hall's to be included, adding, "I hope it does not seem ungrateful when I reveal that we were just as vigorously to have our names kept out of it." Moore, "feeling that the script was not up to his usual efforts and expectations," according to [his wife] Jean Moore, tried just as hard to keep his name off.... Ironically, Hitchcock's resistance to changes had limited the Englishmen's input, and after studying the drafts the guild struck their names.[26]

The fact that most films, whether or not they are directed by Hitchcock, have several writers but only one director paradoxically works in favor of writers who want their names removed from the credits, since there is always another writer around to shoulder the blame. In the case of likely flops such as *The Paradine Case*, *Torn Curtain*, or *Topaz*, however, there was nowhere for Hitchcock to hide. Another director might have availed himself of "Alan Smithee," the fig-leaf pseudonym under which such directors as Don Siegel, Sidney Lumet, and John Frankenheimer have disavowed their work on doomed films. But Hitchcock could not use this disguise because the advance publicity that made him famous had already associated him indelibly with the abortive project.[27] As the placeholder "Alan Smithee" indicates, someone always has to step forward as a film's author, even if that someone prefers to remain anonymous.

Who should prevail when directors and writers clash? As the old joke about a Hollywood starlet so dumb she slept with the writer attests, screenwriters are widely perceived as the least powerful collaborators on movies. When Hitchcock began his career as director, he rarely clashed with playwrights and novelists because he was so clearly subordinate to them. To the end of his life, he recalled his adaptations of well-known plays by Noel Coward (*Easy Virtue*, 1927), Sean O'Casey (*Juno and the Paycock*, 1930), and John Galsworthy (*The Skin Game*, 1931) and of Sir Hall Caine's novel *The Manxman* (1929) with little enthusiasm because he had felt constrained to follow the original properties so slavishly. The director depended as well on the screenwriters, with whom he more actively collaborated. Charles Barr argues persuasively that Hitchcock's incorrigible fondness for piquant but discrete set pieces made him dependent on "the tight organic construction" provided in the 1920s by screenwriter Eliot Stannard and in the 1930s by Charles Bennett.[28] Even the release of *The Lodger* (1926), the signature film Hitchcock told Truffaut was "you might almost say . . . my first picture," was held up by its hostile producers until still another writer, Ivor Montagu, drastically cut the number of intertitles.[29] As early as 1936, however, Hitchcock had achieved enough independence to opine that "I owe much of the success I believe I have been lucky enough to achieve to my 'ruthlessness' in adapting stories for the screen."[30]

This independence faced new challenges when Hitchcock arrived in America and settled in to work on *Rebecca*. Now his biggest battles were with an activist producer, David O. Selznick, who took it upon himself to represent the rights of the absent author. Selznick reacted to the freewheeling treatment Hitchcock drafted in collaboration with the screenwriters Michael Hogan and Philip MacDonald with the withering response, "We bought *Rebecca*, and we intend to make *Rebecca*." The producer's memo continued in the same vein: "The few million people who have read the book and who worship it would very properly attack us violently for the desecrations which are indicated by the treatment."[31] "The five Hitchcocks"—Hitchcock, his wife Alma Reville, his assistant Joan Harrison, and the screenwriters Hogan and MacDonald—returned to successive drafts that hewed ever closer to Daphne du Maurier's novel before Robert Sherwood was called in for the final draft. McGilligan summarizes the collaboration:

> Although Sherwood, the first and most important writer's name on the screen, was undoubtedly the highest paid, the yeoman's work had been done by everybody else. The producer's main contribution was to restore the book's precise dialogue whenever possible. Hitchcock, for his part, had long since accepted that few of his personal story ideas would make the cut in this, his first American film.[32]

Leonard J. Leff, reviewing the terms of Hitchcock's contract with Selznick, concludes that "more than Selznick's memoranda, Hitchcock's financial insecurity shaped his deference to the producer throughout the writing of *Rebecca*."[33] His enforced subservience taught Hitchcock not only that producers could always pull rank on directors but also that the screenwriters on whom the director had once depended were still lower on the totem pole. Hitchcock's long-sought independence from Selznick was also a quest for independence from both the novelists Selznick represented and the screenwriters Hitchcock increasingly sought to dominate.

An essential part of Hitchcock's strategy to establish himself as a producer-director was to free himself from screenwriters who might clash with him. When he and Sidney Bernstein established their own production company, Transatlantic Pictures, he invited Hume Cronyn, an actor and friend with no writing experience, to prepare the adaptations of *Rope* and *Under Capricorn*, the only films Transatlantic released. Just as he frequently cast leading ladies he could dominate, from Joan Fontaine to Tippi Hedren, he often preferred to groom relatively inexperienced screenwriters, such as Czenzi Ormonde (*Strangers on a Train*), Joseph Stefano (*Psycho*), Evan Hunter (*The Birds*), Jay Presson Allen (*Marnie*), and Brian Moore (*Torn Curtain*), instead of working with more experienced professionals. Whether or not he was working with established writers, Hitchcock's customary method of dealing with intractable disagreements was to dismiss the offending writer and hire a replacement.

How could these disagreements best have been resolved? It would be disingenuous to assume that matters always worked out best when the director overrode the writer. Fans of Patricia Highsmith's novel may wish Chandler had prevailed in urging Hitchcock to stay closer to Highsmith's tale of two strangers who each agree to murder a relative the other wants to be rid of. Hitchcock adopted Chandler's suggestion that the story's hero, Guy Haines, only pretend to accept Bruno Anthony's persistent urging that he return Bruno's favor of strangling his unfaithful wife by shooting Bruno's hated father. (In Highsmith's novel, Guy does indeed murder Bruno's father and is eventually caught by the police.) But Chandler complained that the pivotal scene in which "a perfectly decent young man agrees to murder a man he doesn't know" and "has to convince Bruno and a reasonable percentage of the audience that what he is about to do is logical and inevitable" was a "contest between a superficial reasonableness and a fundamental idiocy.... The more real you make Guy and Bruno, the more unreal you make their relationship."[34] Even Hitchcock acknowledged "the weakness of the final script" produced by Czenzi Ormonde and Barbara Keon after Chandler had been sent packing.[35]

The pattern persisted in later Hitchcock films. Instead of working through their disagreements, the director replaced Alec Coppel with Samuel Taylor on *Vertigo*, Brian Moore with Keith Waterhouse and Willis Hall on *Torn Curtain*, and, most notoriously, Evan Hunter with Jay Presson Allen on *Marnie*. The disagreement that led to Hunter's departure concerned Mark Rutland's honeymoon rape of the compulsive thief he has caught and married. Convinced, as he told Hitchcock, that the rape scene *"is out of place in this story,"* Hunter submitted both the rape scene Hitchcock had demanded and an alternative honeymoon sequence without a rape, but realized, as he told himself, that *"you just got bothered by the scene that was his reason for making the movie."*[36] Hitchcock's victory produced one of his most problematic films, yet one that Hunter's alternative scene, emphasizing Mark's compassion over his fetishistic attachment to Marnie, might have weakened still further.

Disagreements between screenwriter and director persisted even on the final film Hitchcock completed, the playful *Family Plot*. Ernest Lehman, returning at Hitchcock's request some fifteen years after the success of *North by Northwest*, realized that both collaborators were more obdurate. "I found myself refusing to accept Hitch's ideas (if I thought they were wrong) merely because those ideas were coming from a legendary figure," Lehman recalled. When he added details designed to strengthen the characters, Hitchcock "put them back in the script and shot them, then edited them out of the picture." Eventually Hitchcock suspended his daily conferences with Lehman, as he told a Universal executive, because "it's too difficult to get Ernie to agree with me."[37] Viewers who recall *Family Plot* as the most lighthearted of Hitchcock's Universal films might be surprised to learn that its source novel, Victor Canning's grim thriller *The Rainbird Pattern* (1972), kills off all its main characters.

Hitchcock's defense of his summary resolution of all these disagreements is implicit in the way he described *The Rainbird Pattern* to Lehman: "I don't have any regard for the book. It's *our* story, not the book's."[38] His determination to recast each of his projects into a Hitchcock film produced endless battles with writers and the producers who stood in for them. Yet even the films on which Hitchcock lost these battles, from *The Lodger* to *Rebecca*, are universally regarded as Hitchcock films by commentators who do not regard victorious combat as a prerequisite of successful authorship.

Given the differences that mark most filmmaking collaboration, what makes a film a Hitchcock film? Hitchcock told Truffaut that "for me to take someone else's script and merely photograph it in my own way isn't enough. For better or worse, I must do the whole thing myself."[39] Hitchcock and Truffaut both perceived a constant tension between the servile labors of the *metteur-en-scène* on behalf of the studio, the stars, or the literary property and the realization of an original directorial vision. This tension was the driving force behind the auteurist approach to cinema under whose aegis Hitchcock was canonized and film studies entered the academy. As Hitchcock's running conflict with Selznick shows, both filmmakers viewed authorship as a function to be reserved for the single leading contributor in a struggle for control. The narrative of his life that Hitchcock shared first with Truffaut and later with John Russell Taylor showed a gifted artist gradually emerging from the forces that sought to stifle him—benighted studio heads, inexpressive actors, authors whose work commanded uncritical respect—to rise to the point at which he could stifle others. A defining mark of Hitchcock's maturity was that everyone who collaborated on a mature Hitchcock film was contributing to a Hitchcock original.

Once Hitchcock had fulfilled the terms of his seven-year contract with Selznick, the principal figures who challenged his authority were writers, especially when they showed signs of independence. Resenting John Michael Hayes's resistance to crediting Angus MacPhail on *The Man Who Knew Too Much* and Hayes's growing fame in the industry because of the very pictures they had made together, he broke with Hayes over his refusal to follow Hitchcock to Warner Bros. for the project that became *The Wrong Man*. He drove George Tabori from his unproduced film *The Bramble Bush* by his constant criticisms. He refused to speak to Ernest Lehman for years after Lehman declined to work on another unrealized project, *No Bail for the Judge*. He cooled toward Joseph Stefano when his television commitments kept him from scripting *Marnie*. And he fired Evan Hunter from the same project when they disagreed about the pivotal rape scene.[40] To Hitchcock, disagreements with his collaborators amounted to personal betrayals by employees who did not know their place.

Few recent commentators have shared the rigidly hierarchical view of collaboration in which all a film's collaborators, like a monarchy's armed services, toil on behalf of a single supreme ruler. Yet none of the ad hoc reassessments by screenwriters like Hunter or historians like DeRosa have dislodged Hitchcock from his roost atop the pantheon of American auteurs. Even theorists who do not believe Hitchcock did the whole thing himself agree that there is such a thing as a Hitchcock film.

In the Hitchcock film that carries her name, Marnie (Tippi Hedren) stares past the embrace of her new husband, Mark Rutland (Sean Connery), in the controversial rape scene that also precedes her suicide attempt.

If all filmmaking involves collaboration, what does it mean to call a film a Hitchcock original? Are some of his films, as he repeatedly averred to Truffaut, less original simply because they are based on better-known novels or plays? Does a literary pedigree actually inhibit adapters' originality, so that authentically Hitchcock films can be fashioned only from second-rate properties? Hitchcock's rote answer to these questions was that the most original adaptations are the most free. Yet many of Hitchcock's greatest successes, from *Rebecca* to *Psycho*, follow their source texts closely. And misfires, from *Champagne* (1928) to *Torn Curtain*, demonstrate that an original screenplay is no guarantee of success, or indeed of originality. It would seem at the very least that terms like "Hitchcock original" or even "Hitchcock film" are more problematic concepts than film scholars have acknowledged.

One way to resolve these questions is to observe that all Hitchcock's films are adaptations—if not of somebody else's novel or play, then of somebody else's original screenplay. Hitchcock's lack of interest in character and his limited facility with dialogue meant that he was always filming someone speaking someone else's words and acting as someone else had bidden. Like the actors and actresses he claimed to treat like cattle, his screenwriters, whether or not they were adapting someone else's work, were always potentially subject to his rivalry and resentment. Ironically, these writers became forgotten foot soldiers in Hitchcock's campaign against the authors of the literary properties he adapted. To the end of his life, Hitchcock divided his films into Hitchcock originals, such as *Psycho*, that transcended their source texts, and flat transcriptions, such as *Juno and the Paycock*, that slavishly followed them, and film theory has generally followed him in limiting authorship to these two functions. But one of the great opportunities adaptation study offers is the possibility of nominating alternative authors whose collaborative contributions recast the whole idea of authorship as more complex than the choice of a single controlling collaborator would suggest.

Why aren't there auteurs of adaptation? On the face of it, this question is absurd. How could adapters, writers who strive to realize someone else's creative vision by subordinating their own ego to serve that vision, be auteurs? Although Andrew Sarris's *The American Cinema: Directors and Directions, 1929–1968* was broadly successful in its call for an evaluative hierarchy of Hollywood directors, Richard Corliss's ensuing call for a cognate pantheon of Hollywood screenwriters, complete with a Sarris-like Acropolis of comparative rankings, fell on deaf ears. Yet Corliss's prescient arguments on behalf of the importance of screenwriters sound even more cogent now than when he advanced them:

> The director *is* right in the middle of things. At the very least, he's on the sound stage while the director of photography is lighting the set that the art director has designed and, later, while the actors are speaking the lines that the screenwriter wrote. Quite often, he steers all these factors—story, actors, camera—in the right *direction*. So why not just say that it's his film, that he is the author? Simply because the director is almost always an interpretive artist, not a creative one, and because the Hollywood film is a corporate art, not an individual one.[41]

Since Corliss wrote, the tendency of film studies has been increasingly critical of the identification of a given film's director as either its author (its maker or creator) or its auteur (its artist, the visionary responsible for its leading ideas or images or its inscrutable essence). So why has Corliss's plea on behalf of screenwriters been so little heeded?

The obvious reason is suggested by Corliss's own preoccupation with evaluative categories. In his eagerness to contest Sarris's directorial hierarchy, Corliss buys into its most slippery premise: that the business of film studies is primarily comparative evaluation. Although he begins by urging closer attention to the contributions of screenwriters, Corliss ends by dividing them as variously worthy of attention according to their merits: "The best screenwriters were talented and tenacious enough to assure that their visions and countless revisions would be realized on the screen. Now it is time for them to be remembered in film history."[42]

Corliss's insistence on evaluation leaves the most damaging traces on his consideration of the "screenwriter who specializes in adaptations." He argues that "as with directors, one can distinguish several different levels of screenwriting: the indifferent work of a mediocre writer, whether an original script or an adaptation (which we may call procrustean); the gem polishing of a gifted polisher like [Donald Ogden] Stewart (protean); and the creation of a superior original script, like Herman J. Mankiewicz's *Citizen Kane* or [Abraham] Polonsky's *Body and Soul* (promethean)."[43] In his determination to rank not just different screenwriters but different screenwriting functions, Corliss loses sight of his original point, that filmmaking is first and foremost a collaborative process rather than a submission to, or a struggle with, the promethean ego of a single creative artist, whether director or screenwriter. In fact, his implicit argument against granting the highest rank to adapters is exactly the same argument that he accurately cites concerning directors, the argument from which Sarris's auteurist claims had rescued them: that they were nothing but interpreters, conductors of someone else's score.[44]

The continuing neglect of screenwriters despite the general decline of directorial auteurism overlooks the principal reason for the decline of the auteur. Both archival research and reinterpretation have repeatedly demonstrated that filmmaking is a radically collaborative enterprise, whatever its most gifted or vocal practitioners may claim. The recent resistance to the imperial power once imputed to pantheon directors should not elevate screenwriters as their equals or replacements but rather should encourage more critical discussion of the nature of authorship in the cinema.

Recent work on Hitchcock and his writers has much to contribute here because Hitchcock's reputation is so firmly established that there is no danger of displacing Hitchcock the auteur by any of his screenwriters. Hence Dan Auiler titles his monumental collection of production materials *Hitchcock's Notebooks*, even though little of the material is by Hitchcock and none of it takes the form of notebooks.[45] None of the three production histories published to date on Hitchcock films has much to say about their source novels, but they all devote considerable attention to the process of adaptation. Stephen Rebello's study of *Psycho* sets the pattern: a brief summary of Robert Bloch's novel, its reception, and its acquisition by Hitchcock, followed by a more extended account of the screenwriting process.[46] In his production history of *Vertigo*, Auiler relies on the 1955 report Allida Allen wrote for Paramount rather than referring directly to the novel, which was not translated into English until 1997.[47] He goes into much greater detail about the screenwriting contributions of Maxwell Anderson, Angus MacPhail, Alec Coppel, and Samuel Taylor, emphasizing the gradual evolution of the story under each of their hands and the politics of the screenwriters' collaboration with Hitchcock. Steven DeRosa follows the same pattern in writing about *Marnie*. All three show Hitchcock collaborating closely with a single writer, often meeting for daily story conferences over a period of weeks or months, until the writer runs into problems that leave Hitchcock discontented enough to dismiss the writer and find a successor. The process reveals Hitchcock to be both an intimate collaborator and an independent producer determined to maintain control of his product.

In chronicling the development of *Marnie*'s screenplay at the hands of Joseph Stefano, Evan Hunter, and Jay Presson Allen, DeRosa intends to "highlight multivocality in the *Marnie* text. . . . I will show how author Winston Graham and screenwriter Jay Presson Allen were major contributors to the film's themes of feminist issues and social injustice."[48] Although DeRosa's account does not consistently support his larger claims, the claims themselves are an important indication of a new direction in Hitchcock studies. If it were generalized, DeRosa's search for multiple voices might well complicate the subtitle Auiler chose for his book, *Hitchcock's Notebooks: An Authorized and Illustrated Look Inside the Creative Mind of Alfred Hitchcock*. Or it might not, since, as the brand name that warrants the attention paid to his screenwriters, Hitchcock the auteur is valorized by the very attempt to nominate other authors for his films.

Charles Barr adopts a different but equally powerful approach to the question of authorship. He attempts to redress the overemphasis on Hitchcock the sole author by "explor[ing] the influence of his predominantly English source materials or of his English scriptwriters" on "the gradual and uneven process of his *becoming* (or anyway starting to become) the Hitchcock we all think we know."[49] Organizing his traversal of Hitchcock's English films according to their principal credited screenwriters, Barr emphasizes the extent to which Hitchcock learned from the novelists and playwrights he always claimed as his formative influence. He marks the ways in which Hitchcock's films take on the coloration of their screenwriters. And he raises the question whose answer the title of this essay assumes: whether Hitchcock's screenwriters are *his* writers any more than he is *their* director. Hitchcock's career would be understood very differently, Barr suggests, if due credit were given to his writers. To this proposal may be added a corollary: The arc of any filmmaker's career would be understood differently in the context of *all* the contributors to his or her films, whether or not they receive screen credit.

In *Hitchcock at Work*, Bill Krohn provides a third new angle on Hitchcockian authorship by using material in studio and production archives to attack the myth of a Hitchcock who planned everything in advance. Krohn repeatedly demonstrates, as he contends of the pivotal moments in *Notorious* (1946), that "unscripted choices made during production grew out of details already written into the script, in the process creating rhymes as one shot or sequence suggested another falling into the same paradigm."[50] In Krohn's account, authorship is not only collaborative but incessant. Even the most obsessively preplanned film is constantly being rewritten as the treatment is being worked out, the screenplay is being revised, the meticulously storyboarded shots are being filmed, music is added, scenes are reshot, and dialogue is changed in postproduction.

If adapters aren't auteurs, what is their distinctive position in the collaborative medium of filmmaking? This question at least has a simple answer. Well-intentioned but misbegotten attempts to claim auteur status for adapters as if they were competing for attention with novelists and playwrights and directors and authors of original screenplays overlook their even more pivotal role. The adapter's function, and only the adapter's function, provides the prototype for all the others because the collaborative adapter offers a more accurate model of all Hollywood filmmaking practice than the dominant director or even the solitary novelist. This is not to claim that the adapter is the true auteur of the film. Instead, the adapter is the paradigmatic collaborator whose function explodes the claims of any single filmmaker to complete authorship by revealing that all filmmakers are collaborators. Now that the academy is no longer dominated by the aesthetic of romantic expressionism under which film studies first gained admittance, it is time for the adapter to replace the director as the paradigm for all filmmakers. At one time the term *director* may have suggested only someone who choreographed or coordinated the shooting of a film. But now that it has grown to suggest vastly more control than most directors actually exercise, it is time to recognize the adapting screenwriter as the contributor whose function best epitomizes the process of making a film. Not all filmmakers are directors, not all of them are auteurs, but every one of them is an adapter.

The trajectory of Hitchcock's career might seem to provide the strongest possible exception to this rule. After all, Hitchcock began in England, at least in his own eyes, as an artisan pressed into serving authors more prestigious than any film director. During his first decade in America, he alternately sought the cachet of celebrity screenwriting collaborators and waged war on the sanctity of novels like *Rebecca* and the producers who pressed their claims. And he gauged his status as a producer-director by his success at subordinating the contributions of writers, however closely he worked with them, to his own authorship. Even though this narrative has become a truism of Hitchcock studies, it is finally untrue. For Hitchcock remains throughout his career a collaborator rather than a solitary author. If "the meaning of an art work," as Robert E. Kapsis maintains, "is the result of an ongoing exchange between the art work and the receiver," then it may well be that the actual Hitchcock who made the artistic decisions by which his films stand or fall was remote from the public relations Hitchcock on whose behalf properties were chosen, a tone struck, and entire screenplays written.[51] But even the actual Hitchcock was always a collaborator with his colleague of longest standing, his wife Alma Reville. Trained as an editor, Reville is credited as assistant director on Hitchcock's first two films, *The Pleasure Garden* (1925) and *The Mountain Eagle* (1926); as principal screenwriter on *Juno and the Paycock*, *Murder!* (1930), and *The Skin Game*; as co-writer on *Rich and Strange* (1931), *Number Seventeen*, and *Waltzes from Vienna* (1933); as continuity coordinator on *The 39 Steps* (1935), *Secret Agent* (1936), *Sabotage* (1937), *Young and Innocent* (1937), *The Lady Vanishes*, and *Jamaica Inn* (1939); as co-writer again on *Suspicion* and *Shadow of a Doubt*; and as adapter of the properties for *The Paradine Case* and *Stage Fright* (1950).

It is possible, of course, that her responsibilities on these films were sufficiently different to warrant such different credits. It may also be true that, as Charles Bennett told Patrick McGilligan, "she never did a damned thing, because continuity was really Hitchcock saying, 'I'll shoot it this way or that way.'"[52] On the other hand, she may have been as actively involved in planning *Strangers on a Train* as in *Stage Fright*, as Whitfield Cook claimed. She may have outlined the car chase in which Cary Grant and Grace Kelly are pursued by the police in *To Catch a Thief*, as Patricia Hitchcock O'Connell claimed. She may have collaborated discreetly but actively on the screenplay for *Marnie*, as Jay Presson Allen claimed.[53] Most of Hitchcock's collaborators who have spoken about Reville have agreed that whatever specific contributions Reville made to individual films, she was the gatekeeper to her husband, the partner whose approval was indispensable to him. As Hitchcock's longtime personal assistant Peggy Robertson observes, "Hitch's wife, Alma Reville, was the most important person to him in everything.... Whatever he had—a subject, a writer, an actor—'What did Alma think?' If Alma approved, we could go on."⁵⁴ O'Connell confirms this judgment numerous times in the matter of adaptation: "Each time my father received a book or a script to consider as a potential project, he immediately gave it to my mother to read first. If she didn't like it, it was instantly rejected. If she liked it, she would pass it on to him."⁵⁵

O'Connell's biography of her mother—more accurately a memoir of her family—offers tantalizingly little in the way of new information about her parents' collaboration. But it is clear, as Charles Champlin wrote, that "the Hitchcock touch had four hands, and two of them were Alma's."⁵⁶ It seems likely that the archetypal auteur Alfred Hitchcock, who was legendary for wooing, bullying, and discarding screenwriters at whim, was indeed the public face of a longstanding and largely unacknowledged creative partnership. Hitchcock is an exemplary filmmaker not because of his single-minded control over his collaborators but because he is the exemplary collaborator with both credited and uncredited colleagues, the author whose authorship is itself collaborative. Film studies have yet to take the measure of the status of Hollywood's staunchest auteur as the ultimate adapter.

NOTES

1. Of Hitchcock's fifty-three completed feature films, only ten—*The Mountain Eagle* (1926), *The Ring* (1927), *Champagne* (1928), *Mr. and Mrs. Smith* (1941), *Saboteur* (1942), *Shadow of a Doubt* (1943), *Lifeboat* (1944), *Notorious* (1946), *North by Northwest* (1959), and *Torn Curtain* (1966)—were based on original stories, although *The Man Who Knew Too Much* (1934) was based on an unpublished story, the originals of *Foreign Correspondent* (1940) and *Spellbound* (1945) were virtually unrecognizable from their screen adaptations, and the relation between *Rich and Strange* (1931) and Dale Collins's novel remains obscure. On this last film, see Charles Barr, *English Hitchcock* (Moffat: Cameron & Hollis, 1999), 12, 118.

2. Apart from Charles Bennett and D. B. Wyndham Lewis's original story on which both versions of *The Man Who Knew Too Much* (1934/1956) are based, and the pairs of television adaptations Hitchcock directed of stories by John Collier (*Wet Saturday* and *Back for Christmas*, both 1956) and Roald Dahl (*Dip in the Pool*, 1958, and *Mrs. Bixby and the Colonel's Coat*, 1960), only two authors supply the source for more than one Hitchcock film: Helen Simpson for *Murder!* (1930) and *Under Capricorn* (1949), and Daphne du Maurier for *Jamaica Inn* (1939), *Rebecca* (1940), and *The Birds* (1963).

3. Budge Crawley, Fletcher Markle, and Gerald Pratley, "Hitch: I Wish I Didn't Have to Shoot the Picture," *Take One* 1, no. 1: 14–17, quoted by Steven DeRosa,

Writing with Hitchcock: The Collaboration of Alfred Hitchcock and John Michael Hayes (New York: Faber and Faber, 2001), ix.

4. Krohn, *Hitchcock at Work* (London: Phaidon, 2000), 9.

5. Barr (22–26) argues persuasively for Stannard's influence on Hitchcock's early films, including *The Ring*, the only one on which he receives no screen credit. For Stannard's likely contributions to *The Ring*, see John Russell Taylor, *Hitch: The Life and Times of Alfred Hitchcock* (New York: Pantheon: 1978), 89, and Patrick McGilligan, *Alfred Hitchcock: A Life in Darkness and Light* (New York: HarperCollins, 2003), 94.

6. McGilligan, 153.

7. DeRosa, 88, 90.

8. The $7,500 figure for *Strangers on a Train* and the $11,000 figure for *The Trouble with Harry* come from Donald Spoto, *The Dark Side of Genius: The Life of Alfred Hitchcock* (Boston: Little, Brown, 1983), 320, 353. John Russell Taylor (213) reports an even lower figure of $2,000 for *The Trouble with Harry*. DeRosa, noting his inability to corroborate the size of the payment to Story, observes: "$11,000 was hardly a modest fee in 1954" (310).

9. Tony Lee Moral, *Hitchcock and the Making of Marnie* (Lanham, MD: Scarecrow, 2002), 8.

10. Taylor, 213.

11. DeRosa, 128, 147.

12. François Truffaut, *Hitchcock*, rev. ed. (New York: Simon and Schuster, 1983), 243. Narcejac disputed this account in an interview with Dan Auiler, "maintain[ing] firmly that that he and his collaborator never had any intention of writing a book especially for Hitchcock." See Auiler, *Vertigo: The Making of a Hitchcock Classic* (New York: St. Martin's, 1998), 28.

13. DeRosa, 162.

14. Quoted in DeRosa, 30.

15. DeRosa, 16–17.

16. "Reflections on *Vertigo*: A Talk by Samuel Taylor, Screenwriter of *Vertigo*," in *Hitchcock's Rereleased Films: From* Rope *to* Vertigo, ed. Walter Raubicheck and Walter Srebnick (Detroit: Wayne State University Press, 1986), 289.

17. Geoff Brown, *Launder and Gilliat* (London: British Film Institute, 1977), 89.

18. DeRosa, 194.

19. DeRosa, 156.

20. Hunter confirmed this account in the 1999 Hitchcock Centennial Celebration. See "Working with Hitch: A Screenwriter's Forum with Evan Hunter, Arthur Laurents, and Joseph Stefano," ed. Walter Raubicheck, *Hitchcock Annual* 10 (2001–2002): 12.

21. For a more detailed account of this latter violation, see Moral, 39–41. DeRosa, elaborating the legal issues more fully, explains that Hitchcock may have violated the spirit rather than the letter of the Writer's Guild of America rules:

Article 8 of the WGA's 1955 Motion Picture Basic Agreement states that a writer and the head of the studio's story department must be informed by the producer of the assignment of any writers to a project.... While Article 8 does not explicitly state that story material created by the prior writer must be made available to subsequent writers, it is presumed by the WGA that any subsequent writer will have had access to prior material whether firsthand or communicated verbally by the producer. (199)

22. McGilligan, 330, 331.

23. McGilligan, 445, 447.

24. Pat Hitchcock O'Connell and Laurent Bouzereau, *Alma Hitchcock: The Woman Behind the Man* (New York: Berkley, 2003), 136–137.

25. McGilligan, 449.

26. McGilligan, 671.

27. For an amusing look at the relation between Hitchcock's authorship of *The Birds* and Smithee's of *The Birds II: Land's End* (1994), see Stephen Hock, "This Is Too Big for One Old Name: Hitchcock and Smithee in the Signature Centrifuge," in *Directed by Allen Smithee*, ed. Jeremy Braddock and Stephen Hock (Minneapolis: University of Minnesota Press, 2001), 175–205.

28. Barr, 25.

29. Truffaut, 44; McGilligan, 84.

30. Hitchcock, "My Screen Memories: My Strangest Year" (1936), rpt. in *Hitchcock on Hitchcock*, ed. Sidney Gottlieb (Berkeley and Los Angeles: University of California Press, 1995), 18.

31. Selznick, *Memo from David O. Selznick*, ed. Rudy Behlmer (New York: Viking, 1972), 266.

32. McGilligan, 241, 242.

33. Leff, *Hitchcock and Selznick: The Rich and Strange Collaboration of Alfred Hitchcock and David O. Selznick in Hollywood* (New York: Weidenfeld & Nicolson, 1987), 55.

34. Chandler, "Extract from Notes Dated 1950 about the Screenplay *Strangers on a Train*," *Raymond Chandler Speaking*, ed. Dorothy Gardiner and Kathrine Sorley Walker (Boston: Houghton Mifflin, 1962), 133, 134.

35. Truffaut, 198.

36. Hunter, *Me and Hitch* (London: Faber and Faber, 1997), 87.

37. McGilligan, 721, 722.

38. McGilligan, 719.

39. Truffaut, 319.

40. See DeRosa, 210.

41. Corliss, "The Hollywood Screenwriter" (1970); rpt. in *Film Theory and Criticism: Introductory Readings*, ed. Gerald Mast, Marshall Cohen, and Leo Braudy, 4th ed. (New York: Oxford University Press, 1992), 606–613, at 607.

42. Corliss, 613.

43. Corliss, 610.

44. Interestingly, when Corliss reprinted this essay as the introduction to *Talking Pictures: Screenwriters in the American Cinema, 1927–1973* (Woodstock, NY: Overlook, 1974)—following a "Preface for a Dialectical Discussion" by Sarris—he presented writer-directors as "a synthesis of these presumably antithetical functions" and suggested that "once the contribution of all these crafts"—acting, writing, and directing—has been examined, "studies of other vital film collaborators could begin and be meshed into a giant matrix of coordinate talents" (xxviii).

45. By far the largest section of Aulier's *Hitchcock's Notebooks: An Authorized and Illustrated Look Inside the Creative Mind of Alfred Hitchcock* (New York: Avon, 1999), "Building the Screenplay" (21–293) is copiously illustrated with pages of treatments and screenplay drafts that are not by Hitchcock.

46. See Stephen Rebello, *Alfred Hitchcock and the Making of Psycho* (New York: Dembner, 1990), 7–14, 31–50.

47. Auiler, *Vertigo*, 30–32.

48. DeRosa, xiv.

49. Barr, 8, 11.

50. Krohn, 97.

51. Kapsis, *Hitchcock: The Making of a Reputation* (Chicago: University of Chicago Press, 1992), 245.

52. McGilligan, *Backstory: Interviews with Screenwriters of Hollywood's Golden Age* (Berkeley and Los Angeles: University of California Press, 1986), 27.

53. O'Connell and Bouzereau, 143, 149, 166, 194.

54. O'Connell and Bouzereau, 182–183.

55. O'Connell and Bouzereau, 102.

56. Champlin, "Alma Reville Hitchcock—The Unsung Partner," *Los Angeles Times*, July 29, 1982, pt. VI, 7.

3

FROM *TRAUMNOVELLE* (1927) TO SCRIPT TO SCREEN— *EYES WIDE SHUT* (1999)

///

Jack Boozer

STANLEY KUBRICK CAME VERY LATE IN LIFE TO THE SCREEN ADAPtation of Arthur Schnitzler's novella, though he had read it and been intrigued by it some thirty years earlier. The arduous process of transforming the novella into an acceptable screenplay and finally into the film, *Eyes Wide Shut*, reveals Stanley Kubrick's method of adaptive collaboration, as well as what he brought to the film as director after the script was completed. Throughout his long career as a recognized auteur, Kubrick consistently relied on the adaptation of literary and popular novels and short stories. He sometimes wrote the screenplays himself, or he meticulously oversaw their written adaptation. This applied whether or not he took credit as a co-author on the screen.[1] He was a constant reader who had an eye for strong stories that were often difficult to adapt. He once commented, "All the films I have made have started by my reading a book. Those books that have been made into films have almost always had some aspect about them which on first reading left me with the sense that, 'This is a fantastic story: is it possible to make it into a film?'"[2] More specifically, Kubrick's highly selective eye sought material that might serve as a platform for his own unsentimental imagination and ideological concerns, which were deeply embedded in matters of major significance to Western culture.

Kubrick's screenwriting and film experience in the twelve years preceding *Eyes Wide Shut* is instructive of both his thematic concerns and his time-consuming methods of project development. His Vietnam War film *Full Metal Jacket* (1987) is based on Gustav Hasford's novel *The Short-Timers* (1979), and Kubrick began discussions with that author and also with the author of *Dispatches*, Michael Herr, as early as 1980. This led to an extended adaptive screenplay collaboration with both that involved ongoing rewrites, over which Kubrick eventually took sole control during shooting.[3] The seven-year *Full Metal Jacket* project was followed by two failed efforts in the early 1990s to bring script adaptations of his own to film. He invited Steven Spielberg to direct his screenplay of what was to be called *A.I.*,[4] but when the project floundered it was Spielberg who eventually bought the short story rights, rewrote the script, and directed the film. Kubrick also wrote a screenplay that he called *The Aryan Papers*, which was based on a novel about Jewish survival during the Holocaust.[5] The tedious development of this project, too, was discontinued when Spielberg came out with a major Holocaust film project of his own, *Schindler's List* (1993).

In 1994, seven years after the completion of *Full Metal Jacket*, Kubrick initiated work on Arthur Schnitzler's *Traumnovelle*. The novella had been published as a magazine serial in Vienna and then as a book in 1926. It was translated into English by Otto P. Schinnerer as *Rhapsody: A Dream Novel* in 1927 and reissued in 1955. This translated edition is the one on which Kubrick based his film project.[6]

Like Schnitzler, Kubrick came to *Traumnovelle* after having established a successful career.[7] He was already familiar with Max Ophuls's popular film adaptation of one of Schnitzler's stage plays concerning sexual, cultural, and interclass relationships and titled, appropriately, *La Ronde* (1950).[8] Kubrick's urban upbringing in the Bronx and his Austro-Hungarian Jewish lineage were also not far removed from Schnitzler's turn-of-the-century Jewish family experience in Vienna. Both Kubrick and Schnitzler were the offspring of cosmopolitan physicians who supported their sons in cultural activity and the arts. The young writer and pianist Schnitzler became a physician and a man about town,[9] not unlike his observant protagonist in *Traumnovelle*. The contemplative Kubrick also loved books and music, but he was not socially gregarious and preferred the technical expressivity of cameras. These men also shared a greater intellectual awareness of the way in which personal experience and religious and political ideologies were shaped by the historical eras in which they lived.

Kubrick no doubt appreciated the strong visual quality of observational psychology[10] in Schnitzler's once controversial novella, which carefully traces erotic impulses through fantasies, dreams, and behaviors that challenge containment within marital, scientific, and class conventions. In films as diverse as *Lolita*, *A Clockwork Orange*, *Barry Lyndon*, and *The Shining*, Kubrick had already shown an interest in psychosexual dynamics, family dysfunction, and social class. His political-military films (*Paths of Glory*, *Dr. Strangelove*, *Full Metal Jacket*) also draw linkages between the male libido and imperialistic hierarchies, a relation hinted at in Schnitzler's novella.

One further connection that may have attracted Kubrick to Schnitzler's short novel was one he repeatedly borrowed from his literary sources, namely, symmetrical story construction. In *A Clockwork Orange*, a wild sexual escapade is eventually followed by an excursion of retribution that is particularly close to *Traumnovelle* in more ways than are immediately obvious. In *Barry Lyndon*, too, the first half follows the ascent of the eponymous character, who is brought low in the second half by most of the same characters who appear in the first half. But Kubrick's adaptation of Thackeray's eighteenth-century English novel is a costume drama and not what he decided to do with the 1927 Viennese novella. That decision, however, also created further problems. Although Schnitzler's 1927 fiction is basically contemporary in its foregrounding of the dreams, temptations, and jealousies of marriage, its cultural milieu is clearly dated, and its social commentary is muted.

Kubrick wanted the help of an appropriate screenwriter who could contemporize the novella and open it up in a way that would also allow him to contribute the full array of his own visual aesthetics. He had Warner Bros. contact Frederic Raphael, born in Chicago and educated in England, who had written the screen adaptations for Thomas Hardy's *Far from the Madding Crowd*, Iris Murdoch's *A Severed Head*, and Henry James's *Daisy Miller*. Raphael also penned two original screenplays of contemporary life in the 1960s—John Schlesinger's *Darling* and Stanley Donen's *Two for the Road*. *Darling* concerns a modern free spirit of sexual affairs (Julie Christie) who ultimately fails to find grounding and commitment in any one relationship. The film won an Academy Award for Best Original Screenplay. Raphael seemed most comfortable, in short, with themes of heterosexual life in the context of class and cultural change. He demonstrated both literary sensitivity in his script adaptations and timely personal and cultural integrity in his original screenplays.

The collaboration between Kubrick and Raphael on the Schnitzler adaptation is carefully recounted in Raphael's revealing book, *Eyes Wide Open: A Memoir of Stanley Kubrick* (1999). Raphael describes his screenplay work with the famous auteur as a thankless, trying, and exhausting twenty-four-month marathon that began in 1994. His memoir is a tightly focused insider's look at the screenplay working procedure, attitudes, and lifestyle of Kubrick. Employing at times direct dialogue from Raphael's conversations with Kubrick or with his own wife regarding the project, the memoir provides a close running commentary. It is also exceptional for its unblinking artistic and personal assessment of the director, particularly under the circumstance of Kubrick's death in March 1999, just days after an initial private preview screening of *Eyes Wide Shut* in Manhattan for the actors and the studio (and at a time when Kubrick may still have intended a few final tweaks to the film's score). It wasn't until his first visit by taxi to Kubrick's secluded home near London that the name of the author whom Raphael was being asked to adapt was inadvertently revealed. Raphael observed firsthand Kubrick's well-known obsessions with privacy and secrecy. For his part, Kubrick has responded elsewhere to questions about where and how he lived relative to his work:

> You read books or see films about people being corrupted by Hollywood, but it isn't that. It's this tremendous sense of insecurity. A lot of destructive competitiveness. In comparison, England seems very remote. I try to keep up, read the trade papers, but it's good to get it on paper and not have to hear it every place you go. I think it's good to just do the work and insulate yourself from that undercurrent of low-level malevolence.[11]

In fact, the biggest mistake Raphael said he made with the director occurred at the point of the full script draft's completion, when he sent a documentation copy of the draft to his representative at the William Morris agency and to a close friend for filing back in the States. This made Kubrick furious because he didn't want the public alerted to what he was doing, and it nearly got Raphael fired before final revisions with the director were completed (Raphael, hereafter parenthetically abbreviated as R., 26–27).

Most significantly, however, during the extended period of their work, Raphael notes Kubrick's failure to be forthcoming about what he wanted from the adaptive screenplay, which necessitated the constant rewrites from which Kubrick seemed gradually to formulate on his own what he might finally be looking for. Raphael saw this as Kubrick's "dread of the 'conceptual': he has no interest in *purpose* and refrains from declaring any big idea" (R., 58). Rather than taking a prescriptive or even supportive role in the collaboration process, Kubrick would simply tell him, after numerous revisions, when they might move forward and begin to deal with the next scene. As Raphael notes, "He always knew what he didn't want, never what he did" (R., 122) He goes on to explain, relative to the infrequency of their face-to-face meetings:

> I was quite unable to guess what he would applaud and what he would ask me to do again. Sometimes he would leave me in doubt for sev-

eral days. As the days and weeks went by, I wrote and I waited and I wrote again . . . it is natural for directors, of whatever skill, to seek to turn writers into their creatures. The frog and the scorpion can never contract out of their allotted roles. (R., 122)

The slavish nature of Raphael's collaboration in the writing of *Eyes Wide Shut* took its toll. He concluded toward the end of his work with Kubrick that "he doesn't want to make anything *with* anyone" (R., 113). Raphael goes on to explain: "I have come to realize, painfully, that I am there to provide a script to which he can then apply himself without me. . . . All he requires of me is a text that can be made audible and visible" (R., 150). His lament is common to screenwriters, who know that directors may change a script at will through the remaining stages of shooting, editing, and sound mixing. During their infrequent script meetings and several phone conversations, Raphael came to believe, especially in light of the often intimate sexual nature of the story material, that "what concerns him is always the furniture, the mechanics of such things, never what anyone might feel" (R., 163). Raphael saw that Kubrick (the sincere family man in real life) was taken by the impersonal orgy in this story, and they researched historical references to the phenomenon. But again, as opposed to Raphael's concerns with character motivation in the screenplay's development, he noted that Kubrick had "an almost solipsistic lack of interest in character" (R., 161). Kubrick was searching for a prevailing story conception during the course of their collaboration, and he hoped that his writer might provide him with a contemporary turn on most of the character and story elements that would make this possible.

Raphael was not alone in being left out of the creative process that went on in Kubrick's mind at the script stage. Kubrick also treated his film cast in much the same fashion during shooting. In the Warner Bros. documentary, *Stanley Kubrick: A Life in Pictures* (2001), Tom Cruise (who also narrates) observes that when actors asked Stanley what he wanted in the typically numerous takes for almost every scene in *Eyes Wide Shut*, his only response was that he "wanted the magic." Nicole Kidman, who played Tom's character's wife in the film (Kubrick wanted an actual married couple for his lead roles, which might suggest his wish to capture a heightened realism in marital jealousy), notes in the same documentary that Stanley's approach on the set "was about a discovery. He wanted to investigate every avenue . . . to perfect it. Stanley hated to explain himself about a scene or the film as a whole." The third member of the lead cast to be interviewed was Sydney Pollack, who believes that Stanley was after something spontaneous and essential "not in a literal but in an imaginary way." Perhaps at this stage Kubrick felt that voicing conceptual perspectives on the set would have squelched the possibility of "spontaneous" illumination in performance, since the adapted screenplay already indicated a clear story structure and theme, if not the precise situational inflection of character that the actors may have been looking to their director to suggest. Notably, here as elsewhere, audiences do not get emotionally close to characters in Kubrick films so much as behold them in a total audiovisual space that is always fully and mindfully articulated. This helps to explain the director's reticence with his writer and his cast to predefine character emotions and thus encourage the spectator's uncritical emotional identification with them. Kubrick's consistently strong denunciation of dehumanizing forces in Western culture is partly realized through a mental distancing from character melodrama.

Meanwhile, as Frederic Raphael continued to write deep into the screenplay, he also came to realize the extent to which Kubrick had "convinced himself that our salvation lies in keeping to Schnitzler's beats . . . he wants as straight a translation as can be" (R., 163–164). With this in mind, therefore, I provide a brief summary of Schnitzler's lesser known novella, which is credited on-screen as having "inspired" *Eyes Wide Shut*. This is not to judge the fidelity of the film to its source but rather to demonstrate where Kubrick and Raphael were starting from, and the process by which their script "collaboration" finally became the guide for the much expanded cultural commentary that appears on-screen.

The novella begins with Fridolin and his wife Albertine attending their young daughter's reading of a fairy tale about a prince who, on a dreamy night, is being delivered on a galley rowed by slaves to a palace for his pending marriage. This sets the mythic tone for Fridolin's actual journey, which begins in marital distrust and the longing for adventure and becomes an episodic, circular rite of passage wending its way back to his marriage bed. Once their daughter is asleep, the couple find themselves briefly reflecting on a masquerade ball and those with whom they flirted the previous night. This leads to admissions by each of them regarding their own sexual fantasies involving strangers while on a recent vacation in Denmark. So upset is Fridolin at the potent revelations of his wife's longing for a sailor she had merely seen there that he finds himself momentarily launched on a restless excursion of his own. Whether his nighttime adventure is specifically for sexual consummation as revenge for Albertine's fantasy is not altogether clear, since he decides against sex with a prostitute, who then refuses payment. Repeatedly, the novella emphasizes the troubling nature of erotic energy in dreams and lived experience as it relates to personal autonomy, marital fidelity, and social desires.

Fridolin's odyssey begins with a call on an elderly patient who has just died, and whose daughter for the first time expresses her love for him before being interrupted by the arrival of her fiancée. After Fridiolin's passing encounter with a street prostitute, he finds himself in a club where a former student acquaintance happens to be playing piano. From him he learns of a strange private costume ball later that night that includes beautiful naked women and is being hosted by a secret society that requires a password for entry. Armed with the password "Denmark,"[12] and dressed in the costume of a masked and black-robed man in a three-cornered hat, he crashes the late-night affair. There, in an unremarkable suburban home, he discovers an intense proceeding that may be "a meeting of some religious sect" but where veiled women dressed as nuns suddenly remove their robes to reveal a variety of nude body types. The masked men, who have given up their black monks' robes to reveal their dress as cavaliers, rush to the women and begin to dance in the voluptuous setting. Fridolin retains his robe because it covers his normal street clothes, and he receives glaring looks, particularly from "two noblemen." One attractive brunette steps forward and whispers urgent warnings for him to leave, on pain of death. Fridolin is soon challenged also by a few angry cavaliers, who threaten him with complete disrobing and worse. The humiliating crisis again brings forth the kind brunette, who offers herself speaking in the religious diction of "atonement" for his apparent "sins." This brave act before the alerted assembly appears to place the woman in great jeopardy, even as it allows Fridolin to go free. On his strange carriage ride home, Fridolin remains mortified by what may have happened to her. He believes that he may in fact be in a delirium and still lying in his bed at home having a nightmare. He checks himself physically: "Fridolin *opened his eyes as wide as possible* [italics mine], passed his hand over his forehead and cheeks, and felt his pulse" (R., 97).[13]

Fridolin finally arrives back home at four in the morning to find his sleeping wife in the middle of a nightmare, which she gradually recreates for him as she "twines her fingers in his." Albertine explains that in her dream, galley slaves row Fridolin to her door to rescue her, but after a night of love together prior to their wedding day, they find themselves the next morning naked and without clothes. She is filled with terror and shame and blames him. Fridolin immediately sets off to find clothing. But this is difficult, because he soon finds himself under a penalty of death if he does not become the paramour of the flaxen-haired "princess of the land." Albertine describes her appearance as similar to that of the seductive young girl Fridolin confessed an attraction to in the past. She imagines Fridolin brutally whipped by the princess even as she herself is left happily alone. Albertine eventually makes love with a man like the one she described in Denmark. At the same time, she feels indifference, and laughs when she notices that Fridolin is now being nailed to a cross by soldiers and priests for his continued rejection of the princess. Although these dream images seem to stem from the couple's sexual competition, they also suggest that Albertine intuits her husband's real adventures earlier that night and thus her enjoyment of his punishment while she commits adultery. But her dream's introduction of the ruling princess and the crucifixion of Fridolin (a Jew) also further elevate the scenario to sociopolitical and sacrificial connotations. Taken together, Fridolin's actual experiences with the street prostitute, and with the monks turned cavaliers and the "nuns" apparently of noble rank at the secret orgy, as well as Albertine's dream references to the couple's naked isolation and to the imagined queen who crucifies Fridolin, all point to issues of physical vulnerability, class rank, social condemnation, and a cabalistic religiosity of the powerful and privileged. There are also the anti-Semitic overtones of the street incident involving Aryan fraternity boys in blue caps, who jostle and mock Fridolin. At this story juncture, however, what remains of greatest concern to Fridolin (besides his wife's licentious behavior and disregard for him in her dream) is the persistent question of what has happened to his lovely rescuer from the troubling sexual escapade.

He sets out first thing the next day to locate the house where the bacchanalia occurred in order to discover the fate of this mysterious woman. Warned away from the house with a threat, he grows increasingly disoriented and begins to feel that all of life is an illusion. He enters a café and finds a newspaper that informs him of the death of a baroness, an "unusually good-looking woman," by poisoning. Two men were seen to have left this woman's apartment at 4 a.m., leading Fridolin to assume that she is the same woman with dark flowing hair who rescued him. Distraught, he makes his way to the city morgue in order to establish her identity. The circumstance at the morgue is described at great length. The presence of an attending physician, Dr. Adler, and his technical research over a microscope runs counter to Fridolin's extreme emotional state. Fridolin now "twines his fingers" in the stiff, cold ones of the Baroness's corpse (paralleling his earlier action with Albertine, and thus the women's psychological association), and he mourns her loss for his sake. The baroness takes on the burden of his transgressions, while Albertine's dream has him sacrificed. Fridolin's disoriented experience with the corpse is the emotional turning point in the story for him, since he now looks upon death in a context that includes both sexual desire and personal and social responsibility for his walk on the dark side. Schnitzler's narrative accomplishes this intensification through its shift from a question of Fridolin's marital fidelity to one of his culpability in setting a woman up for murder, and a baroness at that. The extended and rather gothic scene in the dimly lit morgue follows Fridolin's agitated concern not only for answers to his role in her demise but also for some larger understanding of the reliability of his perceptions, and thus the very ground of reality and of his identity.

Once more Fridolin returns home very late at night, as he wonders if all he has experienced might have been a dream. This time, however, he discovers on his pillow beside his sleeping wife the mask he had worn to the orgy the night before. After a moment of rationalization in his state of exhaustion, he bursts into tears and provides Albertine with a full confession of what his actions may have caused (not reiterated in the text). He asks at last what they should do, and she expresses gratitude that they have come through their adventures unharmed, be they "'real or only a dream.'" For her, "'the reality of one night, let alone that of a whole lifetime, is not the whole truth,'" and "'now I suppose we are awake,' she said," at least "'for a long time to come.'" The morning light shines through their bedroom window, and they can hear their daughter stirring in the next room. And so the tale of the ardent psychic voyager Fridolin concludes with the nurturing words and embrace of his wife, who does not look to social conventions or ideology for answers but trusts rather in her intuitive acceptance of the confusion that she observes as belonging (melodramatically) entirely within their personal domain. This seems to be intended as a consciously romantic assessment of all that has gone before, although Schnitzler hints ironically at the question of whether momentary marital rapprochement could possibly conquer the subconscious forces of desire and dreams, not to mention the persistently troubling ethnic, theocratic, and even paramilitaristic social realities that remain unresolved in the story.

Schnitzler's novella demonstrates, on the one hand, his appreciation for psychological complexity, represented by Albertine's intuitive powers of inspired imagination in nightmarish dreams and their potential to offer a fuller personal awareness. Fridolin, on the other hand, feels compelled to act out his profound restlessness of desire (for liberation?) through direct experience in the tangible world, even as he endangers himself and others in his adventuresome risks. Thus, Schnitzler demonstrates the marriage between physical and psychic experience, whether curative or not. Sigmund Freud, Schnitzler's Viennese compatriot, had read his work and complimented him as Freud's own doppelgänger. He expressed envy that Schnitzler could intuit "secret knowledge" that Freud could discover only after "arduous examination".[14] Schnitzler was not, of course, after case studies of psychological pathologies. Rather, he set his protagonist Fridolin on a journey of desire that finally tests the limits of conscious awareness through experiences of loss, guilt, and the possibility of atonement. This is established through the novella's predominant story emphasis on the psychosexual as well as the social-theocratic aspects of Fridolin's experience and Albertine's dreams, in which the personal stakes of their marriage finally appear to take some precedence over the other broader questions of their cultural circumstances.

In constructing the screenplay, Kubrick and Raphael both recognized the interior dimensions as well as the less developed social aspects of the novella. Raphael felt that he was the one who initially wanted to push the story emphasis beyond individual longing and toward a more comprehensive portrait of contemporary social class and power relations. Nor did Kubrick finally protest, though he had always been wary of being too obvious in character intent, dialogue, and theme, since he never wanted his films to function mainly as reductive ideas. After completing *2001*, he spoke of how he hoped audiences would respond to his work generally: "I think an audience watching a film or a play is in a state very similar to dreaming, and that the dramatic experience becomes a kind of controlled dream ... the important point here is that the film communicates on a subconscious level, and the audience responds to the basic shape of the story on a subconscious level, as it responds to a dream."[15] *Traumnovelle* provided a literal story of oneiric experience, although Kubrick and Raphael clearly did not want their screen treatment to be merely a reflection on the interchangeability of waking versus dream life. Kubrick's choice of title for the film is indicative of his eventual emphasis: *Eyes Wide Shut* might insinuate a potential for psychological awareness through dreams, although the title's dominant allusion is to myopia in perception despite wakefulness. The title change removes the word *Traum* (dream) from the original German in favor of a physical sense of seeing without seeing, of a blindness to social consciousness.

The displacement of personal autonomy and family or community cohesion by alienating forces is repeatedly held up for examination in Kubrick films such as *Lolita*, *A Clockwork Orange*, and *The Shining*. Kubrick, a Jew, knew where Western life had led since 1926 and had experienced deep anguish over the genocidal devastation of the Holocaust. Frederic Raphael, also a Jew, pointedly observed that it would be "absurd to try to understand Stanley Kubrick without reckoning on Jewishness as a fundamental aspect of his mentality, if not of his work in general" (R., 108). This may seem surprising in light of the nearly complete lack of Jewish characters in his films. Here, too, Kubrick specified that Raphael should make the central couple thoroughly gentile and mainstream, with the English-sounding family name of Harford (perhaps coined from the auteur's living area of Herefordshire). When Bill is jostled in the street by a group of young men, he is accused of being gay. Kubrick did not want ethnicity to distract from audience identification with the Harfords' mainstream status and rather typical marital issues; they eventually confront far more suggestive and omnipresent contemporary challenges than does the couple in the novella.

It is in the realm of contemporary character and plot motivation related to the socioeconomic dimension of desire that the contributions of Frederic Raphael were initially crucial. Most important, he was responsible for both creating and developing the character called Victor Ziegler in the screenplay. This new character—who does not exist in the novella—becomes central to the entire contemporary theme that Kubrick eventually put on-screen. Ziegler (Sydney Pollack) appears along with Bill Harford in three key scenes: the first occurs toward the beginning, at Ziegler's Christmas party, in a bathroom of his huge urban home; the second is at the grand orgy at a massive country estate when they are in mask; and the third is the climactic discussion in the billiard room at Ziegler's home, in which Ziegler reveals the identity of the dead woman Bill believes tried to save him. Raphael's idea and intentions here were explicitly addressed to Kubrick:

> It [the novella's plot] was, I argued, seriously unsatisfactory unless, for instance, the man I had called Ziegler was somehow involved both in the orgy and in Bill's escape from danger. To avoid resolving the issue, merely because Schnitzler had left it all in the air, would be to make the same mistake as Antonioni when he failed, at the end of *Blow Up*, to let us have any idea why anyone had been murdered, or by whom. (R., 145)

During the script's composition, Raphael argued not only for the critical billiard room confrontation between Bill and the wealthy Ziegler regarding the dead woman but also for Ziegler's revelation about what group was behind the orgy in which she played a role.[16]

On-screen, Bill and Alice Harford are presented as beautiful, sophisticated, but at first rather naïve citizens in America's urban society. Their expensive apartment and social world in New York City (actually shot in

London) seem at first untouched by the more chaotic world down on the streets. The warm appeal of their home interiors, however, is periodically counterbalanced by neon-lit commercial exteriors along shadowy streets and byways of unpredictable danger. This juxtaposed imagery surrounding Bill's excursions is psychologically suggestive, but it also reflects a rich-poor gap that becomes an important signifier of class differences. To accentuate this diference, Kubrick, unlike the novella's author, has his upper-middle-class Adam and Eve figures play out their drama at Christmastime.[17] He persistently dresses his interior scenes in reds and blues, while often further lighting these tints with blue overtones. The light blue interior wash comes either through windows at night[18] or from above in key scenes and thus creates an expressionistic sense of fantasy and nightmare, of claustrophobically enclosed and uncanny spaces. The Christmas red, in contrast to the blue, is also part of a thematic series of binaries: warmth and cold, interior and exterior, dream and reality, and a personal longing and social exploitation that finally require further elaboration. This begins with the fact that Bill's sexual jealousy toward his wife becomes merely a pretext in the film for an extended venture into a world of seduction, wealth, and power. This is carefully developed through a series of details that assert class difference and mythical economic fulfillment. As if the cold blue contrast to the presence of warm Christmas lights and Christmas trees in interiors were not enough, there are dialogue references to color as a promise of Eden. The models who flirt with Bill at Ziegler's party say very suggestively that they are taking him to "the end of the rainbow," as if sexual gratification and the more typical allusion to a pot of gold were the same thing. The shop where Bill rents his costume and stumbles on an unseemly sexual episode also has painted red-and-blue signage naming it The Rainbow. Even the large bag in which Bill carries his burdensome costume prominently features the store's name. These and other dialogue cues and visual images crescendo in the blue-washed trial scene at the orgy.

 The film opens just as Bill and Alice dress for the gala party at the huge urban mansion of Victor Ziegler (Sydney Pollack) and his wife. The grandiose surface elegance of Ziegler's private party becomes a hallucinatory pleasure garden that overlays some troubling events. Bill and Alice quickly become separated at the classy affair and find themselves in flirtatious circumstances that are extended beyond anything in the novella. In the film, when Bill is summoned upstairs by Ziegler, he tells his two seductive escorts that this is "to be continued." He must tend to another one of Ziegler's beautiful party guests, a momentary sexual partner who has overdosed from drugs and lies naked and inert before the two men and perhaps near death. Her position in a lounge chair imitates a painting of a reclining nude set over an elaborate fireplace, as if she were just another part of the furnishings. Dr. Harford is successful in awakening her and insists she go into drug treatment, but he also continues to kowtow to Ziegler as the older man proceeds to blame the poor victim, named Mandy, and to ask Bill to keep the incident to himself. Meanwhile, the tipsy Alice downstairs averts a heated seduction by her lascivious Hungarian dance partner, Szavost. He wants her to go upstairs alone with him to see Ziegler's "private collection" of artifacts. He is an even more obvious incarnation than is Ziegler of a decadent ownership class that enjoys an institutionalized form of vampirism in art, women, and business. But unlike the way Bill is subtly drawn into a conspiratorial friendship with Ziegler, Alice shows her ability to play with Szavost's temptations while tipsy without caving in to his luxurious charms.

The following day, as Bill and Alice share a joint while dressing for a shopping trip, they discuss what each did at the party, and Bill denies any sexual interest in the girls with whom he flirted. Alice is moved to challenge Bill's denial with a vigorous interrogation. Alice feels eventually driven to tell him her feelings of rapture for a man she merely observed on one of their vacations, and Bill is unable to answer with any similar experience of his own. Whether drinking champagne or stoned on a joint, Alice seems able to move through the turmoil of her desires and subconscious toward their curative possibilities. The film reveals, however, the way Bill's logical thinking and control tend toward repression and denial, an unwillingness to address subconscious truth and authentic feeling. The outwardly more adventurous Bill is nevertheless forced to confront a socioeconomic level of authority to which Alice is not directly privy, or else disregards as of little consequence.

Kubrick always preferred to create at least enough distance and complexity in characters and scenes to encourage active audience contemplation rather than simply character identification. This is particularly apparent in the way he undercuts the titillating potential in his constant resort to glaring images of nudity and sexual embrace, whether seen or imagined. In the opening shot, before the film's full screen title, Alice kicks off her dress and momentarily stands naked with her back to the camera. Both a later scene in which the couple lounge in their underwear in the privacy of their bedroom and again when they share an intimate nude embrace play initially to the viewer's voyeurism. But in the first instance, the couple's near nudity is resisted by Alice's verbal attack on her husband, and in the second scene, during their sexual embrace before their dresser mirror, Alice glances at herself self-consciously just as the aggressive Chris Isaak song, "Baby Did a Bad, Bad Thing," distances the viewer from their intimacy as well as its legitimacy. Much later, as Bill taxies to the mysterious orgy, he has tortured thoughts, shown in black and white, of his wife in bed with her stranger, and each time he imagines this, the image becomes more sexually aggressive than the last. Alienating devices such as these make the nudity and sex uncomfortable and viewer voyeurism self-conscious. So consistently are nudity and sex represented in increasingly degrading contexts of jealousy, fear, sickness, commerce, and finally death that it implicates the entire Christmas setting, normally taken to suggest generosity and good will. Further, the directorial consistency in the images of alienating voyeurism creates a tension at the level of appearances. They evolve into a motif that contradicts visual consumption and prepares the way for an additional level of meaning.

Unlike Schnitzler's bland orgiastic event that Fridolin attends at a modest home to the sounds of a harmonium and sacred Italian song, Kubrick's primary spectacle occurs at a palatial country estate in a great, church-like hall, where an aggressive, single-note piano score collides against a forbidding deep voice chanting in Latin. Here, the now disguised Bill is surrounded by other masked figures on the main floor, while a small group of men and women on an upper level look down on those below. One senior figure stares down at him and nods in a seemingly disapproving recognition that has Bill confused. This large male, in a traditional mask of aristocracy,[19] is later revealed to be the power broker Victor Ziegler. Most of the crowd on the main floor stands in the wings near a central performance by a masked, bishop-like figure in pink liturgical regalia. Pounding with his staff, he directs a circle of masked, leggy models of Barbie doll similarity to drop their cloaks and expose their nudity. While they are still on their knees, he approaches each woman individually and gives the consensual command to rise and seek a partner among the larger group. A debauched reflection of a high church Mass and Eucharist is unmistakable. As Bill wanders from room to room, the continuing displays of nude observers and raw sexual acts seem to follow Raphael's suggestion for the screenplay "that the orgy take the form of a sort of sexual mall, perhaps in the library of the big house" (R., 145). Voyeuristic and active sexual behavior is meant by Raphael to be associated with the casual activity of shopping, which would explain the bored and unfulfilled faces of the nude figures who passively observe the sexual performers. As the acts of copulation (partly screened by cloaked bodies in the American release) are observed indifferently by a shifting audience of couples, Bill's anxiety grows because he is sought out and further warned by one of the masked women with a large headdress. She seems to have recognized him as an outsider and taken pity on him, although soon afterward in the great hall, she is unable to prevent his ritual public unmasking and condemnation. Just before Bill is forced to remove his clothes by another formal command from the presiding "bishop" (who sits on his throne, which has a crown facsimile topped by a cross), however, the same masked woman reappears in an upper balcony and publicly offers herself as a sacrifice in his place. This scene suggests a strange insider morality that advances orgiastic sex, restricts it to lifeless codes of consumption, and backs it all by punishment for the uninitiated.

Kubrick and Raphael, therefore, while sharing with Schnitzler a dreamlike text of hierarchical psychodrama, not only extend the novella's sexual associations to an organized ritual of consumer fetishism but also heighten the threat of a potent but secretive authority that wraps itself in a cloak of twisted religiosity and righteousness. The orgy spectacle asserts no less than a patriarchal, spiritually bankrupt Mass led by the privileged ownership class. The unmitigated and forbidding seriousness of Kubrick's assault here is not to make a moral point about sex and sin but rather to emphasize how the natural appeal of sexuality has been commodified into a form of economic and political weapon. (*Clockwork Orange* carries a similar message, though in an entirely different tonal register.) Nudity and sexuality become bland and shameful under conditions of exploitation, which distorts rather than reveals truth and meaningful connection.

After Bill returns home and hides his mask, Alice awakens and tells him of her nightmare, which is almost the same as the one Albertine tells Fridolin in the novella. The business about Fridolin's being pursued by a princess and nailed to a cross is exempted, however, perhaps because it has now been transmogrified into the religious insinuations of the Rafael/Kubrick orgy already described. In Alice's dream, furthermore, she speaks of being the humiliated nude victim of a sexual assault involving several men, as if she were the one who had to take the responsibility and pay the price for her husband's involvement with their society's "leadership" class. In contrast to the happy Albertine in her dream, Alice is tortured by her husband's absence and what we know of his flirtation with the privileged. Thus, the overwhelming impression of the entire night's adventure is one of Bill's introduction into the unseen vertical structures of economic and political power, where he should tread with great care lest he or Alice be severely punished. Indeed, when Bill retraces his steps in a state of guilt the next day, he is very menacingly followed.

As he seeks to locate those from his first strange sojourn, it becomes increasingly clear that the members of the lower service class he met along the way have suffered physically or worse. When Bill returns his costume, the obsequious vendor Milich stands with his daughter and propositions the doctor regarding her sexual availability; the street prostitute Bill almost had sex with turns out to have just tested positive for HIV; Bill's pianist friend was that morning severely beaten and rushed from the city; and Bill is denied entry at the massive blue gate of the country estate with another dire warning.

The lower orders are humbled while the power figures remain anonymous. Most important, Bill learns from a newspaper story of the drug-induced death of a woman he believes to be the same one who stood up for him at the orgiastic ceremony. Beside himself with concern, he visits the morgue and is sufficiently convinced that it is the same woman.[20] From his perspective of those suffering mistreatment, despair, and loss, Bill is called on his cell phone and asked to pay a visit to Ziegler at his city mansion.

In this climactic scene, Ziegler in a light blue shirt receives Bill in a large billiard room of huge windows filled with blue light. The wealthy man first attempts to soften Bill with an offer of cases of expensive scotch. Ziegler also pushes billiard balls about on his large pink felt table as he answers Bill's increasingly pressing questions about what happened to Mandy. It is probably intentional that the table's felt matches the color of the bishop's cowl at the orgy, and that the centrality of the pool table matches the centrality in the prior scene of the metal slab in the morgue on which Mandy's lifeless body reclined. Ziegler admits that Mandy was the same drug-overdosed girl Bill treated at his party and who spoke for him at the masque. He also tells Bill that he had him followed for his protection, although Bill believes it was to prevent his speaking to the police about the circumstances surrounding Mandy's death. Ziegler increases his threat by explaining that Bill doesn't know what kind of trouble he was in last night, and that if he told Bill the names of the people at the masque, "I don't think you would sleep too well." The implication that the masked attendees at the orgy are the political and business elite is confirmed. Bill now refuses to be cordial and pointedly challenges Ziegler's evasiveness about Mandy's death, about what kind of charade or so-called "faked intervention" by Mandy on Bill's behalf would lead to such a thing. Ziegler simply says she was a hooker and a druggie and "got fucked" by a lot of men before she was taken home after the masque . . . "nobody was killed; life goes on."

Bill now unconditionally recognizes what he saw only with his eyes wide shut at the beginning of the film. In the aftermath of the orgy, in his wife's

In Eyes Wide Shut, *Victor Ziegler (Sydney Pollack) approaches Dr. Bill Harford (Tom Cruise) in warning and supplication, but Bill is no longer to be seduced into that world of exploitative power.*

real and dream revelations, and now in the case of Mandy's death, Ziegler becomes recognizable as the face of a viciously exploitative culture. His family name (not to mention his first name, Victor) is also phonetically close to the German term *Sieger*, or conqueror.²¹ Ziegler refuses to connect Mandy's death "by drugs" with the abuse she has received at the hands of the power figures with whom he associates. Ziegler, steeped in denial, believes that Mandy's death is based on her own inferiority. Bill, however, no longer blames Mandy but rather sees the self-preoccupied indifference in Ziegler's position, as well as how he once colluded with it. Having now taken stock of Ziegler, Dr. Bill returns home, apparently resolved to atone for his involvement. He turns off the Christmas tree lights as he enters their large apartment, but he is shocked to see his mask on the pillow beside his wife. He collapses sobbing in Alice's arms.

The next day, both shaken from their experiences, they give their closing lines in a setting invented by Kubrick for the film. They take their daughter Christmas shopping at a fancy toy store and find themselves surrounded in a pricey toy land of adults and children. Like Fridolin, Bill asks what they should do, and Alice makes the same replies given by Albertina. They should

The circus-like atmosphere of the upscale toy store captures the Harfords' daughter's attention at Christmas time. The presence of white stars on the ceiling against the strong red and blue color tones also adds a note of nationalism.

feel fortunate for having survived their struggle to an awakening, but with the understanding that nothing is certain or eternal. The immediate setting counteracts, however, the sense that full wakefulness can weigh against the forces of identity displacement in a highly seductive social formation. As they converse, their daughter has gotten herself momentarily lost among entire shopping islands of toys. What, then, will the distracted parents' emotional catharsis mean in a world in which children are actively seduced by a class-oriented consumerism?[22] The lush setting of large toys contributes to skepticism.

Alice's final comment to her husband is also original to the film and a loaded reminder of the terror of modern isolation. Alice asks that they go home and "fuck," directly asserting their need to find what connection and basic solace they can amid the debased commerce of distortions that have undermined the good faith and generosity that Christmas was meant to represent. In this his last film, therefore, Kubrick makes a Ulysses-like return to the familial hearth and its potential at least for honest personal intimacy within a greater political economic and pontifical landscape of secrecy and deception. Having completed his directorial travels through films involving war rooms, computer isolation in outer space, sleazy "milk" bars, psychosis-filled hotel landscapes, foreign battlefields, and the final nightmare of political and theocratic depravity, Kubrick has continued to prove his belief that contemporary Western culture is increasingly a paradise lost.

Whereas the 1927 novella's emphasis falls on the psychological dimension of ethical, ethnic, class, and religious experience, Raphael and Kubrick build a contemporary psychological and political blend of these ingredients into a bad dream of false and degraded promise. Their adaptation thus constitutes a realignment and contemporary reaccentuation of the novella. It is hard to imagine that Kubrick could have developed the depth of story that this film became without the exhaustive efforts of Freddie Raphael, whose authorship remains central to its characterization and plot. In the film, Schnitzler's tale is vastly enlarged into a compelling metaphor for the seductive exteriorization of native desire and fulfillment and the consequent loss of meaningful social agency. The "Zieglers" continue to rule. Years earlier, after completing the likes of *Dr. Strangelove*, *2001*, and *A Clockwork Orange*, Kubrick was asked how he thought the world would end. "'I think the danger is not that authority will collapse,' he said, 'but that, finally, in order to preserve itself, authority will become very repressive.'"[23] Such a thought is close to the warning delivered in *Eyes Wide Shut* of a pietistic society of political-economic expediency that depends on class envy (the eroticized promise of the rainbow) for its continuing control and exploitation. Victor Ziegler (partly through his association with the unholy and judicious bishop) personifies all of these linkages so carefully developed in the dialogue, the alienating use of sound, and the blue-tainted mise-en-scène of this adaptation. The film poses a privatized ruling order of grand spectacle that brandishes the signs of its wealth and public rituals even as it masks its debauchery and abuses of power. Perhaps Kubrick's own epic voyage through cinema and into death has found some solace in reminding us of all the essential human connections that have gone missing, and of what might be done on the level of social as well as personal consciousness to begin to recover them.

NOTES

1. Kubrick did his own adaptation of Lionel White's novel *Clean Break* for *The Killing*. Calder Willingham and Jim Thompson helped him with the adaptation of Humphrey Cobb's fact-based novel *Paths of Glory*. The screenplay adaptation

of Vladimir Nabokov's novel *Lolita* is credited to Nabokov, although the film isn't based on Nabokov's published version of his screenplay. Peter George's serious novel *Red Alert* is the basis for *Dr. Strangelove*, and though he is partly credited for the film's screenplay, Kubrick saw the need for satirical treatment of the subject and brought in and also credited comic novelist Terry Southern to help him complete the project. Kubrick brilliantly adapted Anthony Burgess's novel *A Clockwork Orange* on his own, as he did *Barry Lyndon*. He hired Diane Johnson to help him adapt Stephen King's *The Shining*, and for *Full Metal Jacket* he brought in Gustav Hasford, whose work (*The Short-Timers*) they adapted, as well as another Vietnam War novelist, which is discussed further in my text.

2. Gene D. Phillips, *Stanley Kubrick: Interviews* (Jackson: University Press of Mississippi, 2001), 179–180.

3. Greg Jenkins, *Stanley Kubrick and the Art of Adaptation* (London: McFarland, 1997), 109.

4. The source was science fiction writer Brian Aldiss's short story, "Super Toys All Summer Long." A.I. is an abbreviation for artificial intelligence.

5. The script was based on the novel *Wartime Lies* (1991), by Louis Begley.

6. Warner Books published a transcript of the *Eyes Wide Shut* screenplay in 1999 when the film was released, and also included a new translation of *Traumnovelle* by J. M. Q. Davies under the title *Dream Story*.

The references cited here are to the *Rhapsody* translation and pagination.

7. Schnitzler claimed to be working on this story idea for about twenty years. He was sixty-six when the novella was finally completed, and he died at seventy, while Kubrick completed his screen adaptation of it in 1999, the final year of his life at seventy-one.

8. Kubrick also admired Ophuls for the visual sophistication of his characterizations, including in particular his smooth-moving camera techniques, which Kubrick used and expanded upon.

9. In addition to being a physician, writer, and pianist, Arthur Schnitzler became interested in film in his later years and even wrote a fragmentary screenplay from *Traumnovelle* as part of an unrealized plan with G. W. Pabst to bring it to film. As might be expected, Schnitzler's screenplay fragment is a near replica of his fictional story. There is no firm evidence that either Kubrick or his screenwriter read this untranslated and little known partial German script, which nevertheless has fleeting images from the wife's dream of her husband's little escapade in Denmark. Schnitzler's script concludes at the point where he rents his costume and departs for the strange late-night party in a horse-drawn cab.

10. Schnitzler was also an early experimenter with stream-of-consciousness writing as he attempted to trace the swells of heterosexual desire and guilt intermixed with the reasoning processes of the mind.

11. Jenkins, *Stanley Kubrick and the Art of Adaptation*, 201.

12. This password to the orgy in the novella is meant to have direct associations with the couple's summer fantasies in Denmark. The password is changed to "Fidelio" in the film, which is close to Fridolin's name and has the direct sense of fidelity, and is thus further ironic in relation to Bill's marriage. *Fidelio* is also the name of Beethoven's only opera. Since one of the opera's primary themes is loyalty, Raphael/Kubrick may have had in mind the code of silence, which fits the Mafia and, as we shall see, the elite class behind the "sacred" orgy in the film.

13. The idea of a social and psychological awakening is present elsewhere in Schnitzler's work. His short story "The Widower" describes a man who finds a letter from his best friend to his now deceased wife that makes their infidelity apparent. The text describes his reaction in words similar to those in *Traumnovelle*, which may have given Kubrick his idea for the film's title: "And the first word that Richard reads . . . strikes him numb for a moment. . . . With *wide open eyes* he looks around to see if everything in the room is still the same. . . ." (Italics mine.)

14. Leo Carey, "The Dream Master: The Stories of Arthur Schnitzler, the Amoral Voice of Fin-de-Siècle Vienna," *The New Yorker* (September 9, 2002), 154. The words are quoted in the article and apparently are from Freud, but the source is not cited.

15. Bernard Weinraub, "Kubrick Tells What Makes *Clockwork Orange* Work." *New York Times*, January 4, 1972.

16. To make his point to Kubrick about the possibility of a secret society of sexual license among the powerful elite, Raphael wrote an entire story about such a thing using real names and gave it to the director, who believed it to be factual at first because it was so thoroughly laid out (R., 146–148). Although such a society is not spelled out in the film, Kubrick obviously saw that something like this might exist, not to mention its metaphorical possibilities for what eventually became his larger thematic insinuations.

17. Martha Nochimson made suggestions about "the spiritual/consumerist oxymoron of Christmas" that appeared in an early draft of an article she was writing and are gratefully embraced here.

18. Also an effect of shooting interiors where exterior daylight is not color-corrected for interior tungsten.

19. This Venetian type of mask allowed the wearer to drink and eat without removing it. Almost all the masks for the film came from the craftsmen and shops in Venice. See Mario Belloni's *Maschere a Venezia* (Venice: Ca' Macana, 2002), 16.

20. The film is ambiguous on this point since a different actress was brought in to play the corpse in the morgue, although this may have been done because the other actress was not available at the time.

21. Also, *Sieg Heil* (hail victory) was sometimes given as a Nazi salute to another Austrian by birth, Adolph Hitler. Certainly Schnitzler, who understood imperial Austrian nationalism well enough in his own time, would have been appalled at

the level of National Socialist anti-Semitism by the late 1930s. Raphael notes that he named Ziegler after an unpleasant former agent of his called Ziggy (R., 119), although the German language and Nazi associations seem valid and were probably considered eventually by Kubrick. The director had a German artist as his third and most long-term wife, Susanne Christian. Some of her art work appears in this film, as it did in others of his.

22. Kubrick and Raphael also add a scene at home before Bill's second odyssey that involves their daughter's request for a real puppy for Christmas, which she argues could serve as a watchdog. But then she goes back to her homework involving a math problem in subtraction testing how much more money one person has than another. This scene with mother and daughter over homework is also dressed in a strong red, white, and blue—as are others, including especially the closing scene with the family at the toy store.

23. Phillips, *Stanley Kubrick*, 185.

PART II
//

SCREENPLAY ADAPTED
AND DIRECTED BY

> ... we are the guys who dig out the gold. The man in the executive tower cannot do that. The studios are corporations now, and the men who run them are bureaucrats. . . . They go to parties and they hire people who know people. But the power lies with us—the ones who actually know how to make movies.
>
> —George Lucas (quoted in Michael Pye and Lynda Myles, *The Movie Brats*)

A second model of screenwriter participation in the adaptation process is the "written and directed by" combination, which places total creative responsibility in the hands of one individual. This model differs from the auteur configuration discussed in Part I mainly in the absence of a separate writer. If Hollywood auteurs use their writers to help them fill out their only partly realized ideas of adaptation at the outset, writer-directors of adaptations must work through all the details of dialogue, description, and story structure on their own. They must build their adaptation from scratch on the page, even if they may already have an overall sense of how they intend to approach it. The writer-director in adaptation single-handedly performs the functions of interpreting published sources, transforming them into a screenplay, and bringing them to life in production and postproduction. The writer-director must bridge the yawning gap between the private experience of molding an adapted screenplay on the page and the turmoil of endless decision making and public interaction that is directing. To combine these complementary but very different tasks in one person severely tests the focus required for each one, although the writer-director on the set is talking mainly to him- or herself when script changes are made. This may be liberating when the director feels confident in the scriptwriting, or lonely during an exhausting shoot when perspective is hardest to come by. As Patrick McGilligan observes in his introduction to Backstory 4, up until the 1970s, the writer-director was mostly a novelty in Hollywood.

Directors who choose to write their own scripts—not to mention writers who have been able to leverage access to the director's chair with their writing, as Steven Soderbergh did for his original script, *sex, lies, and videotape*—usually do so because the source material is to be given a very personal or very specialized interpretation. In the two case studies presented here, the director's devotion to a unique interpretation of the source becomes a personal mission. Whether such a comprehensive undertaking by one individual and its outcome can be usefully contrasted with what results from other models of adaptive screenwriting must be judged from the evidence provided. The significance of the script remains in any case, as do the same questions of orientation to the source. The director carries the ultimate responsibility for the screen adaptation whether scriptwriting alone or working with or from the script adaptation of someone else.

The two essays here which address the screenwriter-director model demonstrate once again the extent to which the screenplay dominates the formative process of intent. In Chapter 4, Mark L. Berrettini provides a thorough consideration of the politics of the color line in postwar Los Angeles in Carl Franklin's 1995 adaptation of Walter Mosley's 1990 noir throwback novel, Devil in a Blue Dress. *Berrettini notes writer-director Franklin's engagement with the entire noir film tradition that focuses on the gumshoe, the dark side of Los Angeles, and, in particular, the city's racial history from the perspective of a "blues detective" in the making. Though eliding the novel's backstory of the incestuous femme fatale character of the title, Franklin otherwise formulates her mulatto circumstance much as does the novel. She's the tragic focus of several interlocking violent incidents and murders. Berrettini explains how Franklin largely reconstructs rather than reimagines the period setting, off-beat characters, and grim authorial tone of his source.*

Ernesto R. Acevedo-Munoz in Chapter 5 provides an insightful interpretation of Egoyan's sensitive articulation of Russell Banks's novel The Sweet Hereafter, *with special attention to preserving the mysterious quality of the ineffable already present in the source. His discussion helps to elaborate that which is usually hardest to pinpoint in the ultimate success or failure of a relatively close adaptation. It is also notable that adapting writer-director Egoyan produced this film as well.*

4

PRIVATE KNOWLEDGE, PUBLIC SPACE

Investigation and Navigation in *Devil in a Blue Dress*

//

Mark L. Berrettini

WHILE THINKING ABOUT FILM NOIR IN RELATION TO CARL FRANKlin's *Devil in a Blue Dress* (1995), I have returned repeatedly to the considerable ways in which the film represents Los Angeles as a historically resonant and metaphorically rich location. Numerous critics and scholars have explored L.A.'s historic relationship with film noir, both as a major setting for film noirs and as the space in which writers and filmmakers generated the initial material that was to be named noir. In his definitive study of L.A., *City of Quartz*, Mike Davis posits that noir is a film style, a literary impulse, and a type of L.A. intellectual intervention that "made Los Angeles the city that American intellectuals love to hate."[1] Paul Arthur in "Los Angeles as Scene of the Crime" argues for the enduring importance of L.A. as a setting for film noirs, while the first chapter in Foster Hirsch's *The Dark Side of the Screen*, titled "The City at Night," focuses on L.A. and New York City to introduce the topic of film noir.[2]

As a neonoir,[3] Franklin's film develops out of this L.A. film noir history in its use of, among other film noir conventions, L.A. as a setting in which investigational narratives occur. Focusing on crime, corruption, and strained social bonds, *Devil in a Blue Dress* depicts a portion of L.A. culture that, because it lacks moral light, is considered, metaphorically, to be "dark." The film interrogates the very darkness that is central to this metaphor as, simultaneously, it explores the racialized equation of criminality and darkness-blackness through a plot that concentrates on questions that pertain to racialized social relations. This aspect of *Devil in a Blue Dress* informs B. Ruby Rich's consideration of the film, in which she rightly identifies it as a "film noir with a difference": a neonoir that focuses on "'outsider' identit[ies]—African-Americans, non-fatal femmes, gays and lesbians."[4]

To maintain a balance between its film noir generic framework and its emphasis on the lives of historically marginalized figures, *Devil in a Blue Dress* pays significant attention to the sociohistorical aspects of postwar L.A. The use of film noir's critical potential allows for a studied assessment of moments in which the city's "dark" criminal terrain is established by a policing of the color line. Within the film, L.A. serves as a quintessential "American" space in which cultural anxieties about race, gender, and racial purity are contained, explored, and exploded. With these concepts in mind, I shall trace the film's specific use of film noir conventions to explore the prominence of race, gender, and the color line in L.A. circa 1948.

BAD BLOOD, BAD DADDIES, AND THE "PRODUCTION" OF THE TRAGIC MULATTA FEMME FATALE

Both the novel (Walter Mosley, 1990) and the film version of *Devil in a Blue Dress* open as Easy Rawlins (Denzel Washington), an unemployed black man and the protagonist of the narrative, is approached by a white man named Dewitt Albright (Tom Sizemore), who wants to hire Easy to find a white woman who has "a predilection for the company of Negroes." Even though the woman is white like Albright, her preference precludes the white man from actively searching for her and conversely necessitates Easy's (or some other black person's) involvement. Albright's request at this early point in the film highlights the significant impact that race and the color line will have on the progression of Easy's investigation, even though the details of the case have not yet been presented. When Easy meets Albright the next time and agrees to take the job, Albright again directs Easy's attention to racial matters as he verbally marks the woman, Daphne Monet (Jennifer Beals), as white. Albright says that Daphne's fiancé, Todd Carter (Terry Kinney), is worried about her and then supports his comment with a photograph of Daphne and Carter from the newspaper.

This is the second time in the film that a close-up of this photograph is shown; while in Joppy's Bar (the site of Easy's first meeting with Albright) in the film's first scene, Easy briefly looks at the photo of the then-unnamed Daphne and Carter, who has just dropped out of the L.A. mayoral race. Though three times removed from her corporeal being—via mediation by a photographic camera, a newspaper's reproduction of the photograph, and the film camera's reproduction of the newspaper image—these close-ups of Daphne constitute her first appearance in the film. Since, according to conventional narrative cinema, visual evidence equals truth, and, according to the popular notion that news reportage guarantees truth, the filmed photograph supports Albright's description of Daphne and presents her as white, because she is shown in the photograph with the white Todd Carter. Easy and viewers can assume that Daphne is white because, according to the photograph, she has a predilection for the public company of whites.[5] But even as the film directs Easy and viewers to adhere to newspaper and filmic conventions of truth, it invokes the time-honored convention of hard-boiled detective fiction and film, a generic designation signaled at this early point in the film by the mise-en-scène, Easy's voice-over, and the title credit sequence: we cannot always believe what we see. By twice placing significant emphasis on Daphne's photograph in the first few moments of the film, the film sets up the potential subversion of this truth later on.[6]

Daphne's first appearance in the flesh occurs after Easy has obtained some information about her from her friend Coretta (Lisa Nicole Carson). In the first stage of his investigation, Easy sets out to find Daphne at John's, an illegal black jazz club. Easy, a regular at the club, quickly gains entry through a hidden doorway, while an unknown white man is thrown out, as if to verify Albright's reasons for hiring Easy. Once inside, Easy casually asks about Daphne, purposefully misnaming her "Dahlia" and "Delilah" so as to appear uninterested in the woman. His "mistake" is that, although he attempts to conceal his investigation and to cover over his knowledge of Daphne's real name, in two allusions Easy reveals much about how he imagines Daphne. Delilah, the Old Testament's duplicitous, fatal woman who helped bring about the public downfall of her lover, Samson, serves as an ancient predecessor for Daphne, a potentially dangerous woman who has most likely played some role in her lover's decision to drop out of the mayoral race. Building on this ancient reference, Dahlia is a name that seizes on the film's geographic and temporal setting: the name refers to the famous 1947 L.A. murder of Elizabeth Short, named by the press the Black Dahlia.

James Ellroy, whose first best-selling novel *The Black Dahlia* (1987) is a fictionalization of the famous case, explains that Short's torture-murder was reduced by the police and the press to a simple story of a loose woman who "attract[ed] death" and that the Black Dahlia "tag nullified [Elizabeth Short] and vilified her and turned her into a sainted lost daughter and a slut."[7] In addition to this true-crime antecedent, Dahlia also calls up the film *The Blue Dahlia* (George Marshall, 1946), scripted by Raymond Chandler, which focuses on a returning World War II veteran and the murder of his unfaithful wife. Thus, Easy's comments foreshadow for viewers the representation of Daphne as a femme fatale before she appears on screen, but his comments do not depend on complete recognition and understanding on the part of the audience. Rather, the range and depth of his allusions allow for potential viewer recognition that would in turn align viewers' comprehension of Daphne with Easy's perceptions of her.

Easy gets no positive response to his inquiries while he continues to misname Daphne, but then he meets his friends Dupree (Jernard Burks) and Coretta, who both stare at him when he asks about the white woman with a "name that starts with a D." After a momentary pause, Dupree and Coretta change the subject and sidestep Easy's question. At this point, Easy does not seem to notice from their facial expressions that they recognize Daphne's name and description, but later in the evening, after Dupree has passed out from drinking, a seemingly drunk Coretta tells Easy that she knows Daphne. After a quick sexual liaison (and financial transaction), Easy leaves Coretta, having obtained Daphne's address, which he then passes on to Albright. Later that day, Easy learns from the police that Coretta was killed some time after he left her.

Easy is questioned, beaten, and released by the police, and when he returns home he receives a telephone call from Daphne, who asks him to meet her at her hotel. The reason for the meeting, she explains, is that she has learned that Easy is looking for her. As a medium shot of Easy on the phone dissolves to a shot of a hotel hallway, Daphne's voice shifts from dialogue to voice-over as she tells Easy that he must sneak into the white section of the hotel to meet her. Daphne's voice-over directions end as she is shown for the first time—dressed in a blue sheath nightgown, her black hair swept up—in a wide shot taken from Easy's point of view.

Daphne's hair and gown, both reminiscent of Barbara Stanwyck's classic incarnation of the femme fatale in *Double Indemnity* (1944), build on Easy's earlier, suggestive misnaming. With cigarette smoke circling around her blue dress–clad body, Daphne is clearly the devil of the film's title. She greets Easy and wonders if she should think of him as "a friend of Coretta's or a private dick," a double entendre that alludes to her knowledge that he and Coretta had a sexual liaison and characterizes him as a private detective, a profession Easy eschews at this point. Daphne's wordplay also articulates two aspects of her femme fatale persona: the overt sexuality of her character and her proximity to a private detective. Later in the scene, while Easy tries to determine just what Daphne knows about Coretta's murder, Daphne extends the sexual dimension of their exchange, again through wordplay. After Easy asks her what her weapon of choice is, Daphne invites him to search her and find out. Easy smiles, for as he and viewers can plainly see, the only weapon that Daphne could conceal in her "sheath" dress would be her body.[8]

Daphne's body-as-weapon makes its second appearance when she arrives at Easy's home after another murder is linked to him. Easy finds Daphne, again in a blue dress, inside his home and learns that she wants information about blackmail pedophile photographs of Matthew Terell (Maury Chaykin), Carter's opponent for mayor. Easy, in turn, wants Daphne to explain her connections to the murders so that he can clear himself and since he suspects that, at Daphne's behest, Frank Green (Joseph Latimore), the man purported to be Daphne's black lover, killed Coretta. In a scene reminiscent of Jake's confrontation with Evelyn late in *Chinatown* (1974), Easy physically and verbally accosts Daphne about Frank's involvement in the murders.[9] Unable to fend him off, Daphne breaks down and explains, "Frank is my brother. Our mother is Creole, we have different fathers: mine is white. And that's what Terell has on me." Threatened by Easy, Daphne says she is a mulatta, thereby revealing the mysterious trajectory of the narrative: Terell used his knowledge of Daphne's racial background to force Carter out of the mayor's race, and Daphne bought the photographs of Terell as a way to trump his information. Albright, it turns out, actually works for Terell and wants to find Daphne to stop her from blackmailing Terell. Ironically, the photographs of Terell reference the earlier photograph of Daphne. In both instances, the photographs ensure Daphne's white identity, even if this identity exists only in L.A.'s public sphere.

Easy states in a voice-over near the resolution of the film that Daphne explained her racial history "like a sinner who wanted to confess." This confession is not shown in the film, so what film viewers learn about her is mediated through Easy's voice-over. Easy expands on what Daphne has said about herself as he notes that Daphne's real name is Ruby Hanks and that she is from Lake Charles, Louisiana. It is significant that Daphne's confession in the film is a condensed version of the two confessions depicted in Walter Mosley's novel, for this alteration indicates much about Daphne's history and agency. In the novel, Daphne first reveals a portion of her past to Easy as the two hide out together. Engaging in what seems to be idle chitchat, she asks him if he has been to the zoo and then remarks:

> The first time my father took me to the zoo, it was in New Orleans. I was born in New Orleans. . . . At almost closing time, we passed the zebras. No one was around and Daddy was holding my hand. Two

zebras were running back and forth [and then] the male mounted the female.... My daddy and I were holding hands so tight that it hurt me but I didn't say anything about it. And when we got back to the car he kissed me. It was just on the cheek at first but then he kissed me on the lips, like lovers do.... From then on, my whole fourteenth year, he'd take me to the zoo and the park. Always at first he'd kiss me like a father and his little girl but then we'd get alone someplace and act like real lovers. And always, always after he'd cry so sweet and beg me to forgive him.... My daddy never took me anywhere again after that year. He left Momma and me in the spring and I never saw him again. Nobody ever knew about him and me and what happened. But I knew. I knew that that was why he left. He just loved me so much that day at the zoo and he knew me, the real me, and whenever you know somebody that well you just have to leave.[10]

As explained in this confession, the secret "sin" of Daphne's past is incest, not that she is mulatta. Incest, it seems, is a more acceptable, appropriate secret to share. As Daphne's self-disclosure reveals some information about her past and her identity, her comment that her father "knew the real me" simultaneously raises questions about her identity. Who is the "real" Daphne? Though no definite explanation is given as to what constitutes this identity, the novel foreshadows the announcement of Daphne's biracial identity—her real identity?—with a vivid and rather vulgar image: zebras engaged in intercourse.

The zebra image in this passage evokes both the sexualized relationship between Daphne and her father and a vernacular usage of the word *zebra* as a racial slur for someone with a biracial background, linking the animal's black-and-white stripes to the supposed commingling of black and white blood in a human.[11] In the novel, the zebra acts as a bridge between Daphne's first confession and her second confession, in which she explicitly mentions her mulatta status. This later revelation is not self-determined since Easy's friend Mouse reveals the "real" Daphne as he describes her racial background. Mouse remembers Daphne as Ruby, Frank Green's light-skinned sister, prompting Daphne to provide the following amended history:

I'm not Daphne. My given name is Ruby Hanks and I was born in Lake Charles, Louisiana. I'm different from you [Easy] because I'm two people. I'm her and I'm me. I never went to that zoo, she did. She was there and that's where she lost her father. I had a different father.

He came home and fell in my bed about as many times as he fell in my mother's. He did that until one night Frank killed him.[12]

Rejecting the unified body of the zebra in favor of the image of a zebra as having distinct black-and-white stripes, Daphne imagines herself as two people, not one embodiment of black and white. Her two fathers, one black, one white, give rise to this split identity, yet their incestuous relations with their "daughters" in a perverse way allow Daphne-Ruby to maintain some semblance of a unified identity.[13] The incestuous relationships provide a point of cohesion for Daphne-Ruby in that the two daughters are linked by a shared trauma that, in effect, mirrors the sexual relations between their two fathers and their shared mother. Here, Daphne-Ruby embodies social transgression on two levels since she is simultaneously the child "product" of transgressive miscegenation and a participant in incestuous-miscegenationist relationships.[14] Further, according to the tradition of Oedipus and the conventions that accrue around the mulatta in U.S. film and fiction, Daphne-Ruby's life can only result in a tragedy.[15]

As Daphne articulates her mulatta identity in the film, the explicit incest and bad fathers of the novel are elided for a less spectacular yet still dramatic revelation about her identity.[16] While Franklin's earlier film, *One False Move* (1993), insists on there being a connection between incest and miscegenation, Daphne's discussion of incest, her two "bad fathers," and her split Daphne-Ruby subjectivity all drop out of the film version of *Devil in a Blue Dress*. What we are left with is a white father who, we assume, refused to recognize Daphne as his daughter and, perhaps, as the novel tells us, left. This filmic moment maintains the tragedy of the novel by still relating Daphne's tragedy to her status as a mulatta, but here the film elides the element of incest in favor of another form of "illicit" sexual relations and social transgression: miscegenation involving the mulatta as a participant, specifically Daphne's engagement to Carter.

Once Easy forces Daphne to reveal her "invisible" biracial background, he understands one problem that has been at the heart of his investigation, and since he now has the photographs of Terell, he can help rectify Daphne and Carter's social transgression. The photographs will, of course, save Carter's mayoral campaign, but they will not help reinstate Daphne into the white world in which she once traveled. This failure can be seen both as the conventional failure of the detective fully to resolve his case and as the inability of any character to overcome a tragedy, especially when that tragedy stems from seemingly immutable aspects of identity. On one level, then, Easy is unable to "save" the femme fatale Daphne, but, on another level, Daphne is unable to "transcend" her mulatta identity. Within the racialized terrain of L.A., Daphne's unstable identity would always loom over her life with Carter, and Carter cannot renew his private, interracial relationship with Daphne because its existence could always spill over into the public sphere. As Easy aptly sums up the issue, "The color line in America worked both ways and even a rich white man like Todd Carter was afraid to cross it." With this assessment, Easy articulates his understanding of his surroundings and predicaments, which provides viewers with a way retroactively to understand his character throughout the film.

EASY RAWLINS, RELUCTANT PRIVATE DICK

Easy's actions and commentary throughout the film relate primarily to questions of perception and meaning-making, and, as a black detective, he always processes these questions in relation to his particular understanding of race relations. Hence, Easy understands Carter's refusal to reunite with Daphne as a standard response given the legal and social prohibition against miscegenation. In this specific instance and indeed throughout the film, Easy resembles the black detectives Stephen Soitos describes in his study *The Blues Detective*. "The blues detective," Soitos argues, "always delineates the color line as primary in any case of social relations [and is] interested in the social and political atmosphere [as] inscribed by racial prejudice."[17] With Soitos's claim in mind, Easy's actions and commentary throughout the film can be viewed as indicative of his developing characterization as a blues detective. I include the word *developing* here because it is not until the end of the film that Easy accepts his role as a detective; while sitting on his porch in the film's final sequence, Easy tells his friend Odell (Albert Hall) that he plans to do a little private investigating as a new job. Before this moment, as demonstrated in his first meeting with Daphne, Easy is at best a reluctant "dick" who is involved in her case in order to clear his name and protect his home.

Easy's understanding of postwar social interactions and social space in L.A. as defined by the color line informs the hesitancy with which he approaches his burgeoning detective career. In the beginning moments of the film, Easy notes in a matter-of-fact voice-over that something is wrong with the job Albright offered him and that Albright (all bright) is only the second white man he has seen in Joppy's Bar (the other being the landlord on collection day). Making a connection between the space of the bar and Albright's racial status, Easy recognizes that something is amiss. After Albright leaves, Easy

Easy Rawlins (Denzel Washington) is drawn into a web of murder, blackmail, brutal cops, and L.A. politics in Carl Franklin's Devil in a Blue Dress.

makes his distrust of the all-bright white man known and asks Joppy (Mel Winkler) if the job and Albright are questionable, to which Joppy responds, "Ain't nothing to worry about." Rather than calming Easy, Joppy's casual statement only increases Easy's suspicions, for, as he notes in his voice-over, "When somebody tells me ain't nothing to worry about, I usually look down to see if my fly is open." Following from this first scene, Easy (in voice-over) continues to express his concerns about the case in terms that foreground the "fact" of race in relation to the L.A. landscape. And, quite often, these terms include considerations of the general area surrounding Easy's fly.

Race and Easy's fly next become conjoined when he meets Daphne at her hotel, where she calls Easy a "private dick" and invites him to search her body. In response, Easy is embarrassed (laughing slightly as he says that he is no detective), then intrigued, then threatened. Overcoming his initial surprise at Daphne's bold sexual statements, he approaches her to "search" her; however, the scene plays as though the two are about to kiss. After a moment and before they touch, Easy regains his senses and backs away from Daphne, apparently remembering "his place" in relation to her, a white woman who is also a mayoral candidate's ex-fiancée.[18]

The interaction fresh in his mind, Easy then attempts to drive Daphne to Carter's home, at her request. As they pass a police car—a close-up shows

Easy's eyes as reflected in the car's rear-view mirror—Daphne asks Easy if he is nervous. He does not respond to her in dialogue but instead reflects in voice-over: "Nervous? Here I was in the middle of the night in a white neighborhood with a white woman in my car. Naw, I wasn't nervous. I was stupid." When Daphne calls attention to some police, Easy is forced to recognize their threatening presence in relation to the potentially sexualized and supposedly antithetical relationship between his blackness and her whiteness (he still thinks that she is white at this point in the film). But, as the earlier hotel scene indicates, Easy does not need Daphne or the police to remind him about the color line and the potentially dangerous differences between Daphne and himself. Indeed, Daphne's reminders most significantly raise questions about her own slightly suspicious navigation of the color line as demonstrated in the semiprivate hotel room and in the fully public space of the streets they drive through.

By the time Easy meets up with Daphne later in the film, the point at which she reveals her biracial identity, he is fully cognizant of the danger that she represents in general (as a white woman) and in particular (at least two people associated with her are dead), and his perception of her is once again informed by their setting. Their second meeting is at Easy's house, a private dwelling that has figured in his voice-over.[19] Before this moment, viewers have seen Easy's home on several occasions and have heard him speak about it glowingly. When his house first appears (it fills the frame of a wide shot), Easy says, "I loved coming home . . . maybe because I just liked owning something." He goes on to explain that he is one of many new black homeowners who returned from World War II with money and the GI Bill to support them or who migrated from the South in search of jobs in airplane factories and munitions plants. Easy's homeownership is the result of both circumstances, since he moved to L.A. from Houston via the European theater of World War II. By placing Easy in this context, the film comments on the contradictions of postwar America: while the war opened up new economic and social opportunities for blacks, job discrimination, as an early flashback to Easy's firing indicates, and geographic restrictions and containment in the form of redlining and police surveillance countered "advancement."[20] It is in this portion of his voice-over narration that Easy also explains why, against his better judgment, he accepted Albright's job: Easy needs to pay late mortgage payments. In other words, Easy has become a detective because "[his] blackness allows him entry into certain areas of society where whites have little access."[21] I would add that Easy also takes the job because he wants to maintain ownership of his house.

Easy's home is easily the most important element in his life, so it is not difficult to understand why, when Daphne arrives there, he is most in control. Unlike their meeting in Daphne's whites-only hotel room, Easy directs the flow of their interaction and pressures Daphne to divulge important information. In his meetings with Albright, however, Easy is most agitated and aggressive at his home. These are not mutually agreed upon meetings, in that Albright and his henchmen arrive uninvited, so Easy rightly views these meetings as home invasions. Likewise, all the characters who arrive at Easy's house—Daphne, the police, Frank Green, and even a neighbor who tries to chop down trees—are uninvited.[22] The first home invasion occurs when two white police detectives (Beau Starr and John Roselius) appear at Easy's home late at night and arrest him for Coretta's murder. Easy is taken from his yard and brought to the police station by two detectives who beat and taunt him during an interrogation, even though they have no evidence of his role in Coretta's murder. The detectives eventually let Easy go, and he names the confrontation "a game of cops and niggers," noting the police's routine, insignificant, even jocular approach to this task.

This game continues in the fifth home invasion, when the same police detectives arrive on Easy's porch and threaten to plant evidence connecting him to the homicide. This time, the police let Easy go before they take him in because he agrees to help them solve their case. The ease with which the detectives agree to Easy's involvement indicates that this was their plan when they arrived at his house, and, in a manner similar to Albright's, they want Easy to investigate black areas and report back to them.

The home invaders' visits to Easy's home resemble the stream of visitors who often appear at detectives' offices in detective fiction. In his brief comments about Easy, Soitos notes that throughout Mosley's Easy Rawlins Mystery Series, Easy "works for money but does not retain an office nor does he have any official status as a detective."[23] In *Devil in a Blue Dress*, Easy's lack of an office is a practical matter since he is just beginning to work as a detective, but in the rest of the novels he does not ever have one; for the most part, throughout the series, Easy tries to keep his status as a private detective a secret from most of the people in his community. As *Devil in a Blue Dress* demonstrates, Easy's base of operation, against his will, is his home, and although this substitution of home for office is significant in that it marks Easy's status as an unofficial private detective, the collusion of the home and office is not without precedent in hard-boiled detective film and literature.

The Maltese Falcon (John Huston, 1941) includes several important scenes that take place in Sam Spade's apartment, but not because Spade does not have an office. Rather, Spade, a white private detective, holds meetings in his apartment because it seems to be less visible and more private, factors that are important to his clients, who want to avoid the police. More recently, two white police detectives—Nick Curran (Michael Douglas) in *Basic Instinct* (Paul Verhoeven, 1992) and Martin Riggs (Mel Gibson) in the *Lethal Weapon* trilogy (Richard Donner, 1987, 1989, 1992)—check in and out of their offices but do their real investigative work in the field, in homes, and in beds. In "The Synoptic Chandler," a scholarly approach to the subject of detectives, homes, and offices, Fredric Jameson examines Raymond Chandler's Philip Marlowe series and compares the homes of the rich (usually corrupt) characters to the general function of offices as empty spaces of "retreat and withdrawal."[24] In this context, the office "subsumes a much wider variety of social activity than it is normally understood to do," for, as these homes come to resemble offices, they no longer serve as spaces in which characters dwell.[25]

Using Jameson as a guide, what seems to occur in *Devil in a Blue Dress* is the gradual transition of Easy's home from a dwelling to an office, a transition that nearly empties his home of its domestic functions. Just as the classic hard-boiled detective cannot remain outside his investigation and the rich, corrupt characters of Chandler's novels are always more involved in their cases than they initially state, Easy is implicated in his case as he becomes more drawn into the mysteries and crimes that surround Daphne. Recognizing his involvement, he needs to retreat from the investigation in order to sort it out, but since he does not yet consider himself a "private dick," the only private space to which he has access is his home. Withdrawing to his home again and again, Easy brings with him the psychic and literal baggage of his investigation and thereby transforms that private space into a different kind of private space, an office.

In this sense, Easy does not derive from the white detectives mentioned above; he more resembles black detectives for whom homes and offices come into play. The black NYPD detective protagonists of Chester Himes's Harlem series, Coffin Ed Johnson and Grave Digger Jones, live in Astoria, Queens, and work out of the 125th Street police precinct in Harlem but are most at home and do the bulk of their work on the streets and in the restaurants and bars of Harlem. Roger Murtaugh (Danny Glover), the black family man and detective from *Lethal Weapon* who is always on the verge of retirement, owns a large and often-remodeled home that is invaded repeatedly by criminals *and* by his partner, Riggs, despite Roger's attempts to keep his work at the office.

Perhaps the most telling example of the intersection of black detection and the home is found in Gordon Parks's *Shaft* (1970), which opens with a question sung by Isaac Hayes: "Who's the black private dick that's a sex machine with all the chicks?" The answer, as viewers see and as the female background singers exclaim, is, of course, "Shaft!"—John Shaft (Richard Roundtree). Shaft's status as a "private dick" and his relationship to a range of public and private spaces in New York City provide the central focus of this film, which takes viewers on a tour of Manhattan that follows Shaft's investigation and his sexual exploits. Unlike Coffin Ed and Grave Digger, whose authority extends only throughout Harlem, Shaft can travel all over the island, since he lives in the Village, has an office in central Manhattan, and has connections in Harlem. Coupled with his mobility, he is a licensed private investigator, a rank that further supports his ability to move between the underworld and the official police and to operate in significantly different racialized spheres.[26]

I include this discussion of the representation of detectives and of black detectives in particular not so much to suggest that vast similarities exist between them and Easy but to point out the degree to which geographic, temporal, and racial distinctions alter shared representational characteristics of detection—the importance of offices and homes, a liminal position between the police and the underworld. Here, *Shaft* again provides a precise counterpoint to the representation of Easy. On the one hand, Shaft gets the information he wants and solves his case on his own, and at the end of his film, he leaves behind a burning apartment building and a number of corpses, a mess for the police to sort out. He operates in New York City during the era of black nationalism as a licensed private investigator, and the color line is more flexible than it was in L.A. in 1948. On the other hand, Easy cannot simply leave matters as they are at the end of *Devil in a Blue Dress*. He must instead provide the police with an explanation for what has occurred over the course of his investigation. As per his agreement with the police, Easy provides a solution to their case, but he cannot give them an explanation without endangering himself. Beyond the fact that the racist white detectives who harass Easy seem to want to pin the murders on him, it would be difficult for Easy to explain his involvement in the case without indicting himself: he is not a licensed private detective, and he has, as it turns out, been working for the criminals Terell and Albright and not for Carter as he thought, a fact that may cast him in a suspicious light. Also, Easy has been present at each of the murder scenes, before, during, and after. There is, then, the possibility that some evidence links him to at least one murder. Easy has no choice, then, but to rely on the authority of the only powerful white man he knows: Todd Carter. In their first meeting, Carter threatens Easy by stating that the police commissioner regularly has dinner with Carter and his family, and it is this detail that Easy remembers late in the film. Faced with the prospect of jail, Easy asks Carter to sort out his dealings with the police. Carter agrees, and, with his help, Easy is able to create a story for the police so that they will not charge him with murder.

The limits of Easy's authority in his dealings with the police come into play at the resolution of the film. As a black unlicensed detective working in L.A. in 1948, Easy does not have enough credibility to push forth his own version of the case. Instead, he must rely on Carter, the white civic leader who will most likely be the next mayor of L.A. Thus, at the end of *Devil in a Blue Dress*, Easy's relationship to Carter is not presented as problematic but rather as a fact of time and place, just as the color line has been a determining factor throughout the film. And here, despite its critical portrayal of these facts of race, the film imagines 1948 as a simpler and perhaps more innocent era in L.A. than the time and place in which the film was produced.

In his final voice-over, Easy says that at the end of his investigation, he drank whiskey for a while, "forgot all about Daphne Monet, Dewitt Albright, Carter and all them, and [was able to] sit with [his] friend on [his] porch at [his] house." His voice-over plays as he walks offscreen and as the camera (in a crane shot) pulls back to a wide shot that shows children playing and traffic moving on a sun-dazzled, palm tree–lined Central Avenue, a setting that Franklin in the promotional material for the film names as "the heart of the city's black community.... Central Avenue in 1948 was tantamount to Harlem during the Harlem Renaissance of the 1920s and 1930s. It was a crossroads of all cultures—black people, white people from uptown, country folk from the South—all interacting together."[27] This bright, archetypal L.A. image gives way to the end credits as jaunty 1940s-era jazz swells on the soundtrack. These cinematic techniques combine with Easy's comments in this final sequence to present a rather utopian vision of this small portion of L.A.

This aural and visual resolution of *Devil in a Blue Dress* joins with a strain of films noir that enact a nostalgic return to utopian L.A. in the 1930s and 1940s. Quite often, the films that present such utopian moments simultaneously depict relationships between antagonists that are clear-cut "bad guys" (especially bad women) who are punished and conflicts that are resolved in favor of the "good guys." In fact, a nostalgic yearning for noir's "golden age" (L.A. in the 1940s) begins to appear as early as *Kiss Me Deadly* (Robert

Aldrich, 1955), which positions its hero, Mike Hammer (Ralph Meeker), at the crossroads of U.S. culture, between the "good old days" of World War II and the Cold War, a period characterized by government corruption and the fear of impending atomic destruction. More recently, this nostalgic return to a bygone "pure" era has appeared in the neonoirs *Farewell, My Lovely* (Dick Richards, 1975), *The Postman Always Rings Twice* (Bob Rafelson, 1981), and Curtis Hanson's *L.A. Confidential* (1997), which drastically reconfigures James Ellroy's much darker 1990 novel. Relative to these and other films, *Devil in a Blue Dress* ends on a quintessentially light moment of hope and happiness, the kind made famous by Hollywood.

If we juxtapose the resolution of *Devil in a Blue Dress* with some of the "dark" L.A. moments that the film depicts and with a section of the film's end credits, however, this quintessentially light moment slips out of focus and becomes less defined. Along with its copyright date (1995), the final credits of *Devil in a Blue Dress* include the emphatic line "FILMED ENTIRELY ON LOCATION IN LOS ANGELES, CALIFORNIA." I designate this title as emphatic for several reasons: it is all in capital letters, while the rest of the titles are in a mix of upper- and lowercase; it includes the phrase "entirely," to underscore that the film was shot on location; it is centered and set apart from the rest of the end credits; and it spells out Los Angeles, a location that is often written as and recognized by its initials. The end credits thus call attention to the difference in the film's setting and its production date. Along with the violent, disturbing, and critical elements of the film's narrative, these end credits foreshadow a future L.A. that is portrayed in the remaining Easy Rawlins novels. That L.A. is more violent and corrupt, marked by Red Hunts, increasing racial tensions, corporate-urban sprawl, and government corruption, and the later novels connect those events to Easy's more complicated life as he becomes less connected to the black community that thrives on Central Avenue. Viewers can foresee such developments in the film's final moments when the police, who have harassed Easy throughout the film, menacingly drive by his home. At this same moment, Easy's friend Odell is shown sitting on Easy's porch, reading a newspaper with a red headline, suggestive of the practice of redlining, that states "Negroes Angered over New Property Laws."[28] As these visual components gesture toward a threatening future, viewers can hear in Easy's final voice-over some of the suspicious and reluctant qualities of his earlier comments. He is able to forget Daphne and the rest, but only after drinking a lot of whiskey. He is on his own property, but even his ownership cannot stop the police and the city from regulating black neighborhoods and black homeownership. Furthermore, with the benefit of hindsight, contemporary viewers (and the filmmakers) are able to read (create) these moments with the knowledge of what is to come for L.A.—the Watts rebellion, social protests and campus unrest, the Rodney King riots, and numerous scandals involving the LAPD and the L.A. county sheriff's department. Even though these events have not yet occurred at the end of *Devil in a Blue Dress*, audiences and the producers of the film are able to affix this history—Easy's future—to their perception of the film's resolution. What is shown at the film's conclusion is a good moment in Easy's life and in the history of L.A., but, after all, it is only a moment.

NOTES

I would like to thank Marcelle Heath, Kelly Hankin, Sharon Willis, the members of the Rochester reading group, and two anonymous readers from *Cinema Journal* for their comments on this essay.

1. Mike Davis, *City of Quartz: Excavating the Future in Los Angeles* (New York: Vintage, 1992), 21, 18–24, 36–46.

2. Paul Arthur, "Los Angeles as Scene of the Crime," *Film Comment* 32, no. 4 (summer 1996): 20–26; Foster Hirsch, *The Dark Side of the Screen: Film Noir* (New York: Da Capo Press, 1981), 1–21. Marcus Doel and David Clarke note the centrality of L.A. in *Blade Runner*, one of several "generic hybrid[s] of science fiction and film noir" in "From Ramble City to the Screening of the Eye," in *The Cinematic City*, ed. David B. Clarke (New York: Routledge, 1997), 141. On relationships between film noir, L.A., and literature, see Part 2, "Los Angeles and the Detective Novel," in *Los Angeles in Fiction*, rev. ed., ed. David Fine (Albuquerque: University of New Mexico Press, 1995), as well as James Ellroy's *My Dark Places: An L.A. Crime Memoir* (New York: Vintage Books, 1997).

3. Sporadic production of films noir from the late 1950s through the 1960s gave way in the late 1960s to what Edward Gallafent, Christine Gledhill, Leighton Grist, and several authors in *Shades of Noir* have called a modern film noir or neonoir period. These authors cite the release of *Klute* (Alan Pakula, 1971), *The Long Goodbye* (Robert Altman, 1973), *Chinatown* (Roman Polanski, 1974), and *Farewell, My Lovely* (Dick Richards, 1975), among other films, as defining moments of the neonoir period. Many recent neonoirs have developed in an increasingly independent and experimental climate of film production that allows filmmakers to revisit and revise classic noir narratives, settings, and characters. James Naremore suggests that film noir is a discourse, "a loose evolving system of arguments and readings, helping to shape commercial strategies and aesthetic ideologies," that includes a set of genre conventions and techniques, a critical methodology, and an aspect of reception present in contemporary film culture. James Naremore, "American Film

Noir: The History of an Idea," *Film Quarterly* 49, no. 2 (Winter 1995–1996): 12–25, see also 14.

4. B. Ruby Rich, "Dumb Lugs and Femmes Fatales," *Sight and Sound* 5, no. 11 (November 1995): 8, 10.

5. Here, *Devil in a Blue Dress* resembles the opening of Franklin's earlier film, *One False Move* (1993), since both films signal a main character's racial status by linking the character to other, more visibly racialized characters: Daphne is coupled with Todd, while Fantasia (Cynda Williams) in *One False Move* is a light-skinned black woman who is grouped with her four black friends.

6. The discrepancy between what is seen and what is the truth is played out in numerous detective narratives to greater or lesser degree. The classic example that seems most apt here is from *Chinatown* (Roman Polanski, 1974), in which Jake recognizes the woman shown with Hollis Mulwray in the surveillance photographs as his mistress, when she is in fact Kathryn Mulwray, Evelyn's daughter-sister, who was conceived in the incestuous rape of Evelyn.

7. Ellroy, *My Dark Places*, 124. Ellroy also gives a detailed account of the murder, some of the press on the case (including Jack Webb's rendition), and his own fascination with the case; see esp. 122–132, 251–252.

8. Daphne's sexualized wordplay correlates with previous femme fatales: during the classic film noir period, the Production Code banned explicit mention of sex, so conversations were often coded, both out of necessity and for effect. Lauren Bacall, in two scenes from *To Have and To Have Not* (Howard Hawks, 1944) and *The Big Sleep* (Hawks, 1946), has conversations with Humphrey Bogart in which sex is discussed in relation to whistling and horse racing.

9. This is but one of many striking similarities between *Chinatown* and *Devil in a Blue Dress*. I thank Sangita Gopal for drawing my attention to the connections between these films.

10. Walter Mosley, *Devil in a Blue Dress* (New York: Norton, 1990), 189–191.

11. Though there appear to be no documented historical origins of *zebra* as a racial slur, this use shares with the word *mulatto* an equine etymology: *mulatto* is a derivation of the Spanish word for *mule*, a mix between a horse and a donkey. Della Thompson, ed., *Oxford Compact English Dictionary* (New York: Oxford University Press, 1996), 1130. And although there is no written history of *zebra* as a racial term, at least two books use *zebra* in this context: Leon Harris's *Run, Zebra, Run: A Story of American Race Conflict* (New York: Exposition Press, 1959), and *Zebra Project: Articles and Interviews* (London: Zebra Project, 1988), which documents the work of a multiracial Christian group called the Zebra Project. The use of *zebra* as a slur is perhaps most memorable for television viewers of the sitcom *The Jeffersons*. As the "black Archie Bunker," a name used on "*The Jeffersons*' Home Page," George Jefferson (Sherman Helmsly) repeatedly voices his opinions on race relations in Bunkeresque terms that often focus on Tom and Helen Willis (Franklin Cover and Roxie Roker), the Jeffersons' close friends, downstairs neighbors, and "zebra" couple (Tom

is white, Helen is black). As the only regularly appearing interracial couple on the program, Tom and Helen bear the brunt of George's attacks but still remain friends with George, who insists on calling them and their children "zebras."

12. Mosley, *Devil*, 203–204.

13. Mosley's fiction is replete with other representations of disturbed fathers, their abusive relationships with their daughters, and the "specter" of miscegenation and biracial children. In *White Butterfly* (1992), a white father named Vernor Garnett sexually assaults and kills his daughter when she threatens to go public with her biracial child. In *Black Betty* (1994), a wealthy white man named Albert Cain carries on a long sexual relationship with his black maid, Betty, and fathers two children with her but insists that the children never know about their parentage.

14. Joy James describes the embodied identity of the tragic mulatto "as the literal and symbolic embodiment of 'miscegenation'" (34). "Black *Femmes Fatales* and Sexual Abuse in Progressive 'White' Cinema: Neil Jordan's *Mona Lisa* and *The Crying Game*," *Camera Obscura* 36 (1997): 33–47.

15. For an explication of the relationship between Oedipal tragedy and the tragic mulatto, see Werner Sollors, "'Never Was Born': The Mulatto, an American Tragedy?" *Massachusetts Review* 27, no. 2 (1986): 293–316; and Heather Hathaway, "'Maybe Freedom Lies in Hating': Miscegenation and the Oedipal Conflict," in *Refiguring the Father: New Feminist Readings of Patriarchy*, ed. Patricia Yaeger and Beth Kowaleski-Wallace (Carbondale: Southern Illinois University Press, 1989), 153–167.

16. Franklin's casting of Beals in this role is interesting given the actress's history and discussions of her racial status. Although Donald Bogle provides no definitive history of Beals, he comments on her appearance in *Flashdance* and her "assumed" whiteness in this film: "Beals . . . went without any racial features whatsoever in her features. In *Flashdance* (1983)—a drama about a beautiful young welder in Pittsburgh, who aspires to be a dancer—Beals is clearly the tan Other. Next to nothing is known about her background. The film shrewdly graces her with a white mother surrogate, an older woman (Lilia Skala), who encourages Beals to pursue her dreams of being a dancer. When she becomes involved with a white married man, the subject of race never enters the picture. The film is a cheat. In the past, white actresses such as Jeanne Crain and Susan Kohner had played tragic mulattoes. Surely, a light black woman should be able to play any role. Had *Flashdance* fully established her as a white character—with a white family—one might have respected its courage. But Beals plays a woman cut off completely from any kind of roots. In *The Bride* (1985), a remake of *The Bride of Frankenstein*, Beals, as the creation of the mad Dr. Frankenstein (played by Sting), was again a woman coming out of nowhere with no cultural/racial links or traditions." Donald Bogle, *Toms, Coons, Mulattoes, Mammies, and Bucks: An Interpretive History of Blacks in American Film* (New York: Continuum Publishing, 1989), 291–292.

In *Blackface*, Nelson George states that "*Flashdance* introduces the feature film as long-form video, hastens the burn out of break dancing, and introduces Jennifer Beals, one of the many biracial women to become sex symbols in the coming years." Nelson George, *Blackface: Reflections on African-Americans and the Movies* (New York: HarperCollins, 1994), 72. Franklin "clears up" Beals's history, in a way, and, in casting her as Daphne, effectively describes her as biracial. This casting was notable also because this film was a comeback for Beals, who had been absent from Hollywood since *Flashdance*. If we think about Beals's career alongside Dorothy Dandridge's or Lena Horne's, this absence can be read as yet another case in which Hollywood producers were unable to create roles for actresses (and actors) whose visual appearance and/or racial-ethnic background did not "fit" in a black-white schema. One potentially problematic aspect of Franklin's casting of Beals, then, is that although it breaks Hollywood's tradition of casting white actresses as light-skinned black women and tragic mulattas, the casting of Beals to a certain degree maintains a black-white schema: to play a mulatta, an actress must "be" biracial.

17. Stephen F. Soitos, *The Blues Detective: A Study of African American Detective Fiction* (Amherst: University of Massachusetts Press, 1996), 31.

18. Easy comments on Daphne's bold sexual language in Mosley's novel but does not mention it in the film. Her language, in fact, is much bolder in the novel than it is in the film.

19. For a discussion of Easy's home as it appears in Mosley's novel, see Theodore O. Mason, Jr., "Walter Mosley's Easy Rawlins: The Detective and Afro-American Fiction," *Kenyon Review* 14, no. 4 (Fall 1992): 178–179.

20. An interesting complementary novel that explores the conjunction of race, job discrimination, police harassment, and L.A. at the close of World War II is Chester Himes's *If He Hollers Let Him Go* (New York: Thunder's Mouth Press, 1990). Written several years before Himes's Harlem series of detective novels, *If He Hollers* follows Bob Jones, a black man who works in the L.A. shipyards, as he tries to maintain his job and social standing against racial prejudice and a false accusation of rape.

21. Soitos, *The Blues Detective*, 234. Soitos's explanation of Easy's development as a detective links up with Yvonne Tasker's theorization of the term "vendor of information" in Tasker, ed., *Spectacular Bodies: Gender, Genre, and the Action Cinema* (New York: Routledge, 1993), 36. Tasker uses this term to describe black informants in film who gather information for white detectives and thereby carry out the bulk of investigational work (Tasker's astute example is Huggy Bear in *Starsky and Hutch*). Albright approaches Easy in this spirit, but Easy does not fulfill this role. Instead, Easy takes on aspects of this "vendor" at strategic moments in order to maintain his advantage over Albright: Easy tells Albright what he wants him to know and thereby appears to be "reporting" back to Albright, who cannot, after all, gather information in "colored" areas.

22. This seemingly innocent, possibly developmentally disabled neighbor (Barry Shabaka Henley) insists throughout the film that Easy has too many trees, but Easy continually chases off the man before he can cut any down. This neighbor is not in Mosley's novel, and even though he is a minor character, his addition to the film is notable. If we consider the scenes in which a character or group of characters threatens Easy within the space of his own home, we notice that the tree attacker either foreshadows or literally announces the presence of the not-so-innocent home invaders. Late in the film the tree attacker links the home invasions to Easy's supposed overgrowth of trees: he has seen "all them people" and "all that trouble" take place at Easy's, so he reasons that the only solution is to cut down some trees. At the end of the narrative, this parallel between the tree attacker and the home invaders remains. The film maintains this parallel as Easy (in voice-over) wraps up his first disturbing case as a detective, gestures toward the physical and psychic damage he has sustained, and notes that the tree attacker has chopped down two of his trees.

23. Soitos, *The Blues Detective*, 234.

24. Fredric Jameson, "The Synoptic Chandler," in *Shades of Noir*, ed. Joan Copjec (New York: Verso, 1993), 40–41.

25. Ibid., 39, 41.

26. The liminal position between the underworld and the official law that Shaft and Coffin Ed and Grave Digger occupy can be described as "doubly-conscious detection" (Soitos, *The Blues Detective*, 33–37). As one of the four characteristics of the blues detective outlined by Soitos, doubly conscious detection is an activity whereby a black detective both upholds and transgresses the white judicial system. On the relationship between blackness, double consciousness, and criminality, see Paul Gilroy, *The Black Atlantic* (Boston: Harvard University Press, 1993); Ed Guerrero, *Framing Blackness: The African American Image in Film* (Philadelphia: Temple University Press, 1993); Phillip Brian Harper, *Are We Not Men? Masculine Anxiety and the Problem of African-American Identity* (New York: Oxford University Press, 1996); and James Snead, *White Screens, Black Images: Hollywood from the Dark Side* (New York: Routledge, 1994).

27. Carl Franklin, *Devil in a Blue Dress* Web site, www.spe.sony.com/Pictures/SonyMovies/Devil/index.html.

28. For a history of geographic containment as enacted by police surveillance and harassment and of redlining in L.A., see Davis's *City of Quartz* and "Uprising and Repression in L.A.: An Interview with Mike Davis by the CovertAction Information Bulletin," in *Reading Rodney King/Reading Urban Uprising*, ed. Robert Gooding-Williams (New York: Routledge, 1993), 142–154.

5

"STRANGE AND NEW..."
Subjectivity and the Ineffable in *The Sweet Hereafter*

//

Ernesto R. Acevedo-Muñoz

Egoyan's films are almost like books. You don't feel passive when you watch them.
—Russell Banks

STORYTELLING AND THE INEFFABLE

Russell Banks's novel *The Sweet Hereafter* (1991) tells the story of the devastating emotional effects of a school bus accident on the people of the small upstate New York town of Sam Dent.[1] In the accident, children from almost every family in town drown or freeze to death at the bottom of a reservoir when their school bus skids off the road into the man-made lake during the winter freeze. Through the novel's five chapters, four different witnesses relate and analyze the event and its effects on them in first-person narrations, revealing, sometimes directly, sometimes indirectly, their strategies for coping with grief. In some ways, then, the novel is about "the ineffable" (that which is incapable of being conveyed in words), about coping with and expressing the pain and desperation of death and grief in something other than words. Through the process of understanding death, grief, and pain, the narrative analogously reveals other "ineffable" topics, specifically the trauma of incest and sexual abuse.

In *The Mind of the Novel*, Bruce Kawin identifies and analyzes certain tendencies of fiction that address or call attention to the difficulty of expressing the ineffable. There are emotions, experiences, fears, and desires that are too complex, too difficult, and for which the conventional forms and uses of language prove inept or inappropriate. As Kawin writes, "literature's attempts to confront or describe the ineffable . . . at some point generate (as a function of the frustration of those attempts) a sense of their own limits as texts," becoming "self-conscious" or reflexive fiction. Kawin poses the problem in the form of questions: "What are the limits of language? How does an artist's sense of being embattled with these limits affect his (or her) sense of form?"[2] In his quiet, beautiful, and sensitive 1997 adaptation of Banks's novel, Canadian filmmaker Atom Egoyan seems to ask himself the same questions. Faced with the ineffable, what are the limits of cinematic language? And how do these limits affect form? While Banks's novel emphasizes the subjectivity of experience in its narrative structure, Egoyan's film suggests that same subjectivity by distancing the spectator from the events. By violating conventions of classic editing, story time, and identification, the film allows the characters themselves to mediate the telling and judgment of the events for the spectator, without resorting to a false omniscience that may suggest objectivity.

Besides the dramatic content of death and incest, the novel treats the topic of subjectivity itself, addressing the difference between reality (the actual events) and truth (how these events are perceived or interpreted by witnesses). Banks approaches this topic by juxtaposing four different accounts or perceptions of the same and related events. Each of the five chapters is narrated in the first person by one of four witnesses. Alternately we read, as if they were legal depositions or journal entries, the testimonies of Dolores Driscoll, the bus driver; Billy Ansel, a widower and father of two of the dead children; Mitchell Stephens, a New York City lawyer who is interested in representing the townspeople in lawsuits against potential guilty parties; and Nichole Burnell, a sexually abused teenage girl who survives the accident but is left paraplegic. Each of the characters interprets the accident and assesses its meaning and effects on the community according to his or her perspective and beliefs, giving the novel a kind of "*Rashomon*" effect.[3] Paradoxically, from the four first-person narratives, each different in content, style, and tone, there surfaces an omniscient, arguably objective account of the events and their meaning. In the novel's narrative and formal experimentation, within the interplay of subjectivity, opinion, and absolute truth, lie some of the key questions raised by Banks: What is the truth? What is judgment? And especially, who has the authority and the knowledge to answer those questions? The novel deals directly with the redeeming lessons that we learn from loss, grief, and tragedy. Indirectly, it shows how the subjectivity of personal experience may lead to the discovery of some universal moral truth.

Egoyan's film is visibly faithful to the content of the novel. Each of the four narrators appears in the film and tells his or her story, mainly to the lawyer Stephens, who seems, deceptively, to operate as an omniscient interpreter. But the film's structure violates conventions of temporality, telling the story not in a linear but in a seemingly haphazard manner, flashing back and forward, from past to present to future within the story time. Thus the film editing (credited to Susan Shipton), by restructuring temporal and spatial logic, circumvents relations of cause and effect. The effect is alienating to audiences accustomed to linear narrative structure.

In the cinema as in literature, storytelling arguably reaches the limits of its formal capabilities when faced with the ineffable and the subjectivity of personal knowledge. As spectators we cannot experience the emotions or even the effects of these events (death, grief, the trauma of incest) because we are not privy to their real meanings; we are not participants in their causes or affected by their results. We are at best witnesses to their formal mediation. *The Sweet Hereafter* film is, even more so than the novel, "self-conscious," a term defined by Kawin to mean "present[ing] itself as an artificial arrangement of falsehoods which are to be recognized as such, and thereby to generate the paradox that such fiction in fact tells the truth."[4] In this essay I explore the ways in which Egoyan's adaptation of *The Sweet Hereafter* attempts to address the ineffable by emphasizing its inexpressibility. The film presents a structural experiment comparable to Faulkner's *The Sound and the Fury*, in which temporal and narrative relations are subordinate to experience and emotion.[5]

Egoyan's strategy is to refrain from judgment even in the face of such emotionally devastating topics as sexual abuse and the death of children, acknowledging the cinema's incapacity to represent emotional or psychological pain and opting instead to conclude that we cannot know what these characters are feeling. Although there is a clear sense of sympathy among the characters themselves, as spectators we are allowed only limited, mediated access to their emotional or psychological states. I argue that the film's formal strategies (in particular its disruptive manipulation of time and space) are designed to put in evidence the limitations of cinematic language in conveying the ineffable, because even though we may believe that "a picture speaks a thousand words," the ineffable, as Kawin writes, "is experienced, but remains inexpressible."[6]

THE SWEET HEREAFTER, OMNISCIENCE, AND SUBJECTIVITY

Classic film versions of literary works typically do not experiment much with form. The aim is usually to remain faithful to the story, to find ways of covering the material or the events depicted in a novel in a manner that is more descriptive than interpretive.[7] In his book on Orson Welles, André Bazin discussed various strategies used to balance the concepts of form and content in film—in other words, the relationship between the subject matter of a film or story and the aesthetic, formal, and technical decisions a director makes in order to communicate such themes. In Bazin's view the relationship between form and content in a film need not be one of subordination of formal elements to the story but one of finding a balance between the two.[8] In other words, the story is only as effective as the way it is told.

In the case of Atom Egoyan, the celebrated Canadian director of *Exotica* (1994), *Calendar* (1993), *The Adjuster* (1991), and *Speaking Parts* (1989), storytelling is a function of form. The director himself, in a PBS interview with reporter Charlie Rose on the release of *The Sweet Hereafter*, said that for him, the attraction of storytelling comes not only from what the story is but how it can be told from a cinematic perspective. The idea is to "intersect" the story, as Dudley Andrew writes, with properly cinematic expressive elements like time and space, "attend[ing] to the specificity of the original within the specificity of the cinema."[9] Narrative cinema is an art dependent on the expressive manipulation of time because films unfold in time and follow its course as a condition of narrative ("what happens next . . ."). In the same interview, Egoyan also said that cinema "is about how we structure time."

In respect to time, structure, and subjectivity, it is especially interesting to look at Egoyan's adaptation of *The Sweet Hereafter*. The novel was an unusual choice for director and screenwriter Egoyan, who had based his six previous films on his own original screenplays, but Banks's novel held a special attraction for him. On the one hand, it is a story about people coping with a devastating experience in a tender, essential fashion, about people emerging from a tragedy changed and redeemed. It is also about people's secrets and how they balance their ordinary lives with the repression of forbidden desires. These themes Egoyan had already explored in his better known films of the 1990s, *Calendar*, *The Adjuster*, and *Exotica*. On the other hand, the structure of the novel allowed Egoyan to experiment with time and subjectivity, as he had done in his previous work.

The small-town setting helps to focus the novel on personal tragedies with collective consequences. The book reveals the strength of the townspeople on losing their children, as well as the tragic, ineffable revelation to which it leads: the abusive sexual relationship between the fourth narrator, Nichole Burnell, and her father, Sam. The source material is thus potentially melodramatic, since the novel deals with dead children, grief, guilt, greed, and incest. Yet what emerges from the novel's four narratives is a powerful portrait of the town of Sam Dent, of its people, its economy, its idiosyncrasies, its virtues, and its sins. This portrait of Sam Dent—a town with a man's name—as painted by Dolores, Billy, Mitch, and Nichole is also to be seen as a portrait of the larger rural North America. It is what Robert Niemi calls "a typical Banksian rural hamlet—isolated, economically depressed," from which Banks removes the veil of tranquility that often hides something terrible or dangerous.[10] What the novel presents is a somewhat sociological, ironic view of American life. Even as the citizens are trying to cope with and understand their lives, they are being scrutinized and judged by outsiders. The prevailing perspective, however, belongs to the townspeople, and it ultimately reveals the true circumstances of the accident, the sexual relationship between Sam and Nichole, and the traumatic effects of both on the local citizens and the teenager.

In her narrative (which reads like a diary entry), Nichole reflects on the accident and what it has done to her body. The experience of the accident has changed her physically (she is now paraplegic), but Nichole reveals that her wounds go much deeper. She writes candidly (to herself) about how this new relationship with her body has made her aware of and angry about her father's sexual abuse. Nichole becomes the keeper of her father's "worst secret." She arms herself with that knowledge and turns it into a tool to find some dignity and redemption for what her father has done to her.[11] The victims' search for financial compensation for the accident depends on Nichole's deposition. She is the only person besides the driver, Dolores Driscoll, who can testify that Dolores did not do anything unusual that morning. From Nichole's truthful testimony, her lawyer, Mitchell Stephens, plans to extract a possible lie: that somebody else—the town council, the school district, the bus manufacturers—must be liable and made to pay. But at the last moment, Nichole sabotages the lawsuit by declaring falsely that Dolores was driving significantly over the speed limit and under a strong snowfall. With her lie, Nichole eliminates everyone's chances for a generous settlement, although she does it to punish her father privately. She keeps the secret while punishing him for his crime, and in the process recovers some sense of dignity.

The novel's treatment of subjectivity and omniscience makes it a partly reflexive or "self-conscious" novel. According to Kawin the self-conscious novel seems to recognize its own difficulties expressing subjectivity and relies on the multiple-narrator structure to call attention to that particular problem of "the limits of the text." Banks's *The Sweet Hereafter* operates as a self-conscious novel because of its attempt to articulate things that are beyond the limits of structured language. Kawin ultimately explains that because some things are ineffable (the mystical, the sublime, the Holocaust), one way for an artist to suggest that he or she is addressing the ineffable is to "call attention to the limits of that world, and to create characters or narrators who are embattled with those limits."[12]

In *The Sweet Hereafter*, the character of Billy Ansel is perhaps the most hurt, and the one who seems to acknowledge his own incapacity to express pain. Billy, a Vietnam veteran and a recent widower who has lost his wife to cancer, is driven to the ultimate despair by the death of his twins. His narrative appears between those of Dolores Driscoll (the bus driver) and Mitchell Stephens, whose interest in Sam Dent is apparently self-serving. While all the other characters try to cope by redirecting their frustration and anger toward religion, superstition, or destructive lawsuits, Billy is the only one who seems resigned to his own doom. Billy refuses to mask his pain, except temporarily by his excessive drinking, and he is the only character who acknowledges his pain as ineffable. When Mitch Stephens says, "I can help you," Billy replies bitterly, "Not unless you can raise the dead," and he repeatedly states, with a crystal-clear mind, that he "cannot be helped."[13] Billy views his tragedy and that of the town as "wickedly unnatural, so profoundly against the necessary order of things that we cannot accept it.... It's the final contrary. A town that loses its children loses its meaning."[14] The novel's structure serves to underline the self-consciousness of ineffability, and only by balancing the four different accounts, by juxtaposing the fragmented "narrative intelligence," do we as readers come somewhere near to understanding that the ultimate meaning of this story cannot be told.

FORM, STRUCTURE, AND ADAPTING THE INEFFABLE

Films based on novels often have the disadvantage of being compared to their original sources and judged based on their fidelity to the content, structure, mood, or spirit of the story.[15] Although films are based on novels probably more than on any other source, the tendency of common adaptations is to "transform" to film that which is essential to the original, taking few risks as far as formal or structural experimentation is concerned.[16] Generally speaking, novels, short stories, or plays are reduced to details such as the content of the story and its narrative structure. In his adaptation of *The Sweet Hereafter*, Atom Egoyan emphasizes the formal and structural possibilities the story offers. Instead of pursuing a more conventional approach to the literary work by telling the story, Egoyan's film interprets the story by exploring its themes from a formal perspective. Rather than presenting four separate, consecutive segments in which the different parts of the story are told, such as we see in *Rashomon* (1950) or *Citizen Kane* (1941), Egoyan's strategy is to break down the temporal logic of the story time. The edited segments juxtapose events of the past, present, and future without following a classic cause-and-effect sequence of actions. This strategy allows the different accounts to seemingly exist simultaneously while temporally intersecting each other; they are not juxtaposed but interdependent. The overall effect of this apparent discontinuity is that the whole story appears ostensibly free of omniscient judgment.[17]

In an appearance together at the University of Toronto in 1998, Egoyan and Russell Banks spoke about the process of adaptation and what it took for the film to acquire its peculiar structure. A Hollywood producer had already optioned the novel and a screenplay had been written before Egoyan ever laid eyes on the novel. The first screenplay was, Egoyan said, "very well written" but conventionally structured, not as fractured, and the director thought it was not suited to his filmmaking style. When that option ran out, Banks and Egoyan were able to get their project off the ground, and decided to keep the production in Canada, with Egoyan's production company, to ensure independence from Hollywood producers and conventions.[18] Although Egoyan worked alone on the screenplay, he consulted throughout the process with Banks, and even allowed the novelist some authorial presence in the film: both Banks and his daughter Caerthan appear in the film. The screenplay's structure is even more fragmented than the finished film, and only a few sequences did not make the final cut. All of these omissions involved moments in which the characters' actions, thoughts, or dialogue directly expressed their subjective feelings. One sequence had Mitchell Stephens in an airport washroom fondly observing a younger man changing his baby daughter's diaper.[19] The scene directly expressed Mitchell's nostalgia for his "lost daughter" and the time in his life when she still belonged to him or was dependent on her parents for care and protection. Another scene would have shown Mitchell looking sadly at a photograph of his daughter, the photograph triggering his memories and his anger over her fate.[20] There are similar glances at subjective feelings of principal and secondary characters that Egoyan dismissed.[21] The most noticeable formal difference between the final screenplay and the finished film is the exclusion of an ongoing voice-over narration by Nichole Burnell that emerges a number of times in the screenplay as a running commentary. It is significant that Egoyan chose to withhold this narration from the finished film, since it directly and subjectively spells out Nichole's feelings. The film retains Nichole's voice-over of Robert Browning's "The Pied Piper," but it is edited to a shorter version.

There is no discernible direct first-person perspective in the finished film. The film presents different time frames that intersect each other. These are the Sam Dent Harvest Fair the summers before and after the accident; the action of the day before, the day after, and the day of the accident itself; and the arrival of Mitch Stephens in Sam Dent and the subsequent interviews and investigation he conducts through the following spring. Finally, there is Mitch Stephens's own story, which takes us from events many years earlier, when his daughter, Zoe, was a toddler, to the present time of the winter and spring following the accident, and a leap forward to two years later, when Mitch reflects on the events. In this segment Mitch briefly reencounters Dolores Driscoll. These identifiable settings are intersected by timeless segments depicting Billy's children playing in the snow and little Zoe playing with her mother, now long divorced from Mitch.

In terms of cinematic form and structure, the most significant issue is not the presence of these numerous time frames but their intersection as the story evolves. Classic continuity editing is based on visible relations of cause and effect between the different events depicted and is designed to preserve the temporal and spatial integrity of the story's time and setting. The viewer is customarily supposed to know "where and when" to place each episode. But in *The Sweet Hereafter*, Egoyan organizes the story by thematic rather than causal logic. Instead of following narrative requirements of the disclosure of story information, Egoyan's film is structured around emotions, memories, and gestures. We do not see each character's narrative of the events unfolding fully, which would enable us to judge the value of his or her perception (the *Rashomon* effect); rather, we see only glimpses of moments or segments of their experience. These fragments are put together without the use of ordinary editing techniques and formal conventions (dissolves, fades in and out) that usually indicate the passage of time in film. The lack of direct transitional devices or clarifying intertitles (such as "Two years later") suggests not only a sense of simultaneity but of the urgency of these events. The emotions are universal, the experience human yet inexpressible. It seems as if it were all happening in the same instant.

It is the presence of Mitch Stephens (Ian Holm) that links the temporal segments together. Like the reporter Thompson in *Citizen Kane*, Mitch helps to trigger and anchor the disjointed episodes. As a lawyer investigating the events, Mitch attempts but fails to put into words the measure of people's suffering. Mitch is professionally interested in the written law and its mediation of morality and guilt in briefs, settlements, and judicial findings; he wants to adjudicate guilt, to make someone responsible, and to circumscribe

Multiple temporal segments intersect in The Sweet Hereafter. Here, Nichole Burnell (Sarah Polley) practices a song for the Sam Dent Harvest Fair the summer before the school bus accident. Photo: J. Eisen © Courtesy Fine Line Features.

it with words.[22] Yet, as he tells the parents of one of the dead children, "I can only represent you in your anger, not your grief." Mitch's attempt to quantify grief and his failure to do so properly exemplify the incapacities of the written law. By extension, Mitch exposes language's own failure to address, describe, or even "represent" grief.

Mitch offers a point of temporal reference for the stories being told (as in "two years ago"), and that is the only perspective from which the story is interpreted in hindsight. It is through Mitch's conversation with a childhood friend of Zoe's named Alison (Stephanie Morgenstern), whom he coincidentally meets in an airplane, that the viewer is offered a glimpse of Mitch's own personal story—losing his daughter to divorce, drugs, prostitution, and AIDS. The conversation in the airplane establishes a correlation between Mitch's story and that of the people of Sam Dent. The airplane scenes are among the major narrative strategies original to the adaptation. They suggest how time itself is structured in the film as something subjective. Mitch and Alison seemingly move forward, but the past keeps intersecting the present, qualifying it and giving it meaning. In Mitch's conversation with Alison, he captures and treasures his memories of Zoe's childhood before she was "lost." Mitch seems to want to freeze time before his tragedy, just as the people of Sam Dent initially hold on to the memories of their lives before the bus accident. As Mitch slowly opens up to Alison, we learn of his emotional and personal tragedy dealing with a drug-addicted daughter. Despite their differences in education, background, and social condition, the city lawyer and the small-town folk share an emotional connection and a wish to rearrange time that is stronger than any of their differences.

Once the emotional connection between Mitchell and his potential clients is established, Egoyan returns to the structural breakdown of time and space in the film. Paradoxically, the mismatching of temporal segments works to connect the film's characters. The setting moves from the airplane back to Sam Dent, where another narrative device is presented that is not found in the novel: Nichole Burnell (Sarah Polley) reads Robert Browning's 1888 poem, "The Pied Piper of Hamelin," to Billy Ansel's twins while babysitting for them the night before they die in the accident. Browning's poem is particularly apropos because it tells the story of a town that also loses its children. Nichole explains the story to the twins, concluding that the piper was not "mean" when he took the children away, but angry at the injustice done to him. This anticipates the film's climax, in which Nichole recants her initial testimony in a deposition about the accident, ruining everybody's chances at compensation. Like the Pied Piper, Nichole rebels against the lawsuit because she is angry and wants to punish her father for years of sexual abuse. The incestuous relationship between Sam (Tom McCamus) and Nichole Burnell is the most emotionally devastating revelation in the film, yet it is to be judged only by Nichole herself. After baby-sitting for the Ansel children and reading and explaining the moral of "The Pied Piper of Hamelin" to them, Nichole goes home with her dad. On arriving home, Nichole and Sam get out of the car, and she follows him to a barn. After hesitating for a moment, her eyes more tired than scared, Nichole follows her father inside. There, among a dozen burning candles, they kiss romantically. Through the entire scene we hear Nichole reciting "The Pied Piper" in voice-over. She repeats the lines she had read to the Ansel twins, the stanza in which the children of Hamelin are abducted by the piper and disappear into a mountainside. In a poetic voiceover we hear Nichole narrate:

> All the children... ran merrily after / The wonderful music with shouting and laughter... / [And] lo, as they reached the mountainside... / The Piper advanced and the children followed / And when all were in to the very last / The portal on the mountainside shut fast

/ Did I say all? No. One was lame / And could not dance the whole of the way / And in after years, if you would blame / His sadness, he was/ used to say, / "It's dull in our town since my playmates left. / I can't forget that I'm bereft / Of all the pleasant sights they see, / Which the Piper also promised me. / For he led us, he said, to a joyous land / Joining the town and just at hand / Where water gushed and fruit-trees grew / And flowers put forth a fairer hue/ And everything was strange and new."[23]

While the parallel between the Browning fragment and the scene seems clear as Sam misleads Nichole into tragedy rather than joy, it is the treatment of the scene in its entirety that is most significant. Not only is the poem not present in Banks's novel, but there is a seemingly romantic and thus rather disturbing tone to the scene. The candlelight, the slow, suggestive camera movement, Sam's gentle manner, and the docile look on Nichole's face seem to present the theme of incest from a seemingly nonchalant perspective. The only direct reference to incest in the film is the single shot in which the camera slowly moves to briefly reveal Sam and Nichole kissing. In the shot the camera unobtrusively cranes upward from the barn floor slowly showing the dull heaps of hay, until we see the couple up on a landing. Sam is lying down on a blanket, his guitar by his feet while Nichole sits on the floor next to him, delicately leaning on his chest. The camera continues its upward motion steadily until it momentarily slows down to show the couple kissing, as Sam gently pulls Nichole towards him. The shot keeps tracking up while tilting down slightly on Sam and Nichole, suggesting a romantic rather than a criminal, tragic liaison. In the screenplay the shot is described as "SAM and NICOLE are engaged in a sexual embrace. The camera glides past them as NICOLE's voice continues to read from the poem."[24]

The juxtaposition of Nichole's voice-over and the father's kiss adds an ironic perspective, a poetic, aural counterpoint to the visual action that, instead of directly condemning Sam's act, distances the spectator from it, delaying judgment, though he is guilty of incest, rape, and pedophilia. The formal coverage of incest in the film serves to balance Nichole's narration from the book, where she clearly states how much she resents her father and is clearly terrified and traumatized by their relationship to the extent of contemplating suicide. Yet, since there is no clear speaking subject in the film, it is effective to withhold judgment, even on incest, until the whole story is told. Only Nichole, the victim herself, is allowed to judge her father.

In the October 1996 version of the screenplay, Nichole's running voice-over, with the exception of the Browning fragments, is always a direct expression of her feelings, her frustration at her fate, and her anger toward her father's abuse and her mother's complicity, and even toward Mitchell's attempts at manipulating her without understanding her feelings. Nichole's voice-over included, for instance, direct addresses to her father, her mother, and Mitch, such as "I know I'm as well as I ever can be again. So shut up, Mom . . ." and "I'm so sick of looking at my doctor, listening to Frankenstein ask me stupid questions about what I was feeling. . . . He thought it was cute when I called him Frankenstein. It wasn't. I feel like his monster."[25] Almost all of Nichole's voice-over narration, present some seventeen times in the screenplay but deleted from the film, is taken or inspired by her chapter in Banks's novel. Nichole states in no uncertain terms her anger at her father for subjecting her to sexual abuse and for his enthusiasm for the future financial settlement. When her father impatiently asks Mitchell about the potential damages, in the screenplay Nichole was to say in voice-over, "At that moment I hated my parents—Daddy for what he knew and had done, and even Mom for what she didn't know and hadn't done." She addresses Mitchell directly in the continuing voice-over: "You told me it wasn't going to be easy. But as I sat there staring at Daddy, I knew it was going to be the easiest thing in my life."[26] Had Egoyan retained Nichole's voice-over as written in the screenplay the suspense at the film's climax—Nichole's deposition in front of the lawyers—may have lost some of its impact; the attentive spectator could have easily predicted that she was plotting some type of revenge all along. It also would have left no place for confusion as to Nichole's feelings concerning the sexual abuse; the film would have been unequivocally judgmental.

The directorial decision to put aside Nichole's subjective voice-over and substitute for it the Browning fragments amounts to one of the most effective and most difficult elements of the film: its refraining from judgment. Egoyan emphasizes and arguably suggests that nobody has the moral authority, the knowledge, the words, or the perspective to judge other people's fears, desires, tragedies, or even grief. While Egoyan's representation may initially seem to romanticize the incestuous relationship, in a manner reminiscent of Humbert Humbert in Nabokov's (and Kubrick's) *Lolita*, what the film suggests is that we, you and I, should not judge it. At the end, Nichole's swift, smart, and devastating revenge on her father (her sabotage of his chances of a financial settlement) leaves no doubt as to where the film stands on judging sexual abuse. There is no celebration of incest in the film or novel, quite the contrary, but only Nichole can really condemn it.

Egoyan follows the revelation of Sam and Nichole's sexual relationship with the brutal juxtaposition of the bus accident sequence. It is a different kind of ineffable tragedy, yet it treats the same consequences as those of sexual abuse: the destruction of childhood and innocence and the impotence of those nearby to help. Egoyan avoids taking melodramatic shortcuts. Instead of exploiting the potentially sensational formal possibilities of a scene that describes a terrible accident involving some forty children in a school bus, the film minimizes manipulative options in favor of understatement and restraint. In the accident scene, the pain of the characters, both physical and emotional, remains something that the spectator can only imagine but not experience, since we do not "see" anything. Immediately juxtaposed to the intimate representation of Sam and Nichole's relationship (appropriate to its depiction of a young woman's private, painful, terrible secret), the school bus accident scene opens with an aerial extreme long shot of the mountains and woods near Sam Dent. Eventually the tiny yellow dot of the bus is revealed as it advances up the snowy, serpentine road. The shot suggests the scope of the foretold tragedy (a devastating event that touches the whole town) in contrast to Nichole's private pain. They are comparable yet different in reach.

Appropriately, Dolores Driscoll (Gabrielle Rose) at the wheel is like the Pied Piper leading the children, and it is she who narrates the events to Mitchell Stephens in the film. Dolores possesses a kind of omniscience at this point, mediating the town's experience. Her narrative is crosscut between the two time frames of the day before and the day of the accident. Dolores's representation of the town's collective grief is best seen when she tells Mitch her story a few days later and she cannot contain her tears. She chokes while the camera tilts up to reveal the wall behind her full of photographs of the children of Sam Dent, many now dead. Strategically, the shot goes out of focus when the children's photographs are shown to prevent revealing that which no longer is, to undermine melodramatic identification with these characters, and to suggest that the loss of any of them, not just the ones the story reveals, is devastating to the town. From the shot of the out-of-focus photographs the scene cuts to the children inside the bus. The camera tracks slowly through the center aisle, showing the children carelessly and happily interacting. The editing links the faceless still photographs on Dolores's wall to these lively faces seconds before their time ends. But we never see the accident itself. Egoyan juxtaposes shots of the bus with those of Billy Ansel (Bruce Greenwood) driving his truck behind it and a wide aerial shot of the two vehicles making their way up the road. Billy waves at his children through the windshield while the twins wave back from the bus.

Billy, like us, is a spectator here, seeing the action unfold within the frame of his own windshield, and like us he is also distanced, powerless. Suddenly we see the bus skid off the road and Billy's terrified face in the reverse reaction shot. Billy pulls over, quickly gets out of his truck, and looks off frame at the bus skidding over the frozen surface of the reservoir. The reverse shot of the bus is an extreme long shot, dramatically distanced from us and from Billy. It emphasizes the impotence of this man and the spectator's distance from the emotions going through Billy and the children's minds. The bus slowly sinks into the water, under the ice, and we see Billy enter the frame from the right, negating the momentary possibility that this may be Billy's "point of view." The composition and mise-en-scène of this shot are formally significant because they stress that we are not in the same position, that we can only imagine what it means, and especially that there is nothing we can do. Furthermore, instead of exploiting our voyeurism and curiosity to see the children screaming and drowning—what Dolores describes in the novel as the children's "wide-eyed faces and fragile bodies swirling and tumbling in a tangled mass"[27]—we are denied access to those images. What we see instead is Billy's reaction to the sight and sound of the children dying, suggesting that pain is the sole experience of those who suffer it.

Although the accident scene is the dramatic axis of the film, its emotional core is focused on the characters' strategies for coping with grief after the fact. After the visually elusive yet emotionally suggestive accident scene (like that of Sam and Nichole in the barn), the film takes us to the center of Mitchell Stephens's story. Structurally, the scene emphasizes the connection between all the major characters and their experiences as the film cuts sequentially from Sam and Nichole's story to Billy and the accident to Mitch. The effect of the editing is paradoxical. The scene cuts quickly from Billy's desperate and useless run toward the bus to the calm, quiet repetition of the opening shot of the film, which shows the younger Mitch, his wife Klara, and baby Zoe sleeping in bed together. This strategy highlights the atemporal logic of the narrative and enhances the way the story is linked by emotional meanings. This is aided by the fact that the transitions are done without the use of editing conventions that would suggest a chronological shift, in this case to a flashback. The scene then returns to the airplane, where Mitch tells Alison the story of Zoe's brush with death when she was a toddler and his dramatic rescue. Not surprisingly, in light of the film's constant rearrangement of time, Mitch chooses to reflect on an episode of Zoe's childhood in which he protects her from potentially mortal danger. He describes it to Alison rather nostalgically, saying, "It was a wonderful time in our lives."

The episode as told is taken directly from the novel, where Mitch narrates it very much as Egoyan adapts it, but to an unknown listener. Mitch recalls how one summer he and his wife Klara were spending some time with their daughter on the Carolina shore (the film scene represents that time and place) and they woke up to the toddler swelling and gasping for air, having been bitten by baby black widow spiders. Since there was no hospital around, they had to drive Zoe forty miles to find one. On the trip, Mitch holds the child in one hand and a knife in the other, in case he may need to perform an emergency tracheotomy as explained by a physician over the telephone. A medium close-up shows Zoe's little, inquisitive face and Mitch's hand holding the knife. It is reminiscent of the sequence in which Sam leads Nichole to the barn, also to harm her, but in an entirely different context. The shot is very revealing, as little Zoe's face, like Nichole's before her, seems more puzzled than frightened, more contented than threatened. In contrast to the desperate reaction shot of Billy Ansel upon witnessing his children's death, we do not see a reaction shot of Mitch Stephens when he is holding the knife and ready to cut into Zoe's throat. The denial of the reverse shot, a convention of classic editing, is particularly effective here because in her close-up, little Zoe looks straight into the camera, almost defiantly. The lack of the reverse shot of Mitch has an unsettling effect because it becomes connotative rather than denotative of his feelings; we can only imagine his terror at what could happen. As with Nichole in the barn and Billy by the lake, the characters' emotional experience is private, privileged, cinematically ineffable. The distance at which we are kept, the place to which we are relegated as spectators, is a formal way to not sentimentalize or moralize the action and to acknowledge the formal limitations of the cinema to express these emotions.

Mitch relives that one moment, now lost in time, when Zoe was dependent on him and he had the power to protect her. That was the last time he was happy. After that, he lost Klara and began to lose Zoe (whose name means "life"). For Mitch, Zoe's drug addiction has effectively killed her already, and like Billy and the other people of Sam Dent, Mitch knows what it is to be powerless to protect his child. The single close-up of Mitch and Alison together shows simultaneously his heartbreak and her sympathy. The quiet, static shot of the two actors lasts nearly five minutes and is only briefly interrupted by the inserts of little Zoe's face in close-up. Formally, the idea of not breaking down this conversation into a sequence of alternating shots and reverse shots of Mitch and Alison emphasizes the connection that is developing between these two almost-strangers. But the conversation with Alison also reveals Mitch's bitterness, his incapacity until now to "represent"

The lawyer Mitchell Stephens (Ian Holm) faces the incapacity of the written law to represent grief, yet he shares the emotional experience of the people of Sam Dent. Photo: J. Eisen © Courtesy Fine Line Features.

his own grief, so it turns, he says, "to steaming piss." That lesson in grief and healing he will eventually learn from Nichole, Billy, Dolores, and the rest of the people of Sam Dent.

The close-up of little Zoe and the knife is even more intriguing and telling when it becomes one of the transitional shots back to the accident scene. From the airplane setting with Mitch and Alison, the film cuts to the final view of Zoe's face in extreme close-up now, looking straight into the camera, her expression unintelligible in spite of the dangers she is facing. The close-up dissolves to another temporally displaced shot, without any clear connection to the other times and places in the film. The shot shows Klara and Zoe, around the time of the spider bite, playing happily in some pleasant meadow. The shot of Klara and Zoe tilts up to the hazy summer sky and suggestively remains there a few seconds until Billy Ansel, his face distorted by desperation, simply walks into the frame, as if it were the same shot, also looking straight into the camera. It is a low-angle medium shot showing Billy from head to waist. He approaches inquisitively, just like Zoe's eyes before him, and only then do we realize what he is looking at, as the reverse shot reveals a blanket covering his dead children. Billy then walks away amid the sounds of crying and sobbing of other parents whom we do not see, their voices drowned by the sounds of sirens, rescue trucks, and helicopters. The concluding shot of the sequence, after Billy sees his dead children, is another temporally displaced memory: the shot shows Jessica and Mason alive, playing in the snow, running toward and looking into the camera. There is no conclusive evidence as to where this image belongs in the story time; it is winter, but it could have been yesterday, or a year ago, or simply an illusion. Like Billy, we will only remember the children alive, in some timeless happiness, exactly as Mitch wants to remember Zoe. The editing transitions in this extended sequence, from the airplane to little Zoe many years before, to Klara and Zoe, to Billy and his children many years later, do not suggest the passage of time but rather stress the emotional connections between these characters. Their feelings are timeless, and the editing structure makes Zoe, Klara, Mitch and Alison, Billy, and even the twins all seem to be looking into each other's eyes. There is an ineffable sense of intimacy between the dead and the grieving, circular in structure and exclusive of those of us who are not privy to the experience.

What follows in the second half of the film is Mitch Stephens's investigation and interviews with potential lawsuit clients: Dolores, Nichole, Billy, and others. From these meetings surface the people's strategies for dealing with grief. Anger, frustration, resignation, drunkenness, and even greed are evidenced in Mitch's meetings with the Walkers, the Ottos (parents of other victims), the Driscolls, Billy, and the Burnells, respectively. The turning point comes when Nichole's parents seem rather excited by the prospect of a generous financial settlement. Nichole, however, one of a handful of surviving victims expected to testify, stresses that she cannot remember anything about the accident, as if she had effectively repressed the memory. Billy on his part fiercely opposes the lawsuits despite his loss, because the children are irrecoverable and legal battles will only serve to divide the town. Billy tells Mitchell Stephens that he does not want to keep digging into his wounds, and reasons that the process will only prolong grief and cause the town further distress. Dolores Driscoll and her husband Abbot (David Hemblen), who had been incapacitated by a stroke years earlier, believe that only the people of Sam Dent can judge what happened, not the lawyers, judges, reporters, or spectators from outside. Significantly, Abbot's stroke has left him with a severe speech impediment, and yet it is he, in words translated by Dolores, who utters the ultimate truth of the novel and film: that only those directly affected can issue judgment on these events. "Abbot understands these things," says Dolores, who is the only one that understands him. Abbot's brief but significant presence addresses the ineffable from the literal perspective of a speech impediment. Egoyan's screenplay describes Abbot's speech as "an outburst" and "a string of broken syllables and sounds."[28] Abbot cannot speak properly, yet he holds the truth. Mitch can speak, write, rationalize the law, and even describe the events, but he does not have the words, experience, or moral authority to do so.

For Mitchell Stephens, the experience of Sam Dent projects his own motives. By directing other people's rage, as he offers to Billy, Mitch exorcises his own frustration at having lost his daughter to drugs and HIV. Mitch understands what it is like to lose a child, but he wants to make somebody pay; he wants to translate it into legal terms. Ultimately, Mitch's case rests on Nichole's testimony, notwithstanding her repeated warnings about not remembering anything. "I won't lie. . . . No matter what they ask me," she says. Significantly for Nichole, this translates into the possibility of redemption. She can help redeem the town for its loss and herself for the sexual abuse to which she has been subjected. Redemption comes about during Nichole's deposition, which she narrates in the fourth chapter of the book. Banks gives Nichole the strategic position of acting as the teller of the climax, since her chapter contains the deposition where everything is resolved. Nichole's section, which is formatted in the guise of a journal or private diary, allows an intimate glance into the teenager's mind: we learn of her resentment, feelings of guilt, and the true terror of her father's predatory sexual behavior. Nichole describes the instances of sexual abuse in a hazy, oblique manner, as if she "had imagined [it]" or "only dreamed it." She also describes her father's abuse in similes: "I saw him as a thief . . . just a sneaky little thief . . . like he had robbed me of my soul or something."[29] What Nichole's diary suggests is her incapacity to directly describe the terrible feelings of guilt and terror that her father's sexual abuse has evoked in the fourteen-year-old, but she refuses or is unable to put it into specific words. Nichole wishes she could effectively repress those memories the way the memories of the accident have been erased from her mind by the shock. Instead, to punish her father and sabotage the lawsuit, Nichole lies about what happened the morning of the accident. From victim, Nichole evolves into an unlikely heroine, and from her lie there paradoxically emerges a moral truth. Nichole understands, as do Billy and Dolores, that the town is better off left alone to grieve and recover by putting the tragedy behind it. In her deposition Nichole falsely testifies that Dolores was speeding, suggesting that as the cause of the accident. While Nichole's lies seem to put the blame on the driver, Dolores already understands that eventually the townspeople will forgive her. In the novel this information emerges from the characters' narration, and in the screenplay from the aforementioned deleted voice-over, but the film returns to the literary resource of "The Pied Piper" to qualify Nichole's action, allowing the spectator a view of her subjectivity from what seems to be an objective perspective.

When Nichole arrives for her deposition, carried by her father because she is now unable to walk, the soundtrack returns to her voice-over recitation of Browning's poem. The passage is the same one that is heard over Sam and Nichole's "love" scene, about the children being led to the mountain by the Piper. The poem's lines about the lame child "who could not dance the rest of the way" are particularly resonant, since in her diary and deleted voice-over Nichole confesses her occasional desire to die, and even her disappointment at surviving the accident. In the Pied Piper story the lame boy is, ironically, a survivor. Nichole, by contrast, is the character who ensures the town's survival, ultimately helping it return to the routine of earlier life. Nichole's intimate personal tragedy (not the result of the accident, but of sexual abuse) serves as a vehicle for Sam Dent's collective experience.

At the deposition, the people of Sam Dent, dead or alive, are symbolically present in the empty chairs that surround Nichole, Mitchell Stephens, the other side's lawyers, a stenographer, and Sam Burnell. Suddenly and surprisingly, in spite of her previous claims to the contrary, Nichole announces that she remembers "pretty clearly" that fatal morning's drive. Mitch Stephens had expected Nichole to clear Dolores of all guilt because in the absence of other evidence, the investigation would certainly conclude that Dolores did nothing wrong. As Nichole improvises her new testimony, the Pied Piper voice-over narration returns giving some indication of Nichole's feelings and of the town's plight. "It's dull in my town since my playmates left.... I can't forget that I'm bereft of all the pleasant sights they see, which the Piper also promised me." Egoyan creates a counterpoint between the deposition and the Browning poem, emphasizing the drama of deceit and betrayal. Nichole's eyes are full of tears, and the camera cuts to a close-up of Sam Burnell's surprised and resigned look: he clearly realizes that Nichole is punishing him, as if he could hear her mental recitation of the verses. The true feelings of the characters—Nichole's anger and frustration, Sam's disappointment and fear of exposure, Mitch's surprise and anger—emerge paradoxically from Nichole's lies. In the screenplay's voice-over Nichole addresses Mitch directly, explaining what it is that she is doing: "[Daddy] must have tried to tell you that I was lying.... Daddy knows who lied. He knows who the liar is. He knows who's normal."[30] Mitch has been seeking to publicly condemn some-

From Nichole Burnell's factual lies there paradoxically emerges the moral truth for the people of Sam Dent. Photo: J. Eisen © Courtesy Fine Line Features.

one for a crime that never occurred; Nichole privately condemns and punishes her father for crimes no one will ever know about.

The film's climax thus addresses subjectivity and how only those directly touched by the events can judge and understand them. This becomes especially clear when, in one of the most revealing of his narrative strategies, Egoyan combines Nichole's personal, subjective reflection (which has been mostly absent from the film thus far) directly with Browning's poem. "And why I lied he only knew," she says, retaking the rhyme and meter of "The Pied Piper," but with newly improvised verses that speak literally, not metaphorically, about herself. "But from my lie this did come true: those lips from which he drew his tune, were frozen as a winter moon ..." she concludes while the camera focuses tightly on Sam's lips slightly open in surprise. With no one left to sue if Dolores is at fault, the impending legal battles destined to tear the town apart are effectively over. "Everyone's lawsuit is dead!" Mitch warns Sam. "The thing you have to worry about is why she lied. . . . Any kid who'd do that to her father is not normal, Sam" are Mitch's final words. Nichole's personal verses, modeled formally after Browning but different in content, end the film. Sam has been punished, Dolores is forgiven, Billy is at peace, Nichole recovers her dignity, and the town may now heal. The closing sequence returns to Mitch in the present-day setting, now exiting the airplane and listening, though somewhat distant, to Alison's goodbye. A casual, silent encounter between Mitch and Dolores at the airport (she now drives hotel shuttle buses) is reduced to an exchange of acknowledging glances. Nichole's voice-over returns for the last time, and again she addresses Mitch directly. Her concluding narration, spoken to Mitch, gives her some omniscience, a narrative power that no other character has in the film, leaving the spectator, subjectively and poetically, with a final thought. "As you see her," Nichole says to Mitch, "two years later, I wonder if you realize something? I wonder if you understand that all of us, Dolores, me, the children who survived, the children who didn't, that we're all citizens of a different town now. A place with its own special rules, its own special laws, a town of people living in the sweet hereafter. . . ." Instead of ending the narration there the film returns to Browning and once more intertwines the personal with the collective, the real with the poetic. Thus, Nichole concludes with a direct quote from "The Pied Piper": ". . . a town of people living in the sweet hereafter . . . where waters gushed and fruit trees grew, and flowers put forth a fairer hue, and everything was strange and new. . . . And everything was strange and new." We then see Billy Ansel finally disposing of the wrecked bus, a restrained yet meaningful look of satisfaction in his eyes, and we see Nichole at the Sam Dent summer fair, perhaps a few years later. Over the final lines of her narration, her little smile suggests that indeed, everything is strange and new in this sweet hereafter but she is redeemed, safe, and maybe even happy now.

"STRANGE AND NEW": TIME, SUBJECTIVITY, AND NARRATION

In his book *Mindscreen*, which preceded *The Mind of the Novel*, Bruce Kawin describes the concept of the "first person film" and the significance of subjectivity and narration as ways of telling stories that are counterpoints to the fallacy that the camera is "objective" or in the "third person."[31] In the cinema, subjective stages are presented through a consistent number of optical and aural effects ("ripple" dissolves and unnatural echoes, for instance) or by clearly assigning the subjective mediation to a fictional character within or without the diegesis. As Kawin writes, "when the voiceover narration is assigned to a fictitious speaker, it expresses not the filmmaker's judgment on his material but the character's interpretive response to his own experience. . . . [O]ne understands that the film is limited to this character's point of view." These practices of voice-over narration are usually combined with formal visual strategies that also suggest or offer (if never actually rendering) subjectivity. Based on some formal conventions (such as hand-held wide-angle shots, for example), the camera pretends to show us either the characters' physical point of view or that of his or her mind's eye.[32] In *The Sweet Hereafter*, Nichole Burnell's narration, although presented in voice-over format, is less about storytelling than conventional voice-over (since she never tells any part of the actual story) and more about subjectivity. It is also formally poetic in its adoption of Robert Browning's "Pied Piper" form and thus metaphorical or referential, rendering not her angle of vision but rather a limited, oblique access to her state of mind, a type of "mindscreen."[33] This category is different from conventional voice-over narrators, who may be considered storytellers, especially since Nichole in the finished film, unlike in the screenplay, never actually tells the story itself.[34]

The subjective structure to which *The Sweet Hereafter* owes its greatest formal debt is that of Welles's *Citizen Kane*. Unlike Kurosawa's *Rashomon*, none of *Citizen Kane*'s characters whose mindscreens we access (Susan, Thatcher, Bernstein, Leland, Raymond the Butler) have any final knowledge of Kane's actual thoughts. Not one of them (unlike the spectator) ever discovers the meaning of "Rosebud." Although the novel *The Sweet Hereafter* offers itself structurally as a potential *Rashomon*, Egoyan's choice of the *Citizen Kane* model serves to emphasize the problems of addressing subjectivity. In the film, Mitch Stephens operates in an analogous fashion to Thompson, the *Citizen Kane* reporter. But unlike Thompson in his quest for some essential knowledge of Kane, Stephens is not interested in the truth, nor is he totally alien to the life experience that he is investigating. Like the people of Sam Dent, Mitch knows loss, and he ultimately sees everything about the townspeople mediated by his own pain. In further contrast to *Citizen Kane*, where some truth about Kane emerges from the audience's knowledge of Kane's cryptic last word, *The Sweet Hereafter* film, unlike Banks's novel and Egoyan's screenplay, always conceals the mystery of the characters' true feelings, fears, and desires. While *Citizen Kane*'s narrative structure seems to avoid been deciphered because of its "conflicting appraisals" about Kane and its "involuted chronology," it fails because the camera keeps "trespassing" and "asserting its curiosity" regardless of the narrative's resistance.[35] Where the fictional characters fail, the audience succeeds in "knowing" something about Kane. In Egoyan's *The Sweet Hereafter*, the camera is not allowed to trespass; it remains forever suggestive but distanced, evocative but oblique, never direct. Unlike the meaning of "Rosebud," in *The Sweet Hereafter* the spectator is ultimately left to guess or to imagine the ineffable, only allowed to conclude that we do not know, cannot know what these feelings really are. The film's constant rearrangement of narrative time without the customary framing devices for subjective scenes or even without the assignment of the mindscreen to any specific character, serves as a representation of the subjectivity of experience and suggests formally the difficulty or the limits of the cinema's capacity to show emotion and to speak the ineffable.

In keeping with the film's sense of intimacy and subjectivity, the final shot is paradoxically both revealing and intriguing. It returns to the day before the accident, to Nichole putting the Ansel children to bed in their room. The shot concludes the action started earlier in the film, continuing to the scene's ending, which we had heretofore not seen. Nichole has finished reading "The Pied Piper." She closes the book and tenderly bends over each of the twin beds to kiss the sleeping children good-night. She then exits the room, and the camera pans and tracks with her as she walks down the hall toward a window through which a light is seen entering (presumably Billy's car headlights as he returns home). As Nichole walks toward the window, the light becomes very bright for an instant, before a sharp cut to a black screen. This entire final scene exemplifies the communion of form and subjectivity in the film. It reorganizes the structure of time and its relationship to narrative once again, flashing back to Nichole and Billy Ansel's children, even after the story time proper is concluded. In this final sequence the realignment and juxtaposition of Nichole's, Sam Dent's, and Browning's stories, rather than raising conflict, makes their connections more intimate. On one hand, the stories are cemented together; on the other hand, the spectator is alienated by the temporal discontinuity that violates conventions of editing and narrative structure: we are not allowed access into these characters' feelings. As with the evasive visual representation of the sensational topics of incest and death, the film's conclusion stresses empathy rather than sympathy.

In *The Sweet Hereafter*, spectator identification comes more from understanding than from "experiencing" the characters' lives. Egoyan's films avoid the possible shortcuts of classic narrative structure and the facile designs of melodramatic identification, yet *The Sweet Hereafter* is an emotionally compelling film. The distinction may come from Egoyan's efforts to refrain from judgment, which paradoxically give the story further moral authority. Structurally, the narrative is organized around themes rather than actions, and formally the editing suggests universality and omniscience rather than causality and subjectivity. As a result, what remains with us after experiencing *The Sweet Hereafter* is a sense of understanding the deeper meanings of the characters' lives, motives, feelings, and emotional development rather than an identification with their dramatic arc. Although the novel by Russell Banks and Egoyan's screenplay suggest a more subjective perspective that facilitates sympathy and narrative identification (particularly with Nichole as victim-turned-heroine and her periodic voice-over interventions), the film expands that focus to underscore not just the story itself but also its meaning.

NOTES

I am grateful to Melinda Barlow and Ella Chichester for their valuable comments and suggestions, and to Grace Niu of Fine Line Features for permission to use still photographs.

The epigraph by Russell Banks is quoted in Atom Egoyan, *Exotica: The Screenplay* (Toronto: Coach House Press, 1995), cover flap.

1. Russell Banks, *The Sweet Hereafter* (New York: HarperCollins, 1991).

2. Bruce Kawin, *The Mind of the Novel: Reflexive Fiction and the Ineffable* (Princeton, NJ: Princeton University Press, 1982), 21–22, 5.

3. *Rashomon* (In the Woods) is the 1950 film by Japanese director Akira Kurosawa in which the story of a woman's rape and a man's murder in some remote woods is told from the perspective of several people (including the victim, the accused murderer, and other witnesses). In *Rashomon*, each version of the story plays out consecutively, so that we can see the differences in the perception and personal manipulation of the events recounted. A similar effect occurs in Orson Welles's *Citizen Kane* (1941), where several different accounts raise more questions than they answer about the life of the fictional newspaper magnate Charles Foster Kane.

4. Kawin, *The Mind of the Novel*, 14.

5. See the critical edition, William Faulkner, *The Sound and the Fury: An Authoritative Text* (New York: W. W. Norton, 1987). See also Bruce Kawin, *Faulkner and Film* (New York: Frederick Ungar, 1977).

6. Kawin, *Faulkner and Film*, 30.

7. Deborah Cartmell and Imelda Whelehan, eds., *Adaptations: From Text to Screen, Screen to Text* (London: Routledge, 1999), 7.

8. André Bazin, *Orson Welles: A Critical View* (New York: Acrobat Books, 1991), 81–82.

9. Dudley Andrew, *Concepts in Film Theory* (Oxford: Oxford University Press, 1984), 99–100.

10. Robert Niemi, *Russel Banks* (New York: Twayne, 1997), 162–163.

11. Banks, *The Sweet Hereafter*, 179–181.

12. Ibid., 25–26.

13. Ibid., 84, 76.

14. Ibid., 78.

15. Imelda Whelehan, "Adaptations: The Contemporary Dilemmas," in *Adaptations*, 9–11.

16. Dudley Andrew, *Concepts in Film Theory* (Oxford: Oxford University Press, 1984), 100.

17. I am leaving out of my discussion a few episodes of the novel and film, such as the love affair between Risa Walker and Billy Ansel and the episodes with Wanda Otto, her husband, and adopted child. Although these episodes are important thematically because they reveal intimate truths about people's virtues and faults in Sam Dent, formally they are not very different from the scenes I cover.

18. "Before and After *The Sweet Hereafter*" in *The Sweet Hereafter* (DVD). New Line Home Video, 1998.

19. Atom Egoyan, screenplay, *The Sweet Hereafter* (Ego Film Arts, 1997), 4–5.

20. Ibid., 30.

21. Ibid., 35, 36, 49.

22. In an interview for Canadian television Banks stated that his novel is periodically taught in some law schools in the United States, particularly in courses on legal ethics. See the DVD.

23. Robert Browning, *The Pied Piper of Hamelin* (London: F. Warne, 1888), 47–52. Reproduced on *The Sweet Hereafter* (DVD).

24. Egoyan, screenplay, 39.

25. Ibid., 57–58.

26. Ibid., 70–71.

27. Banks, *The Sweet Hereafter*, 35.

28. Egoyan, screenplay, 56.

29. Banks, *The Sweet Hereafter*, 174, 175, 180.

30. Egoyan, screenplay, 89.

31. Bruce Kawin, *Mindscreen: Bergman, Godard, and First Person Film* (Princeton, NJ: Princeton University Press, 1978), 4–6.

32. Ibid., 6–7.

33. Ibid., 10.

34. For more, see Sarah Kozloff's *Invisible Storytellers: Voice Over Narration in American Fiction Film* (Berkeley and Los Angeles: University of California Press, 1988), 49–53.

35. Ibid., 28, 33. In Kawin's view, Kane's conflict between what is told and what is known makes the film more akin to the "reflexive fiction" mode in literature discussed in his later book, *The Mind of the Novel*.

PART III
//

WRITER AND DIRECTOR COLLABORATIONS: ADDRESSING GENRE, HISTORY, AND REMAKES

> *The best answer to that problem [story conference strategies] is to work with your friends, because no matter how much moxie you've got, if you're with a guy who is fundamentally not congenial to your point of view, or if he's worried about what somebody else is going to think, it just doesn't matter. So if you can side-step such things, it's best to work with people you know and trust—and who know and trust you—and to work from that vantage point. There are going to be disagreements, for sure. But there is also mutual respect.*
>
> —Robert Towne, *The Craft of the Screenwriter*

The most frequent pattern of adaptive screenwriter and director collaboration since the studio era entails a separate writer and a director (not necessarily an auteur). The working relationship of these individuals may fall under one of several diverse arrangements, as reflected in the individual studies of English-language films presented in Part III. The first four chapters explore either obtrusive narrative approaches to film adaptations or intriguing remakes of adaptations. The next four chapters address either unique variations in producer-writer-director dynamics of authorship or collaborations particularly concerned with marginalized populations and their points of view. These two groups of studies suggest the diversity of current collaborative approaches to film authorship in adaptation.

The astutely named film, Adaptation *(2002), is unusual in that the adapting writer, Charlie Kaufman, is also a co-executive producer on this film, which Jonathan Demme produced and Spike Jonze directed. For this film, very loosely based on the nonfiction book by Susan Orlean,* The Orchid Thief, *Kaufman did numerous script revisions (evident in the unpublished script, which is archived at the Margaret Herrick Library in Los Angeles), and a very close collaboration between writer and director in the latter stages of script development was required. In Chapter 6, Frank P. Tomasulo constructs a sophisticated analysis of this recent project, which he finds to be a self-reflexive, postmodernist take on the nonfiction source material. Tomasulo's chapter explores the complex and layered thematic and cinematic thinking that went into this transformation.*

Among the many different intentions that may prevail in an adaptation is the updating of older fiction and drama to comment on more immediate cultural circumstances. Barton Palmer in Chapter 7 analyzes the alternation of time frames as a significant factor in screenwriter Harold Pinter's and director Karel Reisz's film adaptation of The French Lieutenant's Woman. *Palmer details their radical cinematic approach to the nineteenth-century story with a contemporary narrative perspective found in John Fowles's novel. Palmer's discussion of the narrative framing of the story from novel to film illuminates this bold experiment in cinema's capabilities vis-à-vis the literary source.*

In Chapter 8, Rebecca Bell-Metereau takes on the two very different film adaptations of Vladimir Nabokov's ironic but controversial novel Lolita (1955). Her informed discussion details Kubrick's experience with Nabokov's own screenplay, as well as with movie censors in 1962, when his film was finally released. Director Adrianne Lyne's version of 1998 had problems with the public's response to a romanticized form of pedophilia. Bell-Metereau explains the many complexities surrounding the characters and tone of the novel and the different characterizations and thematic, structural, and stylistic approaches of the film versions. She registers a closing concern with both adaptations.

In Chapter 9, Mark Gallagher's comprehensive study of the American film Traffic, a "remake" of the British television miniseries Traffik, includes a compelling discussion of the effect of changing the story's international setting. The adapted screenplay, by Stephen Gaghan, and the film, directed by Steven Soderbergh, demonstrate the radically different cultural, economic, and political orientations of the two works, in part resulting from a change in locations from the South Asian and European settings in the British TV miniseries to Mexican and U.S. settings in the American film. Gallagher also emphasizes the unique politics of the American "war on drugs" in light of the personal tragedy of drug addiction for obsessed American consumers and their families.

6

ADAPTATION AS ADAPTATION
From Susan Orlean's *The Orchid Thief* to Charlie (and "Donald") Kaufman's Screenplay to Spike Jonze's Film

//

Frank P. Tomasulo

> *Adaptation is a profound process.*
> —John Laroche, *The Orchid Thief*

NO LESS AN AUTHORITY THAN ANDRÉ BAZIN WROTE TWO ESSAYS on the process of filmic adaptation, "In Defense of Mixed Cinema" and "Adaptation, or the Cinema as Digest."[1] These articles, and others in Bazin's corpus of theoretical writings, suggested that filmic adaptations of literary works should be less concerned with strict formal fidelity to the source material than to *"equivalence in meaning of the forms."*[2] Bazin went on to point out that a crucial distinction had to be made between adaptations designed for the cinema and those designed for the audience. He noted that "most adapters care far more about the latter than about the former."[3]

A discussion of adaptation from the perspective of a film's fidelity (or lack thereof) to its literary progenitor is bound to be tedious. As Brian McFarlane avers, "Discussion of adaptation has been bedeviled by the fidelity issue."[4] The changes that appear in even the most faithful versions of novels, plays, and other prose fiction are ultimately not that significant in terms of the meanings of the two distinct works. As Dudley Andrew notes, the two forms—written prose and cinema—derive from "the absolutely different semiotic systems of film and language."[5] Furthermore, as Keith Cohen points out, "film technique . . . relates to a way of thinking and feeling—about time, space, being, and relation . . . that has become a part of the mental life of an entire epoch in our culture."[6] Thus, from a textual standpoint, both literature and film rely on theme, characters, situations, and imagery. Similarly, although they are processed in different ways, both art forms require analysis and connotation on the part of the reader or spectator to be understood and appreciated.

Thus, the two questions raised by Bazin—about the style and meaning of a work when it is transmogrified by cinematization, and about its artistic aspirations versus its box-office marketability—are crucial to the analysis of any filmic adaptation. They are especially apposite for an analysis of *Adaptation*, the 2003 film written by Charlie Kaufman (and his nonexistent brother "Donald") and directed by Spike Jonze, from the 1998 nonfiction book *The Orchid Thief*, by *New Yorker* essayist Susan Orlean. Indeed, few movies exhibit so frankly the dialectical marks of their artistic and industrial production as the paradoxical *Adaptation*.

> *The answer to everything [is] adaptation.*
> —Susan Orlean, Foreword, *Adaptation: The Shooting Script*

If Susan Orlean's *The Orchid Thief* is an unadaptable literary property, both in the real capitalist world of movie studio commercial imperatives and in the fictional world of the movie *Adaptation*, then it stands to reason that a Hollywood film about adapting it to the screen would be an exercise in postmodernist pastiche and self-reflexive intertextuality. Orlean has even compared the adaptation of her book to the changes that follow the adoption of a child, especially since "orchids ... happen to be complex organisms."[7] Her first-person bestseller is a veritable bricolage or hybrid of several genres: journalistic reportage, lowbrow botany and biology tract, historical essay, character study, autobiography, poetic meditation, and sociology tract.[8] There is no story line to speak of, no dramatic crisis, and the events are told in a meandering format that departs from traditional narrative causality.[9] Indeed, Orlean's description of her orchid-hunting travels to Florida's Fakahatchee Strand is a metaphor for her book's structure. Rather than take a direct route, she

> preferred going the other way, zigzagging across [various counties], rounding the bottom of Lake Okeechobee, then cutting across the Everglades ... through the Seminole reservation near Immokalee, past the ghostly signs for long-gone tourist stops ... on the small state roads that go off at right angles every few miles as if they had been drawn by a box cutter. *It is slow going but broadening.*[10]

This is also the circuitous narrative structure of *Adaptation*, at least until screenwriting guru Robert McKee (Brian Cox) appears on the scene and convinces the diegetic Charlie Kaufman (Nicolas Cage) to abandon his desire to preserve the spirit of Orlean's literary nonfiction and make a more commercial movie. The real-life McKee summarized the process of adaptation in *Adaptation* as follows, "Taking a cue from Orlean, Kaufman decided to layer his self-inquisition over her self-inquisition."[11]

MCKEE OR NOT MCKEE? THAT IS THE QUESTION

Early in the script, Donald Kaufman (Nicolas Cage) had taped a copy of Robert McKee's pseudo-religious and formulaic "Ten Commandments" of screenwriting above Charlie's work area, but Charlie tore them down and crumpled them up—even though Donald had assured him that McKee's "principles" (like the Bible's Ten Commandments) "work and [have worked] through all remembered time." Charlie initially eschews such recipes ("Screenwriting seminars are bullshit. . . . There are no rules."). He also believes that "people don't change, they don't have epiphanies. They struggle and are frustrated, and nothing is resolved," as in the "real world."

By the end, however, Charlie has adapted many of McKee's principles for *Adaptation*, including the idea of mixing genres. He attends one of McKee's seminars in New York and is even seen reading McKee's screenwriting primer, *Story* (while Donald reads *The Orchid Thief*). Charlie also learns, by interacting with other human beings, some of McKee's "life lessons," that in "the real fucking world" there *is* conflict and crisis: "People are murdered every day. There's genocide, war, corruption. Every fucking day . . . somebody sacrifices his life to save somebody else" (just as "Donald" sacrifices his life to save Charlie's script).

Nonetheless, at the outset of the script (and throughout most of its narrative), the putative protagonist, Charlie Kaufman, attempts to preserve Orlean's "book about flowers" from the clichéd commercial formulas of the Hollywood assembly line. As he tells his producer Valerie Thomas (Tilda Swinton),

> I think it's a great book . . . and I'd want to remain true to that. . . . Y'know, I just don't want to ruin it by making it a Hollywood thing. . . . Like an orchid heist movie or something, or, y'know, changing the orchids into poppies and turning it into a movie about drug running. . . . *Why can't there be a movie simply about flowers?* I don't want to cram in sex or guns or car chases. You know? Or characters learning profound life lessons.

In Adaptation, *Charlie Kaufman reads Robert McKee's book* Story *while his "brother" Donald reads Susan Orlean's* The Orchid Thief.

In that vein, many passages from Orlean's book are quoted faithfully, if not verbatim, in the screenplay and film, particularly her introspective moments focusing on her relationship with flowers. Later, on the verge of selling out his original purist intent to be true to the spirit of *The Orchid Thief*, however, Charlie is advised by Robert McKee, "Don't you dare bring in a *deus ex machina!*" But the semicommercial film version does just that: it must contain gratuitous guns, sex, drugs, car chases, life lessons, and a deus ex machina—an alligator who chomps on the villain's leg and then proceeds to devour him half a second before he fires a fatal rifle shot at the hero.[12] Although the alligator ex machina seems to save the day, Donald Kaufman later dies in a car crash—a reprise of the shocking car crash shown at the beginning of the film that caused the death of John Laroche's mother and uncle, put his wife in a coma, and left him toothless.

Similarly, McKee provides another screenwriting "secret" to Charlie, just before the final act of *Adaptation*: "The last act makes a film. Wow them in the end and you've got a hit." That tacked-on third act inscribes almost all of the negative plot and character elements that Charlie had railed against throughout the screenplay, thereby putting in question whether *Adaptation* itself is a conscious metatext that critiques the Hollywood system (and itself) or one that capitulates to Tinseltown's standard shibboleths. As Natalia Skradol put it, "We are not sure whether that which was announced as a self-conscious meta-film turns into kitsch, or whether that which was introduced to us as kitsch manifests itself as a tragic reality."[13] This is not the only instance in which the potential for an allusive and understated artistic expression is jettisoned in favor of an obvious concession to imitative box-office formulas, whether the screenwriter's ironic tongue is in his cheek or not. Within "the reality of this movie, where there's only one character," Charlie is able to overcome his writer's block only when he introduces himself and his own personal and artistic concerns into Orlean's text. Even the larger theme of human and vegetative adaptation is introduced only when Charlie starts to muse about where *he* came from, starting with the "primal ooze."

Finally, Charlie Kaufman (the screenwriter and fictional character) does not follow another McKee injunction: the ban on voice-over narration. During McKee's lecture (and later on in the script), he says, "God help you if you use voice-over in your work, my friends! . . . It's flaccid, sloppy writing! Any idiot can write voice-over narration to explain the thoughts of the character." And, of course, *Adaptation* begins and ends with Charlie Kaufman's voice-over narration. Later, at an orchid show, we hear Susan's disembodied voice-over from her book: "One [orchid] looks like a turtle. One looks like a monkey. One looks like an onion." Then we hear Charlie continue her recitation, but with his own preoccupation—women: "One looks like a gymnast. One looks like that girl in high school with creamy skin. One looks like a New York intellectual." These sorts of expository voice-overs dot the aural landscape of the entire movie, as Charlie muses on his script and his life—and makes explicit some of the screenplay's more abstract concepts, such as the analogy between orchids and people. Indeed, when we finally see the ghost orchid, it is shaped like a woman—with two white petals as its open legs, two "arms" coming out of each side, and a little "face" in the center of its flower. Most of the time, Charlie's recitations reveal material that cannot be conveyed visually, for example, "It is a journey of evolution. Adaptation. The journey we all take. A journey that unites each and every one of us."

The screenplay and film contain several instances of Susan Orlean's narration. The first such instance occurs during our first view of the author, who recites the opening words of *The Orchid Thief* in her office at the *New Yorker* magazine: "John Laroche is a tall guy, skinny as a stick, pale-eyed, slouch-shouldered, sharply handsome despite the fact he's missing all his front teeth." Later, when Laroche tells her about how he is able to change, adapt, and drop his various enthusiasms (flowers, tropical fish, turtles, fossils, antique mirrors) without a second thought, Susan thinks aloud, "Sometimes I wish I could do the same." We also hear her voice reciting from her book several times as we watch Charlie reading the volume or as we observe

Orlean (the character) with her husband or Laroche. Even Charles Darwin has a voice-over narration: "Therefore, I should infer from analogy that probably all the organic beings which have ever lived on this earth have descended from some one primordial form into which life was first breathed."[14]

"ALL THE WORLD'S A (SOUND)STAGE"

If a picture is worth a thousand words, then a book such as *The Orchard Thief*, which is replete with lengthy, detailed, and highly repetitious verbal descriptions of the sights, sounds, and smells of flora and fauna, is bound to be visually upstaged by a film that can show an orchid bloom in slow motion—or flowers growing magically through time-lapse photography, as in *The Wizard of Oz* (1939). The movie's "image system" (Robert McKee's phrase, used throughout *Adaptation*) is packed with such visual motifs, unlike Orlean's book, which depends on more overt verbal statements, such as "I hate hiking with convicts carrying machetes"[15] or a pages-long description of explorers hunting for orchids that can be condensed into a few quick shots in a movie.

Thus, a weak, rambling narrative is found in the source book, the screenplay, and the film. *The Orchid Thief* is filled with repetitions, diversions, and digressions—the very antithesis of a carefully structured "through line." In contrast, plot is an ironic and self-conscious construct within the diegesis of both the script and the film, to the extent that the characters Charlie and Donald Kaufman represent respectively the polar extremes of serious modernist and lighthearted (and lightheaded) postmodernist narrational strategies and styles. Indeed, at one point Donald even calls his brother "my friend," a phrase he undoubtedly picked up from Robert McKee, who uses it frequently in his seminars. Charlie tells his brother, "Don't say 'my friend.'" Throughout most of the story, Charlie attempts, mostly unsuccessfully, to avoid McKee's principles and vocabulary; he yearns to write an authentic personal screenplay, while Donald "borrows" all of his plotlines and characters from clichéd B-movies.

In fact, Charlie specifically acknowledges a private side to his script when he says, "I've written myself into my screenplay," while Donald incorporates every stock motif of the thriller genre into his script, *The 3*: a serial killer, multiple personality disorder, chase scenes, cop-and-criminal-share-one-psyche theme, and so on. Indeed, Donald's premise for *The 3* can be construed as a comment on *Adaptation* itself, in that Charlie, Susan (Meryl Streep), and John Laroche (Chris Cooper) are "the three" who animate its narrative and who, in a way, share one psyche.[16] Susan, who, like Charlie, is emotionally stagnant but successful as a writer, and John, like Donald, who is a passionate but unsuccessful hobbyist, represent the two life paths that Charlie can take, and, in a sense, the two poles of the one psyche: Charlie/Donald.[17] Even the real-life Robert McKee accepts this reading: "[The screenplay] reads like a filmic stream of consciousness, an allegory starring the contentious facets of Kaufman's psyche."[18] Of course, in this interpretation, Charlie and Donald are essentially warring aspects of one character—internal *doppelgängers*, so to speak—who are twin sides (the artistic and the commercial) of American independent cinema circa 2002. (It is therefore noteworthy that both Charlie and Donald have each, in their own way, written a script in which all the characters are aspects of the author.)

Indeed, the whole idea for this "odd couple," who represent the art-versus-commerce poles of film praxis, may have come from *The Orchid Thief*. Referring to the differences brought about when Laroche had to give up his nursery business, Orlean notes,

> None of the plants at the nursery now had the mangy, fantastic look that Laroche's ... all had. [The new owner's] plants were clean-cut and regular and looked like plants that a normal person would be able to grow.... [Laroche] had a lot of impractical plans. He filled the nursery with weird things that were never going to sell.[19]

In this sense, the toothless and unkempt dreamer Laroche is akin to Charlie Kaufman, whose "mangy" looks and "weird plans" (uncommercial screenplays) are "never going to sell." Indeed, Laroche is established as having a problem with both "personal hygiene" and a "funny smell" in his van, while Kaufman refers several times to the fact that he sweats too much. Laroche claims to be "the smartest person I know," while Charlie's condescending air (especially with his brother) *acts as though* he is the smartest person *he* knows. Laroche, who appears not to require human companionship, shares that trait with Charlie, who is too shy to even accept an offer of a nightcap from his "girlfriend" Amelia (Cara Seymour).[20] In addition, Orlean believes that Laroche is "obsessed with his dead mother," while Charlie and "Donald" are obsessed with their live mother, who is referred to several times in the narrative. Finally, another similarity between the two characters is that Laroche is always willing to reinvent himself, giving up stale passions to take on new ones, just as Charlie forsakes his artistic integrity in favor of adapting to commercial realities.

In a key line of dialogue with self-reflexive connotations, Charlie says, "In the reality of this movie, where there's only one character"—leaving the audience to determine whether "this movie" refers to Donald's script *The 3* or to *Adaptation* itself. In addition, Charlie's repeated use of terms such as "narcissistic" and "solipsistic" confirms that this is all happening in one mind (or mindscreen).[21] Without accepting Lucas Hilderbrand's odd premise that *Adaptation* is "a masturbation narrative," one can still concur with his assertion that "Charlie's twin brother and co-screenwriter Donald is a fantasy alter-ego adept at Hollywood screenplay structure and happy-go-lucky in romance."[22] Similarly, Arthur Lazere has argued that, "the playoff between the two brothers is surely intended as ego and alter-ego, as two sides of the same conflicted writer battling for control."[23] More accurately, though, Donald may not be an actual (that is, diegetic) alter ego (the Hollywood facet of his persona) fantasized by Charlie but just a cinematic means to dramatize Charlie's inner conflicts to an audience.[24]

The first time we see Charlie, he is on the soundstage of the real-life Kaufman's earlier movie, *Being John Malkovich* (Spike Jonze, 1999). Charlie is awkward and out of place on the movie set and is actually thrown off the soundstage for interfering with "the eyeline" of the camera. His nervousness is conveyed both by Cage's performance and by the director's use of a jittery handheld camera. This camera technique, which calls attention to the artifice of cinematography, serves also to remind the audience that they are watching a film. Later, Donald, who has no official business being on a film set, is allowed to stay and even flirts with and picks up Caroline (Maggie Gyllenhaal), an attractive makeup artist.

"THE FILM'S THE THING . . ."

> *My genre's thriller. What's yours?*
> —Donald Kaufman, to Charlie, in *Adaptation*

Adaptation is also an example of a compound genre—"mixed cinema," to return to Bazin's pithy phrase. Indeed, it is mixed and multiple at its core, as is its source, *The Orchid Thief*. There are identical twin brother screenwriters, rather obvious *Doppelgänger* figures (and sibling rivals), who dominate the action—even as one of them writes a clichéd script about multiple personalities. This self-reflexive turn is accentuated by an obscure (but telling) reference to Ourobouros, the Gnostic symbol of a snake that swallows its own tail. This "image system"—Robert McKee's term for recurring motifs—also applies to Charlie, who swallows his own tale, by writing about himself writing about Susan Orlean writing about John LaRoche.

The opening voice-over monologue, delivered over a black screen as credits appear, is a painfully solipsistic introduction to Charlie's unbridled neuroses, his "self-loathing and pathetic existence":

> Do I have an original thought in my head? My bald head? Maybe if I were happier, my hair wouldn't be falling out. Life is short.... I need to turn my life around. What do I need to do? I need to fall in love. I need to have a girlfriend. I need to read more, improve myself.... Why should I be made to feel I have to apologize for my existence? Maybe it's my brain chemistry.... I need to get help for that. But I'll still be ugly, though. Nothing's gonna change that.[25]

Human, animal, and plant adaptation (in that other sense of the term) are hardly possible if "nothing's gonna change." The very meaning of the screenplay's title is alive with doubled possibilities. At one level, it refers to the troublesome process of adapting a book to the screen; just as important, *Adaptation* refers to the troublesome process of growing and maturing as a person—and as a species. This latter self-reflexive theme is loosely found in *The Orchid Thief*, in passages such as the following:

> Sometimes this kind of story turns out to be something more, some glimpse of life that expands like those Japanese paper balls you drop in water and then after a minute they bloom into flowers, and the flower is so marvelous that you can't believe there was a time when all you saw in front of you was a paper ball and a glass of water.[26]

> [Laroche] especially loved working on hybrids—cross-pollinating different types to create new orchid hybrids.... "Mutation is great. It's the way evolution moves ahead."[27]

Mutation is also the way that the script for *Adaptation* develops within the film; the screenplay ends up as the composite vision of Charlie and Donald. So, people mutate just as readily as flowers. Furthermore, as J. Hoberman points out, the writing styles of the two "brothers" are completely opposite; Charlie writes slowly and painfully (until Donald's and McKee's advice is sought), while Donald seems to bang out his script without effort (like Susan Orlean).[28] As Orlean notes,

Many wild orchids don't like to live away from the woods. They will usually flourish and produce seeds only if they are in their own little universe.[29]

Similarly, at the beginning of the story, Charlie lives in his own private universe, alienated from relatives, friends, other people, and the Hollywood community.

Such doubling is found not only in the twin brothers but in specific motifs that dot the narrative landscape of the screenplay and film: (1) two fatal car crashes (one at the beginning, one at the end); (2) an odd *Doppelgänger* connection between Orlean and LaRoche, who are opposites in many of the same ways that the Kaufman brothers are foils to each other (one, Charlie, is an intellectual, a serious writer, like Susan; the other, Donald, is a somewhat crude and flaky eccentric); and (3) both Charlie and Susan seem to suffer from anhedonia, the inability to experience pleasure or passion. In many ways, the LaRoche-Orlean "odd couple" resembles LaRoche's description of the pollination process: "Every one of these flowers has a specific relationship with the insect that pollinates it. There's a certain orchid looks exactly like a certain insect, so the insect is drawn to this flower. Its double. Its soul mate. And wants nothing more than to make love to it." LaRoche adds, "And neither the flower nor the insect will ever understand the significance of their lovemaking," just as LaRoche and Orlean will never understand the nature of their attraction to each other.

Another, subtler recurring motif is one of shattering glass. Donald mentions wanting to incorporate an Image System of broken mirrors in his script—just as Charlie gazes into a mirror on the wall of their shared home—to show the fragmentation of the protagonist's self;[30] of course, Donald himself is killed when he flies through the windshield of a car.

Orlean's book is filled with first-person reflections on her lack of passion. As one example, the author's own jaded existence is only hinted at in the following passage:

> I felt that I was meeting people who didn't at all seem part of this modern world and this moment in time—the world of petty aggravations and obligations and boundaries, a time of bored cynicism ... they sincerely loved something, trusted in the perfectibility of some living thing, lived for a myth about themselves and the idea of adventure, were convinced that certain things were really worth dying for, believed that they could make their lives into whatever they dreamed.[31]

Charlie Kaufman sees Susan Orlean in an elevator but is too mortified to speak to her. Charlie and Susan have certain similarities: they are both intellectuals, serious writers, and both seem to suffer from anhedonia, the inability to experience pleasure or passion.

At one point in the book (related in voice-over narration in the film as she stares at herself in a mirror), she even states, "I wanted to want something as much as people wanted these plants. But it isn't part of my constitution. I suppose I do have one unembarrassed passion: I want to know what it feels like to care about something passionately." The apparition-like ghost orchid becomes her Holy Grail, and her journey of self-discovery.

Likewise, her ideas mirror Charlie's anomie, as well as his indecisive and rudderless approach to his quest—a perfect screenplay—in another passage:

> The sheer bigness of the world made me feel lonely to the bone. The world is so huge that people are always getting lost in it. There are too many ideas and things and people, too many directions to go. I was starting to believe that the reason it matters to care passionately about something is that it whittles the world down to a more manageable size . . . not huge and empty, but full of possibility.[32]

Like the fictional Charlie, the real-life Susan Orlean (as well as her on-screen incarnation) lives in a world of "petty aggravations" (Charlie's balding, his aches and pains, his nervous perspiration, his agent; Susan's complacent relationships with her husband, friends, and co-workers). Their escape from that world-weary ennui is through discovering a fervor—for flowers, people, and life. So, even though Charlie initially eschews "life lessons" and believes he can write a script "without dramatic arcs and conflict," his final draft—and the film we witness—has all these things. In fact, in the book, Susan Orlean develops at least one passionate desire, to see the elusive ghost orchid: "I was so excited to finally see a ghost orchid that I wouldn't have waited a minute longer."[33] Of course, at the book's conclusion she never gets to see one: "At this point I realized that it was just as well that I never saw a ghost orchid, so that it could never disappoint me, and so that it would remain forever something I wanted to see."[34] Not exactly a Hollywood happy ending, based as it is on frustration and irresolution, but a slightly upbeat and optimistic finale to a tale of disappointment. Even a denouement like this is inappropriate for a Hollywood movie, even one that supposedly breaks (or bends) the rules.

Not only does Susan Orlean (the character) see a ghost orchid at the end of the screenplay and movie, when she does so, she is extremely disappointed: "It's just a flower." In the end, she must also suffer the death of her lover, Laroche,[35] and be arrested for her crimes. In contrast, Charlie must be uplifted by his brother's (literal or figurative) death, learn the profound, adaptive life lesson that Donald conveys ("You are what you love, not what loves you"), complete his script, and reach out to Amelia. In short, he must develop passion—in line with McKee's commercial advice, "You cannot have a protagonist without desire! It doesn't make any sense! Any fucking sense!"

Needless to say, most books—fiction or nonfiction—do not come with soundtracks. Cinema has an important advantage over literature in its ability to convey mood, theme, character, and narratological information through diegetic and extradiegetic music. *Adaptation* uses four songs to communicate information to the viewer: "Wild Horses," by the Rolling Stones; "Allison," by Elvis Costello; "Dead Melodies," by Beck; and, most important, "Happy Together," by the Turtles. These pop culture hits contribute to the film's theme about mass-produced and mass-marketed commercial entertainment and also provide clues about the movie's characters and other themes. The lyrics of "Wild Horses," for instance, are heard on Laroche's van radio as he drives Susan around Florida. The song's refrain—"Wild horses couldn't drag me away"—suggests an intensity and passion that Laroche has and that Susan wants to acquire. In addition, the motif of horses "rhymes" with Donald's awkward statement of his theme in *The 3*: "Technology versus ... horse." "Happy Together" is actually heard three times in the film: first it is sung by Donald, in an attempt to befriend his antisocial twin brother by reminding him of their more fraternal youth; after Donald's "death," Charlie sings it in a melancholy manner, as if to revive him from the dead or to commune with the soul of his late brother; and, finally, the song (sung by the Turtles) is heard over the final shots and end credits, as if an authorial expression of the movie's coda and moral. The lyrics are instructive:

> *Imagine me and you, I do*
> *I think about you day and night*
> *It's only right*
> *To think about the girl you love*
> *And hold her tight*
> *So happy together.*

In its penultimate rendition, as Donald lies dying in his arms, Charlie modifies (adapts?) the lyrics and sings, "It's only right to think about *the one* you love." Then, in its final presentation immediately following Amelia's profession of love to Charlie ("I love you too, y'know?"), the "girl" of the song seems to be Amelia, but this does not explain its two previous versions, which relate to the love between the two "brothers." Of course, the possibility for homoerotic incest is present but since Charlie and Donald are one and the same, the lyrics suggest a self-love merging of the opposites within a single psyche rather than a taboo relationship between actual twins.[36] Although the other songs are not specified in the screenplay and may have been selected by director Spike Jonze or composer Carter Burwell, "Happy Together" is explicitly referred to in the screenplay.

Another cinematic technique that reveals theme and character that is not found much in the source book or in the script is set design. As one major example, Charlie spends a good deal of screen time in his home office/bedroom. It is interesting to note that there is almost nothing on the walls: no movie posters, art reproductions, or photos. This is not to suggest that he is a John Lockean tabula rasa. These blank white walls seem more to be a subtle visual representation of Charlie's writer's block as he tries to begin his orchid screenplay, or perhaps of his empty personality, a reading supported by the absence of open windows in his closed-off, insulated environment. Charlie seems to come alive only when he meets with Donald and Donald's makeup artist girlfriend in the colorfully wallpapered kitchen with open windows and the sun streaming in.

CONCLUSION: ALL'S WELL THAT ENDS WELL

Toward the end of the film, when Charlie goes out to a bar for a beer with McKee and the script sage offers free advice, Kaufman reads aloud what is ostensibly the concluding line of *The Orchid Thief* to his newfound mentor: "but a little fantastic and fleeting and out of reach." McKee then asks the proverbial screenwriting question "Then what happens?" Charlie replies that it is the end of the book. However, the cited passage is *not* the end of the book.[37] *The Orchid Thief* actually ends with Orlean and Laroche lost in a prelapsarian swamp, as follows:

> It was pure vivid gorgeousness, a bounty, a place so rich no one could help but pass through it and say to himself, I will find something here. After hours or minutes or forever, we splashed through the last black water and onto the dry levee. First we turned to the right but saw only cypress and palm and saw grass, so we turned to the left, and there, far down the diagonal of the levee, we could see the gleam of a car fender, and we followed it like a beacon all the way to the road.[38]

Why would the real-life Charlie Kaufman use the "but a little fantastic and fleeting and out of reach" line as the supposed conclusion to *The Orchid Thief*? The obvious answer is that to use Orlean's actual last words would have her and Laroche escaping from their predicament, returning from nature to civilization. No car chase, no deaths, no major life lessons. The full "fantastic and fleeting" quotation from the book can be instructive: "Life seems to be filled with things like the ghost orchid—wonderful to imagine and easy to fall in love with—but a little fantastic and fleeting and out of reach."[39] Here the self-reflexivity is more apparent: to Susan, Laroche and his passion have become "easy to fall in love with."

The actual ending of *Adaptation* shows nature—in the form of morning glories in an urban planter—continuously opening and closing as day shifts to night and back again in time's (speeded-up) diurnal rhythms. Nature adapts and even thrives within a smog-filled civilization, Los Angeles. Likewise, Charlie eventually adapts and even thrives in that same stultifying Hollywood milieu. He has changed and tacked on a happy ending that includes reconciliation with Amelia, closure to his screenplay, and (like Laroche) a concern with who will play him in the film version (Gerard Depardieu, without a French accent). His final upbeat voice-over lines show the degree to

Charlie reads aloud the concluding lines of The Orchid Thief *to screenwriting guru Robert McKee.*

which he has matured (or sold out): "So Kaufman drives off from his encounter with Amelia, filled for the first time with hope. I like this. This is good."

Thus, both the script and the movie resolved André Bazin's commercial-artistic conundrum by capitulating to the audience (or, more accurately, the movie industry) rather than by preserving cinematic purity. Indeed, the screenplay was so successful in this regard that it garnered an Academy Award for Best Screenplay, Adaptation, at the Oscar ceremonies in 2003. (Interestingly, the Motion Picture Academy seemed to play along with the screenwriter's in-joke by awarding the gold statuette to Charlie Kaufman and his fictitious brother, Donald.)

In this regard, an author and a filmmaker's complementary comments are noteworthy. Norman Mailer once said that "Film and literature are as far apart as cave painting and a song"; Ingmar Bergman agreed, stating, "Film and literature have nothing to do with one another; the character and substance of the two art forms are usually in conflict."[40] At the opposite end of the spectrum are Herbert Read and Béla Belázs. Read wrote,

> Those people who deny that there can be any connection between the scenario and literature seem to me to have a wrong conception, so much of the film as of literature.... Reduce the art of writing to its fundamentals and you come to this single aim: to convey images by means of words. But to *convey images*. To make the mind see.[41]

In a like vein, Belázs noted that an adaptation should be a new, different work, with its own aesthetic integrity: "[If] the [film] artist is a true artist ... [he/she] may use the existing work of art merely as raw material, regard it from the specific angle of his own art form, ... and pay no attention to the form once already given to the material."[42]

In the case of *Adaptation*, both sets of commentators seem to be accurate. On the one hand, the screenplay and resulting film seem to have little to do with Susan Orlean's "book about flowers." On the other, screenwriter Charlie Kaufman has turned the source volume into an authentic vehicle of self-expression, a new statement. After all, to adapt (in both the cinematic and biological senses of the term) is to change.

NOTES

1. André Bazin, "In Defense of Mixed Cinema," in Bazin, *What Is Cinema?*, ed. and trans. Hugh Gray (Berkeley and Los Angeles: University of California Press, 1967), 53–75, and idem, "Adaptation, or the Cinema as Digest," in *Film Adaptation*, ed. James Naremore (New Brunswick, NJ: Rutgers University Press, 2000), 19–27.

2. Bazin, "Adaptation," 20.

3. Ibid., 21.

4. Brian McFarlane, introduction, *Novel to Film: An Introduction to the Theory of Adaptation* (Oxford: Clarendon Press, 1996), 8.

5. Dudley Andrew, *Concepts in Film Theory* (New York: Oxford University Press, 1984), cited in Andrew, "Adaptation," in *Film Adaptation*, ed. James Naremore, 34.

6. Keith Cohen, *Film and Fiction: The Dynamics of Exchange* (Charlottesville: University of Virginia Press, 1979), xii.

7. Susan Orlean, foreword to Charlie and Donald Kaufman, *Adaptation: The Shooting Script* (New York: Newmarket Press, 2002), vii.

8. Orlean even admits that there is no central focus in her volume: "What was the book about? Was it about orchids? Was it the biography of John Laroche, orchid thief? Was it about passion in general?" Kaufman, *Adaptation*, viii.

9. Again, Orlean acknowledges that her book is "a nonlinear, eccentric story ... too subtle and convoluted for movie-making." Orlean, foreword, vi.

10. Susan Orlean, *The Orchid Thief* (New York: Ballantine, 1998), 107; emphasis added.

11. Robert McKee, "Critical Commentary," in Kaufman, *Adaptation*, 133.

12. The deus ex machina device is specifically proscribed to Charlie by screenplay guru Robert McKee in the script and film: "Don't cheat. And don't you dare bring in a *deus ex machina*. Your characters must change. And the change must come

from them." Kaufman, *Adaptation*, 70. If *Adaptation* is supposed to be the script that Charlie wrote, then it is interesting that so much of its ending seems to fit McKee's "principles" (and Donald's kitschy B-movie "taste").

13. Natalia Skradol, "*Adaptation*, 'Adaptation,' and Adaptation: Žižek and the Commonplace," www.film-philosophy.com/vol8-2004/n27skradol.

14. Actually, this voice-over is not meant to be Charles Darwin's. It is the British narrator of the audiocassette, *The Writings of Charles Darwin*, seen in Laroche's van at the beginning of the movie.

15. Orlean, *The Orchid Thief*, 132.

16. It may be that "the three" are also the Freudian superego (Charlie/Donald), ego (Susan), and id (John). In fact, as the film goes on, *Adaptation* comes to resemble *The 3* more and more, with Charlie/Donald in the role of the detective who spies on and tails Susan, with Orlean representing the helpless heroine who is kidnapped by the villain (Laroche). Indeed, not only does *The 3* take on more relevance as the film progresses, but its screenwriter, Donald, gains increasing control and dominance within the narrative. Charlie and Donald go through a role-reversing gradual metamorphosis (or adaptation) in which Charlie first asks Donald to help him with his flower script and then begins to read McKee's book *Story* while Donald reads *The Orchid Thief*. Thus, Donald can be killed off in the end, since Charlie has adapted and absorbed all his twin's commercial instincts, as well as his social skills.

17. It is instructive to remember that in their initial meeting, when Laroche suggests that he can propagate enough ghost orchids to make them available commercially, Susan writes "delusions of grandeur" in her notebook. Likewise, Charlie believes that his brother's harebrained schemes of Hollywood screenwriting success are nothing more than pipe dreams.

18. McKee, "Critical Commentary," in Kaufman, *Adaptation*, 132.

19. Orlean, *The Orchid Thief*, 225.

20. When Charlie decides to include the creation of the universe in his script, to "tie all of history together," he speaks it into his mini-recorder: "All is . . . lifeless. And then, like, life begins. . . . Oh, and it's before sex, 'cause, like everything was asexual." Of course, this is not only the "journey of evolution," it is also Charlie's individual story. He appears to be "lifeless" and "asexual" at the beginning, unable to express his love for Amelia until the very end.

21. For more elaboration on the concept of a mindscreen as a first-person narrational device in the cinema, see Bruce F. Kawin, *Mindscreen: Bergman, Godard, and First-Person Film* (Princeton, NJ: Princeton University Press, 1978).

22. Lucas Hilderbrand, review of *Adaptation*, *Film Quarterly* 58, no. 1 (fall 2004): 38.

23. International Association of Art Critics Web site, www.culturevulture.net (accessed November 6, 2004).

24. For more on the authorial inscription of narrational agency, see Frank P. Tomasulo, "Narrate *and* Describe? Point of View and Narrative Voice in *Citizen*

Kane's Thatcher Sequence," in *Perspectives on* Citizen Kane, ed. Ronald Gottesman (New York: G. K. Hall, 1996), 504–517.

25. Kaufman, *Adaptation*, 1.

26. Orlean, *The Orchid Thief*, 7. This meta-analogy is also found in the film's dialogue.

27. Ibid., 17.

28. J. Hoberman, "The Truths about Charlie," *Village Voice*, December 4, 2002, www.villagevoice.com/issues/0249/hoberman/php.

29. Orleans, *The Orchid Thief*, 24.

30. Although the multiple personality is a cliché of the thriller genre, as Charlie tells his brother ("The only idea more overused than serial killers is multiple personality"), it would be natural for an identical twin (Charlie or Donald) to conceive of a multiple personality plot line. Aren't authors frequently advised to "write what you know"?

31. Orleans, *The Orchid Thief*, 201.

32. Ibid., 109.

33. Ibid., 160.

34. Ibid., 281.

35. Laroche dies in Susan's arms, in a *Pietà*-like tableau.

36. Although I do not accept the repressed homosexual interpretation of the twins' relationship—since I do not believe they are separate characters—that view can be buttressed by recalling Wong Kar-wai's *Happy Together* (*Chunguang Zhaxie*, 1997), a Hong Kong film about a gay couple in which one partner achieves success while the other's life falls apart. (Coincidentally, that film also features poetic time-lapse cinematography.) See Kent and Nathaniel Jones, "Hearts and Flowers," *Film Comment* 38 (December 2002): 24–27, and Jeremy Tambling, *Wong Kar-wai's* Happy Together (Hong Kong: Hong Kong University Press, 2003), 65–104.

37. The passage actually appears on page 41 of the 282-page volume, not at the end. Orlean, *The Orchid Thief*, 41.

38. Ibid., 282.

39. Ibid., 41.

40. Norman Mailer, quoted in Morris Beja, *Film and Literature: An Introduction* (New York: Longman, 1979), 51, and Ingmar Bergman, "Film Has Nothing to Do with Literature," in *Film: A Montage of Theories*, ed. Richard Dyer McCann (New York: E. P. Dutton, 1966), 144.

41. Sir Herbert Read, *A Coat of Many Colors* (London: Routledge & Kegan Paul, 1945), 230–231. Read's final sentence is reminiscent of both Joseph Conrad's and D. W. Griffith's oft-repeated (and similarly stated) artistic goals: "Above all, to make you *see*." See George Bluestone, *Novels Into Film* (Baltimore: Johns Hopkins University Press, 1957), 1–2.

42. Béla Belázs, *Theory of Film: Character and Growth of a New Art*, trans. Edith Bone (New York: Dover, 1970), 263.

7

FROM OBTRUSIVE NARRATION TO CROSSCUTTING

Adapting the Doubleness of John Fowles's *The French Lieutenant's Woman*

//

R. Barton Palmer

DESPITE THE STRENUOUS EFFORTS OF THE AUTHOR TO INTEREST screenwriters and producers in the property (and the important agreement of Karel Reisz to direct, very early in the process), John Fowles's novel *The French Lieutenant's Woman* came to the screen only in 1980, more than a decade after its publication in 1967. This difficult second birth had nothing to do with the predictable cinematic appeal of this historical romance, set in 1867 England. A chorus of praise from academic critics and the general reading public alike had greeted the novel's appearance, and there was no reason to believe that a film version would not be received with comparable acclaim. Fowles's tale is replete with fascinating, complex characters who are involved in a plot that is at once generic (turning as it does on a "mysterious" woman beyond the social pale of respectable society) and unusual (because the narrative refuses to close in any conventional sense). No doubt, *The French Lieutenant's Woman* offers suspense and surprise in substantial and pleasant portions and therefore presented potential filmmakers with the opportunity to create an emotionally satisfying narrative. Such an engaging form of storytelling is an important element in the art film of the *Masterpiece Theatre* variety, which is the subgenre for which the novel, with its Victorian setting and deep engagement with intellectual and cultural themes of the period, seemed ideally suited.[1]

Fowles himself offers the most compelling explanation for what proved to be the almost Sisyphean task of getting the novel filmed. The book's unusual popularity, he remarks, quite early put it "in grave danger of becoming sacrosanct," which meant that what would be required was an eminently faithful approach to adaptation that took account of not only story but style, broadly considered. And yet Fowles reveals that he wrote the novel "at a time when I began to develop strong and perhaps idiosyncratic views on the

The Karel Reisz adaptation of John Fowles's novel The French Lieutenant's Woman *offers a glamorized visualization of the nineteenth-century story of sexual dissatisfaction.*

proper domains of the cinema and the novel." The result was that *The French Lieutenant's Woman* depends on "word things the camera will never photograph nor actors ever speak." Indeed, as he goes on to say, it has been the case in general that the twentieth-century novel "has been more and more concerned with all those aspects of life and modes of feeling that can *never* be represented visually."[2]

Despite this statement, Fowles was hardly interested only in the modernist preoccupation with subjective states, "the modes of feeling" or "aspects of life" that can only be described, never photographed. His novel also deeply engages the antirealist aesthetic that would subsequently be known as postmodernism. The book's effects depend on an obtrusive narrator who both breaks and furthers the illusion of the story world, exceeding the always intrusive functioning of noncharacter narrators in general.[3] How to represent a point of discourse, ontologically distinct from the characters, that dominates readers' experience of the story? This was the central problem faced by director Karel Reisz and, especially, screenwriter Harold Pinter, as we shall see after a closer look at the idiosyncratic design of Fowles's novel.[4]

THE FLIGHT FROM REAL REALITY

When he published *The French Lieutenant's Woman* in 1969, John Fowles had already established himself as a novelist of considerable intellectual substance through his six previous books, and was being taken up as a suitable figure for serious literary study by the academic community. *The French Lieutenant's Woman* much advanced his growing reputation as an existentialist with a mannerist's flair for technical experimentation, a writer who was seen to bear comparison with such disparate notables as Albert Camus, Iris Murdoch, and John Barth. It is not coincidental that major studies of Fowles's fiction appeared in the wake of the outstanding critical success achieved by *The French Lieutenant's Woman* and often focused on that novel.[5] Surprisingly, however, the book found a much wider audience than his critically admired earlier efforts, such as *The Collector* (1963) and *The Aristos* (1964), becoming, against all odds for a book of such complex ideas and stylistic *sprezzatura*, a runaway bestseller. Reportedly, its 1970 sales were exceeded in the fiction category only by Erich Segal's *Love Story*. Indeed, in the flurry of interest that followed the appearance of the book, an academic roundtable devoted to exploring *The French Lieutenant's Woman*'s (dis)connections to Victorian fiction opined that "the novel presents us with that rare phenomenon—a highly intellectual work of fiction that is also a highly popular work of fiction."[6]

Fowles, to be sure, had achieved something quite different from Segal, whose *Love Story* is perhaps only a cynical exploitation of popular taste for sensationalized and simpleminded romance, a "literary" effort hardly worth the fabulizing energies of a respected professor of Classics, who seemed slightly embarrassed about his "slumming" and the notoriety it brought. Both novels, in due time, were brought to the silver screen, where they achieved substantial success, although of different kinds. In any event, like Segal, Fowles structured his novel around a transgressive romantic liaison; in each case the suspenseful plot not only traces a difficult courtship but is concerned with the social price that the upper-class male protagonist must pay for the love he bears for an intriguing and unconventional woman of lesser rank. As in the case of *Love Story*, the story of *The French Lieutenant's Woman* is easily summarized, but—and here the two books radically diverge—any plot outline must take into account the extent to which Fowles's fascination with narratorial self-consciousness determines the reader's experience. Segal does not deal in such textual complexities, preferring, with his shameless appeal to the emotions, a somewhat low-level Aristotelianism to the more Brechtian play with ideas and values that preoccupies Fowles.

Amateur naturalist Charles Smithson, a bachelor of independent means, has determined that to avoid a lonely old age he would be wise to marry, a change of life he has resisted into his thirties. Ernestina Freeman, daughter of a wealthy tradesman, has caught Smithson's eye, and after a quick and intense courtship they become engaged, a match that suits not only their sensibilities but their economic and social prospects as well. Yet even as plans are being made for their life together in the provincial town of Lyme Regis, Smithson becomes acquainted with Sarah Woodruff, a beautiful woman who is educated but seemingly of dubious repute. The townspeople are convinced that she became the lover of a certain French naval officer who then deserted her, hence the name by which, in its politer form, she is generally known and which provides the book with its title. Charles is seduced as much by her helplessness (in some measure a mask she dons to trap him) as he is by her unwillingness to conform to "respectable" standards of behavior. Defying the strict mores of his class, Smithson determines, after a brief but passionate sexual encounter that surprisingly reveals Sarah's virginity, to break off his engagement with Ernestina. He abandons his legal and personal commitment to the marriage, for which he will suffer enduring public shame.

But Charles is desolate when Sarah disappears and, apparently, then resists his strenuous efforts to locate her. Suddenly, after several years, her alias and whereabouts are communicated to him. She has found herself a home and employment in the household of Dante Gabriel Rossetti, and Charles is granted a meeting with the much more independent and confident Sarah in which he reveals that, despite his desperate anger, his desire for her is unchanged. Charles's complex emotions, and Sarah's refusal to be swayed either by their power or by his position, reveal her as someone who defies all known social categories. These include the role in which she had earlier seemed to cast herself, that of the "scarlet woman," who should be eager for the kind of legitimating marriage for which her previous "indiscretions" conventionally disqualified her.

At this moment of turning, as at several others in the course of the novel, the narrator abandons telling the story to meditate on the difficulties of his position. The tale, he reminds us, does not precede his narration in some completed form. It is no object whose inalterable series of events and disclosures he has simply to convey. Such a view is a mirage thrown up by the position of seemingly unassailable mastery that he enjoys as a noncharacter narrator. He adopts the all-knowing and all-disposing pose of the "voice of God," a directing presence separated from his creatures only by the literary equivalent of the *primum mobile*, the ontological barrier that means he can know them but they cannot know him. As readers, we are well aware of but persuade ourselves to ignore what is actually the truth. The story must be confected as he proceeds, and it has only come into existence because of his desire, but in an earlier passage he either declines to name his motives or finds himself perhaps unable to identify what they might be.[7] As God, his principal quality would seem to be that his actions, indeed his being, are unlimited—a quality that defies the very nature of the concept of "quality," as William of Ockham observed. Tied to his creation, however, this narrator/God is limited by the obligation to decide. Just as Charles, rejecting a conventional life with Ernestina, experiences the "anxiety of freedom," realizing that "being free is a situation of terror," so the narrator is brought to acknowledge the Camusian quality of his own situation, for his being is defined by the necessity of choice (341).

And yet the narrator, unlike his fictional creations, confesses that the moral paradox of his situation renders him unable to choose. The reason is simple. As a God-like figure, he has bestowed freedom of choice on his creations, and this constrains his own. And so, while "what Charles wants is clear ... what the protagonist wants is not so clear" (406). Perhaps Sarah wants Charles and a life that would now conform more closely to accepted social custom. Perhaps she wants her complete freedom from such constraints on behavior. Even though acknowledging the freedoms of Charles and Sarah that limit his own, the narrator must still choose. And his choice is to refuse to decide between the two plausible endings for his tale of custom-breaking passion. As a result, he provides both a happy conclusion (Charles, Sarah, and their child are reunited) and an unhappy one (Charles is turned away by a Sarah who will not surrender her independence), tossing a coin to determine which should come last and thus have the presumption of "correctness" (chance, so he reports, decides in favor of the unhappy resolution).[8]

The book's self-conscious stylings and existentialist musings are obtrusive features that even the most singleminded reader entranced by the plot could hardly ignore.[9] And yet, expertly melded with a conventionally realist tale, Fowles's unabashed literariness and intellectuality apparently contributed substantially to its popularity with the general reader. Here was a historical romance with an attractive, intellectual difference, similar to yet quite unlike other contemporary entrants in the genre, such as the string of bestsellers turned out during the same period by James Michener, including *Hawaii* (1959) and *Centennial* (1974).

The text's doubleness goes much deeper, beyond its appeal to two different groups of readers.[10] In fact, with this novel Fowles anticipated the call issued more than a decade later by John Barth for a "literature of replenishment," a postmodernist program that was to depend on the "synthesis or transcension of these antitheses which may be summed up as premodernist and modernist modes of writing."[11] One of the most enthusiastic admirers of this program, as it took significant shape within Anglo-American literature, has been theorist Linda Hutcheon, who has commented that postmodernist fiction manifests a "wholesale, 'nudging' commitment to doubleness or duplicity," offering both a traditional form of narrative and some form of self-conscious commentary that undermines any simpleminded claims to the truth value (the representation of life "as it really is") that such a story might be thought to provide. In addition to underlining the arbitrary and contingent nature of narrative, its status as discourse rather than illumination, the postmodernist project, in her view, aims to "de-naturalize some of the dominant features of our way of life."

In fact, postmodernist texts like *The French Lieutenant's Woman*, as Hutcheon observes, often "juxtapose and give equal value to the self-reflexive and the historically grounded," calling attention to the difference between but the inseparability of art and life.[12] Such doubleness in Fowles's novel is centrally figured in the narrator, who is both the authoritative source of the story that elicits our interest and investment, if limited, of belief and a point of resistance to such blandishments. In the concise formulation of Philip

Cohen, the narrator "asserts the fictiveness of his fiction but also the means by which he does this." As a result, the novel offers "a sophisticated realism which repudiates neither naïve realism nor anti-realism but rather presents a balanced opposition of the two modes."[13]

The French Lieutenant's Woman is a novel about the Victorian era, or, more accurately, a pseudo-Victorian novel about the Victorian era (and thus a realist novel about the kind of realist novel produced during the high tide of that aesthetic's domination of the literary world). Fowles's work, however, self-consciously adopts the stylistic *tours* of that era's "realist" fiction (and one of its most characteristic subjects, the events that "place" a young man in society) while simultaneously advertising its own textuality as a modern imitation. The work's antirealism may be said to reside not only in this hyperauthenticity but also in the text's undermining of the illusion of reality that realist technique takes pains to foster. The narrator historicizes the very conventions he employs by addressing readers of the late 1960s as coevals, whose distance from the age they are invited to "know" must be closed by a number of devices, including ostensibly era-bridging commentary about social manners, political events, and the *Weltanschauung* of a past quickly receding from memory.

And yet these often elaborate, detailed disquisitions are only in part devoted to detailing the iron rules of historical evolution, firmly establishing the borders between supposedly distinct "periods" of human experience as customary modes of thought and fashion are displaced in favor of constant innovation. Instead, the narrator's commentary more often underlines the reader's developing and disorienting sense of the paradoxical sameness of the apparent stark differences in worldview between the Victorian and the modern. Like Charles, who steps outside the role his culture ordains he should play, the reader too comes to see beyond "the great human illusion about time, which is that its reality is like that of a road," thereby glimpsing a perhaps less comforting truth, "that time is a room, a now so close to us that we regularly fail to see it" (320). For narrator and readers alike, then, the fiction Fowles creates becomes more an object of knowledge resulting from a complex act of literary archaeology and textual pastiche and less a distant, self-enclosed story world whose truth, in the manner of a Jamesian or Conradian text, simply manifests itself to be "seen" and thereby sympathetically entered.

The novel, however, is not simply deconstructively experimental. In the conventional manner of historical fiction, Fowles provides a huge amount of detailed information about the era's customs and fashions, appending passages from notable Victorian authors as epigraphs that are designed to evidence and illuminate the "truths" of the story (in this way the book comes not only to reference but also to embody Victoriana). This strenuous effort at authentication, in addition to emphasizing the difficulty of the literary reconstruction here attempted, heightens the sense of the *vraisemblable* in the narrative, deepening the reader's connection to the characters. But, once again, these are reality effects that advertise their status as reality effects. For the narrative voice that Fowles invents for the novel's telling constitutes a kind of book in itself, an explanatory framework whose rhetoric is direct address and whose expansive space finds room for, among other forms of discourse, disparate forms of antirealist or anti-illusionist commentary, including an entire chapter (Chapter 13) in which the narrator explores the problematic nature of the fictional enterprise on which he has embarked.[14] To put it simply, *The French Lieutenant's Woman* offers a particularly appealing form of postmodern doubleness: an engaging story and an equally engaging story about the story (and about storytelling in general). If, as the narrator suggests, fabulizing is a universal activity because "we are all in flight from the real reality," then in this book Fowles both illustrates that compulsive desire for escape and analyzes the (dis)contents of this project at amusing and illuminating length (97).

The cinema, in contrast, offers scant opportunity for analysis of this kind because its extradiegetic space simply cannot accommodate such a voluble and strident voice. But any meaningful screen adaptation of the novel would have to find some way to represent a historical romance whose claims on authenticity would be both upheld and denied, or, more precisely, denied by what upholds them.

THE WORK OF THE "DEMON BARBER"

Having for years failed to arrange for the adaptation of his novel, Fowles had almost been persuaded by some old hands in the movie business, notably screenwriter Robert Bolt, that the book (if not the story strictly speaking) was unfilmable. But then, nearly a decade after first contacting Harold Pinter to write the screenplay, Reisz secured the playwright's participation, and a screenplay was duly produced. Like others who had given the matter much thought, Pinter also proved unable to devise direct cinematic equivalents for many of the novel's "word things," which are largely the province of its obtrusive, voluble, and very self-conscious narrator. The narrator, of course, is not a character and therefore must address the reader from outside the ontological space of the story as its point of origin. Even though this figure relentlessly thrusts himself into the reader's consciousness, film could re-present his verbal traces only through voice-over. This would be possible because the soundtrack, unlike the image track, makes room for both nondiegetic and diegetic effects. And yet voice-over, even though it is part of the layering that the sound (but not the visuals) allows, does not lend itself to extensive use. Obviously, an occasional and only commenting voice would not be an adequate equivalent for a narrator who marks out a discursive space nearly equal to the diegesis whose production is his principal but not sole aim. Pinter, however, did hit on a remarkably creative solution that met with Fowles's strong approval. In fact, the novelist termed it "the only feasible answer" to the central problem any adaptation would have to solve were it to remain meaningfully faithful to the novel's most obvious formal feature.

Literary texts can be adapted for the screen because written fiction is usually dominated by its narrative, which can be rendered, mutatis mutandis, fairly straightforwardly in cinematic terms. The simple reason is that both art forms are linear (that is, they unfold in time) and deploy, although through often radically different means, characters, events, and settings. But the process of adapting a literary text also involves, at least at times, the discovery of properly cinematic equivalents for literary means. For these there are often no properly cinematic analogues. If such structures are to find a place in the film text, they must do so figuratively, as Fowles himself suggests when he affirms that the script (and the resulting film) is not so much a "version" of the novel as the "blueprint . . . of a brilliant metaphor for it," the result of "an imaginative leap." What his perhaps unfilmable novel needed, and found in the person of playwright Pinter, was "a demon barber . . . someone sufficiently skilled and independent to be able to rethink and recast the thing from the bottom up" (xii). Pinter's solution was to reconceive the otherwise unfilmable narrator in theatrical terms familiar to anyone who knows the production history of Shakespearean plays such as *As You Like It*. In these dramas, as originally staged, boys played women characters who (usually in order to join two disparate aspects of the plot) assume male masks, producing a richly comic, and narratively indispensable, transvestitism of the second degree. Similarly, the key to Pinter's adaptation lay in his creative exploitation of the rich signifying capacity of actors (and other realia) in performance art.

Because of that capacity, the playwright was able to devise a diegetic structural equivalent for the narrator's omnipresent but extradiegetic voice. His screenplay dramatizes, if only in small part, the story of the film's making and thus creates a modern frame to contain the period romance. This strategy preserves, among other things, what the novelist terms the book's "stereoscopic vision," its melding of two viewpoints, one mid-Victorian (the world of the story) and the other modern (the space occupied by the narrator, who emphasizes his contemporaneity with the book's readers). The novel juxtaposes and therefore relativizes two distant (but evolutionarily connected) cultural moments, and the film does much the same. Though faithful to its source because it finds an equivalent for its most distinctive formal feature, Pinter's innovation is also a radical departure, offering two story worlds for the novel's one. As a result, the film is structured differently, its organization determined by the principle of alternating syntagmas or, less academically, crosscutting.

This is a time-honored filmic device, one whose power derives from the capacity of the cinema to shift instantaneously from one set of time and space coordinates to another and, through doing so a number of times, to set up two lines of action that, even though one or the other is at any moment not on-screen, can be given a continuing and simultaneous forward motion that utilizes the same coordinates of time, if not of space. In other words, crosscutting entails disjunction and interruption (and the creation of unfilled gaps or ellipses in the story that are often extensive). Even so, in important ways crosscutting can further rather than impede a continuing narrative forward motion, imparting a dynamism that, when combined with accelerating editing rhythms, has contributed to exciting conclusions in action films since the days of D. W. Griffith and Sergei Eisenstein. Crosscutting from one line of action to another is a feat less facilely managed in written fiction, which does not enjoy the considerable advantage of the immediate ability of the image-driven cinema to "place" its viewers. Readers must be oriented instead by the linear provision of narrative information in language, a process that is cumulative because it necessarily unfolds more slowly and depends on iron linguistic protocols, notably grammatical closure, that postpone meaning. If the obtrusive narrator is characteristically literary, a "word thing" that can never be pictured or dramatized, crosscutting is characteristically (if not exclusively) cinematic. But Pinter's use of the device in this instance is hardly customary.

In the cinema, crosscutting usually involves shifting back and forth between different spaces within the same story world. In the film version of *The French Lieutenant's Woman*, however, the alternating sequences are drawn from two different story worlds or, more accurately, from, first, an evoked "contemporary" reality, whose project is the making of a film, and, second, the reconstructed "historical" reality of the film being made. But it is also true that these two different worlds are different aspects of the same. Reisz's screen version of the novel in effect deploys the device of the mise-en-abîme, with the modern story self-reflexively standing in for the same processes (adaptation, filming) that, if radically different in detail, produced the film that we watch. Reisz and Pinter thereby suggest the permeability of the realms of life and art, which is the central idea around which the juxtaposition of the two story worlds is organized.

The Victorian tale of temptation, broken vows, unfathomable motives, and difficult intellectual growth, set within the framework of its own cinematicization, shows the "fictional" couple joined by an irresistible attraction "played" by actors who themselves begin an affair that increasingly parallels that of their fictional alter egos. Jeremy Irons plays the actor Mike who plays the character Charles, while Meryl Streep plays the actress Anna who plays the character Sarah. As Charles, Mike plays at falling in love with Anna as Sarah. But as "himself," Mike falls in love with Anna, perhaps (so the film often hints) because he has fallen in love with her embodiment of Sarah. Part of the genius of Pinter's idea is that, contrary to normal industry practice, the film within the film is shown as being shot in the same sequence in which the plot unfolds.[15] The beginning of the novel is thus filmed first, and the production ends with the shooting of the story's conclusion. And so the sequences that trace the Victorian story succeed one another in the same order in which they are being shot within the frame story. In this way, the segments that limn the fictional story world are also the "products" of the on-location shoot. These segments then become story and frame at the same time. And so the modern story can be evoked with very few additional segments that treat the off-set relationships between the actors, especially Anna and Mike, and the work that otherwise constitutes the making of the film. It is the case, however, that the segments shot *en costume* and with the complete occulting of the apparatus (camera, technicians, and so forth) belong primarily to the story and not to the frame.

A double understanding of the diegetic action is thus set up from the film's first sequence, which initially (yet very briefly) shows Anna as Sarah prepping with a technician before an elaborate long take. As this dramatic and complex traveling shot unfolds, all traces of the productive apparatus disappear, the musical score is first heard, and thus the shot assumes its other meaning as the story, but without losing its function as the shot. The story and the frame are thus shown to be unfolding at the same time and in (at least in part) the same space. And—this is the crucial point—story and frame also dispose of the same physical presences (actors, set dressing, location, costumes). What the film thereby calls attention to is a central fact of performance art: the inseparability of what we might call the performance product (such as the actor's transformation of himself into a signifier) from the existential physicality of performance (such as acting as a form of work for which the actor is rewarded and paid). A related point is that performance art results from the stipulation (constituting an implicit contract between producers and consumers) that the "real" now means something "other."

The film's diegetic doubleness is similar to, but ultimately different from, literary fiction that deploys an embedded narrator. There, most commonly, a frame story (itself narrated, of course) represents a narrator who tells a story to the other characters. This tale within the tale involves what we might call characters of the second degree. That is, the characters of the framed story are characters not only for readers but also for the characters within the frame story, who listen to the tale. Another way of putting this is to say that such texts feature not only a story (the tale the embedded narrator tells) but also the story of the story (which is related in the frame that situates and dramatizes the act of storytelling).

As a performance art, film offers only something of an analogue for such embedding. In its most basic terms, acting can be described as a form of being of the second degree, as the construction (or assumption, in some styles) of a pretended other self and a hypothetical other life. So, from an existential point of view, acting is radically different from telling, which is the less involving and more distancing evocation of an alternate reality, not its bodily enactment. The teller always remains distinct from the tale, and storytellers make use of language, a system of signs, to convey meaning. Actors, in contrast, transform themselves into signs; meaning comes to reside in them. Acting is thus more deeply, and dangerously, personal, a well-known fact that serves as one of the psychological premises of Pinter's screenplay and Reisz's film, as Mike and Anna begin to experience the blurring of the boundaries between their real and their fictional selves. What they mime becomes what they do. And what they do affects how (and perhaps what) they mime. And yet there is no simple parallel between life and fiction, as is intriguingly exemplified in a key passage of the film. Mike and Anna are rehearsing the scene in the Undercliff (a wooded area where Charles and Sarah meet by accident and later by design), in which the key movement, heavy with symbolic meaning, is Sarah's tripping on the path, only to be caught by Charles, as the relationship between them begins to deepen. After one awkward attempt, Mike and Anna, who are already lovers, manage the action more convincingly, and there is an immediate cut to the scene as played (or is it "lived"?) with great intensity in the film. Mike and Anna are shown to transfer their mutual affection to acting their roles, and yet these roles (Sarah as elusive object of pity and desire, Charles as her compulsive rescuer and pursuer) affect their performers. Their affair bears at first all the marks of a self-limiting casual romance. Yet it becomes for Mike an all-consuming passion that ends desolately with his anguished cry of "Sarah!" as Anna flees him in the film's final scene. That scene is enacted, fittingly enough, on the set where, in the story, Charles and Sarah were reunited just before the production "wrapped."

The ending of the film thematizes a central fact of performance art, which, because it makes use of human beings and other realia as signs, can deploy what we might call embedded resignification, in which a signified becomes a signifier of the subsequent degree. Such a process is potentially endless, as well as both seamless and cumulative.[16] As the film industry discovered early to its immense profit, stars represent "themselves" even while they play a character. Because the body remains the same at every level of playacting, the physical signification involved in performance art creates not separate levels of meaning but rather a rich simultaneity of meanings. And so Pinter's structuring of the screenplay through crosscutting creates more than a parallelism between the modern story of production and the mid-Victorian one of representation. Parallelism (geometrically speaking, the failure of intersection), of course, would be the only literary possibility because "characters" in a written work are verbal constructs, not physical realities. The signifier in a written fictional text is not a body but a collection of traits as evoked in language. Thus, in literary fiction, one character cannot "represent" another at an embedded fictional level.

As viewers of the film, however, we are always aware that "Mike," in addition to being himself, is also "Jeremy Irons." And, once the film's two story worlds are established, we are aware as well that "Charles" is "Mike." These three "selves" are, in fact cannot help but be, simultaneously evoked by the same physical presence, the same irreducible signifier, which is the body of Jeremy Irons.[17] The film's two seemingly distinct story worlds are thus not only "frame" and "story" (though to be sure they are that too). They also constitute a continuum of performance and "being" that works against the separation inherent in parallelism. This mutual imbrication of life and art is suggested by, among other devices at the level of story, what seems to be the banal theme of the location affair, a cultural commonplace that has become a staple theme of fanzine exposés.

Performance and being are separable but permeable human states, and this is a fact of life as well as a fact of art. Mike and Anna have the opportunity to become lovers because they are contracted to play at being the unconventional couple, Charles and Sarah. We accept without much question that the intensity of the make-believe they indulge in that is acting (and the couple's experience of working closely for some weeks) creates a powerful intimacy. That is because in performance, the absolute division of the self into signifier and experiencing human being is difficult, if not impossible (even undesirable) to maintain. In fact, good acting often depends on the so-called chemistry between the players, which is nothing less than the attraction they share and the connection they establish as persons rather than characters (or, perhaps more radically, as this film seems to intimate, as both persons *and* characters).

In Reitz's film, an important theme (perhaps the most important theme) is the slippery but ineluctable connection between art and life. This is an idea that is hardly neglected by Fowles, for the novel's double structure (its self-conscious construction of an alternate reality) evokes the essential contradiction of realist fictionalizing. Such texts proffer another world whose seeming claim to exist as a reality that is somehow "there," ready to be seen, and therefore worthy of (limited) belief is always undermined by the secure knowledge of artist and reader alike that all is illusion.

The double structure of the film version of *The French Lieutenant's Woman* may be a "brilliant metaphor" for the novel's juxtaposition of the represented, reconstructed mid-Victorian world with the narrator's obtrusive extradiegetic modernism. Nevertheless, a central question is still begged: How faithful is this metaphor to the literary means it signifies? Traditionally, of course, film adaptation studies have been preoccupied with fidelity as an evaluative protocol, producing a body of often whining complaints about how film versions fail to "equal" their literary sources. The premise of such analyses has recently come under devastating attack.[18] Given the great fame of Fowles's novel and the startling innovations of Pinter's screenplay, it is hardly surprising that a relevant example is not far to seek. In an essay revealingly titled "Karel Reisz's *The French Lieutenant's Woman*: Only the Name Remains the Same," Tony Whall, though conceding that the film "possesses enviable strengths," argues that it fails because of the "miscalculated use of the frame-tale as a cinematic substitute for the novel's distinctive point of view." He suggests that this device befuddles or disappoints viewers.[19] More seriously, Whall charges that because the filmmaker "disregards the function of the novel's narrative point of view, he has made a film that has virtually nothing to do with its source"(81). He has not been alone in dismissing the film's accomplishments for this reason.[20]

I would argue instead that the frame story interestingly reproduces the nature of obtrusive narration, even if it cannot mime its depth or complexity. I do so not to make the rather empty point that the film is more faithful to the book than some critics might allow. In the vein of the postmodernist critique of classic realism, the narrator (or, more accurately, this point of discourse) insistently reminds readers that literary art is a product whose making is fueled by complex forms of desire, that it involves transactions between the author and not only readers but also his creatures. His function in the novel is thus more multileveled than what Whall terms "a narrative point of view."

Though prominent in the Victorian fiction that Fowles imitates, the obtrusive narrator is a device that was largely discredited by influential adoption by Henry James of a quite different position. Thereafter it was largely ignored as James's followers and popularizers, particularly Percy Lubbock, redefined novelistic excellence. Consider Lubbock's view that since "a novel is a picture of life," then, "using our taste," we have only to "judge whether it is true, vivid, convincing—like life in fact" (9). Modern realist fiction, adapting itself to this aesthetic, has developed various occulted forms of storytelling, the most discussed and celebrated of which is indirect free discourse. Fowles's narrator, by way of contrast, is a device resurrected from the literary past that is equally suited to the postmodern present. As a formal feature, it perfectly suits the novel's stereoscopic vision and the work's commitment to the doubling and distancing effects of postmodernist fabulation. In both its forms, *The French Lieutenant's Woman* demystifies the transparently false claims of realism and yet furthers the irresistible appeals of that aesthetic, interestingly confirming while refuting James's critique.

OBTRUSIVE NARRATION AND THE "FICTIONAL EFFECT"

In Chapter 13, the narrator reveals himself as the novelist and confesses that he has only pretended that he "stands next to God," a pose that now appears to be a literary convention. Though he admits that the story he is "telling is all imagination" (95), he still refuses the judgment that he has "disgracefully broken the illusion." Instead, the narrator/novelist declares that "my characters still exist, and in a reality no less, or no more, real than the one I have just broken." "Fiction is woven into all"—this is the cultural commonplace he offers by way of an explanation, meaning, presumably, that the border that separates the imagined from the lived is an artificial construct, a comforting but distorting binary ripe for the appropriately deconstructive gesture (97).

But the product of such deconstruction is hardly the dismantling of common sense. For the conventional belief is surely that the fictional and the real are distinct ontological realms. Yet this accepted taxonomy is subverted by literary realism, whose aim, deploying so-called reality effects, is to convince the reader that the story world is "there to be seen," that it is in some sense real. This, then, is the "illusion" that the narrator breaks and yet preserves. We might say however that this revelation merely restores conventional belief to itself, reconfiguring the fictional as the product of imagination, the proper object of a narrative urge (these are truths novel readers, of course, already know). The narrator's antirealist move might then best be termed a "fictional effect," and Chapter 13 offers not a break in his conception of his role, just the most obvious and self-analytical account of an important function he provides throughout the novel, which is nothing more radical than to remind the reader at all times that she is reading a book.

The analysis offered above runs counter in some ways to the most influential account of obtrusive narration since the theory revolution: Colin MacCabe's attempt to "define the structure which typifies the nineteenth-century realist novel" and, having done so, to propose strategies for the subversion of realism in both its literary and cinematic forms. MacCabe starts with the definition of classic literary realism "as one in which there is a hierarchy amongst the discourses which compose the text and this hierarchy is defined in terms of an empirical notion of truth." The noncharacter narrator who calls attention to himself offers a metalanguage "that can state all the truths in the object language ... and can also explain the relation of this object language to the real."[21] So the metalanguage is the inarguable source of Truth, while the object languages (more plainly, the words that belong to characters in the story world) may contain truths of various kinds, but the extent to which they do so is to be determined by the narrator's commentary, by his "placing" of their speech. What the narrator says is, to use MacCabe's term, "transparent," and this is so because "the metalanguage is not regarded as material" but is "dematerialised to achieve perfect representation" (35). But in precisely what sense is the narrator's speech dematerialized, that is, relieved of its status as having a human origin? How can we really conceive of such language as unmarked by its unfolding in time and space and also devoid of contingency, that unfinished quality of all human utterances that Bakhtin terms "answerability"?

MacCabe attributes dematerialization to a time-honored philosophical problem, the "separation between what was said and the act of saying," which allows the narrator's commentary to "simply allow reality to appear," even as it denies its own status as articulation (36). Thus in the classic realist novel "no discourse is allowed to speak for itself but rather it must be placed in a context which will reduce it to a simple explicable content." Working within the hierarchy of textual discourses, the intrusive or obtrusive narrator furthers the claim of realist fiction directly and simply to "present us with the truths of human nature" (37).

But surely this is to accept that my reader, holding a copy of the book in her hands, thinks that any of the words contained within, whatever their place within the hierarchy of discourses, is dematerialized, originless, lacking subjectivity, somehow a direct conduit to indisputable knowledge about a world? Does any reader forget that works are authored? The author's connection to her novel, we might point out, is never occulted or dematerialized, a fact of reception that relentlessly subjectifies the complex speech act contained between the covers. Moreover, could any film spectator forget that films are produced, not found? Does any spectator really believe that, as MacCabe suggests, the operations of the cinema can be summed up in this simple formula: "the camera shows us what happens?" And thus, to make the obvious point, as readers of novels and viewers of films we already know that these objects of our attention are not "the real." Only a Madame Bovary, seduced by the textual escape to which she submits, would mistake the conventions of cheap romantic fiction for reliable scientific truth.

We may refuse to credit fictional worlds as true (for if we did they could not be "the flight from real reality" which, as Fowles points out, is the appeal of art). And yet, granting MacCabe's point in part, it is also true that, as we read, the narrative metalanguage is in effect dematerialized, the bearer of unquestionable truths. But that is because we understand that this metalanguage issues from outside the simulated contingency of the textual world. The narrator speaks to us from that space where he creates his fiction, and of this fiction he is in truth an all-ordaining divinity, a fact that as readers we cannot deny. At the same time, we also know (however we may be encouraged to forget) that what ventriloquizes this textual mystification that is the narrator is the human agent we term the author.

The obtrusive narrator in *The French Lieutenant's Woman* dethrones himself as a fabulizing God, but this dethroning does not relieve him of the burden of absolute freedom to confect the text—even though the very exercise of this freedom ironically leads him to undecidability. The narrator limits but does not undermine our already limited belief in the fictional world that he brings to self-conscious and self-deconstructing life. The novel thus offers an experience of art and an experience of that experience, and Fowles exploits the analytical space occupied by the narrator in order to provide a profound commentary on the contract between himself as the novelist, on the one hand, and his characters and readers on the other.

In the film, the slippery connections between art and life are not analyzed but dramatized. Unlike the novel, the film is thus unable to meditate on its meditations, but it replicates its source's engagement with self-consciousness, with the textual doubleness that is the central element in the postmodern aesthetic. For the film-within-the-film device marks every segment of the fiction as simultaneously story and frame, as both artistic activity and artistic product, mimicking the principal function of obtrusive narration.

If the realist aesthetic in the cinema produces a sense of "thereness" and a lack of contingency in the image, its subversion would involve an unmasking rematerialization such as Pinter and Reisz provide. As MacCabe, speaking of cinematic realism, observes, "the whole text works on the concealing of the dominant discourse as articulation," that is, cinematic realism depends on an occulting of the apparatus (47), a mystification that this film, persistently self-reflexive, will not allow. It is clear, however, that no political agenda is involved here. Fowles does not contest the aesthetic power or the epistemological usefulness of realist fiction. In Reisz's film, Mike becomes captivated by Anna as Sarah, falls in love, to be more precise, with the Sarah whom Anna becomes. So doing, he becomes the intratextual representative of our fascination with and engagement in the fiction he helps bring to life, modeling the transforming power of art.

SCREENING IN THE MIND

Revealing in Chapter 44 that the morally conventional ending he has proposed for his story (Charles rejecting Sarah and living contentedly if not happily thereafter with Ernestina), the narrator reminds the reader that "we have a habit of writing fictional futures for ourselves . . . screen in our minds hypotheses about how we might behave" (339). And why, we might ask, do we write "fictional futures for ourselves," imagining thereby a life that can never be and whose appeal, presumably, is that it is unrealizable? Why is it that we are all novelists or poets, as he declares (339)? Why, to put the question more generally, does life need art? The narrator has no explanation to offer.

But perhaps an answer of no little eloquence is to be found in the fiction he creates. If the narrator manages to give life and depth to the extratextual space he occupies, a place that has its own peculiar history, customs, and ideology, his central aim remains the construction of a fiction, of a world that must be made to appear, and which manages in some important ways to be, real, more real (at least in terms of depth, complexity, and detail) than the shadowy realm where he locates himself. Unlike the characters he creates, the narrator permits himself no life, confessing instead to be a function of their having one. He is, after all, a god whose freedom must be subordinated to their own, a Creator who draws life from his creations.

Judging from the modifications he has made in the screenplay, Karel Reisz shows every sign that he understood this important aspect of the novel better than Pinter, who wished to establish more (and often ironically interesting) connections between the frame and the story. Several commentators have suggested that, as Peter Conradi tellingly puts it, the subtleties of the screenplay have "not always survived the relentlessly demoticising urgencies of the medium itself" (53). Thus, for example, Reisz has omitted a scene, ostensibly at first from the "story," where Mike and Anna "break" character when Charles says the line "May I introduce myself?" Sarah replies, according to script, with "I know who you are," and immediately dissolves into hysterical laughter, presumably because Anna already "knows" Mike. An off-screen voice shouts "Cut!" (26). According to Conradi, what the director has left out are some of the "prosperous complications" of the screenplay (56). Pinter himself does not admit to a dissatisfaction with the resulting film, but the fact that he arranged for the printing of the unmodified screenplay perhaps indicates that he also did not think of Reisz's deletions as an improvement.

What is beyond dispute is that in Reisz's handling, the frame story has been tellingly reduced. Perhaps a consideration for the filmmakers was the overall length of the film, and it may be true as well that they felt the cinema-going public would be distracted by too much emphasis on the frame. And yet the stylistic approach Reisz has taken to the project suggests otherwise. The modern world Mike and Anna inhabit is filmed in a flat visual style, without glamorizing setups or costuming. It lacks both elaborate camera movements and a rich musical soundtrack. The film's recreation of 1867 England, however, is lushly pictorial, following the conventions of art films of this kind, with the exterior and interior sequences alike designed to exhibit the arduous labor of the filmmakers in reconstructing the period authentically. A haunting classic theme sets the emotional mood for a drama developed with more intensity than the romantic intrigue between Mike and Anna.

Were the frame story allowed to become too prominent, this carefully developed sense that the more important and engaging of the worlds in the film is the fiction, not real life, would be destroyed. Conradi himself provides the grounds for dismissing his criticism of Reisz's approach to the screenplay.

As he points out, "if it seems logical at the start to speak of the modern story 'enclosing' the Victorian one," this distinction will not hold true at the end, when Mike, entering the set where as Charles he reunited with Sarah, fails to halt the flight of the woman who has now become for him more character than person. It is then that "the boundary between 'inside' and 'outside' has teasingly disappeared" (50). Of course, Pinter draws (perhaps too boldly) this tenuous boundary in the film, which is the sign of postmodern doubleness. And yet its erasure, though indicated by the playwright with his ending, is furthered by Reisz, who has noted well Fowles's point that life pales in comparison to the art we create to escape from it.

The "flight from real reality" in novel and film, though revealed as such in all three forms the text takes, exerts, we might say, an irresistible attraction in its deceptively apparent fullness of meaning, depth, and color. And this is why we are encouraged to long for that which both is and yet never can be. Like Mike, we are satisfied and yet left unfulfilled by the impossible reconstruction of a past that is always the present. Like that past, whose authentic reconstruction the novelist (because he is not of that moment) fail to achieve, the Sarah that we come to desire eludes our grasp. Finally, Sarah is not decisively embodied even by Anna, her ostensible embodiment. Her flight from Mike *is* the flight from real reality, the act that defines fiction, especially that of the archaeological variety, as a presence with no substance, as a discourse grounded finally in nothing but itself. It is this central point about art, history, and desire that the film version perhaps makes more tellingly and affectingly than either of its written sources.[22]

NOTES

1. Terry Lovell remarks that "Bestsellers are coveted properties among film producers. But they are not usually made into the kind of film which *The French Lieutenant's Woman* became—the literary adaptation." Following the typology of adaptations devised by Dudley Andrew, she goes on to say that "What is common to literary adaptation and what above all is transposed from novel to screen in this genre, is the 'aura' of the original: that which registers its claim to high cultural status as literature.... The film-makers strive to be 'faithful' by retaining as much as possible of the original. Story, plot, characters obviously, *but also language*" (emphasis mine). "Feminism and Form in the Literary Adaptation: *The French Lieutenant's Woman*," in *Criticism and Critical Theory*, ed. Jeremy Hawthorn (London: Edward Arnold, 1984), 121–122.

2. John Fowles, "Foreword," in Harold Pinter, *The French Lieutenant's Woman: A Screenplay* (Boston: Little, Brown, 1981), viii–x. Further references to the screenplay and introduction are noted in the text.

3. See note 21 for further clarification of the differences between intrusive and obtrusive narrators.

4. This is not to say, however, that the adaptation process did not encounter other difficulties, only that these were more generic (such as what to omit and retain as the necessary abridgement went forward) and thus more conventionally resolved. For details, see Steven H. Gale, "Harold Pinter's *The French Lieutenant's Woman*: A Masterpiece of Cinematic Adaptation," in *The Films of Harold Pinter*, ed. Steven H. Gale (Albany: State University of New York Press, 2001), 69–85. For an interesting meditation on the film's reduction or elimination of some of the novel's central themes, see Marie-Claire Simonetti, "The Blurring of Time in *The French Lieutenant's Woman*," *Literature/Film Quarterly* 24, no. 3 (1996), 301–308. Reisz's modification of the screenplay at key points is discussed in the last section of this essay.

5. See, for example, Robert Scholes, "The Illiberal Imagination," *New Literary History* 4 (1973): 521–540, and Ronald Binns, "John Fowles: Radical Romancer," *Critical Quarterly* 15 (1973): 317–334.

6. Patrick Brantlinger, Ian Adam, and Sheldon Rothblatt, "*The French Lieutenant's Woman*: A Discussion," *Victoria Studies* 15 (1972): 339, from which source the information about 1970 sales is also taken.

7. The narrator has this to say about his own raison d'être and those of his fellows: "novelists write for countless different reasons: for money, for fame, for reviewers, for parents, for friends, for loved ones.... Only one same reason is shared by all of us: *we wish to create worlds as real as, but other than the world that is*," John Fowles, *The French Lieutenant's Woman* (Boston: Little, Brown, 1969), 96.

All subsequent references to the novel are to this edition and are noted in the text.

8. Properly speaking, the novel actually has three endings if we include what is subsequently revealed to be the life Charles only supposes he will live should he never see Sarah again and marry Ernestina (Chapter 44).

9. Brantlinger et al., "*The French Lieutenant's Woman*," 339.

10. The narrator even suggests, with insight and plausibility, that such doubleness was a feature of the very age that it is his chosen task to describe, for "every Victorian had two minds," as can be glimpsed in the period's "endless tug-of-war between Liberty and Restraint, Excess and Moderation, Propriety and Conviction." Thus, in his view, "the best guidebook to the age [is] very possibly *Dr. Jekyll and Mr. Hyde*. Behind its latterday Gothick lies a very profound and epoch-revealing truth" (368–369).

11. John Barth, "The Literature of Replenishment, Postmodernist Fiction," *The Atlantic Monthly* 245 (January 1980), 70.

12. Linda Hutcheon, *The Politics of Postmodernism* (New York: Routledge, 1989), 1.

13. Philip Cohen, "Postmodernist Technique in *The French Lieutenant's Woman*," *Western Humanities Review* 38, no. 2 (1984): 149.

14. Such a novelistic structure, what we might describe as an expanded frame that contains a story world otherwise limned in the manner of traditional realism, flagrantly violates Jamesian strictures against fiction in which narratorial commentary plays an important role. Cf. Percy Lubbock's famous complaint about the comparable method utilized by Tolstoy in *War and Peace*: "He whose power of making a story *tell itself* is unsurpassed, is capable of thrusting into his book interminable chapters of comment and explanation.... But the reader at last takes an easy way with these maddening interruptions; whenever 'the historians' are mentioned he knows that several pages may be turned at once" (*The Craft of Fiction*, rev. ed. [New York: Viking, 1954], 35). Further references are noted in the text. But in its recycling of cultural givens, the "readymades" of an already expired literal tradition and the culture it once represented, *The French Lieutenant's Woman* abjures modern forms of superrealism that debunk prominent features of nineteenth-century realism such as ideological closure. The novel's preference for ambiguity and the open ending is presented as more faithful to lived experience (a protocol with which James and Lubbock would certainly agree), especially since the characters, though recognized as characters, are imagined as having a life of their own, including the power of self-determination.

15. As Peter Conradi remarks, "The film depends upon the useful convention—a quite false and artificial one surely, though perfectly plausible in its context—that a given film is likely to be shot in chronological sequence. Thus the action of *both* plots can then move from Lyme to Exeter, from Exeter to London, and finally to Lake Windermere" ("*The French Lieutenant's Woman*: Novel, Screenplay, Film," *Critical Quarterly* 24, no. 1 [1982]: 54). Further references noted in the text. This observation is correct but does not in my view go far enough. For it is not only true that both "plots" move through the same spaces and in the same chronological order. It is also the case that each individual shot is thereby given two narrative values, is "layered," so to speak, for it simultaneously figures as an element within the story and as an element with the story of the story, that is, its filming.

16. Although the film version of *The French Lieutenant's Woman* has generated a significant body of critical commentary, not much has been made of this seemingly central point except by Seymour Chatman, who observes that "the film's self-consciousness . . . rests on the fact that the medium permits a given signifier—an actor—to signify more than one character. Obviously, that cannot happen in literature, which is made of words, not actors" (*Coming to Terms: The Rhetoric of Narrative in Fiction and Film* [Ithaca, NY: Cornell University Press, 1990], 165). Chatman, however, does not go on to explain that this difference between the two media rests on the fact that film (like theater) depends on the Aristotelian principle of "the imitation of an action" (one action standing for another) while literary narrative must

use language to re-present action. Theatrical imitation involves the simple signifying process of iconic stipulation (on the stage, the actor implicitly stipulates he is playing someone else), but literary representation involves the mobilization of a semiotic system whose signs are conventional rather than iconic.

17. Interestingly, though the film establishes Meryl Streep first as an actress playing a character (with the names of each "person" supplied later), the film establishes Jeremy Irons first as Charles (in the scene where he successfully proposes to Ernestina), only then revealing him as Mike (when he is shown in bed with Anna). This pattern not only contests any presumption of the frame story as the primary source of information, but exemplifies the complex imbrication of the two story lines. For the first scene with Mike and Anna suggests that these two are the principal performers in the film, the man and the woman who conventionally become the romantic couple. This presumed pairing suggests that the engagement scene between Charles and Ernestina may soon be disrupted, as it is, by the affair that begins between Sarah and Charles. That this apparent sealing of a romantic bargain comes first in the narrative (rather than, more conventionally, at its end) also, of course, suggests its lack of solidity, its ripeness for a disruption to take the story in a different direction.

18. Theorists have recently questioned the value of faithfulness as a critical protocol, most notably Robert Stam, who observes, "the notion of fidelity is problematic for a number of reasons," particularly that such a position on adaptation is open to the objection that "an adaptation is automatically different and original due to the change of medium" ("Beyond Fidelity: The Dialogics of Adaptation," in *Film Adaptation*, ed. James Naremore [New Brunswick, NJ: Rutgers University Press, 2000], 55). Stam's critique of faithfulness is particularly relevant to the aspect of adaptation we are here tracing, which has to do with "means" rather than "narrative." As Stam goes on to point out, "The shift from a single-track, uniquely verbal medium such as the novel, which 'has only words to play with,' to a multitrack medium such as film, which can play not only with words (written and spoken), but also with *theatrical performance,* music, sound effects, and moving photographic images, explains the unlikelihood—and I would suggest even the undesirability—of literal fidelity" (56; emphasis mine).

19. Tony Whall, "Karel Reisz's *The French Lieutenant's Woman*: Only the Name Remains the Same," *Literature/Film Quarterly* 10, no. 2 (1982): 75. Further references noted in the text.

20. In "Pinter Fails Fowles: Narration in *The French Lieutenant's Woman,*" *Literature/Film Quarterly* 16, no. 3 (1988), Susan E. Lorsch declares that the playwright's "metaphor ... promised to achieve the spirit of Fowles's novel but which ... ultimately fails to live up to that promise." The filmscript is thus full of "disappointing shortcomings" (145). Peter Conradi similarly suggests that "the film does not quite provide the questioning commentary on the realism or illusionism of its form that

either the novel attempts or the screenplay gestures towards: the two contrasted epochs, of suppositious constriction, and of notional release, do not lastingly illuminate one another, and indeed *stay obstinately separate*" (56; emphasis mine).

21. Colin MacCabe, "Realism and the Cinema," in *Tracking the Signifier: Theoretical Essays: Film, Linguistics, Literature* (Minneapolis: University of Minnesota Press, 1985), 34–35. Further references noted in the text. The non-character narrator is by nature intrusive, that is, this point of discourse *outside* the diegesis calls attention to the fact that the text contains *more than* the diegesis, which is to say that such a narrator articulates the relationship between two discursive spaces: the story of which he is not a part and the space that permits direct communication with the readers and from which he tells the story. The intrusiveness of such a figure, however, is a matter of degree, moving toward obtrusiveness, which point may be said to have been reached when the reader's attention is consistently and compellingly drawn as much toward the narrator as toward the fictional world he produces.

22. In this regard the narrator's comments in regard to Charles's experience of the beauties of the landscape are perhaps relevant. He suggests: "We could not expect him to see what we are only just beginning—and with so much more knowledge and the lessons of existentialist philosophy at our disposal—to realize ourselves: that the desire to hold and the desire to enjoy are mutually destructive. His statement to himself should have been, 'I possess this now, therefore I am happy,' instead of what it so Victorianly was: 'I cannot possess this forever, and therefore am sad'" (69). There may be a philosophy of art contained in these musings.

8

THE THREE FACES OF *LOLITA*, OR HOW I LEARNED TO STOP WORRYING AND LOVE THE ADAPTATION

//

Rebecca Bell-Metereau

IN 1962, THE CATHOLIC LEGION OF DECENCY WAS BOUND TO CONdemn Stanley Kubrick's adaptation of Vladimir Nabokov's *Lolita*, the story of a middle-aged pedophile who marries a widow, loses her, and then becomes the lover of his adolescent stepdaughter. Thirty-six years later, Adrian Lyne's 1998 remake confronted a number of the same problems that Kubrick faced in terms of adaptation, censorship, and distribution. The two film adaptations of Vladimir Nabokov's *Lolita* do not exactly follow the old sexist adage about women—the beautiful ones aren't faithful and the faithful ones aren't beautiful. In fact, Stanley Kubrick's 1962 film was neither particularly beautiful nor faithful, at least in superficial terms. Robert Stam has questioned the legitimacy of the entire concept, arguing that "we need to be less concerned with inchoate notions of 'fidelity' and to give more attention to dialogical responses—to readings, critiques, interpretations, and rewritings of prior material."[1] When Kubrick released *Lolita*, the film's audiences, critics, and would-be censors could not agree on how true to the novel Kubrick's version was, but fidelity was not the most pressing issue at the time. Kinky sex was the sticking point for many readers and viewers, and although some "felt cheated that the erotic weight wasn't in the story," Production Code arbiters objected to its supposed tawdriness.[2]

Lolita's path from novel to film was riddled with compromises and accommodations, beginning with the decision of collaborators Stanley Kubrick and James Harris to move the production from the United States to England, where artistic freedom and financial advantages kept Kubrick for the remainder of his career. Kubrick and Harris had worked successfully together on *Paths of Glory* and then on *Spartacus*, a project they took over to buy their way "out of a five-picture contract [they] had with Kirk [Douglas]."[3] Kubrick wanted to film *Lolita* because he viewed it as one of the great love stories of the twentieth century, so he and Harris purchased the film rights.[4] At a publicity luncheon, Nabokov met Harris, who was introduced to him as the purchaser of *Lolita*, and Nabokov, assuming he had simply bought a copy of the book, told him, "I hope you enjoy reading it."[5] Later, Kubrick commissioned Nabokov as screenwriter, then took Nabokov's 400-page script and used only about twenty percent of it, according to Nabokov. Nevertheless, Nabokov did not publicly condemn the film, even claiming that he was envious of some of Kubrick's ideas. Moreover, Nabokov himself received an Academy Award nomination for Best Adapted Screenplay, and the film was widely acknowledged as a cinematic masterpiece. Nabokov eventually published his edited original screenplay, "not as a pettish refutation of a munificent film but purely as a vivacious variant of an old novel."[6]

Fast-forward to 1998, when Adrian Lyne's worshipful attempt to be both beautiful and faithful resulted in a film described by one critic as "a particularly somber episode of *The Red Shoe Diaries*," a comment referring to the gloom of romantic sentimentality and the soft pornographic atmosphere that characterize Lyne's revisioning of the tale.[7] Lyne took pains to be more faithful to the novel, but in the view of many critics his efforts came to life somewhat anemically, under the double shadow of Nabokov's original masterpiece and Kubrick's groundbreaking adaptation. In the commentary track on the DVD, Lyne scrupulously avoids referring to Nabokov or Kubrick, calling the 1962 work simply "the other film," in the way a betrayed wife might refer to "the other woman."[8] Stephen Schiff, Lyne's screenwriter, seems equally reluctant to acknowledge any anxiety of influence, stating that he "didn't look at the screenplay Nabokov wrote" since he "wanted to be influenced no more by his take on himself than by Kubrick's take on him."[9] Schiff also states that most of his company "actually looked upon the Kubrick version as a kind of 'what not to do.'"[10] Schiff became the screenwriter for the project after Lyne decided not to use the contemporary version by James Dearden (Lyne's screenwriter for *Fatal Attraction*), the production company had rejected Pinter's "fluent" yet "icy and off-putting" script, and David Mamet had been hired and fired.[11] Because of his relative inexperience, Schiff had the virtue of being an inexpensive replacement on a production that was heading way over budget.

The sexually sensitive material proved to be a source of problems for both adaptations, although the directors dealt with the challenges in vastly different ways. Kubrick turned to satire, and Lyne emphasized sentiment, but neither tactic kept censors at bay. Kubrick notes, "At the time I made it, it was almost impossible to get the film played. Even after it was finished, it laid around for six months."[12] The delay could be attributed to the film's combination of pedophilia and humor—a confusing mix for censoring agencies and critics alike. A film version of *Lolita* might be expected to take on the patina of art and respectability with the passage of time, but this was not the case. More than three decades later, Lyne's version had not made it into theaters. The film's release was crippled by the passage of Orrin Hatch's Child Pornography Prevention Act of 1996, a rider attached to a spending bill.[13] Two years after the film was ready for screening, Showtime finally made it a feature of its "No Limits" campaign, a series designed to let audiences see what some considered outrageous fare on Showtime. In an echo of the uproar over Kubrick's film, the National Coalition for the Protection of Children and Families stated that the film would "increase child molestation and have a harmful effect on healthy men."[14]

After all the delays over racy content, most viewers found both adaptations relatively tame. The differences between the two films, however, reveal the delicate line Nabokov successfully walked in his depiction of a grown man's obsession with a twelve-year-old nymphet. Whereas Kubrick went for black humor by centering on James Mason's wry sarcasm and Peter Sellers's comic virtuosity, Lyne attempted to capture a mood of romantic nostalgia, focusing on erotic and emotional elements. Robert Stam argues that "if Kubrick misses the style of the novel, Lyne misses its humor."[15] Kubrick's vision included a satirical comment on the vapidity of middle-class American society, while Lyne's work reflected his own private obsession with obsession. Neither version captured the element of surprise that Nabokov considered essential to the structure of his narrative: the discovery, toward the end, that Humbert Humbert, far from being simply a cynical child molester fixated on young girls, actually loved Lolita herself. As Stanley Kauffmann puts it, "Humbert Humbert is not, in the movie, a 'gonad nomad,' but has become a 'trusty, trustful Tristram.'"[16]

In order to satisfy the censors, Kubrick was forced to downplay the erotic nature of the relationship, inadvertently giving the impression that Humbert actually cared for Lolita, regardless of her age or physical attributes. And Lyne, somewhat freer to explore the more pornographic elements of the story, nevertheless chose from the start to emphasize the elements of romantic love inherent in the relationship. Thus, both filmmakers failed to adequately emphasize an unexpected turn that both Nabokov and Kubrick saw as essential to the dramatic development of the story. Kubrick's version also normalizes Humbert, as Francis Russell observes: "The book is degenerate 'porno-picaresque,' a version of the *Satyricon*. The audiences for the movie are,

"*Promise me you'll never leave me?*" Lolita (Sue Lyon) asks Humbert (James Mason) after she learns of her mother's death in Stanley Kubrick's Lolita (1962).

thus, seeking lubricious details. Actually, though, the movie is more normal than the book."[17] Along these lines, Hollis Alpert explains that Sue Lyon is "too old to play Lolita, so Humbert seems less sick and less grotesque, more human."[18] By creating a more sympathetic or normal character, the film may have lost another element besides narrative tension—the liminality in Nabokov's characters. Always fascinated with complexity, Nabokov introduced a set of characters whose motivations are multifaceted; they cannot be pigeonholed as innocent or depraved, kind or cruel, insane or criminal. Comparatively speaking, Kubrick, through his use of humor and ironic distancing, comes much closer than Lyne does to capturing the thematic depth and moral ambiguity inherent in Nabokov's original work. Even at that, Robert Stam maintains that Nabokov's "screenplay is more prone than the Kubrick film to comic interruption and dedramatization."[19]

While literary and film critics often admire such enriching ambiguities, it may be argued that the continued fame of the mercurial figure of Lolita owes at least as much to the scandals surrounding the beleaguered film adaptations as it does to Nabokov's original literary masterpiece. Long after the novel's critical acceptance in the literary world, film and digital technologies gave Lolita new incarnations. Given the number of Web sites and organizations devoted to the iconic adolescent, it seems that Nabokov has joined Bram Stoker, Mary Shelley, and Lewis Carroll in creating a character and a phenomenon that live beyond the original novel. In providing a compilation of Web sites, Suellen Stringer-Hye comments, "Lolita in fact leads a life of her own."[20] James Naremore comments on the intertextuality of Lolita's character as he notes one of the more obscure cross-references, describing "Richard Kwieniowski's *Love and Death on Long Island*, which tells the story of a sheltered British novelist who goes to see an E. M. Forster adaptation at the local Cineplex and wanders by mistake into *Hot Pants College II*"... in a film "based on a novel by Gilbert Adair . . . a rewriting of Mann's *Death in Venice* and Nabokov's *Lolita*."[21]

The persona of Lolita, like that of Alice in Lewis Carroll's famous works, has spurred admiration and a swirl of controversy since the figure's inception. The popularity of such liminal female figures owes to an ambivalent longing for a combination of naiveté and naughtiness that resides within American culture itself. If both film versions of *Lolita* fall short of truly capturing the interior of her character, Nabokov's novel could also be accused of this same shortcoming. Stephen Schiff explains one of the difficulties he had in creating lines for Lolita in Lyne's version of the film: "Because Nabokov's Humbert lives in a kind of exalted subjectivity, Lolita herself is so much a figment of his imagination that she barely exists on the page."[22] Only at rare moments does the poignancy of Lolita's plight break through Nabokov's witty prose, giving the reader intimations of a creature who is presented primarily as an iconic face, on which Humbert projects his own fears, desires, and dreams. The popularity of Lolita's character points to the love-hate relationship between a male-dominated society and the figure of a female child who should be easy to bully and yet who holds much of the psychological power in the relationship.

The desire to represent this phenomenon is not new, and a number of critics have attempted to pinpoint earlier sources for Nabokov's famous tale. The social milieu from which Nabokov's tale of Lolita arose is the closing of the flapper era, during the 1930s, when a certain boyish quality in young rebellious women was considered enormously attractive. Indeed, Lolita combines elements of the "modern" woman of the prohibition era and the rebellious teen of the forties and fifties. It may have been this complex combination that first inspired Nabokov's interest in the original concept of the seductive quality of an adolescent female on the verge of womanhood. Tim Dirks dates *Lolita*'s origin somewhat earlier by suggesting that "the well-known scandal at the start of the century of actor Charlie Chaplin's second marriage and subsequent divorce to under-age actress Lolita McMurry [sic] may have been the original reference point for Nabokov's novel."²³ Chaplin's second wife was actually named Lillita McMurray, and Nabokov denied any association between his literary Lolita and the real-life actress. Michael Marr notes that a novella published by Heinz von Eschwege (under the alias Heinz von Lichberg), a journalist during the Nazi regime, has the same title and basic scenario as Nabokov's *Lolita*. Both authors "lived in the same area of Berlin for fifteen years, which Mr. Maar believes makes it possible that the Russian read the earlier work."²⁴

Given Maar's assertion that the 1916 short story of the Lolita tale by Heinz von Eschwege may be a source for Nabokov's novel, one could argue that Nabokov has not produced an original story. However, to make that claim would require ignoring the richness and depth of Nabokov's novel. As Maar writes, "What you can see is that the theme itself is nothing. The first novel is not of great artistic merit but then the master takes the subject and creates a work of art."²⁵ While Maar's assessment of Nabokov's literary genius is on target, his claim that the theme is "nothing" may exaggerate the case. Indeed, the symbol of the nymphet itself is so overdetermined that the subject is often skirted or ignored precisely because it engenders such extreme responses, even years after the novel's original publication. The film adaptations brought Nabokov's tale to a wider public, revivifying and further canonizing a literary work that caused a scandal in its original release. Although there are a few striking surface similarities between von Eschwege's story and Nabokov's novel, there is no proof that Nabokov ever read the story.

Nabokov himself claims a later and more convoluted origin:

> The first little throb of Lolita went through me late in 1939 or early in 1940, in Paris, at a time when I was laid up with a severe attack of intercostal neuralgia. As far as I can recall, the initial shiver of inspiration was somehow prompted by a newspaper story about an ape in the Jardin des Plantes who, after months of coaxing by a scientists, produced the first drawing ever charcoaled by an animal: this sketch showed the bars of the poor creature's cage.²⁶

Lolita paints a portrait of the bars of Humbert Humbert's own psychological cage, a picture of his own obsession rather than an account of another human being's life. Nabokov also includes the narrator's self-reflexive and literary explanation for his obsession with the figure of his childhood sweetheart, Annabel, an allusion to Edgar Allan Poe's eponymous child bride memorialized in his poem "Annabel Lee." In yet another vein, Carl Proffer notes that "Lolita was suggested to Vladimir Nabokov by Boris Ivanovich Shchyogolev, a not particularly intelligent character in one of his Russian novels (*Dar*) written in the years 1934–37."[27] These and other theories of influence are not mutually exclusive, for the material resonates deeply and widely. Appel argues that the distinguishing mark of Nabokov's treatment of the delicate subject of girl love is "Nabokov's profoundly humane comic vision."[28]

Despite his "comic vision," not everyone was laughing when they saw Nabokov's initial manuscript. The novel *Lolita* came into the literary world with considerable difficulty. Nabokov, who in the 1950s was a professor of Russian and European literature at Cornell University, sent his manuscript to a number of editors, but he could find no American publisher willing to touch the work. In 1955, Olympia Press, a Parisian company that specialized in pornography, published *Lolita*, and most reviews focused on whether the work should be considered pornographic. The book was subsequently banned in Paris in 1956. After placing excerpts in the *Anchor Review* in 1957, Nabokov succeeded in publishing the work that year in the U.S. and it was so successful that he was able to retire from teaching to live off royalties.

If the inspiration for and the path to distribution of Nabokov's novel are murky, the adaptation process from novel to film and remake took an even more tortuous route, not only because of the controversial subject matter but also because of the strength of artistic vision expressed by both Nabokov and Kubrick. Nabokov's original novel uses multiple references to cinematic imagery, and Kubrick, always on the lookout for literary masterpieces ripe for adaptation, recognized the inherently filmic nature of Nabokov's vision and commissioned the initial screenplay from him. Nabokov's original script would have required about seven hours of filming, so Kubrick suggested cutting major portions. Even after editing, Nabokov could not resist including background scenes, such as one in which Humbert's mother is struck by lightning, her ghost then floating "up above the black cliffs, holding a parasol and blowing kisses to her husband and child who stand below, looking up, hand in hand."[29] As poetic as this image is, it would be logistically quite difficult to shoot, and the scene would have no place in Kubrick's more or less naturalistic film. In addition, extensive development of Humbert's background is simply not feasible in a film that already pushes viewers' attention span at two and one-half hours.

Aside from the task of cutting out five hours' worth of content from Nabokov's screenplay, Kubrick viewed his first challenge as structural, for the original novel's narrative comes to a premature climax when Humbert sleeps with Lolita. Although this precipitous conclusion of romantic foreplay may not be a problem in the novel, it poses a number of difficulties in the cinematic medium, which generally places such climactic scenes toward the end of the film, at least in the latter third. Kubrick attempted to solve this problem by structuring the narrative as a flashback. In both Nabokov's screenplay and Kubrick's film, the story opens with a scene from the novel's epilogue in which the narrator, Humbert Humbert, shoots his nemesis, Quilty. But even before this scene, Kubrick establishes the film's mixture of romantic and erotic elements, tinged with an undertone of playful whimsy, in one of the most daring opening credit sequences in film history. The foot of a young woman, held by a man's hand, takes up the entire screen as the title *Lolita* appears. The man's hand holds the foot with excruciating care, sensuously stuffing a bit of cotton into the crevices between each toe, and delicately painting each nail, all to the accompaniment of Bob Harris's sweepingly romantic string score. The combination of eroticism and fetishism inherent in such a scene was unprecedented in 1962. Years later, Susan Seidelman used a similar opening in *Desperately Seeking Susan* (1987), perhaps as an intentional or unconscious homage to Kubrick. The tender prurience of the scene, combined with the ironic use of the soundtrack, encapsulates the nature of the relationships in the film. The incongruity of this opening, which juxtaposes the close-up of a man subserviently painting a woman's toenails and the standard romantic music of melodrama, alerts viewers immediately to the dark humor that marks Kubrick's treatment of the narrative.

In a sense, Kubrick's opening flies beneath the radar of such censoring groups as the Catholic Legion of Decency, which barely recognizes the underworld of submissive/dominant relationships or foot fetishists. Kubrick regretted that he was unable to emphasize the erotic attraction as much as the novel had done, explaining that

> the eroticism of the story serves a very important purpose in the book, which was lacking in the film: it obscured any hint that Humbert Humbert loved Lolita. One was entirely satisfied to believe that he was erotically obsessed with her, and one believed his repeated comments that it would be necessary to get rid of her when she was no longer a nymphet. It was very important that Nabokov delayed an awareness of Humbert's love for Lolita until the end of the story. I'm afraid that this was all too obvious in the film. But in my view this is the only justifiable criticism.[30]

Kubrick believed that the film should be as erotic as the novel, but he was constrained by censors to eliminate most of the sexual content.

One of the most frequent criticisms of Kubrick's version is common to practically every adaptation of a great novel, and that is infidelity to the original. This might be countered by the fact that Nabokov nominally wrote the screenplay, but the film version nevertheless strays dramatically from Nabokov's novel and screenplay throughout. In describing the "instabilities of textual production," Robert Stam queries, "If a novelist has written a novel, but also provided a screenplay which is already 'unfaithful' to the novel, to which text is the filmmaker to be 'faithful?'"[31] In spite of numerous gaps in interpretation and artistic vision, Kubrick and Nabokov maintained a remarkably amicable relationship, which was no doubt lubricated by the $150,000 Kubrick and James Harris paid for the rights to the novel, the Acadamy Award nomination for Nabokov's adapted screenplay, and subsequent recognition the film garnered. In his 1973 forward to his original screenplay, Nabokov states, somewhat sardonically:

> A few days before, at a private screening, I had discovered that Kubrick was a great director, that his *Lolita* was a first-rate film with magnificent actors, and that only ragged odds and ends of my script had been used.[32]

Not wanting to bite the hand that fed him, Nabokov continues, "My first reaction to the picture was a mixture of aggravation, regret, and reluctant pleasure."[33]

Nabokov expresses some frustration over the fact that he labored so long over scenes that never made it into the film, and he seems unwilling to admit that Kubrick improved the script by slimming down his original product, not simply in terms of size but also in terms of what was eliminated. Particularly in the opening, Nabokov's original screenplay would have produced a slow, talky and painful film. Kubrick conveys the description of Quilty's mansion with a few shots, whereas Nabokov's version would have Lolita's voice-over describe the place. Then, instead of demonstrating Humbert's singleminded madness, as Kubrick does, Nabokov's screenplay inserts the character of Dr. Ray, who begins to explain his pathology. Next, in a lengthy narration by Humbert himself, Nabokov's screenplay explains Humbert's original fixated attachment to his first love, the adolescent Annabel.

This prologue—which details their abrupt separation and his subsequent failed marriage to Valeria, then returns to Dr. Ray's analysis—goes on for twenty pages. Kubrick does Nabokov the enormous favor of cutting all this. In defense of Nabokov's intentions, it must be acknowledged that many viewers feel the need for some explanation for Humbert's obsession, especially those who have read the book and thus know his backstory. The effect of omitting this key information is to diminish the viewer's sympathy for Humbert, and it is precisely this skepticism and distance that Kubrick cultivates, perhaps as a substitute for the more blatant sexual predation that the book could recount and the censor-ridden film could not. Despite the fact that Kubrick ignores large chunks of Nabokov's screenplay version, the opening of the film sets the comically black tone for the film in a way that is remarkably true to the ironic flavor of the novel.

After the toe-painting opening credits, the film flashes forward to a foggy point-of-view shot of Humbert driving through mist to Quilty's mansion. A number of critics have noted Kubrick's penchant for fairy-tale references, and certainly the opening scene establishes a surreal quality to the otherwise realistic narrative style.[34] The mistiness of the setting mirrors the murkiness of Humbert's mental state. The shot of Humbert's car traveling along an isolated road and up to a castle-like mansion also recalls the fairy-tale journey to the house of the beast. His entrance into the house, uninvited, resembles the opening sequence of Jean Cocteau's *Beauty and the Beast* (1946), and Quilty's sudden appearance as he emerges from an armchair covered with a sheet recalls the mysterious human furniture of Cocteau's film as well. Thematically, the ghostly scene also establishes Quilty as the *doppelgänger* who will shadow and taunt Humbert throughout the film. Robert Stam notes that "through a kind of displacement from narrative to character, Quilty becomes a kind of ambulatory intertext, a performative embodiment of the Nabokovian style, no longer as literary citation but rather as allusive improvisation."[35]

While Nabokov's original screenplay opening made extensive use of voice-over, Kubrick was surprisingly stingy in employing a device that directors adapting novels often use excessively. Mario Falsetto observes that, of the thirty-five narrative units or scenes, only five involve Humbert's voice-over. One shows Humbert writing in his diary, and the other four are direct addresses to the viewer. The audience first receives information specifically excluded from Humbert's view in scene eight, in which the camera closes in on a photograph of Clare Quilty. Falsetto argues, "There is a clear difference between how the viewer and Humbert interpret many events depicted in the film, and this difference of interpretation is tied specifically to many of its narrative patterns. Complexities in structure and narrative organization help make *Lolita* one of Kubrick's most accomplished and resonant films."[36]

The casting of actors is another artful element of Kubrick's film, for he had to strike a balance between biting humor and a certain tenderness for his subject. After looking at photos of more than eight hundred girls, Kubrick picked "Sue Lyon after seeing her on *The Loretta Young Show*."[37] Lyon as Lolita was a choice that Nabokov himself approved immediately, describing her as a "demure nymphet."[38] Kubrick reassured Nabokov that she could be made to appear more "grubby," in keeping with the tomboy nature of her character. Given censorship and commercial pressures, it is not surprising that Kubrick cast an older actress and failed to make her look even slightly grubby. One of the most frequent objections to the film was the casting of Lyon as a much older Lolita, a change that made Humbert's passion "normal, not perverse."[39] The first version of the screenplay, by Calder Willingham, bowed to censors by having Humbert and Lolita marry in the end. Originally, Kubrick and producer James B. Harris offered to show Lolita and Humbert getting married in a state where marriage to minors was legal, so that the Production Code Authority would approve the film. Ultimately, this ending didn't appeal to anyone, so Kubrick returned to the original version, agreeing to change Lolita's age from preteen to teenager to placate the censors.

In looking at the effect of censorship on the production history of *Lolita*, another issue that arises is whether Sue Lyon was unduly exploited by having her appear in a film that may have either stunted or prematurely jump-started her acting career. Sue Lyon was fourteen when the film was cast, and it certainly does not call on her to display any overt expressions of sexuality with her aging co-star. Nevertheless, this was a topic of concern at the time of the film's release. As for Nabokov, he declared himself to be completely satisfied with the casting of Lyon, whose pouty mouth and heart-shaped sunglasses featured prominently in publicity posters for the film. Whether or not Lyon was a true nymphet, movie stills of Sue Lyon as Lolita occupy a number of Web sites today, testimony to the visual magnetism of her portrayal. What may have begun as a concession to censors ended up creating a distinctive female icon for generations of film and nymphet aficionados. At the time, the most common assessment of her performance was that it was merely "acceptable."

The casting of Humbert's character was another challenge, for the part called for a European type who could convey a combination of naiveté, salaciousness, sophistication, and charm. Laurence Olivier and David Niven were considered for the part, but James Mason was cast as Humbert, perhaps because his physical appearance was more in keeping with the character's beastly qualities. This was an important enough feature for Kubrick to insert a reference to his hairiness into the screenplay, when Lolita asks why Humbert shaves twice a day, to which he replies, "All the best people do." What might seem to be a comic throwaway line actually underscores themes that pervade the novel and the film as well: the distinction between Humbert's upper-class persona and the contrasting bourgeois American quality of his surroundings, and the delicate line between man and beast, in a subtle allusion to Humbert's resemblance to Dr. Jekyll and Mr. Hyde.

A blowzy Shelley Winters was cast as Mrs. Charlotte Haze, whose doomed aspirations to acquire the status and sophistication of her European lodger make her simultaneously pitiable and laughable. The audience learns eventually that both Charlotte and her daughter Lolita admire intellectual, artistic types. Before the action of the film, Charlotte has brought the genius Clare Quilty (Peter Sellers) into her home, where Lolita first becomes infatuated with him. Later, when the suave European professor Humbert arrives, Charlotte hopes to impress him by waving her cigarette holder at the works of art in her home and making proclamations about the "advanced" culture of the town. With the help of her greatest work of art—Lolita—she draws yet another sophisticated predator into her home, where he tries to dupe both mother and daughter.

Nabokov makes Humbert witty and oddly appealing, but he also makes perfectly clear the moral depravity of his character. Kubrick's Humbert is less depraved and more suave, and the threat of his murderous impulses is diminished by the film's portrayal. One significant alteration in this regard is Kubrick's depiction of Humbert's failed and half-hearted murder fantasies. Rather than show Humbert attempting to leave Mrs. Haze stranded and drowning, he shows Humbert contemplating a shooting "accident." Changing the drowning scene to a scene of guns in the home presents fewer logistical challenges, and it also focuses attention on the American setting and its contrast to the very European Humbert. Charlotte talks of her deceased husband as a great lover of firearms, and Humbert's deadpan quizzical response constitutes part of the subtle humor of the exchange. Charlotte's absurd hypocrisy makes her annoying enough that Humbert seems justified in wanting to get rid of her. When Charlotte snoops in Humbert's diary and reads his description of her as "the Haze woman" and the "fat cow," viewers tend to identify with Humbert's anxiety rather than with Charlotte's pain and humiliation.

In this scene preceding Charlotte's death, Kubrick embellishes Nabokov's screenplay very slightly to make it much more effective dramatically. Instead of muttering to himself, as Nabokov's version suggests, Kubrick has

Humbert speaking to Charlotte, whom he assumes is in the other room. This exchange, where Humbert and the viewer imagine an off-screen Charlotte in the house, heightens the surprise of Humbert arguing on the telephone that his wife cannot be dead. Nabokov's screenplay suggests crosscutting at this point to a shot of an instructor explaining the details of the accident to a roomful of police officers. Kubrick wisely eliminates this distracting and somewhat confusing narrative tactic and simply makes it clear dramatically how the car hit Charlotte. Kubrick goes on to place the audience in the position of co-conspirator with Humbert, as the viewer witnesses him playing the role of grief-stricken husband. The next shot—pure Kubrick—shows Humbert in a bathtub, attempting to tilt a full martini resting on his hairy chest to his lips without using his hands. When friends Jean and John Farlow (Dianna Decker, Jerry Stovin) come into the bathroom to comfort Humbert, they see the gun that he had considered using on Charlotte right before her death. Assuming he is contemplating suicide, they urge him not to do anything rash in the aftermath of his grief. At this point, the father of the man who ran over Charlotte rushes in, hoping to avoid a lawsuit, and offers to pay funeral expenses. Humbert explains graciously that he wouldn't dream of filing a lawsuit. The man seems quite relieved until Humbert continues that he would be happy to have the man pay for burial costs. The entire scene prompts laughter and an unwilling viewer identification with Humbert, who has garnered sympathy from his fellow characters, even as he delights in what for him is nothing but a series of lucky accidents giving him sole control over Lolita.

Humbert's cool indifference in this scene begins to suggest a villainous cynicism that is quickly undermined through ironic humor. The scene implicates the viewer, insofar as he or she finds this sequence comical. The viewer's attitude aligns itself with Humbert's cold-blooded distance and sense of superiority or indifference to poor Charlotte, who is shown to be a cold mother, ready to ship out her own daughter to camp and boarding school until she grows up. The dramatic irony of the neighbors' sympathy for the secretly relieved Humbert makes the viewer complicit with Humbert. Because Kubrick's film and Shelly Winters's performance make Charlotte a buffoonish and exaggerated figure, the audience is unlikely to feel much sympathy for her plight or sense of loss over her death.

Another significant change in Kubrick's rendition of Nabokov's novel is the downplaying of Humbert's violence toward Valerie, his first wife, and later against Lolita. Again, censorship considerations influenced Kubrick and all filmmakers at the time, making them hesitant to portray on-screen violence against women. Kubrick also diminishes sympathy for Lolita in subtle ways. For example, throughout the scenes of traveling across the country with Lolita, the musical "Yaya" score in the background makes Lolita's character seem like a shallow, spoiled teenager, and it makes Humbert's arrangement of this journey seem like a harmless romp. At the same time, these changes and other minor omissions soften and normalize Humbert's character, thus removing a great deal of the moral ambiguity and shock value of the story, an effect that Kubrick wants to counteract. Kubrick's solution to this dilemma is to infuse the narrative throughout with black humor and thereby undermine the melodramatic potential of the story. If he errs on the side of slapstick in creating a caricature in Charlotte or in flattening Lolita's personality, Kubrick nevertheless draws viewers into a deeper engagement with moral issues by encouraging audiences to laugh at the exploits of a murderous pedophile.

Kubrick does not create Lolita as a victim or an object of sentiment. Richard Corliss observes that Lyon's Lo is "in charge." In his words:

> In a 1962 interview, Lyon said of Lo, "I feel sorry for her. She's neurotic and pathetic and she's only interested in herself." Yet as an actress she never editorialises (as Shelly Winters sometimes does), never lets you see her disapproval of the character. She shows imagination and authority in all Lolita's gestations: temptress, dominatrix and brat. Lyon fails only in suggesting, at the end, that the girl, like Humbert, is a victim of misapplied passion. But then, in this Lolita, she is meant to be nothing like that. Humbert is the injured party; Lo is one of the conspirators in his misery.[40]

The literate viewer may chuckle at Humbert as a scoundrel and see in subtle details of mise-en-scène limitations in the character's perceptions. For example, while Humbert moons over Lolita in her abandoned bedroom, the camera shows us photographs of Vladimir Nabokov and Peter Sellers (as Quilty) in the background. This sly, self-reflexive poke in the ribs from Kubrick is the cinematic equivalent of Nabokov's humorous allusions throughout the novel.

Robert Stam argues convincingly that Adrian Lyne's self-conscious manipulation of the camera comes closer to capturing the self-reflexiveness of Nabokov's novel than Kubrick's realist style does. However, when Nabokov uses distancing mechanisms, he does so to undermine and ironize the romantic aspects of his tale. Lyne's 1997 *Lolita*, on the other hand, uses equiv-

Director Adrian Lyne has Dominique Swain wear a retainer to make her Lolita appear younger and to lighten his film's tone.

alent filmic techniques in the service of enfolding viewers more securely in the story, with all its romantic and sentimental elements intact. Lyne's rendition is a much more somber tale, placing greater emphasis on the misery of both Humbert and Lolita. The most important difference between Lyne's version and Kubrick's version is in characterization. At one end of the spectrum, Kubrick tries to alienate his viewer from the material and the players, maintaining a cool distance. At the other end, Lyne does everything he can to manipulate, direct, and draw his viewers into a strong identification with the emotions and situations of the characters. Thirty-four years after Kubrick's dry satirical work, Lyne was left to create another Lolita in the shadow of two artistic giants, and the result of that double anxiety of influence on adaptation is a work that captures a surface disruption and sense of self-consciousness. Respectful of his source material to the point of being worshipful, Lyne's version looks as if he had read the many critiques of Kubrick's film that lament the loss of Nabokov's lovely prose. Consequently, he weights the picture with excessive voice-over narration, even at times when the on-screen action would readily convey the sentiment expressed through Nabokov's and Jeremy Irons's mellifluous voices.

Nabokov, Kubrick, and Lyne all depict a sexually precocious Lolita taking the lead to seduce Humbert.

Kubrick's spare use of interior monologue discourages viewers from identifying with Humbert's point of view. Another element that may distance viewers from the characters in Kubrick's film is the apparent cynicism of both Humbert and Lolita. Kubrick makes Humbert more urbane than the character in Nabokov's novel, and the same sort of slant occurs with Kubrick's jaded depiction of Lolita herself. From the initial shot of Sue Lyon's Lolita peering seductively over her sunglasses, the viewer has a sense that this girl is wise beyond her years. Lyon's version of Lolita is more flat and wisecracking than Nabokov's character, more cynical and calculating than Dominique Swain's portrayal. In contrast to the knowing, seductive gaze of Lyon's Lolita, Swain's grin at a complete stranger is surprisingly wholesome, revealing a retainer that was added to make her seem younger than her actual years. Some viewers find Swain's depiction more satisfying and rich, because of the character's complexity and depth. Jeremy Irons's tortured Humbert takes a page from a series of other characters in the actor's repertoire, from his early role as a hopelessly infatuated gay man in the BBC's *Brideshead Revisited* (1981) to the unwitting lover of a female impersonator in David Cronenberg's *M. Butterfly* (1993). Lyne's casting certainly elicits more sympathy for Humbert and Lolita, but in the process, layers of irony are stripped from the work.

The hair, clothing, and makeup styles of the two Lolitas have a profound effect on character as well. Whereas Kubrick's Lolita wears her hair in a slightly bouffant flip, with the Peter Pan collars and full gathered skirts of the late 1950s and early 1960s, Lyne's Lolita has braids and wears clothes reminiscent of the pinafores of Dorothy in *The Wizard of Oz* (1939). Lyne's authentic period clothing fails to ring true, however, because he uses a film style that is distinctly characteristic of the late twentieth century. Soft focus, pastel hues, and the use of slow motion and lens distortion all mark the film as a product of the late 1990s. Kubrick's use of black-and-white photography and a relatively static camera sets the action in a sort of timeless "beatnik" era of American filmmaking. The black-and-white photography also emphasizes the film's noir elements of mystery, a femme fatale, seedy locales, and even seedier activities. The foregrounding of Clare Quilty's character, with his mysterious companion Vivian Darkbloom (Marianne Stone), spoofs the noir and beatnik traditions by making the duo look a bit like the spies Boris and Natasha in the *Rocky and Bullwinkle* television cartoons (1959–1961). When Quilty imitates a police officer, his nervous laugh and pseudo-intellectual repetition of phrases make him seem at least as disturbed as Humbert. His imitation of a psychiatrist also sends up Freudian jargon, a jab at psychoanalysis that would please Nabokov, who often declared his disdain for modern psychiatry and psychological symbolism.

Quilty's character is far less important in Lyne's film, no doubt in part because he did not have the brilliant Peter Sellers to improvise and flesh out the character. Lyne comments on this influence in an interview: "Kubrick's film is much more about performance bravura by Peter Sellers as Quilty. I wanted to make a movie where Quilty was much more in the background and where you focus really on Humbert and his relationship with Lolita, which was what I thought was important."[41] While Frank Langella did not contribute substantially to the character of Quilty, Lyne acknowledges that a number of the mannerisms of Lolita were contributed by the improvisations and suggestions of Dominique Swain. Both Kubrick and Lyne took full advantage of the talents and ideas of their actors, and their collaborations resulted in additions beyond both the novel and the original screenplays. Stephen Schiff comments on the actors "stumble[ing] into an inspired improvisation," while they and Lyne remain "as true to [the] screenplay as they can be."[42]

Although Lyne, Schiff, and the actors all attempted to capture Nabokov's subtle humor, Lyne's *Lolita* contains barely a hint of irony from opening to closing. Ennio Morricone's sentimental score plays at key points throughout, with a haunting opening melody reminiscent of the score from Jean-Jacques Annaud's *The Lover* (1992) and the Lolita theme song an echo of Andrea Morricone's melody from Giuseppe Tornatore's *Cinema Paradiso* (1989). Lyne pays tribute to Kubrick in several key scenes, even though screenwriter Stephen Schiff claims that he avoided viewing the original Kubrick film before writing the screenplay. Lyne reread Nabokov's work a number of times, and in the places where he deviates from the novel, it is clear that he is intimately familiar with Kubrick's film as well. The opening scene, in which Humbert (Jeremy Irons) weaves along a small road in the misty countryside, is an homage, however unconscious, to Kubrick's opening scene. The action is sensationalized a bit by featuring a blood-spattered Humbert, a near accident with a haywagon, and some endangered livestock. Irons delivers the voice-over in a much more guilt-ridden, elegiac tone than the dispassionate timbre of Mason's Humbert. Throughout Lyne's film, the voice-over and acting emphasize Humbert's sense of guilt and remorse, and in the pivotal hotel scene, minor alterations establish a religious backdrop to the action. Instead of populating the hotel with the state police convention of Kubrick's film, the hotel is filled with guests from a flower show and a "Glory of Christ" convention, a nod to Nabokov's description of the lobby as filled with "old ladies and clergymen."[43]

Lyne alters Nabokov's take on Lolita's experience, picturing her in close-up, filled with apparent sexual passion.

Both filmmakers soften the character of Humbert, in a variety of ways, and probably for multiple reasons. Certainly Kubrick was constrained by censors to eliminate the more sordid aspects of Humbert's sexual obsession. Given the loosening of censorship by the 1990s, it is not clear why Lyne contrives to have the sexual relationship between Humbert and Lolita appear more consensual than as depicted in the novel. The narrator of the novel describes Lolita's lack of enjoyment of their sexual encounters: "Never did she vibrate under my touch, and a strident 'what d'you think you are doing?' was all I got for my pains."[44] One scene described in the novel, in which Lolita reads the comics while sitting on Humbert's lap having sex with him, is altered significantly by Lyne's film. At the beginning of this scene she appears at first to be laughing at the comics and then laughing at Humbert, but by the end of the encounter, she is pictured in close-up, her face quivering with apparent sexual passion.

Other omissions further normalize Humbert and the relationship. For instance, neither filmmaker includes Humbert's fantasy of impregnating Lolita in order to produce future nymphets for his enjoyment. The films also fail to depict Humbert's habit of paying Lolita to caress him while he gazes at other young girls, a practice that might have been easily captured in a scene that serves as a turning point in the novel: "I sat beside Dolly just behind that neck and that hair, and unbuttoned my overcoat and for sixty-five cents plus the permission to participate in the school play, had Dolly put her inky chalky, red-knuckled hand under the desk."[45]

Both filmic portrayals of the couple's odyssey across America eliminate one of the most moving descriptions of Lolita's unhappiness, as Humbert describes it in the novel: "Our long journey had only defiled with a sinuous trail of slime the lovely, trustful, dreamy, enormous country that by then, in retrospect, was no more to us than a collection of dog-eared maps, ruined tour books, old tires, and her sobs in the night—every night, every night— the moment I feigned sleep."[46] This statement captures a major theme of Nabokov's novel, demonstrating how Humbert destroys Lolita even as he captures her, a deterioration that is embodied through the increasingly tawdry settings. The couple's physical journey is effectively detailed by Lyne's American location shots, in contrast to Kubrick's English countryside montage, but both directors gloss over the hidden sadness of Lolita's character. Nabokov, hardly a proto-feminist, nonetheless at least hints at the absence of Lolita's point of view in the narrative. In contrast, both Kubrick, the Enlightenment director, and Lyne, the romantic director, produce works that are firmly rooted in the phallocentric vision of woman as an obscure object of desire, implacable and ultimately inscrutable—a face without interiority.

If there is a certain degree of realism in Lyne's depiction of American landscapes, the director undermines this quality by calling attention to the filmmaking process, stylizing editing, color saturation, and camera speed. His nighttime scenes are shot with a heavy blue filter that gives them a surreal comic book aspect. In a dream sequence, the camera lens distorts and warps the picture drastically. In the climactic scene at the hotel Enchanted Hunters, Lyne violates the laws of continuity editing by creating a jump cut, showing Humbert entering the bathroom clothed and immediately exiting in pajamas, in imitation of Nabokov's own cinematic description of the moment: "I seemed to have shed my clothes and slipped into pajamas with the kind of fantastic instantaneousness which is implied when in a cinematographic scene the process of changing is cut."[47] The manipulation has a distancing effect, even though it captures the character's subjective experience of the moment. Kubrick creates similar distance during this scene by adding a slapstick routine with a folding cot collapsing as he tries in vain to fall asleep, tortured by his desire for Lolita. Nabokov disliked Kubrick's rendition, but Nabokov himself emphasizes the humor of the moment by writing of the hotel sounds—deep-throated toilets flushing and couples making vociferous love in nearby rooms.

Lyne plays most of the film for sentiment and sensuality, punctuated by whimsical moments of the couple playing tennis or Humbert pushing Lolita's feet out of his face as she lounges in the backseat of the car. Lyne's detailing of the couple's deteriorating relationship makes Humbert's physical violence toward Lolita look like part of the couple's passionate play, a sadomasochistic pattern that Lyne set in his earlier blockbusters *Nine and a Half Weeks* (1986) and *Fatal Attraction* (1987). Because most of the film is awash in so much melodrama, tears, and sentiment, the ending seems anticlimactic. In contrast, Kubrick's *Lolita* plays most of the film for laughs, practically eliminating the physical violence of Nabokov's novel and laying on slapstick at the most embarrassing and anxiety-laden moments. In the conclusion of Kubrick's work, however, the film surprises the viewer with a moment of real emotion, as we watch the cynical, rascally Humbert try to cover his sadness and desperation. He makes his first and last act of true generosity in the entire narrative, as the sentimental score swells, this time playing without irony, to stunning effect. For Kubrick, this scene is the climax, and the ensuing pursuit and murder of Quilty are merely the denouement. Lyne, on the other hand, makes ineffective use of the poignant reconciliation between Humbert and Lolita, focusing instead on the gore and melodrama of the final confrontation between the two men. In Lyne's universe, the climax is the shootout (if a lopsided affair), and Quilty's gushing blood is engineered to serve as the visual high point in much the same way that slow-motion depiction of death works in Arthur Penn's *Bonnie and Clyde* (1967). Lyne's use of stylized visuals in the closing scenes undermines his claim that he wished to keep the focus on the relationship between Humbert and Lolita. The extended gun play, spurting blood, and hysterical emphasis on Quilty's violent ending seem at odds with the earlier role of the character, whom Robert Stam describes as seeming "like a generic extraterrestrial, someone who seems to have wandered in from another studio's backlot."[48]

Lyne's sense of what plays well with audience is keen, and many contemporary viewers prefer Lyne's version to Kubrick's, probably in part because it has a more modern feel, more explanatory backstory, and a clearer appeal to emotions. Some viewers who have read the novel prefer Lyne's relative faithfulness to the original source. Lyne's *Lolita* also contains the kind of visual interest and mobile camera that fans of MTV and VH1 appreciate, in stark contrast to the cool detachment of Kubrick's distanced, unobtrusive camera. The theme of tragic obsessive love is an easier pill for modern audiences to swallow than is the bitter poison of Kubrick's social satire on the decadence of American society and the impossibility of pure love. It is clear that for both filmmakers, adapting *Lolita* was both a labor of love and a daunting challenge. Nabokov acknowledges the tensions of adaptation, along with the difficulties inherent in the enterprise:

> The modifications, the garbling of my best little finds, the omission of entire scenes, the addition of new ones, and all sorts of other changes may not have been sufficient to erase my name from the credit titles but they certainly made the picture as unfaithful to the original script as an American poet's translation from Rimbaud or Pasternak. I hasten to add that my present comments should definitely not be construed as reflecting any belated grudge, any high-pitched deprecation of Kubrick's creative approach. When adapting Lolita to the speaking screen he saw my novel in one way, I saw it in another—that's all, nor can one deny that infinite fidelity may be an author's ideal but can prove a producer's ruin.[49]

Squabbles over whose *Lolita* is the real *Lolita* may obscure the important and often overlooked fact that the eponymous character of Lolita remains inscrutable and unknowable in all versions. One might argue compellingly that among the three faces of Lolita—Nabokov's, Kubrick's, and Lyne's—each successive rendition of the spirit within the sylph becomes more blurred and distorted. Devotees of the great auteur Kubrick maintain that his *Lolita*, despite its bouts with censors, captures the essence of Nabokov's wit and darkness more truly than Lyne's sappy manipulation. Defenders of Lyne's version might counter that he simply amplifies the sentimentality and steamy sensuality lurking in Nabokov's rendition. I would assert that all three artists capture only a glimmer of the humanity behind the icon—the suffering, complexity, and wry wisdom masked by the haunting face of Lolita. So, although censorship prompted some of Kubrick's omissions and sensationalism fueled some of Lyne's excesses, what created the vagueness of all three artists' portraits of Lolita was an utter inability to inhabit the interior of the female mind in the way that allowed Gustav Flaubert to say "Madame Bovary, c'est moi." Mario Falsetto argues that "the character of Quilty is a major presence in *Lolita*, perhaps *the* presence, and more often than not viewers feel his presence by his absence."[50] But even more absent is Lolita herself, for viewers see and hear more about the surface of what other characters see than they do of what she perceives. Just as Nabokov's narrator Humbert expresses his failure to capture in words the essential object of desire, "I could not parade living Lolita,"[51] the filmmakers are humbled before their subject. Even with this shortcoming, however, both films make a lie of Nabokov's final words for Humbert: "And this is the only immortality you and I may share, my Lolita."[52] Stanley Kubrick and Adrian Lyne bring to life two new faces of Lolita, lending her and Humbert's vision of her yet another incarnation, yet another immortality, yet another face whose interior being eludes us.

NOTES

1. Robert Stam, "Beyond Fidelity: The Dialogics of Adaptation," in *Film Adaptation*, ed. James Naremore (Piscataway, NJ: Rutgers University Press, 2000), 75–76.
2. Tim Dirks, "Lolita," in *The Greatest Films*, www.filmsite.org/greatestfilms.org (2004).
3. Gene Phillips and Rodney Hill, *The Encyclopedia of Stanley Kubrick* (New York: Facts on File, 2002), 126.
4. Alfred Appel, "Lolita: The Springboard of Parody," in *Modern Critical Interpretations: Vladimir Nabokov's Lolita*, ed. Harold Bloom (New York: Chelsea House Publishers, 1987), 50.
5. Ibid., 35–51.
6. Vladimir Nabokov, *Lolita: A Screenplay*, 1st international ed. (New York: Vintage, 1977), xiii.
7. Coury Turczyn, "Adrian Lyne's Controversial Lolita Finds Its True Home—Cable TV," http://weeklywire.com/ww/08-10-98/knox_guru.html.
8. Adrian Lyne, commentary track for *Lolita*, DVD (Vidmark/Trimark, 2002).
9. See discussions in Suellen Stringer-Hye, "Vladimir Nabokov and Popular Culture," in *Discourse and Ideology in Nabokov's Prose*, ed. David H. J. Larmour (London: Routledge, 2002), and "An Interview with Stephen Schiff," in *Zembla: The Nabokov Butterfly Net*, CoLOlations, in *The Lolita Effect*, http://www.libraries.psu.edu/nabokov/loleff.htm (accessed September 17, 2001).
10. Stephen Schiff, *Lolita: The Book of the Film* (New York: Applause Books, 1998), xiv.
11. Ibid., xii.
12. Turczyn, "Lolita," 1.
13. See Schiff, introduction to *Lolita*, xix.
14. Turczyn, "Lolita," 1.
15. Robert Stam, *Literature Through Film* (Oxford: Blackwell, 2005), 238.
16. Stanley Kauffmann, "Humbug Humbug," *New Republic*, July 2, 1962, 29–30.
17. Francis Russell, "Petronius Redivivus," *National Review*, September 11, 1962, 198–200, 199.

18. Hollis Alpert, "The Bubble Gum Siren," *Saturday Review*, June 23, 1962, 40.
19. Stam, *Literature Through Film*, 228.
20. Stringer-Hye, www.libraries.psu.edu/nabokov/colo.htm.
21. James Naremore, ed., *Film Adaptation* (Piscataway, NJ: Rutgers University Press, 2000), 13.
22. Schiff, *Lolita*, xv.
23. Tim Dirks, "Lolita," in *The Greatest Films*, www.filmsite.org/greatestfilms.org. www.timsite.org.tott.html (2004).
24. Michael Marr, "The Reading Experience: Originality," *Times Literary Supplement*, April 2, 2004, 1. See also www.smh.com.au/articles/2004/03/21/1079823238702.html.
25. Marr, "Reading Experience," 1.
26. Alfred Appel, Jr., "The End of the Road: Dark Cinema and 'Lolita.'" *Film Comment* 10, no. 5 (1974): 25–31; idem, "Lolita: The Springboard of Parody," 50.
27. Appel, "Lolita," 50.
28. Ibid., 51.
29. Nabokov, *Lolita: A Screenplay*, xiii.
30. Phillips and Hill, *Encyclopedia*, 236.
31. Stam, *Literature Through Film*, 229.
32. Nabokov, *Lolita: A Screenplay*, xii.
33. Ibid., xiii.
34. See Mario Falsetto's discussion in *Stanley Kubrick: A Narrative and Stylistic Analysis*, 2nd ed. (Westport, CT: Praeger, 2001), 8.
35. Stam, *Literature Through Film*, 230.
36. Falsetto, *Stanley Kubrick*, 12.
37. "A Tribute to Stanley Kubrick—Lolita," http://itwebmaster.iit.edu/kelccthe/design/filmography/Lolita.htm (accessed April 4, 2004).
38. Nabokov, *Lolita: A Screenplay*, xi.
39. Bosley Crowther, "Screen: *Lolita*, Vladimir Nabokov's Adaptation of His Novel," *New York Times*, June 14, 1962, 23.
40. Richard Corliss, *Lolita* (London: British Film Institute, 1977), 2.
41. Rod Armstrong, "Adrian Lyne on Kubrick, Nabokov, and a Girl Named Lolita," www.reel.com/reel.asp?node=features/interviews/lyne (2004).
42. Stringer-Hye, 2.
43. Vladimir Nabokov, *Lolita*, 2nd international ed. (New York: Vintage, 1997), 117.
44. Ibid., 166.
45. Ibid., 198.
46. Ibid., 176.
47. Ibid., 128.
48. Stam, *Literature Through Film*, 240.
49. Nabokov, *Lolita: A Screenplay*, xii, xiii.

50. Falsetto, *Stanley Kubrick*, 111.
51. Nabokov, *Lolita*, 308.
52. Ibid., 309.

WORKS CITED

Alpert, Hollis. "The Bubble Gum Siren." *Saturday Review*, June 23, 1962, 40.
Appel, Alfred, Jr. "The End of the Road: Dark Cinema and 'Lolita.'" *Film Comment* 10, no. 5 (1974): 25–31.
Appel, Alfred. "Lolita: The Springboard of Parody." *Modern Critical Interpretations: Vladimir Nabokov's Lolita*, edited by Harold Bloom, 35–51. New York: Chelsea House Publishers, 1987.
Armstrong, Rod. "Adrian Lyne on Kubrick, Nabokov, and a Girl Named Lolita." www.reel.com/reel.asp?node=features/interviews/lyne/ (accessed September 4, 2004).
Caldwell, Christopher. "Who Invented Lolita?" *New York Times Magazine*, May 23, 2004, 11.
Cleaver, Hannah. *The Telegraph*, March 22, 2004. www.smh/com.au/articles/2004/03/21/1079823238702.html (accessed February 24, 2004).
Corliss, Richard. *Lolita*. London: British Film Institute, 1977.
Crowther, Bosley. "Screen: *Lolita*, Vladimir Nabokov's Adaptation of His Novel." *New York Times*, June 14, 1962, 23.
Dirks, Tim. "Lolita." www.filmsite.org/greatestfilms.org (accessed January 14, 2004).
Falsetto, Mario. *Stanley Kubrick: A Narrative and Stylistic Analysis*. 2nd ed. Westport, CT: Praeger, 2001.
Kauffmann, Stanley. "Humbug Humbug." *New Republic*, July 2, 1962, 29–30.
Kubrick, Stanley, dir. *Lolita*. DVD. Los Angeles: Warner Bros, 1961, 2001.
Lyne, Adrian, dir. *Lolita*. DVD. Pathe, Showtime, Trimark Home Video, 1998.
Nabokov, Vladimir. *Lolita*. 2nd international edition. New York: Vintage, 1997.
———. *Lolita: A Screenplay*. 1st international edition. New York: Vintage, 1977.
Naremore, James, ed. *Film Adaptation*. Piscataway, NJ: Rutgers University Press, 2000.
Phillips, Gene, and Rodney Hill. *The Encyclopedia of Stanley Kubrick*. New York: Facts on File. 2002.
Russell, Francis. "Petronius Redivivus." *National Review*, September 11, 1962, 198–200.
Stam, Robert. "Beyond Fidelity: The Dialogics of Adaptation." In *Film Adaptation*, edited by James Naremore. Piscataway, NJ: Rutgers University Press, 2000.
———. *Literature Through Film*. Oxford: Blackwell, 2005.
Stringer-Hye, Suellen. *CoLOlations*. 9/17/2001. In *The Lolita Effect*. www.libraries.psu.edu/nabokov/colo.htm (accessed April 10, 2004).

Turczyn, Coury. Movie Guru. "Adrian Lyne's Controversial Lolita Finds Its True Home—Cable TV." http://weeklywire.com/ww/08-10-98/knox_guru.html (accessed February 22, 2008).

"A Tribute to Stanley Kubrick—Lolita." http://itwebmaster.iit.edu/kelccthe/design/filmography/Lolita.htm (accessed April 4, 2004).

9

TRAFFIC/TRAFFIK
Race, Globalization, and Family in Soderbergh's Remake

//

Mark Gallagher

THIS ESSAY CONSIDERS A RELATIVELY RARE FORM OF MEDIA ADAPtation, from television miniseries to feature film. The 1989 British television miniseries *Traffik* scrutinizes the global drug trade through narratives set in Europe and Asia, while North American settings provide the backdrop for its adaptation, the 2000 Hollywood film *Traffic*. The transformation of the sprawling television serial *Traffik* into the lengthy but contained feature *Traffic* involved condensation, reemphasis, and, arguably, misrepresentation. The U.S. *Traffic*, directed by Steven Soderbergh, adopts Hollywood films' longstanding pattern of recasting social and political issues in accessible, morally legible, melodramatic terms. This transformation contributed to *Traffic*'s popular appeal but at the same time aligned the film with problematic formations of race, culture, and gender. The British *Traffik*, by contrast, explicitly represents the Third World of Pakistan and Afghanistan in its characters, narratives, and settings. The British serial, produced by the Channel Four network and directed by Alistair Reid, has a Eurocentric focus that dilutes the cultural specificity of its Asian plot. Still, the miniseries remarkably implicates the West in a global system of economic and social exploitation, a connection the U.S. film does not make.

Film adaptations of television miniseries almost never occur. More common is the opposite trajectory, with popular films providing the basis for television series or miniseries.[1] The miniseries format exploits television's strengths: relatively long program durations, allowing extensive and detailed narratives; a small-screen format privileging character interactions and dialogue; and segmentation through commercials, facilitating crosscutting among multiple story lines. Adaptations of British television series to U.S. films are rare; since the 1990s, major U.S. films adapted from British television have included only the campy action-spy films *The Avengers* (1998) and

In British television's miniseries Traffik, *co-protagonist Fazal (Jamal Shah) first appears tending a field of opium poppies.*

The Saint (1997), both adapted from 1960s' series. U.S.-based media conglomerates own no portions of Britain's broadcast networks. *Traffik* producer Channel Four is operated by a nonprofit corporation but is supported in part through advertising. Its programming is thus subject to market dictates, making *Traffik*'s complexity all the more notable. The original *Traffik* efficiently sketches out political and economic conflicts through its characters' interactions, and the condensed adaptation is more economical still, relying on many brief scenes that begin in medias res, gesturing toward complexities not fully on view.

The transformation of *Traffik* into *Traffic* follows three principal trajectories, each traceable in turn to the film's producers, its screenwriter, and director/cinematographer Soderbergh. First, two separate production efforts arose for a film about the politics, military involvement, and street-level consequences of the drug trade in the Americas. In the mid-1990s, U.S. independent producer Laura Bickford initiated one effort, while the established production team of Edward Zwick and Marshall Herskovitz initiated another; these projects ultimately merged. Bickford claims to have seen the initial broadcast of the *Traffik* miniseries while living in London and to have been intrigued by its multiple intersecting story lines. In years following, she says, she compiled news articles about the drug trade.[2] As the film's production took shape late in the 1990s, the trio of producers enlisted

New York Times Mexico correspondent Tim Golden as story consultant. Some scenes in the produced film represent Golden's anecdotes rather than Gaghan's screenplay. The film incorporates a patchwork of journalistic and governmental accounts compiled at the producers' behest. A staged Washington, D.C., cocktail party scene featuring actual U.S. politicians nicely encapsulates the film's implicit claims of authenticity, along with its selective treatment of its subject. This scene mixes fact and fiction in intriguing ways: most of the brief polemics from *Traffic*'s screenplay do not appear in the film (some do, such as the sound bite-worthy "Addicts don't vote"), replaced by brief polemics improvised by Massachusetts governor William Weld, California senator Barbara Boxer, and others. These major politicians' actual policy positions compete with the film's more sensational elements originating in the screenplay.

The second notable trajectory relates to the work and autobiography of screenwriter Stephen Gaghan, a recovered narcotics abuser born into a comfortable upper-middle-class life, who in the 1990s became a writer for network television police and legal shows. Gaghan had also written a screenplay about wealthy young self-abusers, "Habit," which had reached Zwick and Herskovitz, and parts of which survive in *Traffic*. In interviews surrounding the film's release, Gaghan repeatedly emphasized his tumultuous history.[3] Gaghan's public disclosure of his past narcotics abuse helped reframe media discussions of *Traffic* during its theatrical run: rather than focusing on the adaptation of a little-known British miniseries, articles considered the film's contemporaneity and authenticity vis-à-vis Gaghan's autobiography. The released film is largely a remake of its predecessor—most plotlines, characters, scenes, and dialogue appear in both texts, with some material altered but much reproduced almost exactly—but the deployment of Gaghan's autobiography into journalistic discourse encouraged emphasis on his adapted screenplay rather than on the original *Traffik* script or miniseries.[4]

Gaghan's subjective interest in the avowedly tortured lives of affluent adolescents contributes to *Traffic*'s areas of emphasis, as does his experience scripting characters involved in law and law enforcement. Combining Gaghan's television-genre specialties with his autobiography, *Traffic*'s screenplay foregrounds criminal activity, police investigation, political and legal maneuvering, and the effects of these activities on privileged yet vulnerable teens. Gaghan's involvement in the project commenced after Bickford began developing the film. Soderbergh claims to have become interested in the subject of drugs at the same time as Bickford, and eventually Bickford and Soderbergh began to work together on the project. They learned of Gaghan's drug-related script in circulation and the writer's collaboration with Zwick and Herskovitz. The projects coalesced, with the three producers overseeing Gaghan's adaptation of the *Traffik* screenplay. Gaghan's screenplay includes more than 260 scenes; though not all were shot, the film includes crosscutting among its four narratives about every two minutes. Some scenes take up only a minute or so of screen time, in contrast to the television *Traffik*, in which many sequences play out at length in a single setting.

The film's third discernible influence is traceable to Soderbergh, whose films have evinced remarkable directorial autonomy, particularly in light of their modest box-office performances. (Long after the 1989 success of *sex, lies, and videotape*, Soderbergh secured major-studio funding and A-list casts for films such as *Out of Sight* [1998], *Erin Brockovich* [2000], and *Traffic*, despite weak returns for all his films throughout the 1990s.) *Traffic* offers multiple protagonists, strong narrative ambiguity, and an overall semidocumentary aesthetic combined with antirealist color.[5] These narrative and formal techniques follow from U.S. and European films Soderbergh has cited repeatedly as influences on his work, both prior to and during *Traffic*'s production: *The Battle of Algiers* (1965), *Z* (1969), *The French Connection* (1971), and *All the President's Men* (1976).[6] Soderbergh's sensibility is one of refinement and reconceptualization. *Traffic*'s status—as adaptation, as reconception of Vietnam- and Watergate-era thrillers, as continuation of the filmmaking styles of prominent U.S. directors in the pre-blockbuster era—owes much to this sensibility. Like many contemporary filmmakers, Soderbergh has directed films adapted from previous texts made both within and outside the Hollywood system. Yet even amid the U.S. industry's ongoing mania for remakes of existing films, Soderbergh's willingness to remake earlier films borders on the obsessive. He has directed remakes of the 1949 film noir *Criss Cross* (as 1995's *The Underneath*), the 1960 Rat Pack caper film *Ocean's Eleven*, and Andrei Tarkovsky's dense 1972 film *Solaris* (and its source, Stanislaw Lem's 1961 novel of the same title). Other Soderbergh films adapt other media: *Kafka* (1991), *King of the Hill* (1993), *Out of Sight*, and *The Good German* (2006) all originated as novels, and *Gray's Anatomy* (1996) continued a series of films of Spalding Gray monologues. Notwithstanding the critical and box-office failure of *Solaris* (2002) and *Full Frontal* (2002), Soderbergh remains one of the most significant directors of popular U.S. cinema. *Traffic*, in terms both of its critical reception and the complexity of its source text, is arguably the most notable remake directed by Soderbergh to date.

Both *Traffik* and *Traffic* rely on a sprawling narrative structure. The miniseries *Traffik* narrates the workings and consequences of the drug trade through three intersecting plotlines. First, the series offers the story of a Pakistani opium farmer, Fazal, his family, and his eventual drug-trafficker employer. A second, Germany-based narrative involves German undercover policemen's efforts to imprison a wealthy heroin importer who masquerades as a businessman, coupled with the attempts of the smuggler's wife to pay her husband's massive debts by becoming a trafficker herself (one might regard these as two separate story lines, but they intersect to a far greater degree than do the other narratives). Third, the series presents the story of a British cabinet minister whose daughter is a heroin addict. The series shifts between personal and political registers, consistently engaging the political consequences of personal choices and vice versa. In comparison, the U.S. *Traffic* redefines a global social and political issue as a personal issue of concern principally to a small group of Americans (and one Mexican, played by the Puerto Rico–born Benicio Del Toro). In addition to transforming a six-part, five-and-one-half-hour narrative made for British television into a star-driven, two-and-one-half-hour U.S. feature film, the producers of the U.S. *Traffic* restage the story's content in a more circumscribed geographic region, constructing a U.S.-Mexico focus with far different racial and political inflections than the original's Western European and Central Asian settings.

The differences between the two texts follow in particular from the narrowing of geographic emphasis. The original *Traffik* devotes substantial time to heroin production: the farmer Fazal (Jamal Shah) first appears tending a field of opium poppies, and later, when he becomes a driver and assistant to trafficker Tariq Butt (Talat Hussain), Fazal and viewers watch as another man performs the process by which harvested poppies are transformed into raw heroin. Viewers also witness the destruction of Fazal's crops by Pakistani troops, Fazal's inability to find work in impoverished, overpopulated Karachi, his arrest when Pakistani authorities intercepts a heroin shipment, and Tariq Butt's strongarmed negotiations with an Afghani heroin manufacturer and with would-be trafficker Helen Rosshalde (Lindsay Duncan). Fazal is a complex figure who sacrifices his ethics for money (and its attendant but short-lived comforts for his family), and finally loses his wife. He gains nothing; though he eventually kills Tariq Butt, the series never suggests that Butt's death will markedly affect the heroin trade. Overall, through Fazal's trials and the interactions of British cabinet minister Jack Lithgow (Bill Paterson) with other Pakistanis, *Traffik* represents the troubled relations between Great Britain and its former colony, Pakistan.[7]

In place of the complex Third World narrative, the U.S. *Traffic* narrates the independent police work of Javier Rodriguez Rodriguez (Benicio Del

Toro) and his subsequent affiliation with the corrupt Mexican army general Salazar (Tomás Milian). Javier's contact with American DEA agents leads to the end of Salazar's activities, and shortly thereafter to the general's death. Ultimately, the film suggests that one or two major Mexican traffickers have been put to rest. An intelligence briefing attributes limitless resources to traffickers, but the film identifies only the two cartels, so their demise promises some sort of victory and narrative closure. The total absence of Colombia from the film—the country is never mentioned—facilitates this closure. As for Mexico, *Traffic* includes one diplomatic interaction, a meeting between U.S. drug czar Robert Wakefield (Michael Douglas) and Mexico's General Salazar. This brief meeting of the film's most influential American character and its most diabolical villain helps the various narratives cohere but only by recourse to thriller genre convention, with power brokers from different spheres squaring off in an official setting. Overall, *Traffic*'s U.S.-Mexico focus can be attributed to the need to contain the various narrative threads, the narrow view of screenwriter Gaghan (whose script "Habit" concerned wealthy U.S. drug users, not the global political economy of the drug trade), and the influence of story consultant Tim Golden.[8] Golden recounted, for example, a story of the Mexican army's suspicious interception of a drug shipment, which became *Traffic*'s memorable opening scene.

Upon the television rebroadcast of the British *Traffik* in the United States, many critics unfavorably compared the U.S. film's moral clarity to the more complex political and moral terrain of the miniseries.[9] Rather than asserting which text is more complex or satisfying, I wish to compare the formations of gender, race relations, and political-economic ties among nations in the British miniseries and the U.S. film, and to understand how the adaptation process contributes to the texts' substantial differences. Beyond rendering social and political conflicts in melodramatic terms, the U.S. *Traffic* offers a conservative notion of a white, patriarch-led family as the solution to its conflicts. In comparison, the British *Traffik* makes the family the primary site of violation, and the terminal nature of this violation partly overshadows the final representation of the family as the unit around which resolution occurs. In their insistence on the resilience of the patriarchal figure and their complementary ambivalence about women's agency, both texts fall short of explicitly progressive stances regarding gender. Both texts' resolutions suggest that even filmmakers who support progressive challenges to dominant institutions remain committed to the legitimacy of patriarchal authority. This ideological entrenchment suggests further directions for criticism of mainstream film texts that purport to advance progressive stances.

Both versions of *Traffic/k* build fictional narratives around the international narcotics trade, setting events in two or more nations and defining characters according to racial as well as national identities. The U.S. characters in Soderbergh's *Traffic* include an affectless drug smuggler, Carlos Ayala (played by Cuban-born Steven Bauer); his unscrupulous white lawyer (Dennis Quaid); a white patriarchal hero, incoming drug czar Robert Wakefield; and two DEA agents of color (played by African-American Don Cheadle and Puerto Rican-American Luis Guzmán). In its Mexico plot, the film depicts characters as almost universally corrupt, with the exception of the incomparably noble policeman Javier Rodriguez. Del Toro delivers most of his lines in Spanish and adopts a thick foreign accent for his few scenes in English.[10] While recognizable to U.S. viewers from his many English-language supporting roles in Hollywood films, in *Traffic* he performs as a Mexican, constructing a linguistic and cultural distance from his preexisting star persona. Because of this preexisting persona, though, his role anchors the Mexico scenes with a recognizably American (that is, U.S.-American, English-speaking) presence. The film thus deploys ethnic and cultural signifiers in contradictory ways: in particular, its substantial usage of Spanish-language dialogue extends most Hollywood cinema's informal limits on representations of ethnic and national identity.[11] Still, the film partly recuperates this range by linking its morally positive figures to U.S. origins, either as characters or performers.

Race representation informs not only the U.S. *Traffic*'s mobilization of audience sympathies but also its provision of pleasure to viewers. The two nonwhite DEA agents, Gordon (Cheadle) and Castro (Guzmán), provide the bulk of the film's comedy, their offbeat banter partly conforming to comic-minority stereotypes but also intermittently disrupting the film's overall grave tone. Other comic moments come from figures either playing or read as people of color: Carlos Ayala's wife, Helena (Catherine Zeta-Jones), and his underling, Eduardo Ruiz (Miguel Ferrer). Constructions of race, and the parallel implication of otherness, thus underwrite the film's deployment of humor. Whereas comedy offers a range of expression for performers figured as other and a source of pleasure for viewers, it also marginalizes the characters in a film whose tone is principally serious to the point of humorlessness. The comic moments productively unsettle the film's ideological project, but they also rob the characters of the ability to matter, to weigh in rhetorically on the film's subject of the narcotics trade. Ruiz offers some lucid rhetoric about the futility of U.S. efforts to stop drug trafficking, but his status as an imprisoned cocaine smuggler substantially dilutes the moral weight of his polemics.[12] The British *Traffik*, in comparison, lends an acid wit to many of its characters, granting equivalent value to their distinct anger, ruthlessness, and frustration.

The U.S. *Traffic*'s conservative racial politics and moralizing tone surrounding substance use complement its prudishness about sex and sexuality. Notably absent from both the U.S. *Traffic* and the British *Traffik* are representations of romantic relationships or of sex, except to the extent that such relationships lead to drug abuse and victimization. Accordingly, the drug addiction of the white government official's daughter, Caroline (Erika Christensen in the U.S. film, Julia Ormond in the British series), in both versions results in her sexual debasement. In both she turns to prostitution, and in the U.S. version she appears engaged in sex with a naked black man from whom she procures narcotics, a scene that melodramatically embodies anxieties about miscegenation and white female purity. In both texts, sex appears only as a consequence of drug use, and the U.S. film shows Caroline's boyfriend Seth (Topher Grace) plying her with drugs, then encouraging her to have sex. In both texts, too, the only other sexual subplot involves a disreputable lawyer's machinations to coerce his drug trafficker client's wife, Helen/Helena, into sex. Despite, or because of, the rhetoric of family circulating in both texts (most explicitly in the U.S. version, in Wakefield's closing speech, in which he asserts that a war on drugs requires "waging war on our own children"), sexual relationships appear unseemly at best, and always as the exercise of a diabolical male privilege. Rather than issuing an explicitly feminist critique of women's positions in the economy of drug trafficking, though, the texts suggest that drug use leads women to victimization, a route they take after rejecting the protection of patriarchal figures. Since no male drug users turn to prostitution in either text, viewers can infer that women are particularly susceptible to hard drugs. Notably, the compromised position of Helen/Helena does support a feminist reading, in that her vulnerability results from her husband's criminal activities and subsequent arrest, which leaves her at the mercy of a series of rapacious or murderous men. In this respect, both versions of *Traffic/k* resolutely show patriarchy not to be on Helen/Helena's side. However, threats to her evaporate with the return of her husband, who immediately polices against other men's sexual or violent advances.

The British *Traffik* periodically invokes issues of gender inequity, but the U.S. film appears blind to the ways the drug trade, like other economic systems, disproportionately renders women vulnerable to abuse and exploitation. The U.S. *Traffic* reserves its greatest outrage for victimized women of the upper-middle class, the teenager Caroline and the mother Helena, but contextualizes their credulity-stretching plights in archly melodramatic terms. Only the British *Traffik* depicts male criminality as a lethal threat to women's bodies. To pay for her husband's release from jail, Fazal's wife, Sabira (Ismat Shah Jahan), is forced to serve as a drug mule, a role requiring her to swallow dozens of heroin-filled condoms. One of these packages leaks, causing her death and leaving her two young children temporarily parentless. The choice of a Third World woman as the penultimate victim of the drug trade allows the series to maintain a fantasy of white invulnerability, or at least of extraordinarily good fortune. In historical reality, white European women are markedly less vulnerable to a range of bodily threats—whether from disease, male violence, or other sources—than are women in impoverished nations. Nevertheless, the construction of the Third World woman as hapless victim rather than agent of her own destiny reiterates longstanding tropes of paternalistic or imperialistic Western discourse, as well as the most conservative exploitation-film conventions. As in many other texts, the melodramatic frame of the television miniseries and the Hollywood feature transforms the subaltern's historical subjugation into a minor narrative device for the mobilization of viewers' outrage. Rather than appearing as a complex agent of historical forces, Sabira functions as an emotional punctuation mark in a Eurocentric text.

Both texts oscillate between an emphasis on strong-willed individual characters and these characters' connections to their nuclear families. In the British *Traffik*, the farmer Fazal, demoralized after the loss of his crops and a subsequent beating, becomes an underling of trafficker Tariq Butt, a choice that leads, as already noted, to Sabira's death. Consequently, the narcotics trade poses a physical threat to the families of suppliers as well as users. In both versions, Caroline's drug addiction leads to her family's dissolution and then reunion, with the father's obstinacy contributing to the breakup and his change of heart aiding the reunion. (In both texts too, Caroline's mother appears as a quiet dissenter who eventually leaves her home and husband; in the U.S. film she reappears without explanation later.) In both as well, Helen/Helena, the wife of the imprisoned Western trafficker, herself becomes an agent in the drug trade, ostensibly to preserve her familial and financial stability.[13] The British version stands alone, however, in depicting its characters of color in family and community relationships. Amid its cast of hundreds, Soderbergh's *Traffic* features four principled men of color: DEA agents Castro and Gordon, and Mexican policemen Rodriguez and his partner Manolo Sanchez (Jacob Vargas). In a configuration that is typical of U.S. popular texts, these men appear only in the public sphere, removed from romance and family. Manolo's wife, Ana (Marisol Padilla), appears twice, but he is absent in both cases: first she worries about his safety, then she mourns his death. The film's implication that drugs cause fissures in the family makes these men's utter autonomy particularly notable. They are key narrative agents yet are wholly removed from the family economy. Since drugs appear only to harm families, viewers can only imagine that abstracted prosocial interests motivate the men; they have virtually no self-interest. The related conceit that black and Latino men are the drug war's unsung heroes rather than its most frequent casualties represents a deliberate evasion and masking of historical reality. Overall, in reconceiving drug trafficking and abuse as threats principally to white family cohesion, the film egregiously misapprehends pressing criminal and public health crises.

The adaptation process crucially alters the texts' meanings surrounding race, family, and gender, particularly evident in the U.S. film's treatment of the Caroline Wakefield character. While the television series' multicharacter, multinarrative format allowed shifting points of emphasis and no specific emotional center, the film *Traffic* calls for a narrower emotional register, with the suburban teenager substituting for all young Westerners, affluent or disempowered. As scripted, Judge Wakefield and DEA agents Castro and Gordon are stock figures out of political dramas and cop films. Performance and direction enrich these characters, but only Caroline Wakefield is offered as a figure for close emotional identification, partly owing to actress Erika Christensen's nonstar status. The film represents Caroline's misadventures as visceral and momentous: her sexual victimization at the hands of the black drug dealer is shot from her hazy, first-person perspective, and the scene immediately follows a scene of her father's desperate vigilante search for her. Comparatively, the film eschews explicit views of her date-rape encounters with her prep school boyfriend Seth; they embrace or kiss, then the film cuts to other scenes not involving her father. Similarly, the film shows the deaths of male characters in Mexico discreetly. An out-of-focus close-up, a gunshot sound, and a brief view of a falling body illustrate Manolo's death. Late in the film, a medium-long shot, framed in a doorway, shows General Salazar about to receive an injection, and a few shots later, another medium-long shot, of about two seconds' duration, shows his body slumped over on a bare mattress. In short, Caroline's plight matters more to the film than do other characters', particularly those of Latinos and blacks. The film's view of the international narcotics trade takes shape accordingly. That the drug trade scars the black urban underclass is taken as self-evident; that it invades spheres of affluence is offered as revelatory and unsettling.

The penultimate scene in Steven Soderbergh's Traffic *showcases the reunion of the privileged Wakefield family.*

Traffic partly effaces its position along the racial divide by foregrounding the DEA agents' efforts and by offering the possibility of white culpability. One brief scene conveys the film's ambivalence about race. Following Carlos Ayala's arrest, Castro and Gordon monitor his wife's conversations from a surveillance van parked outside her house. While listening to one of Helena's discussion, Castro remarks, "I have actual dreams about this, about busting the top people, the rich people, white people." Gordon joins in to echo his partner's last two words. The comic tone of the exchange helps veil a substantial contradiction: the scene involves their investigation of a woman we regard as Latina, not white. In fact, they investigate or arrest only Latinos. By the end of *Traffic*, viewers are left with a veritable pile of Latino bodies: the informer Ruiz, agent Castro, Mexican policeman Sanchez, and the Mexican army general Salazar. In this light, the death of a single white character, the lawyer Arnie Metzger, seems a token gesture on the filmmakers' part (and a cruel twist: the Latin villain continues to wreak havoc on the lives of affluent whites). Metzger is the only white character involved in the drug trade, and Carlos arranges his murder near the end of the film. Thus, while the film rhetorically supports the punishment of wealthy white criminals, it largely withholds this group from representation. The British *Traffik*, in contrast, fully demonstrates its white characters' involvement in the drug trade at all levels, as well as the legal protections their economic privilege allows them.

In removing virtuous black and Latino men from the realm of family, the U.S. *Traffic* also liberates them from the film's family values rhetoric. Instead, they can engage in comedy and take action against criminals aligned with dominant interests (the U.S. business sector, and the Mexican government and army). At the same time, removed from family, they are afforded few stakes in the overall battle. In seeking to punish affluent "white people," as Castro and Gordon say in unison, they serve the interests of a marginally different set of affluent white people. Castro is eventually killed by a car bomb intended to silence the informant Ruiz (a similar fate befalls Castro's equivalent in the original *Traffik*, a white German policeman). The film registers Castro's sacrifice principally through a brief scene of his mother crying at his funeral. Rodriguez's similar risk taking—he betrays his superior, the villainous General Salazar, to the DEA—earns him only a children's baseball field, a romantic gift that the film implies will later cost him his life. Near the end of the film, after the captured, bound Salazar receives his injection, Javier finds Salazar lying alone, dead. The film gives viewers no reason to believe that Javier will elude such a fate himself but suggests rather that the hard-won baseball field represents his sole legacy to future generations. Javier's sacrifice, visually punctuated by his appearance at a nighttime baseball game in the film's final, dialogue-free scene, functions as both a sentimental and a cynical device of closure. Dispensing with subjects of politics or the drug trade, the scene returns the region south of the U.S. border to more innocent associations with the mythology of children's baseball, a mythology that circulates in both U.S. and Mexican cultures.

Another memorable scene in *Traffic* articulates through dialogue and mise-en-scène the film's curious perspective regarding Mexico. Meeting with two American DEA agents in San Diego, Javier insists on exchanging information in a location of his choosing. After one agent asks him, "Where do you want to go, Javier?" Javier grins mischievously, and the next shot shows the two Americans bare-chested, standing in shoulder-high water in a hotel swimming pool. With their serious expressions and unrelaxed stances, the agents look out of place in the cheery, playful setting. Meanwhile, Javier appears relaxed; he stands comfortably and speaks authoritatively, but with a sly comic undertone, as he makes a speech about children's baseball parks, which he uses as a metaphor for his interest in U.S.-Mexican solidarity. Shots of the agents show behind them the sun-dappled water and adults in poolside lounge chairs. Meanwhile, groups of white children, many blond, play in the water behind Javier, clearly visible even when the camera shifts from a medium shot to a close-up of his face. He ends his brief speech by swimming backward, in the children's direction. Del Toro's performance and body language help to naturalize his body in an exposed situation, which his character has chosen and which renders the agents vulnerable instead. Meanwhile, the presence of children defines Javier as unthreatening: he speaks of safe parks for children and says "kids can play" while children do play innocently behind him. Javier's interests are thus compatible with those of the United States. Both want to protect children (contrasting, for example, the Mexican thug who briefly takes Helena's son hostage). At the same time, the scene infantilizes Javier, visually aligning him with children. The scene calls up the familiar trope of the childish Third Worlder or ethnic other, though Del Toro's commanding presence favorably complicates the situation.

Both texts' discourses surrounding globalization emerge from hegemonic, U.S.-centric or Eurocentric worldviews. Thus, narrative or thematic elements that might function in specific ways within Mexican or Pakistani culture instead serve as parallels or counterpoints to elements in the texts' U.S. or European plots. The U.S. *Traffic* offers the family as a universal locus of viewer sympathy, but the white, upper-middle-class nuclear family stands in for all others. The British *Traffik* presents family more expansively, supplementing its view of the privileged family of Minister Lithgow with intermittent scenes of the diffuse family of German drug trafficker Karl Rosshalde (George Kukura) and his English wife, Helen. In this second family, the Rosshaldes' children appear rarely, usually in the company of the family's domestic servants. In the British series as in the U.S. *Traffic*, duty to family perversely underwrites a once-lawful wife's foray into the criminal subculture. This decision temporarily jeopardizes her child and later results in her own invasive strip-search by German customs agents, leaving her physically compromised but unharmed. In comparison, Sabira's plane flight ends with her death just after landing. This parallel underscores the legal and economic support system that protects Western families and its unavailability to the Third World woman, a figure whose absence from the U.S. *Traffic* curtails the potency of its invocation of the family.

The U.S. *Traffic* lacks a range of Third World figures because it focuses on the shipment of cocaine across the U.S. border, not the drug's production in Colombia.[14] The Channel Four series takes a broader view, linking Pakistani and Afghani opium farming and heroin processing to Germany as a European transit point—the "k" in the title *Traffik* represents Germany—and then to sale and consumption in England. In its narrower focus on the final stages of the drug trade, Soderbergh's film reflects screenwriter Gaghan's personal view of drug abuse as a U.S. public health issue rather than a global phenomenon combining Third World farming, international criminal trafficking and trade, and use and abuse by both affluent and poor Westerners.[15] Despite its title, then, the U.S. *Traffic* deals only superficially with drug trafficking. Instead, it visualizes traffic in the most literal sense, with repeated long shots of cars massed at the Tijuana border crossing. In contrast, the British series explicitly links the actions of Central Asian farmers and processors to Western European economic and social concerns. Nonetheless, the focus remains primarily Eurocentric in this version as well. The Germany- and England-based narratives together receive more screen time than the Pakistani plot. However, the Third World plot frames the series. *Traffik* begins with a helicopter shot of a hilly opium-farming area in Pakistan, and Fazal's reunion with his children supplies the series's closing scene. Similarly, the series mobilizes strong emotional investment in the plight of Fazal and his family. In this respect, though, the series defines the Third World as the repository of sentiment and pathos, contrasted with the West's chilly detachment, logic, and reason. Thus, viewer investment in the Pakistan segments is of a far different order than for the London and Hamburg segments.

Traffik uses its British protagonists' incomprehension to guide viewers across its Third World narrative. Conversely, the series's European plots deploy generic elements—of family and domestic melodramas, as well as the international police thriller—not available to the Pakistan plot. The less familiar tale of ex-opium farmer Fazal's relationship with the nefarious but charismatic businessman and drug exporter Tariq Butt largely escapes the pitfalls of generic narratives, but also lacks their accessibility and cultural currency. (In *Traffik*'s final episode, however, Fazal ambushes his former employer Butt and injects him in the neck with a massive overdose of heroin. Here, a conventionally satisfying revenge fantasy denouement provides one of the series' last views of the Third World.) At key moments, Fazal's story intersects with those of Helen Rosshalde and Jack Lithgow. Fazal is arrested when police seize a drug shipment that Helen arranges, and his subsequent corporal punishment is witnessed by a passing Lithgow. Repeatedly, too, scenes featuring Jack Lithgow end with transitions to those involving Fazal. For example, at the end of the first episode, Jack sits glumly on a plane back to England, and the program cuts to a shot of Fazal lying prostrate, being beaten. In the fifth episode, back in Pakistan, Jack wakes up in a plush hotel room and surveys the surrounding area, and the next scene shows Fazal and his family waking up in their confined room in Tariq Butt's compound. With these narrative intersections, the British characters' experiences literally make Fazal's trials legible. At two other points, scenes set in Pakistan carry a voice-over from Jack. In both cases, viewers hear his voice as asynchronous images appear. The first occurs near the start of the second episode as he leads a government briefing. The scene cuts away from Jack to an outdoor shot of Fazal treading a long dirt road, but Jack's remarks about aid to Pakistan continue in voice-over. Scenes such as this define the Third Worlder in terms of his body (with a large pack of belongings over his shoulder, the fatiguing nature of Fazal's long journey is emphasized), while the British minister is apprehended through his authoritative voice. In a second scene, Lithgow's internal monologue accompanies a series of images (a plane landing, a view of the airport terminal, a car in motion), including some in which he appears in long shot. In voice-over, he narrates his own return visit to the country, admitting that "I loathe this place—I don't understand it." The series applies the familiar literary and filmic device of framing images of the Third World in terms of colonialist discourse. However, as Lithgow's statement explicitly links disdain and incomprehension, the moment acknowledges a key contradiction of colonial relationships.

The British *Traffik*'s cognizance of the colonial relationship implicitly excuses the text's Eurocentric perspective. To show how a myopic, Eurocentric view mystifies the drug trade's point of origin, the series reproduces the Western onlooker's confusion. *Traffik* does represent Western Europe as the site of drug consumption and thus the cause of the Third World's economic subjugation. This admission seeks to justify the series's inattention to Third World narcotics use and its limited attention to larger issues of poverty and underdevelopment. Scenes depicting Fazal and his compatriots do visualize the region's inhospitable landscape, its primitive infrastructure, and, in one episode, a crowded, filthy shantytown. The program defines Fazal within this world and narrates its effects on those around him. However, *Traffik* regularly views the conditions surrounding Fazal through the framing perspective of Jack Lithgow. Crosscutting and narrative overlaps indicate the interdependence of world events but also deprive the Pakistani characters of sovereign status. Viewers experience what Lithgow learns on his diplomatic visits, and the series reminds viewers of his need for greater knowledge by cutting from Fazal's narrative to his. In this light, Fazal's life represents part of the larger picture from which Lithgow is shielded. Consequently, we support Lithgow's choice to seek out the "real" Pakistan, guided by a crusading female Karachi lawyer and her cousin, ostensibly bypassing diplomatic public relations filters. Remarkably, this episode includes a scene in which Lithgow agrees to smoke opium, which leaves him in a pleasantly drugged haze incompatible with his political duties.[16] The opium-smoking cousin articulates a specific if somewhat facile political and philosophical position regarding global drug use. Even here, Pakistani characters function as conventional native informants, acting and speaking for Lithgow's edification, a foreign culture mediated though a white Westerner's presence.

Traffik's perspective is colonialist and thus compromised, yet it contrasts favorably with the U.S. *Traffic*'s myopic view of the world beyond the U.S. border. In the film, Mexico serves as a surrogate for all Latin America, and hence the Third World. At one level, Mexico functions as an ally of the rich United States, linked to it politically and economically, with the border crossings providing a metonym for NAFTA and international trade. The nation also serves as a virtual representation of the Third World, defined by arid landscapes, official corruption, and general disorder or lawlessness.[17] The British *Traffik* narrates the physical and economic interactions of characters across its three settings. The U.S. film instead offers the Altmanesque device of serendipitous visual proximity. The staging of such clever intersections substitutes for a fully articulated social argument. More than once, U.S. and Mexican characters coincidentally pass through the same space, as when Helena and Javier cross paths on a Tijuana street, each oblivious to the other's presence. Another time, as Helena waits in a line of cars at the border, a car with Javier in it waits on the other side. The definition of Mexico chiefly through border zones leads to a subsequent narrowness of perspective. The film presents drug abuse as a U.S. issue, hence one that is manageable in that it is subject to swift viewer apprehension. Unwilling to represent a squalid and underdeveloped Third World, *Traffic* finds one within the United States, depicting the Cincinnati neighborhood where Robert Wakefield undertakes his urban vigilante search for his daughter as a lawless zone populated by black men who shout challenges and gesticulate aggressively at the white politician.[18] The London slums of the British *Traffik*, by comparison, are eerily quiet, with no invocation of racial difference to signal poverty and criminality.

Director Steven Soderbergh has consistently worked on films that compellingly reinterpret classic, postclassic, or non-U.S. texts, principally for popular consumption in the U.S. The expressive visual palette and nonlinearity of *The Underneath* reframes the stylistics of 1940s' film noir. *Solaris* combines conventions of science fiction and doomed romance dramas for a dreamy meditation on loss and desire. Even the arrested-development male camaraderie of *Ocean's Eleven* (2001) and its sequels cannily resuscitate a moribund conception of interracial male friendships and teamwork. *Traffic*'s contribution to this process is more problematic, principally because of the substantially higher expectations of cultural verisimilitude for contemporary texts dealing seriously with the international narcotics trade. Visually, the U.S. *Traffic*, on which Soderbergh served as cinematographer under a pseudonym, borrows the paint-by-numbers color scheme of the British series, which rendered London in dull grays, Hamburg in a steely, industrial blue, and Pakistan in warm, saturated earth tones and reds.[19] These color distinctions serve the series's frequent shifts of setting well, mitigating against the disorientation such transitions might cause on the small screen. With few exceptions, the series eschews establishing shots of its disparate locations, instead using color and other precise visual cues to situate viewers in narrative space.[20] Many of Soderbergh's films—in the late 1990s, *Out of Sight* and *The Limey* in particular—employ similar devices of extensive crosscutting, limited establishing shots, and stylized color. In *Traffic*, though, the choice of not only different color schemes but also different film stocks and exposure settings for the U.S. and Mexico scenes effectively defines Mexico as an alien world. In this world, the unrelenting sun literally alters perspective, as does the stroboscopic effect of the forty-five-degree shutter used during filming. The shutter eliminates motion blur and thus represents movement as surreally halting, and the larger scale of the theatrical screen compounds the effects. The extreme differentiation of the two settings accords with the film's ideological project, the representation of Mexico as an unknowable land, bereft of culture, in which a ruthless Darwinism prevails. Such a construction facilitates ignorance of the imbalanced economic relations between nations, and obscures too the systemic economic disenfranchisement that occurs within both countries.

Traffic is exceptional in its ability to link multiple narratives and to offer something approaching a social perspective within the boundaries of the U.S. feature film. The film also contains elements consistent with the Soderbergh remake, a virtual subgenre of American cinema of the 1990s and 2000s. Soderbergh repeatedly asserts the presence in his films of "main characters that are out of sync with their environments."[21] *Sex, lies, and videotape* and *Schizopolis* (1997) rely most explicitly on such figures, though they appear in nearly all the director's films. Both versions of *Traffic/k* too deploy legions of frustrated, alienated characters as vehicles for audience engagement, characters out of place in their families, in politics, and abroad. In the U.S. film, Soderbergh's handheld camerawork magnifies the instability of all its locations, whether in the United States or Mexico. In both versions, social and geographic spaces offer no inherent comfort or solace; characters we follow are perpetually in conflict with their environments.

Soderbergh's remakes consistently curtail the social perspectives of their source films while sometimes taking on rather audacious challenges of scope. Culturally, both *Criss Cross* and the Rat Pack *Ocean's Eleven* are very much products of their time, the former informed by the postwar current of male disenfranchisement, the latter supportive of the Eisenhower-era fantasy of freewheeling play as a bulwark against deep inequities. Soderbergh's remakes respond by closing off the outside world. *The Underneath*, shot and set in Austin, Texas, mobilizes little of that city's particular flavor. Soderbergh describes the city, somewhat inexplicably, as "a city that does not really have a face. It's just a place where you live."[22] In some respects such an attitude suits the film, which as its title suggests shows disregard for surface qualities and takes an interest instead in subtexts and psychology. The remade *Ocean's Eleven* similarly disregards the larger social world, highlighting instead the plastic surfaces of contemporary Las Vegas and making only hasty stops at other locations. Even the science fiction film *Solaris* is originally anchored in the cultural world of the Soviet Union, with the twin foundations of a cold socialist bureaucracy and a mournful romanticism supporting the film's study of human contact and faith. In Soderbergh's remake, set in an indistinct near future, contemporary views of science and of romantic partnerships are only dimly present. *Traffic*, too, provides passing views of social and political conditions, in contrast to the original's detailed social interest. Whereas the remakes tend toward narrower social views than their sources, they also aim for a wide narrative and thematic scope. Despite the obvious reductions from *Traffik*'s serial narrative to *Traffic*'s single text, Soderbergh's film represents with some complexity a range of families, social classes, professions, and nations. In one shot in *Traffic*, the camera turns upside down as it shows a U.S. delegation's helicopter landing atop the presidential palace in Mexico. The shot (which was unplanned) metaphorically suggests the dizzying power relations inherent in the film's subject and the feature film's limitations in apprehending them.[23]

In *Culture and Imperialism*, Edward Said argues that a world system, producing culture, creates what he calls "out of scale transnational images that are now reorienting international social discourses and processes."[24] *Traffik*, a nonprofit television miniseries with a limited international viewership, participates in this world system, though its images might not be described as massively "out of scale." The U.S. *Traffic*, a production of the semi-independent USA Films but also a $49 million film shepherded by major producer Edward Zwick, clearly deploys the outsized images Said identifies. With its cameos from U.S. politicians and its brief tour of the El Paso Intelligence Center (aka EPIC, one of the United States' key sites of antitrafficking activity), *Traffic* promises a wholeness of perspective it does not, or cannot, deliver.

The meanings of *Traffik* and *Traffic* diverge in large part because of their respective treatments of family, race, and nationhood. The transformation of *Traffik*'s white undercover policemen into *Traffic*'s black and Latino agents contributes strongly to the U.S. film's meanings. Racial taboos, not invoked in the British series, similarly inform *Traffic*'s meanings, distinguishing the two texts' constructions of family. A series of opportunistic suitors take sexual advantage of the teenage Caroline Wakefield, emphasizing the white woman's bodily violation. The British *Traffik*, on the other hand, repeatedly demonstrates Caroline Lithgow's abjection—showing her trapped outdoors in the rain, for example, and shooting heroin in a grimy toilet stall—but puts less emphasis on her status as a sexual commodity. Both versions depict Caroline's greatest despoliation as a junkie prostitute, but Caroline Wakefield's younger age, her multiple sexual partners, and the taboo of miscegenation produce greater emphasis on sexual violation in the U.S. film. In both versions too, Caroline's mother is fairly ineffectual, her relative tolerance overwhelmed by her husband's obstinacy; her strongest act is to leave home (and until a final reunion in the U.S. film, the narrative as well). Meanwhile, both white patriarchs, Robert Wakefield and Jack Lithgow, appear diligent even in their excesses. Both men's final softening, in tandem with their climactic rescues of their imperiled daughters, makes possible the family reunion.

Constructions of race and nationhood in realist fictions such as *Traffik* and *Traffic* merit continued scrutiny in light of the heightened national security climate and widespread paranoia surrounding foreignness after September 2001. In the United States, official anxieties about the possible illegal activities of people of color who are not U.S. citizens have reached levels not seen since World War II. In December 2002, the U.S. government implemented a strict registration program for immigrant men over the age of fifteen, targeting almost exclusively men from Arab or Muslim nations. The program sparked a massive flight of immigrants, principally Pakistanis, to Canada. Because of Canadian immigration authorities' inability to process the large numbers of asylum seekers, most were sent back to the United States, where they were immediately arrested for visa violations and scheduled for deportation.[25] Equally of interest, and receiving substantially more media coverage than the Muslim deportation initiative, was the highly visible U.S. immigration debate of 2006, which resulted in the passage of legislation for greater surveillance and control of the U.S.-Mexico border. Such sudden and largely uncontested shifts in political attitudes toward immigrants of color working in the U.S. demand commentary. Given the cultural reach of film and television, progressive media scholarship can call crucial attention to mainstream texts' contributions to processes of marginalization or their resistance to such processes.

In light of North America's current security climate and political relationships between Western and Arab or Muslim states, the U.S. *Traffic*'s fidelity to caricatures of racial and Third World representation appears all the more troubling. In contrast, the strategy of the British *Traffik* to acknowledge the hierarchical relationship between Europe and the Muslim Third World and the effects of continued exploitation of human and economic resources appears all the more vital. Both texts fall prey to political didacticism and regressive racial and gender politics. The texts' melodramatic address and popular narrative forms contribute to these shortcomings but also to their virtues. To their credit, both introduce discussions, however limited, of the political-economic underpinnings of race and global relations into mainstream television and film. Moreover, the apparent reductiveness of the adaptation *Traffic* successfully expands the film's reception, providing potent set pieces and emotionally charged situations that render its complex subject in accessible terms that viewers may negotiate. The film's overall ambiguity encourages viewers to regard its melodramatic episodes skeptically rather than uncritically, and in some economic context if not with benefit of a comprehensive political and historical view. As an adaptation, Soderbergh's film substantially narrows the scope of its source text, but it also generates a cultural discussion far broader than that which accompanied the original (and indeed, the U.S. *Traffic* indisputably raised the visibility of its British source, as high-profile adaptations typically do). On balance, then, we can regard the adapted *Traffic* as a worthy contribution to politically aware Western media.

NOTES

Thanks to Elaine Roth and Jack Boozer for their insightful commentary on this manuscript.

1. For example, a *Traffic* miniseries, borrowing the multiple-narrative format and visual style of the film, but with different characters and strongly different subject matter, appeared on the USA Network in 2004.

2. Bickford relates her involvement in the production on a producers' commentary track accompanying the film (*Traffic* DVD, The Criterion Collection, 2002). Additional material on *Traffic*'s production history appears in "About the Production," liner notes, *Traffic* DVD (USA Home Entertainment, 2001); the producers' commentary track on the Criterion *Traffic* DVD gives a similar history. Another related account appears on the DVD supplement "From *Traffik* to *Traffic*," *Traffik* DVD (Acorn Media, 2001). See also Sharon Waxman, *Rebels on the Backlot: Six Maverick Directors and How They Conquered the Hollywood Studio System* (New York: HarperEntertainment, 2005), which includes discussion of *Traffic*'s production.

3. See, for example, Rick Lyman, "The Screenwriter for 'Traffic' Says He Drew on His Past of Drug Use," *New York Times*, February 5, 2001, www.nytimes.com/2001/02/05/oscars/05GAGH.html (accessed February 16, 2001). Gaghan also cites his autobiography on Criterion's DVD commentary track, observing that many episodes involving the impressionable Caroline Wakefield came directly from his own privileged, boisterous adolescence. Simon Moore, whose substance use is not a matter of public record, scripted the British version.

4. For more on the distinction between remake and adaptation, see Andrew Horton and Stuart McDougal, eds., *Play It Again, Sam: Retakes and Remakes* (Berkeley and Los Angeles: University of California Press, 1998). Reviews of *Traffic* tend not to use the term "remake," opting for phrases such as "based on" (David Edelstein in *Slate*) and "inspired by" (Roger Ebert in the *Chicago Sun-Times*) when referring to the British series.

5. *Traffic* includes different sequences shot with tobacco filters to lend a brownish tint. Other sequences use film stocks that appear a rich indigo blue after film processing. Parts of the film also use desaturation processes, popularized in late 1960s' and early 1970s' U.S. film, that produce muted colors. Soderbergh notes some of these visual choices in his co-commentary track with Gaghan on the Criterion DVD, and a featurette, "Film processing demonstration: Achieving the look of the Mexico sequences," gives additional information.

6. Other Soderbergh films mine the same era of film history. *Schizopolis* in part pays homage to director Richard Lester, most prominent in the mid-1960s. *The Limey*, showcasing 1960s' star Terence Stamp, aesthetically mixes elements of the French New Wave and the style of British director John Boorman, also most active in the late 1960s and early 1970s.

7. India gained independence from Britain in 1947 and at the same time was split into India and Pakistan, in the event known as Partition.

8. The Criterion *Traffic* DVD's producers' commentary track also features the film's two story consultants, Golden and former DEA chief of intelligence Craig Chretien. Bickford claims that conversations with Golden helped steer the film's focus to Mexico and not Colombia. She refers to Mexico's proximity to the United States and the growth of Mexican drug trafficking in the 1990s (following the 1993

death of Colombian drug kingpin Pablo Escobar) as specific reasons for the North American emphasis. Bickford refers to Gaghan's pre-*Traffic* drug-film script in this commentary as well.

9. *Traffik* aired on Channel Four in June 1989 and on American PBS stations' *Masterpiece Theatre* in April 1990 (Internet Movie Database, www.imdb.com, accessed March 1, 2003). It re-aired on PBS in spring 2001, after the U.S. *Traffic*'s strong box-office performance and multiple Academy Awards. Two *New York Times* writers supply representative views of the two texts: Steve Vineberg observes that the newer *Traffic* bears a "glossy, melodramatic style" and a "preachy, social-problem-picture tone" not present in the original, while Julie Salamon declares the newer film "stern and moralistic" in comparison to the British series (Vineberg, "Before 'Traffic,' an Earlier Drug Saga, With No Easy Answers," *New York Times*, February 11, 2001, www.nytimes.com [accessed 12 March 2001], and Salamon, "Before Hollywood's 'Traffic' Came the Elegant 'Traffik,'" *New York Times*, July 6, 2001, E26).

10. Del Toro alters his own Puerto Rican–accented Spanish to give Javier a Mexican accent, and the thick accent he adopts for his scenes in English helps define Javier as a non-native English speaker. Thanks to Michael Aceto for this observation.

11. Comparatively, the British *Traffik* features characters who speak in English, German, and Urdu, though the Pakistani characters speak most frequently in English, attesting to the region's colonial legacy.

12. In their Criterion DVD commentary track, Soderbergh and Gaghan imply that the provision of relatively accurate policy statements to criminal characters (Ruiz, Arnie Metzger, Mexico's General Salazar) contributes to the film's ambiguity and complexity. Other viewers and critics have found this device merely heavy-handed. In this respect, the film bears traces of Gaghan's past work as a writer for the social issue television dramas *NYPD Blue* and *The Practice*.

13. In the original *Traffik*, Helen states that she "won't let them [law enforcement] destroy all that we've fought for," and in the U.S. version, a visibly pregnant Helena asserts that she "won't bring a child into the world I was brought up in."

14. The absence of Colombia severely undermines the film's putative authenticity vis-à-vis the international cocaine trade. Colombia, which produces 80 percent of the world's cocaine (Peru and Bolivia account for the rest), was called in May 2004 "by far the biggest humanitarian catastrophe of the Western Hemisphere" by the UN's Undersecretary for Humanitarian Affairs. (See Peter Canby, "Latin America's Longest War," *The Nation*, August 16/23, 2004, 31.) Its inclusion in *Traffic* would have lent the film an unprecedented verisimilitude; its exclusion results in a predominantly false view of cocaine trafficking.

15. In a *New York Times* interview coinciding with the film's release, Gaghan observes, "'If there's a message to the movie, I guess it's that drugs should be considered a health care issue rather than a criminal issue'" (Lyman, "Screenwriter for 'Traffic' Says He Drew on His Past of Drug Use").

16. *Traffic*'s screenplay includes a similar scene, with Robert Wakefield sampling cocaine he finds in his daughter's bedroom, but it does not appear in the film. See Gaghan, *Traffic: The Shooting Script*, 115.

17. Ironically, the United States even serves as a stand-in for Mexico. Gaghan and Soderbergh's DVD commentary notes that the Mexican desert scene that begins the film was shot outside Las Cruces, New Mexico (San Ysidro, also in New Mexico, was used for other Mexico scenes), and driving sequences set in Mexico City were filmed on roads outside San Diego. Along with some footage shot in Tijuana and Nogales, a helicopter flyover shot of Mexico City does appear, but even this shot is followed by a helicopter landing shot filmed in downtown Los Angeles.

18. Gaghan's subjective view of drug use informs the scene. His introductory remarks in the published screenplay attest to his undisguised racial paranoia. He claims that drug addiction "will take you into the inner city where everybody is a different race than you, everybody has antipathy toward you, everybody is armed, and people are engaged in illegal operations with drugs and death around it all the time. You're leaving your comfy, million-dollar house in your upper-middle class suburb and actively seeking danger" (Gaghan, *Traffic: The Shooting Script*, xiii).

19. This contrast is also noted in Salamon, "Before Hollywood's 'Traffic' Came the Elegant 'Traffik.'" To Soderbergh's credit, a similar tonal range appears in his earlier films, including *Out of Sight*, *The Limey*, and *Erin Brockovich*. *Traffic*'s coloration is thus consistent both with Soderbergh's oeuvre and with the original British *Traffik*.

20. In a brief 1990 interview, writer Moore quotes director Reid as saying "I want to be able to show a close-up of an ashtray and we'll know where we are," and the finished program manifests this intent ("Interview with Writer and Producer," *Traffik* DVD).

21. Quoted in Michel Ciment and Hubert Niogret, "Interview with Steven Soderbergh: *King of the Hill*," in *Steven Soderbergh: Interviews*, ed. Anthony Kaufman (Jackson: University Press of Mississippi, 2002), 60.

22. Quoted in Michel Ciment and Hubert Niogret, "Interview with Steven Soderbergh: *The Underneath*," in *Steven Soderbergh: Interviews*, ed. Anthony Kaufman (Jackson: University Press of Mississippi, 2002) 73.

23. Soderbergh discusses the shot in Anthony Kaufman, "Man of the Year: Steven Soderbergh Traffics in Success," *Steven Soderbergh: Interviews*, ed. Anthony Kaufman (Jackson: University Press of Mississippi, 2002), 161. The camera, operated by a remote head, was intended to show the landing right side up; the results differed, and the filmmakers were pleased by them. Soderbergh notes of the shot that "it's probably the only undiluted lyrical passage in the whole film" and that "it's the first time that the camera is not eye-level." Soderbergh relates similar comments in his co-commentary track on the Criterion *Traffic* DVD.

24. Edward Said, *Culture and Imperialism* (New York: Knopf, 1993), 375.

25. See Susan Sachs, "U.S. Crackdown Sets Off Unusual Rush to Canada," *New York Times*, February 25, 2003, www.nytimes.com/2003/02/25/national/25DETA.html (accessed February 25, 2003). Recorded immigration from Muslim countries fell sharply in 2003, then rebounded slightly in 2004. See Andrea Elliott, "More Muslims Arrive in U.S., After 9/11 Dip," *New York Times*, September 10, 2006, www.nytimes.com/2006/09/10/nyregion/10muslims.html (accessed September 10, 2006).

PART IV
//

VARIATIONS IN SCREENWRITER AND DIRECTOR COLLABORATIONS

In the film adaptation of Nick Hornby's novel High Fidelity, John Cusack not only plays the lead role but is listed as co-writer with three others, as well as co-producer with two of those other writers. Actors sometimes feel compelled to take an active hand in locating and seeing through properties in which they can star. The small United Artists studio was founded in part on that principle in 1919. Today, many stars hire their own screenplay readers, including agents and managers, to help locate material for them. The drive to produce and write the screenplay (and play the leading role) may explain a great deal about the narrative slant of such films, which can serve among other things as "star vehicles." An actor's motivation to adapt and produce a certain source text may also be primarily to advance cultural and ideological observation, even to the point of risking commercial failure. For the actor/co-writer/co-producer in High Fidelity, as well as all the other adapting writers and directors discussed in this book, the effort to reveal personal and cultural insights through the narrative devices of film and through its gauntlet of commercial pressures continues to take many forms.

In Chapter 10, Cynthia Lucia carefully investigates the developmental process that led to the film High Fidelity. Her research included an interview with one of the screenwriters, D. V. DeVincentis. Lucia explains that although director Stephen Frears did not take screenwriting credit, he was apparently instrumental in shaping the film. At a critical point in the screenplay's development, and with the screenwriter present, Frears suggested a method of direct address for the main character rather than the voice-over that had been incorporated in the earlier drafts. This technique in the film has a dualistic effect on viewers, one that Lucia precisely delineates in relation to other modifications of the central story line involving the protagonist's personal, gender-defined struggle.

Shelley Cobb in Chapter 11 offers an insider's look at the development of the film adaptation of Helen Fielding's popular novel, Bridget Jones's Diary, which originated in her newspaper column. Fielding served as executive producer on this film comedy and was also one of its three writers. The friendship between Fielding and the director, Sharon Maguire, did not change the dominant position of Fielding and her two other writers on the project, all of whom had more experience, as Cobb carefully explains, than the novice director Maguire. The typically inferior *position of screenwriter(s) vis-à-vis the director, therefore, is reversed in this case. Cobb constructs elaborate textual interconnections to demonstrate how this adaptation became a kind of intertextual franchise, particularly in relation to the critical debates surrounding feminism and postfeminism.*

Elaine Roth's sensitive consideration of Sherman Alexie's adaptation of his own short stories into the screenplay for the film Smoke Signals *in Chapter 12 provides a fitting close to the perspectives on adaptation offered in earlier chapters. This essay goes a long way toward clearing up his thinking and his debates with the director over issues of ethnic identity, media influences, and character and narrative emphasis. In effect, Roth provides the reader with a roadmap to the way Alexie and director Chris Eyre represent the issues that constantly face culturally repressed Native Americans, who have little visibility or space for identity of their own making in an environment dominated by white, Anglo-Saxon mass media images. Roth reveals how* Smoke Signals *reflects exactly that problem, through its interrogation of the mythic notion of authenticity.*

10

ADAPTING NICK HORNBY'S *HIGH FIDELITY*
Process and Sexual Politics

//

Cynthia Lucia

IN ITS PLAY ON THE SEVERAL MEANINGS OF *FIDELITY*, THE TITLE of Nick Hornby's 1995 novel hints at the top two obsessions driving its protagonist: popular music, and winning back his live-in girlfriend Laura, who walks out as the novel begins. The novel traces the reversal of these priorities in the life of Rob Fleming, a cool-aspiring but rigidly opinionated thirty-five-year-old marooned in adolescence. Gradually Rob learns to commit himself to personal relationships with the same fidelity that he brings to the pop musicians he reveres. Alluding to Rob's pop culture preferences, the title also announces *High Fidelity*'s dualistic position as a work that is both grounded in a realist, "hi-fi" narrative tradition and inflected by a postmodern sensibility. The title asserts a reflexive and ironic awareness of what it means to live and create in an age with virtually infinite possibilities for reproduction and referentiality, whether in music, movies, books, or romance. Furthermore, as if anticipating cinematic adaptation, the title draws attention to the critical bugbear that has haunted adaptation studies until fairly recently, that of fidelity to the source work.

The theme of protracted adolescence is not a new one for the London-based Hornby, whose first work, *Fever Pitch* (1992), is a memoir describing his own casting about for direction. Its popularity paved the way for the critically acclaimed *High Fidelity*, Hornby's first novel. Following *High Fidelity*, Hornby continued to explore the theme of extended adolescence in *About a Boy* (1998), again from a male perspective, while in his third novel, *How to Be Good* (2001), Hornby adopts the perspective of a female protagonist caught in a midlife crisis that thrusts her back into a kind of temporary and destabilizing adolescence. Although Hornby treats serious, complex subjects in all of his work, including his 2005 novel, *A Long Way Down*, he does so with playful and sardonic humor, exploring issues of substance through entertaining and seemingly effortless prose.

Deftly capturing Hornby's substance and humor in the screen adaptation of *High Fidelity* (2000), British filmmaker Stephen Frears (best known for *My Beautiful Laundrette*, *Dangerous Liaisons*, *The Grifters*, and *The Queen*), although not credited as screenwriter, had a significant role in shaping its early progress. In adapting the novel, screenwriters D. V. DeVincentis and Steve Pink also worked with their longtime friend, actor John Cusack, who was slated to play Rob (Gordon in the screenplay).[1] The novel's realistic approach to first-person narration and structure within a larger postmodern context is perhaps what prompted an experimentation with possible approaches during the adaptation process. Screenwriters grappled with a twofold challenge: how best to capture Rob's intimate, conversational—often conspiratorial—direct address to readers while simultaneously allowing for Hornby's deft distancing of readers, enabling them to recognize Rob's protracted adolescence and the limitations of vision and long-practiced self-deception that state involves. A product of multiple revisions, the screenplay in its early versions relied on conventional voice-over narration as a means of capturing the informal first-person perspective of the novel, as Rob "converses" with the reader. Eventually, however, Frears suggested that direct address replace much of the voice-over, in order to retain the "wonderful bits" of the novel. Frears credits DeVincentis with having done "the real work on the screenplay,"[2] and DeVincentis speaks about a weekend during which he and Frears cloistered themselves in a London hotel room and hammered out the first direct-address version, pointing out that "the London draft resembles the final result, as the first draft with direct address, but is one point in a long road," with further revisions to follow.[3]

The crucial transformation from voice-over to direct address not only injects an edgy immediacy to character and theme, forging a strongly intimate connection between Rob and the viewer, it also grafts a postmodern sensibility onto the relatively conventional story and mildly unconventional structure of the film. With its multiple implications for the adaptation of *High Fidelity* in particular and the adaptation process in general, this transformation subtly reshapes viewers' perceptions of Rob as he travels from middle-aged adolescence toward adulthood, and somewhat alters ways of understanding the film's sexual politics in relation to those expressed in the novel.

MASCULINE CRISIS: ECONOMICS, SELF-DECEPTION, AND THE *BILDUNGSROMAN* TRADITION

Rob's extended adolescence is both the result of and a manifestation of an underlying masculinity crisis, a crisis painfully heightened when Laura leaves him. An anxiety infusing much popular literature and many films (often drama or action films) during the decade spanning the mid-1980s through the mid-1990s, the masculinity crisis is here placed in the context of romantic comedy—a playfully dark comedy in the novel that is transformed to a more breezy and optimistic comedy in the film, which, according to Frears, has to do with "the more optimistic way Americans live,"[4] in keeping with the shift from Hornby's London setting to the film's Chicago setting.[5] As expressed in other genres, the masculinity crisis is grounded in the male protagonist's sense of anxiety and failure (or, alternatively, the overly determined need to assert dominance), whether in relationship to career, earning power, family life, sex, or romance.

Both the novel and the film present a view of Rob's crisis and his limited understanding of that crisis while allowing a deeper insight into its source. Rob's feelings of inadequacy in his relationships with women stem from his belief that they hold all the power—a power he willingly confers, particularly in the novel, believing that "women are going to save me, lead me through to a better life, that they can change and redeem me."[6] In the face of rejection, Rob feels uncomfortably (or, as we may come to see, comfortably) emasculated, longing for the control that *"proper* men" exert—the "men who don't call," who appear "not to give a shit"[7]—while at the same time realizing that he is not one of them, and doesn't want to be. After Laura leaves, Rob attempts to convince himself that "if I don't have to go around feeling hurt, and powerless, and miserable, I can cope without her. In other words, I'm unhappy because she doesn't want me; if I can convince myself that she does want me a bit, then I'll be OK again, because then I won't want her ..."[8] Through actor John Cusack's performance as simultaneously dogged and sheepish in Rob's pursuit of Laura and in his humorous, self-deprecating approach to Rob's character, the film likewise conveys Rob's contradictory anxieties.

As Roland Barthes observed, "'In every man who speaks the absence of the other, the feminine declares itself: he who waits and suffers is miraculously feminised.'"[9] Although Rob may sometimes wish he were otherwise, *High Fidelity* does not present Rob's feminization in negative terms. At first glance the novel seems to link such feminization with Rob's protracted adolescence, in the absence of power that state implies. Ultimately, however, the novel suggests that Rob's emotional maturation lies in his learning to place less importance on masculine power, which, paradoxically, will free him from adolescent limitations and masculine crisis—two states the novel does equate. Although the film implies causal links between Rob's masculinity crisis and his extended adolescence—linkages that direct address helps to convey—the film fails to fully develop the novel's concern with (and critique of) masculinity as it is linked to the desire for economic power.

Initially, Rob is unable to see beyond the double limitations of protracted adolescence and masculine crisis, attributing his failure in romance instead to a perceived failure in career and earning power, and vice versa. Although he loves pop music and dealing in vintage recordings, Rob tells us that he's "sick of the sight" of Championship Vinyl,[10] the record store he owns in north London's Holloway, in the novel, and on the corner of Chicago's Milwaukee and Honore, in the film. In believing that the real power in his life belongs to the women he's known, Rob perceives his career failure as rooted in his doomed college romance with Charlie Nicholson. When they met, Charlie legitimized Rob's longed-for self-image as a mildly countercultural twentysomething urbanite—an image he had hoped to cultivate in moving to London. Struggling with his identity as rooted in "a suburban shit hole—and hating it" (a bit like Hornby, himself, who grew up in the suburbs before relocating to London), Rob felt "old enough to have a history" with Charlie, unlike at home, where he "didn't have a history, just stuff that everybody already knew, and that, therefore, wasn't worth repeating," Yet in the company of the artsy, opinionated Charlie, Rob confesses feeling like "a fraud . . . as though I was going to be found out at any moment," a feeling seemingly confirmed when, after two years, Charlie dumps him for Marco, with whom she "matched," according to Rob.[11]

Five years later, and still on the rebound, Rob takes up with Sarah Kendrew, who, also depressed and depressingly on the rebound, seems to match Rob's own sense of himself as embodying "a whole lot of averageness" in "one compact frame." Though he and Sarah "couldn't fill a room," they cling together in mutual fear, at age twenty-six, of "being left alone for the rest of our lives." When Sarah leaves Rob for another man, Rob explains that "all I saw then was that I'd moved down a division and it still hadn't worked out." Rob confesses that, ultimately, he never did get over Charlie, and "when I came around, after a couple months of darkness, I found to my surprise that I had flunked my course and was working in Record and Tape Exchange in Camden," musing that, like the victims of Pompeii "I'm stuck in . . . this shop-managing pose, forever, because of a few short weeks in 1979 when I went a bit potty for a while."¹² He attributes his inertia to Charlie's active rejection of him—a pattern he feels he's been consigned to repeat ever since Alison Ashworth dumped him when they were twelve or thirteen. The Charlie incident in both novel and film shines a spotlight on Rob's feelings of disempowerment—his own sense of having failed to "measure up" sexually, socially, and in the end, economically.

While he imagines that Charlie's power has led to his seemingly eternal despondency, his acknowledgment of Laura's power to "change and redeem" him enables Rob ultimately to transcend both adolescent limitations and masculine crisis. Rarely able to see his store as anything other than a mark of his own failure, both professionally and romantically, Rob has difficulty acknowledging the pleasure he derives from his work, although it does erupt at moments, as on one Saturday when he admits "a little glow . . . maybe because this is after all my work."¹³ Laura helps Rob accept himself as one of those rare individuals who gets to work at something he enjoys—an insight further confirmed by the comic pleasure we, as readers and viewers, derive from images of Rob's work, particularly as he interacts with his employees Dick and Barry, perfect comic foils for each other and for Rob as they too live lives of protracted adolescence. "Rob, Dick and Barry's obsessiveness is the movie's constant gag," *Salon* reviewer Stephanie Zacharek points out, "and yet it's never in doubt how much pleasure they get from the music."¹⁴

In her excellent monograph on the novel, Joanne Knowles identifies its place within conventional realist *Bildungsroman*,¹⁵ although with a protagonist some twenty years the senior of, say, Holden Caulfield or Huck Finn. Knowles points out that "paradoxically . . . the ability to move on allows Rob to choose to stay exactly where he is: managing his record shop and in his relationship with Laura," for, like the conventional *Bildungsroman* protagonist, he recognizes the value of what he already possesses.¹⁶ When he grudgingly adds Laura to the list of his "desert-island, all-time, top five most memorable split-ups"—after earlier asserting, in an apostrophe to Laura, that "those places are reserved for the kind of humiliations and heartbreaks that you're just not capable of delivering"¹⁷—Rob takes an important first step away from self-deception and toward emotional maturity. And very much like Holden or Huck, Rob exhibits mixed motives in his address to readers, wavering between honest reflection and convenient self-deception as he slowly arrives at this recognition. On the one hand, he just wants someone to talk with in order to "sort it out," an attitude forging intimacy with the reader that is heightened in the film when Rob continually breaks the illusionist space, at one point casting the audience as drinking buddies and

In High Fidelity, *Rob (John Cusack) and Barry (Jack Black) endlessly debate their musical and other pop culture preferences, generating a comic energy that works to counter Rob's complaints about his seemingly accidental path in life as owner of a vintage record shop.*
© Touchstone Pictures, Inc., 2000.

addressing us from across the bar after a particularly dispiriting drop along his downward spiral of despair. Beyond just wanting to talk, however, Rob also seeks sympathy, and the implicit validation and self-justification that go along with it. Addressing readers and viewers as co-conspirators, Rob further attempts to maneuver sympathy into a kind of automatic absolution, something we may not be ready or able to deliver in the unambiguous terms he's hoping for—and it is here that issues of gender come more deeply into play in the adaptation process.

Knowles argues that the novel "paints a more complex picture of masculinity" than its initial reception as "a definitive guide to the crisis of the contemporary male" would seem to indicate.[18] When the novel first appeared, it was seen by many British critics as a defense of the early 1990s concept of the "New Lad," which Knowles defines as an "anti-intellectual" backlash response both to feminism and to the 1980s image of the "New Man," which adopted "a progressive model for masculinity as someone who would share housework and other 'feminine' tasks ... and who regarded women as partners and equals."[19] When Rob articulates his desire for women "who talk back, women with a mind of their own, women with snap and crackle and pop," he defines himself as a New Man. At the same time, however, he longs for women "who seem to need the love of a good man," imagining himself powerful enough to rescue and redeem this type of woman, much as he conversely seeks a woman who can "change and redeem" him.[20]

Does this desire for mutuality, even if somewhat idealized, imply feminist undercurrents flowing beneath the perceived surface of the novel? Frears answers the question unambiguously in the affirmative as far as the film is concerned, saying that *High Fidelity* is feminist because "it's a cry for men to grow up," adding that "it's been politicized."[21] The relative absence of Laura from the film compared with her much greater presence in the novel has, however, led some critics to question such claims, leading one, for instance, to assert that "it's almost criminal the way the central relationship . . . has been left such a void."[22] DeVincentis admits that "Laura is not meant to be a mystery in the book, but she comes off that way a bit in the movie," in part, he suggests, because the movie is a point-of-view story.[23]

The differing terms of address in novel and film in a small, seemingly throw-away moment illustrate the complications of filtering feminist undercurrents through Rob's consciousness as he floats between the contradictory emotional anchors of self-deception and honest reflection. Rob speaks of women's underwear, in the novel saying, "I never really recovered from the shock of discovering that women do what we do: they save their best pairs for the nights when they know they are going to sleep with somebody. When you live with a woman . . . your lascivious schoolboy dreams of adulthood as a time when you are surrounded by exotic lingerie for ever and ever . . . crumble to dust."[24] In his use of the inclusive "you" and, as Knowles points out, in his use of "we," Rob addresses a male audience[25] with whom he assumes a tacit solidarity.

Addressing the camera and viewer directly in the film, Rob says, "I used to dream I'd be surrounded by exotic women's underwear forever and ever. Now I know they just save their best pairs for the nights they know they're going to sleep with somebody." The subtle shift modulates the implicit terms of address (in part, perhaps, a concession to box-office realities), from that of unambiguous male camaraderie—wherein Rob feels a guaranteed absolution in the novel—to that of a mixed-gender jury in the film, opening space for a more ambivalent response. The film's visual track adds further resonance. As Rob speaks, he picks up clothing of Laura's, heaped on a chair and absently sniffs it—a tiny, seemingly unconscious gesture that recontextualizes his words within a subtle sense of longing, speaking "the absence of the other." This longing shifts to irritation as he tosses Laura's clothes toward both the camera and viewers. His annoyance is directed at the absent

Laura, but also at those women in the audience who "save their best pairs" as Laura does—now something "women" do, not something that "we do" also. Yet Rob's bitterness is perhaps most profoundly directed toward himself, as expressed through this gesture that, on one level, acts to displace self-censure. A simple expression of male solidarity in the novel now becomes a complicated mixture of anger at Laura that extends to women in general, and anger at himself for having failed with Laura and the other women in his life. This small moment also underscores the limitation of fidelity as a critical approach in adaptation studies, as Robert Stam aptly argues, pointing out the "multitrack" nature of film—with sound, image, music, and spoken as well as written language at its disposal—in contrast to the single-track medium of the novel involving written words on a page.[26]

Rob's (unconscious) uses of self-deception at the same time reveal a nearly opposite dynamic operating in the "dialogue" between novel and film as he and Laura argue about her career as a lawyer, particularly her new job with a city firm, and "the restaurants and the expensive suits" that go along with it, which Rob places in opposition to "the spiky haircut" and "the black leather motorcycle jacket"[27] worn during her days as a legal aid attorney. In his claim that "if I was being obtuse, I'd say that money changed everything... she suddenly had loads, and... I had none," and in his further admission that "really, it wasn't the money. It was me,"[28] Rob simultaneously confesses and denies the underlying truth he'd rather not examine too closely. The possibility that the job and the money do matter perhaps leads Rob back to attitudes grounded in his suburban boyhood that he would rather overtly eschew than admit having covertly absorbed. And the novel allows us to recognize his doubly self-deceptive strategy—in admitting wrong-headedness, he hopes to release himself from having to look much further into conclusions that continue to influence his thinking, though he is loath to acknowledge it. When he asks Laura, in both the novel and the film, how she could have lived in his "dump" of an apartment in light of the salary she is now earning, both works make clear that to Rob, the money really does matter.

As they continue their argument in the novel, Laura expresses herself in amorphous terms that resist pat conclusions—"I left because we weren't really getting on, or even talking, very much, and I'm at an age where I want to sort myself out, and... you seem incapable of sorting yourself out."[29] To these nearly identical sentiments in the film, Laura adds, more pointedly, "You're the same person you used to be... at least you used to talk about the future," here grounding her grievances as much in the mode of future-oriented American values as in the need for introspection or reflection.

When Rob learns that Laura has left him for their former upstairs neighbor Ian (known also as Ray), who in some ways embodies the kind of de jour lifestyle Rob holds in contempt—with musical tastes Rob characterizes as "African, Latin, Bulgarian, whatever fucking world music fad was trendy that week"[30]—both novel and film testify to Rob's static position. Here, however, the novel draws attention to Rob's cultural insularity, as Knowles points out, arguing that his musical preferences "represent a backlash against the need for contemporaneity in music" and that his "antagonism is toward music outside what is either actual, or aspirational, for him. Therefore politicized music . . . records which are not British or American . . . are anathema since they would require him to expand his horizons."[31] The film, in contrast, deflects this potential critique of Rob, through its representation of Ian (played by Tim Robbins) as a caricature of the New Age guru, whose occupation in "conflict resolution" and whose graying pony tail, Asian-inflected costuming, and calm, even-toned speech rhythms devoid of emotional investment set him apart as "other," in contrast to Rob, Laura, Dick, and Barry, who are defined as "real" and emotionally engaged, against Ian's counterfeit cool. The film further represents Ian as a caricature of the New Man who cooks the meals, soliciting Laura for a "second opinion," and who suppresses authentic (read as manly?) anger in response to Rob's obsessive phone calls to Laura. In representing the New Age/New Man persona as inauthentic by comparison to the more authentic crisis-ridden Rob, the film (and the novel, though less overtly) suggests that if Rob does indeed become a New Man (or approach New Manhood), he will do so through genuine struggle, not through counterfeit cool or adherence to a prefabricated social template or formula as Ian seems to have adopted.

As Rob addresses us, the novel, more explicitly than the film, locates the darker consequences of his vision within a Western capitalist context in which success is defined in material, competitive, and gendered terms. This shift is made explicit when Laura's friend Liz challenges Rob with "How come you hate women who have better jobs than you, Rob?" or when having dinner with Charlie and her friends, years after their breakup, Rob asserts, "Do I want some of what they've got? You bet. I want their opinions, I want their money, I want their clothes. . . . I want to go back to 1979 and start all over again."[32] In the film the last line is dropped, once again placing less emphasis on reflection and "revision." The earlier lines, spoken in voice-over, are nearly the same but are now reconstituted as the grounding for Rob's ultimate realization that "Charlie is awful," a conclusion he reaches quite a bit earlier in the novel, after a phone conversation with her.

In replacing the last line, expressing Rob's desire to start over from the point where he and Charlie had broken up with a line pronouncing judgment on Charlie herself, the film removes Rob as an object of his own criticism, thus to some degree shifting the darker, self-contradictory ideological terms of his crisis. Whereas the film here hints that the problem has always been Rob's perception of Charlie, the ultimate judgment is directed at Charlie herself, a judgment enabling Rob to free himself from the imagined power she has held for so many years and from the implications of his wanting what she and her friends have acquired. In the novel, however, Rob pronounces judgment on himself—on his own behavior in response to Charlie's rejection of him. Although the film neatly resolves this source of crisis, the novel exposes more complicated layers of crisis located not within Charlie's character but within Rob's character as it shapes his perceptions of both Charlie and himself.

DIRECT ADDRESS, NARRATIVE STRUCTURE, AND THE ADAPTATION PROCESS: SEXUAL POLITICS IN A POSTMODERN WORLD

The film's use of direct address, however—as in the underwear monologue—does enable more complicated, more layered, and perhaps somewhat darker readings of Rob's character than simple dialogue or voice-over narration are able to provide. In light of the exclusive reliance on voice-over in early versions of the screenplay before the eventual shift to direct address, the voice-over/direct-address interplay becomes an important point of study.

In film, voice-over generally allows for subtle gaps or outright contradictions between narration and image, capturing multiple layers of self-deception and delicious ambiguities on the part of the narrator, as in *Gilda* (1946), for instance, and in numerous other examples of film noir especially. Yet, as used in the final cut of *High Fidelity*, those instances of voice-over still retained rarely exploit these possibilities. In film and literature, the self-conscious narrator who addresses us directly, who confides in us, courting our sympathy, or who winks at us in a shared ironic detachment from events and other characters, poses a postmodernist threat to the very stability of classic realist narrative formulas—a condition adding resonance to our relationship with Rob in *High Fidelity*. This resonance is most richly realized in the film as Rob embarks on the "project" of meeting up again with all of the women on his "top five" list of break-ups, of which his dinner with Charlie and her friends is the climactic instance. What the finished film ultimately accomplishes through direct address becomes particularly apparent when it is compared with an earlier voice-over version of the screenplay (dated 9/98) and an early direct-address version of the screenplay (dated 11/11/98).[33]

To further contextualize this shift, it would be fair to say that Hornby's writing is influenced by certain models of cinematic style and structure, most obviously Woody Allen's *Annie Hall*. Although he references any number of pop culture figures throughout the novel, Rob uses Allen as a means of defining *himself*—his own "genius" for being average—implying that, unlike "lots of blokes" who "have a Woody Allen sense of humor but look like Woody Allen," he has Allen's humor without the wiry, bespectacled appearance or the neurotic mannerisms.[34] (Rob's insularity echoes that of Allen's Alvy Singer in *Annie Hall*, with his masculine crisis grounded, in part, in sexual anxieties.)

Woody Allen masterfully explores his perpetual art/life, fantasy/reality musings through direct address to audience members as *Annie Hall* opens, and through occasional interruption of narrative events as he steps out of the story and addresses us, posing questions, rhetorically seeking answers or advice, asking us to witness and verify his reading of events, or simply laying out theme or exposition—all forms of address that appear influential in Hornby's mode of self-conscious address, and adapted to strong effect in later versions of the screenplay. Just as Rob's relationship with Laura appears to be ending as the narrative opens, so Alvy, in his opening direct-address monologue, tells us that he and Annie have split.

As both men attempt to sort out the reasons for their break-ups and their feelings for Laura and Annie, respectively, we initially sense their limited understanding and acknowledgment of the women themselves as having their own fully formed needs and desires apart from the relationship. Alvy and Annie split, reunite, and split once again for good. Rob and Laura split and reunite—with the threat of a second break-up looming when Rob finds himself attracted to the young reporter writing about his former work as a D.J. (she was one of his fans) and his one-night return to that world he loved as part of an event Laura has orchestrated.

As if in dialogue with Allen and *Annie Hall*, Hornby, in the novel, rewrites the story of Annie and Alvy, forcing Rob to ask (presented almost verbatim in the film's direct address), "I'm going to jump from rock to rock for the rest of my life until there aren't any rocks left? I'm going to run each time I get itchy feet? Because I get them about once a quarter, along with the utility bills," and leading him to conclude that "what's wrong with Laura is that I'll never see her for the first or second or third time again."[35] Finally proposing to Laura, Rob acknowledges that "I know I want to stay with you and I keep pretending otherwise, to myself and you, and we just limp on and on."[36] In *Annie Hall*, Alvy arrives at similar conclusions and also proposes marriage—a proposal Annie unambiguously refuses, just as Laura refuses, implying, however, that when she can count on Rob's stability, she may accept.

Structurally, Hornby's novel opens with a thirty-two-page "prelude," in which Rob describes each one of his "top-five most memorable split-ups, in chronological order."[37] The prelude ends with a paragraph written in apostrophe to Laura: "And then I met you, Laura, and we lived together, and now you've moved out. But, you know, you're not offering me anything *new* here; if you want to force your way onto the list, you'll have to do better than this."[38] Following this prelude, Rob begins the present tense narrative in chapter one by saying, "Laura leaves first thing Monday morning."[39] Rather than group Rob's flashbacks detailing the "top-five" break-ups together as the novel does, the film interweaves two of the top five (Charlie and Sarah) at later points within the present-tense narrative, and almost completely elides number three, Jackie Allen, whom Rob had stolen away from a relatively long-term romance with his best friend Phil in high school—an elision, perhaps, aimed at forging stronger audience sympathy with Rob. In the film Rob merely mentions Jackie, while in the novel Jackie represents Rob's coming to terms with disillusionment and with his own capacity for betrayal. Rob points out that his stealing Jackie—in whom he'd lost interest the moment he had won her—was a crucial moment for himself and his group of friends who had, as a result, grown mildly cynical about romance: "In a few short weeks, mock-marital status had ceased to be something to aspire to, and had become cause for scorn."[40] The novel continues forward, chronologically, unlike the film, which interrupts the narrative with short flashbacks or fantasies as Rob narrates.

Both 1998 versions of the *High Fidelity* screenplay—the September 1998 version with voice-over as its dominant narrative mode and the November 1998 version with direct address as its dominant mode—begin with an image of Rob's flailing about in the mud, hiding from Laura on the night of her father's funeral. This image, to which both screenplays return near the end (where it is positioned, appearing only once, in the finished film), represents Rob's (literally) lowest point before reconciling with Laura. In opening with this image (rather than with Rob's direct address, as in the final version of the film), both earlier versions of the screenplay adopt a broadly comic, borderline-slapstick approach in attempting to define Rob's misery. In eventually opting for a direct-address opening, with Rob speaking to us just as Laura leaves the apartment, the film, like the novel, gives precedence to the very act

As if in acknowledgment that postmodern contingency and referentiality shape even romance, Rob (John Cusack) retreats to the project of reorganizing his record collection on his first night alone after Laura's departure. © Touchstone Pictures, Inc., 2000.

of narration, to the direct and immediate relationship forged with audience. When Rob asks, "What came first, the music or the misery? Did I listen to pop music because I was miserable or was I miserable because I listened to pop music?" (a line that appears well into the prelude of Hornby's novel) Rob announces his mission of attempting to figure out how it all went wrong.

Hornby's novel flirts with the postmodern through content and the sometimes abrupt discontinuity in action and tone from chapter to chapter or even within chapters, capturing something of what it means to live in a fractured, postmodern world, in which personal relationships seem as contingent and as shaped by "intertextual" referentiality as are popular culture and art. Rob comes to recognize how Marco and Charlie "wrote Sarah, in a way, because without Marco and Charlie there would have been no Sarah, and how Sarah and her ex . . . wrote me, and how Rosie . . . [during a brief affair while Rob was living with Laura] wrote Ian."[41] Knowles elaborates by pointing out that whereas *High Fidelity* is a popular novel refusing the highbrow language and devices often associated with postmodern literature, it nevertheless captures the nature of the "postmodern subject," as exemplified by Rob, who "as a consequence of certain historical and cultural developments, lives with the fact that certain barriers have been broken down and the fixed ideas about truth, justice, art, and progress are impossible to sustain,"[42] a factor, perhaps, further contributing to his crisis.

That the voice-over version of the screenplay fails to convey the implications of a postmodern condition is evident at several points when the self-consciousness of Rob's narration and the self-deception embedded within it are muffled. Several comparative examples, as Rob embarks on his mission to meet up with the women on his top-five list, work well to illustrate the greater power of direct address in capturing this condition. The voice-over version of the script, as if to overtly illustrate its deflection of Rob's novelistic self-conscious address and his motives, includes a chance meeting between Rob and Alison Ashmore's (Ashworth in the novel) mother in a bar, where he learns, by accident, that Alison has married her eighth grade sweetheart, Kevin Bannister—the boy for whom she dumped Rob. In all four versions—novel, voice-over screenplay, direct address screenplay and finished film—this knowledge momentarily liberates Rob, who now sees Alison's rejection of him as an act of fate in which he bore no responsibility. This sense of euphoric liberation drives him forward on his mission—a mission he consciously and deliberately initiates in the novel and film, when he picks up the phone to call Alison's mother. Rob's purposeful action here captures his own sense of postmodern contingency and his conscious effort, perhaps, to construct an alternative reality, an alternative narrative of his life in an attempt to "paper over the cracks" of such contingency, to borrow Robin Wood's apt expression.[43] Paradoxically, he wishes to construct an alternative that will provide the very coherence and closure postmodern narrative often denies. At the same time, however, in the context of sexual politics, Rob initially wishes to subvert conventional cause-and-effect patterns in order to displace his own agency, positioning himself instead as a passive receptor who bears little emotional or moral responsibility for the break-ups that transpired—a desire fueled and legitimized by his reading of "fate" as the true agent in his break-up with Alison.

Direct address in the film and self-conscious narration in the novel, however, complicate the process, inviting us to recognize Rob's "game," which we, as viewers and readers, sometimes are positioned to play and at other times are positioned to sit out and observe from a critical distance. His date with Penny, the high school sweetheart he broke up with, is especially revealing. At age sixteen, Penny resisted Rob's sexual advances, prompting Rob to break up with her in both novel and film saying, "What's the point? . . . It never goes anywhere,"[44] and leaving Penny heartbroken. A few weeks later in chemistry class, on hearing that high school stud Chris Thomson has "knobbed" her, Rob revises the story of his active rejection of Penny to a narrative focused on his own passivity and failure. When he has dinner with Penny, now also in her thirties, and asks why she dropped him for Chris, she reminds him that *he* left her, revealing that with Chris, "I was too tired to fight him off, and it wasn't rape because I said OK, but it wasn't far off," lines that follow closely in the film. Rob's reaction, on her leaving the restaurant in anger, is simply to declare, "So that's another one I don't have to worry about. I should have done this years ago"—a response that clearly indicts Rob as blindly narcissistic in his denial of emotional or moral culpability.[45]

The example involving Penny in all versions—novel, both screenplays, and film—works to reveal Rob's delight in rediscovering an agency he's convinced he was never capable of exerting (now behaving like a "proper man ... who appears not to give a shit"),[46] an identity in which he revels, if only for a moment). When he speaks his lines in direct address to the audience, adding initially, "She's right! I *did* break up with her!"[47] the film, even more powerfully than the novel, aligns us with Penny, whose pain is made sympathetically apparent by Joelle Carter's performance. Here, direct address works to heighten our critical distance from Rob. Oddly, in the voice-over version of the screenplay, Rob speaks the original lines from the novel (omitting "She's right. I did break up with her") to an off-screen waiter, followed immediately by his terse request for the check.[48] This version tends to deflect the full effect of arrogant narcissism that direct address so powerfully conveys—a narcissism heightened by Rob's misplaced confidence that, merely by virtue of addressing us, our complicity and absolution will follow. The novel achieves a similar effect, yet in terms that indict Rob less severely, given its single-track form and the power of Penny's physical presence in the multi-track medium of the film. The novel, moreover, deflects sustained contemplation of Rob's action at this moment (unlike its generally more intensive reflection throughout) by immediately shifting attention from Rob to Barry's quest for a band with which to perform as the next chapter opens—an abrupt shift that echoes contemporary cinematic form.

The voice-over and early direct-address versions of the screenplay have Rob move immediately on to a date with Sarah, while in the finished film he briefly addresses us with "Next up, Charlie, but I'm not quite ready for that," followed by a shot of Sarah's answering the door to Rob. Reminding us of his too insurmountable heartbreak, this transitional line modulates, though doesn't wholly alter, our critical stance toward Rob. Both novel and film further counterbalance Rob's response to Penny's anguish through his refraining from sleeping with Sarah, who is clearly vulnerable and despairing of her single status, and through his admission in the novel that "there are no hard feelings here, and I'm glad she ditched me and not the other way around."[49] At the same time, however, we see that he is as much concerned with absolving himself as he is with expressing sincere concern for Sarah.

The same could be said of a key moment in the novel and film in which Rob lists his four sins against Laura, a confession triggered when Laura's friend Liz storms into Championship Vinyl in the film (a pub in the novel), calling Rob an "asshole"/"arsehole." Rob explains Liz's action by confessing her probable knowledge that he had slept with another woman while Laura was pregnant; that the affair very likely prompted Laura to end the pregnancy; that he borrowed five thousand dollars from Laura and had not yet repaid it; that he hinted before Laura's leaving that he wasn't entirely happy in the relationship. While confessional, the terms of address in the novel place Rob in an intimate yet an aggressively challenging stance with respect to the implied male reader when he asserts, "And before you judge, although you have probably already done so, go away and write down the worst four things that you have done to your partner . . . in the plainest language possible. Finished? OK, so who's the arsehole now?"[50] Thus, he forges an unhappy complicity with his reader, whose judgment of Rob is now at least partially held in abeyance.

Although this challenge to the viewer remains in place in the early direct-address version of the screenplay, in the earlier voice-over version, Rob addresses his words to Dick, Barry, and customers in the store, with an interesting editing strategy. After saying "Time's up," Rob is shown seated in a bar, drinking a scotch, with the line, "Okay, so who's the asshole now?" spoken in voice-over.[51] The challenge to other characters and to viewers is dropped entirely in the film's final version, where editing patterns emphasize rather a comic effect derived largely from Joan Cusack's performance as Liz. Intercut with Rob's naming each of his offenses against Laura is a restaurant scene in which Laura repeats each offense to Liz, followed by Liz's incredulous and increasingly angry but nonetheless exaggerated responses, which do strike a humorous chord.

In all versions, Rob attempts to explain and justify each of his four offences and, in the early direct-address version of the screenplay, Rob's address is intercut with a scene in which he and Laura discuss their relationship. Editing patterns in the early direct-address version are perhaps aimed at creating a cause-and-effect relationship beyond what Rob is willing to acknowledge, thus exposing his self-deception and conscious attempt to sidestep responsibility. In the voice-over version, Rob enters into a dialogue with Liz, attempting to explain how these events transpired, followed by his challenge to his mates in the record store. As he addresses us in the film, Rob ends with the line, "Who needs a drink?" as the subway train he rides plunges into a tunnel, an image followed immediately by a scene set in Rob's apartment where he asks us, "What's wrong with me?... Why am I doomed to be left?"—questions that prompt his mission to seek out the women from his past, but, more important, that function to displace his role as agent (in the case of his "sins" against Laura at least) so that he can once again assume the position of passive object or receptor in his relationships with women.

Rob actively and deliberately denies his own agency, thus raising questions as to what constitutes agency in gendered terms. In denying agency, is Rob simply renouncing conventional masculinity, or is he more deliberately repudiating his role in hurting another person (much as he does in the case of Penny), with all the attendant implications and responsibilities in a larger context of sexual politics and debates on masculinity? While Rob is quick to admit his wrongs and ready to conclude that there's little justification for his actions, he nevertheless seeks absolution, mostly from himself, which he can find only by recasting himself, again, as the object "doomed to be left," to be acted upon. In the novel, however, Rob reflects on a conversation with Laura in which he once asked—in the context of the pregnancy issue—why she had stayed with him. She replied that she had wanted to stick with it, to get through a "bad patch," followed by Rob's rhetorical question to his readers, "And why had I stuck with it? Not for reasons as noble or as adult as that.... I stuck with it because, suddenly... I found myself really attracted to Laura again. I needed Rosie to spice Laura up a bit.... I could see her losing interest in me, so I worked like mad to get it back, and when I got it back, I lost interest in her all over again. That sort of thing happens to me a lot.... I don't know how to sort it out."[52] In an ironic form of agency, Rob asserts himself—as reactive—yet expresses discomfort with his own morally questionable reactions, preferring instead the ability to actively choose as Laura has done on several levels. This momentary recognition is one of a number of incremental movements in the novel leading Rob to eventually embrace his agency—both the power and the responsibility it brings—which ultimately results in his choosing a more feminized rather than a masculinized sense of what that agency can mean.

About midway through the novel, when pressing Laura for answers about their break-up and her relationship with Ian, Rob is frustrated with her lack of clarity, saying (in conspiratorial terms with his male reader again), "Why are people—let's face it, women—like this? It doesn't pay to think this way, with all this mess and doubt and gray, smudged lines where there should be a crisp, sharp picture."[53] In choosing commitment to Laura over jumping from "rock to rock"—even with the edge of excitement it promises—Rob ultimately asserts his agency, but in terms that appreciate the smudginess, the impossibility of a "crisp, sharp picture." He thus becomes simultaneously feminized and empowered.

FEMINIZED AGENCY AND POSTMODERN CONTINGENCY

The final version of the film—in part to counterbalance our potential alienation from Rob and, perhaps, in its need to define more "crisply" the nature of Rob's growing commitment to Laura—includes a scene that is neither in the novel nor in the two earlier versions of the screenplay. Just after Laura has moved the last of her belongings from Rob's apartment and has gently prodded him to think of "record store owner" as among his top-five dream jobs, Rob, in direct address, lists the qualities he most misses about Laura: her dry but "warm and forgiving" sense of humor, her loyal and honest character, her unaffected grace, her smell and taste that make her feel "like home." Through this scene, the film positions Rob as the desiring male. Yet, while his words articulate a longing echoing Barthes's notion of the feminized male, his longing remains fixed on Laura as object of his desire, made more apparent in his implied address to a male audience—one of the few such instances within the film—acknowledging that he could also list his complaints against Laura, which are merely the "garden variety female" things. The novel, through its smaller incremental steps, is able to create a more coherent position for Rob's feminized "agency" in the end. While the implied conspiratorial male reader of the novel may establish a more masculinist tone than does the implied mixed-gender audience of the film, early versions of the screenplay appear to grapple with this issue—as if uneasy with both the conspiratorial masculine address and with the ultimate position of feminized agency the novel stakes out for Rob.

As noted earlier, both the early direct-address and the earlier voice-over versions of the screenplay open with an image of Rob hiding in a muddy flowerbed just after the funeral of Laura's father, setting a tone that is perhaps more masculinist in its externalized comic expression of Rob's pain and loss, although when it is repeated near the end, the image is meant to invite a retrospective reading that places Rob in a more feminized position. This scene appears just once near the end of the finished film and seems to suggest both a comic sense of loss and feminization. Yet the film backs away from this more masculinist vision of earlier drafts, both of which also place much greater emphasis on a narrative line involving Justin and Vince, two teenage skateboarders and aspiring musicians who annoy Rob by hanging outside the record store, from which they occasionally shoplift. Justin and Vince—

characters absent from the novel—are created by the screenwriters seemingly to replace the novel's Johnny, an "Irish drunk" whom Rob routinely kicks out of the store in scenes, as he describes them, that "have become choreographed and scripted routines."[54] Knowles observes that Rob is fearful of becoming like Johnny,[55] as is most evident when Johnny unwittingly taps into Rob's anxieties by asking, "'You think I'd be in this fucking state if I had a wife?'"[56]

In earlier versions of the screenplay the more pervasive presence of Justin and Vince appears as a means of further modifying Rob's coming to terms with a more feminized position, as he is forced to, if even unconsciously, when confronted with Johnny. Although Justin and Vince are less prominent in the final film, the film does juxtapose Rob's monologue about missing Laura with the developing Justin/Vince narrative, which is further juxtaposed with a phone call from Laura telling Rob of her father's death. While this structuring adeptly maintains a lightness of tone even in the midst of melancholy circumstances, it nevertheless dilutes the more serious contemplation of gendered agency that the novel invites. In juxtaposing the relatively carefree world of (male) adolescence with the world of (predominantly female) adult responsibility, the film does, however, assert that Rob stands uncomfortably suspended between the two.

In the novel, the death of Laura's father and Rob's response function as an extended and uninterrupted turning point in his coming to terms with himself and his feelings for Laura. He initially asserts that "if people have to die, I don't want them dying near me," until he recognizes that death is "something I've always managed to put off. Now I can see that it's something I'll be doing for the rest of my life," and most poignantly that "I saw, for the first time, how scared I am of dying and of other people dying, and how this fear has prevented me from doing all sorts of things, like . . . sticking with a relationship."[57] This recognition resonates tellingly with Rob's earlier acknowledgment that "I have disappointed myself; I thought I was going to turn out to be worth a bit more than this," expressing his urge to apologize to "the little guy" he sees in childhood photos: "'I'm sorry, I've let you down. I was the person who was supposed to look after you, but I blew it: I made the wrong decisions at bad times, and I turned you into me.'"[58] As he sits in the rain at a bus stop following the funeral, Rob admits, in the film's direct address, "I can see I never really committed to Laura. It made more sense to . . . keep my options open . . . and that's suicide by tiny, tiny increments." While these words echo Rob's more sustained recognition in the novel, the depth of his internalized expression of fear, vulnerability, longing, and regret are somewhat diluted—perhaps because the comic image of Rob's flailing in the mud has greater power in this multitrack medium, thus undermining the novel's more introspective tone.

The novel further complicates Rob's response as Laura drives by, asking Rob to have sex with her—an act that seals their reconciliation in the film. In the novel, however, just as they are about to begin, Rob expresses hesitation, ostensibly grounded in his concern for safety, now that Laura has been with another man whose sexual history Rob cannot know. He later reflects that "in truth it was the symbolism that interested me more than the fear. I wanted to hurt her, on this day of all days, just because it's the first time since she left that I've been able to."[59] In the context of the novel's *Bildungsroman* trajectory, Rob's already ingrained masculinist understanding of action and reaction—of jockeying for empowerment—coexists with and is eventually displaced by his deeper recognition and acceptance of a more feminized sense of empowerment.

Self-reflexively placing the (realist) *Bildungsroman* tradition within a postmodernist context, Hornby has Rob contend that "Dick and Barry and I agreed that what really matters is what you like, not what you *are* like." When Rob asserts that "these things matter,"[60] the novel acknowledges the difficulties of pursuing "growth" in a postmodern cultural context where referentiality is all. As part of the *Bildungsroman* tradition, however, Rob is able to distinguish between a good date and a meaningful relationship and, like the typical *Bildungsroman* protagonist, "discovers the need for 'something more,'" as Knowles points out, and while that "'something more' has been music" he comes to accept "the idea of the right partner as being the 'something more' he seeks."[61]

Rob manages to arrive somewhere in between a *Bildungsroman* state of mature recognition and a postmodern sense of fragmentation. And while Knowles aptly points out that Hornby ironizes the *Bildungsroman* tradition, most overtly by presenting us with a protagonist whose goal has been "the delaying of the *Bildungsroman* process,"[62]—an effect that direct address enables within the film at those times when Rob doesn't always embrace the implications of own narration—Hornby nevertheless situates Rob more securely, and more conservatively, within an acceptance of himself and his social context than do Salinger and Twain, for instance. Whereas Holden and Huck remain suspended in a state of ambivalence regarding their place in a society they respectively see as "phony" and hypocritical, Rob's newfound maturity lies in his desire to construct an emotionally stable and meaningful position within the larger context of postmodern contingency. In the context of gender in *High Fidelity*, just as in the context of race in Twain's novel, this more mature position requires that Rob inhabit and empathize with the desires and needs of the "other."

As both the novel and the film close, Rob imagines making a compilation tape for Laura, "that's full of stuff she's heard of, and full of stuff she'd play," ("stuff she'd like . . . stuff that would make *her* happy," in the film) adding, in the final line of both works, "tonight, for the first time, I can sort of see how it's done."[63] The postmodern and the realist *Bildungsroman* thus merge when, rather than imposing what he would like her to like, Rob is able to recognize the value of what *she* likes and, more important, of what she's like as fundamental to a meaningful relationship with her. In his newfound approach to compilation, Rob metaphorically turns away from a masculinized sense of agency, embracing instead a more feminized understanding of an agency that promises, paradoxically, greater stability and greater flexibility in the context of postmodern contingency.

NOTES

1. Although Nick Hornby did adapt the 1997 U.K. production of *Fever Pitch* (directed by David Evans), he did not involve himself in the *High Fidelity* screenplay other than to provide valuable feedback as the work evolved, according to co-screenwriter D. V. DeVincentis.

I thank co-screenwriter D. V. DeVincentis for a long and very informative telephone interview in August 2004, during which he shared details concerning the film's production history and the many steps involved in the process of adaptation.

2. Stephen Frears, "The Complexities of Cultural Change: An Interview with Stephen Frears" by Cynthia Lucia. *Cineaste* 28, no. 4 (2003): 8–15.

3. A much earlier version of the screenplay had been written by Scott Rosenberg, who is credited as co-writer primarily, according to DeVincentis, because in the case of adaptation, whatever material is used from the novel is credited to the first screenwriter to have adapted it. Although the screenplay DeVincentis, Pink, and Cusack created has little in common, stylistically or structurally, with the Rosenberg screenplay, Rosenberg's name does appear on the credits.

4. Stephen Frears, Interview, on *High Fidelity*, DVD (Touchstone Home Video, 2003).

5. Frears remarks in a supplemental DVD interview that he was at first skeptical about moving the action from London to Chicago, since for him, Hornby's novel was ultimately a novel about London. Co-screenwriters Cusack, DeVincentis, and Pink grew up in Chicago, where they attended high school together. Cusack remarks, also in a DVD interview, that, as he read the novel, he continually envisioned Chicago

locations corresponding to those in London. While it's fair to say that Frears and the screenwriters did capture the various Chicago settings quite naturalistically, it can also be said that the film is not "about" Chicago in the same way that the novel—with its far more developed political and social class context—is "about" London.

6. Nick Hornby, *High Fidelity* (New York: Riverhead Books, 1995), 63.
7. Ibid., 157.
8. Ibid., 110
9. Stephen Neale, *Genre* (London: British Film Institute, 1980), 60.
10. Hornby, *High Fidelity*, 39.
11. Ibid., 136, 22, 29.
12. Ibid., 24–32 passim.
13. Ibid., 97.
14. Stephanie Zacharek, "High Fidelity," *Salon*, March 31, 2000, www.salon.com/Ent/movies/review/2000/03/31/high_fidelity.
15. Joanne Knowles, *Nick Hornby's* High Fidelity (New York: Continuum, 2002), 19.
16. Ibid., 27–28.
17. Hornby, *High Fidelity*, 3.
18. Knowles, *Nick Hornby's* High Fidelity, 17.
19. Ibid., 15–16.
20. Hornby, *High Fidelity*, 196, 63.
21. Frears, "Complexities," 13.
22. David Edelstein, "Broken Record," *Slate*, March 31, 2000, http://slate.msn.com/id/78277/.
23. D. V. DeVicentis, telephone interview, August 2004.
24. Hornby, *High Fidelity*, 46–47.
25. Knowles, *Nick Hornby's* High Fidelity, 25.
26. Robert Stam, "Beyond Fidelity: The Dialogics of Adaptation," in *Film Adaptation*, ed. James Naremore (New Brunswick, NJ: Rutgers University Press, 2000), 59.
27. Hornby, *High Fidelity*, 89.
28. Ibid., 25.
29. Ibid., 108.
30. Ibid., 71.
31. Knowles, *Nick Hornby's* High Fidelity, 47.
32. Hornby, *High Fidelity*, 193, 199.
33. Co-screenwriter D. V. DeVincentis very generously shared two versions of his *High Fidelity* screenplay with me: an early voice-over version, dated 9/98, and a version dated 11/11/98, which he refers to as the "London draft."
34. Hornby, *High Fidelity*, 28–29.
35. Ibid., 315.
36. Ibid., 318.
37. Ibid., 3.

38. Ibid., 31–32.
39. Ibid., 35.
40. Ibid., 19–20.
41. Ibid., 132.
42. Knowles, *Nick Hornby's* High Fidelity, 52–53.
43. See Robin Wood's "The Incoherent Text: Narrative in the 70s," in his *Hollywood from Vietnam to Reagan* (New York: Columbia University Press, 1986).
44. Hornby, *High Fidelity*, 13.
45. Ibid, 173–174.
46. Ibid., 157.
47. D. V. DeVicentis, Steve Pink, John Cusack, and Scott Rosenberg, adapts., *High Fidelity*, by Nick Hornby, unpublished screenplay, November 11, 1998, 81.
48. D. V. DeVicentis, Steve Pink, John Cusack, and Scott Rosenberg, adapts., *High Fidelity*, by Nick Hornby, unpublished screenplay, September 1998, 47.
49. Hornby, *High Fidelity*, 185.
50. Ibid., 93.
51. DeVicentis et al., unpublished screenplay, November 1998.
52. Hornby, *High Fidelity*, 101–102.
53. Ibid., 108.
54. Ibid., 40.
55. Knowles, *Nick Hornby's* High Fidelity, 30.
56. Hornby, *High Fidelity*, 56.
57. Ibid., 232, 236, 247.
58. Ibid., 204–205.
59. Ibid. 255.
60. Ibid., 117.
61. Knowles, *Nick Hornby's* High Fidelity, 28.
62. Ibid., 25.
63. Hornby, *High Fidelity*, 323.

11

ADAPTABLE BRIDGET
Generic Intertextuality and Postfeminism in *Bridget Jones's Diary*

//

Shelley Cobb

> *This is intertextuality with a vengeance.*
> —Molly Haskell, "The Innocent Ways of Renée Zellweger,"
> *New York Times*, April 8, 2001

IN HER GLOWING REVIEW OF THE FILM ADAPTATION OF *BRIDGET Jones's Diary*, Molly Haskell delights in the intertextuality of the film and the ways it plays with audience knowledge of the book, its author, and the film's screenwriters and stars. Following her lead but turning it onto a broader subject, we might momentarily consider intertextuality's ability to wreak vengeance on our expectations of adaptation studies. Much of the critical literature on adaptation continues to reflect expectations that films should simply translate their source material, and a film's value is assessed according to how faithfully it reproduces the original text. Scholars have called repeatedly for a move away from a criterion of faithfulness because of its limitation as a mode of criticism and its implied prioritizing of the literary over the cinematic, a hierarchy that allows little room for the popular novel adaptation.[1] However, one of the reasons fidelity criticism remains prevalent in scholarly literature is the academy's emphasis on adaptations of canonical and literary novels. When a book has sold thousands of copies to the same audience that will go to see it on-screen, there is no longer a high culture imperative for textual faithfulness, and a language of authenticity (which allows for successful adaptations that do not strictly translate the novel to film and focuses on the audience's approval of the film) often replaces the language of fidelity. Not only does fidelity criticism limit the critic, it also limits the text, confining the adaptation to a compare-and-contrast analysis. Most adaptations, whether considered highly canonical or fashionably popular, resist this simplistic assessment, and from a different perspective, an adaptation could be seen productively as a dynamic (if not vengeful) display of intertextuality. I propose that intertextuality is necessary for a move away from the binary of fidelity because "any text is constructed as a mosaic of quotations; any text is the absorption and transformation of another."[2] Nowhere is the notion of the absorption and transformation of another text more obvious, explicit, even self-conscious, than in adaptations.

Bridget Jones's Diary is built on multiple layers of intertextuality. Bridget originated as Helen Fielding's "alter-ego" in a newspaper column in *The Independent* (one of Britain's national broadsheet, quality newspapers); the novel is a kind of adaptation in its own right (as Fielding herself said, "I shamelessly stole the plot from *Pride and Prejudice*"). Moreover, the 1994 BBC adaptation of Jane Austen's novel appears in Fielding's novel: Colin Firth plays Bridget's Mark Darcy in the same stiff, upper-class manner he played Elizabeth's Mr. Darcy in the BBC version (he is also mentioned in Fielding's novel via a tabloid story of an affair with his *Pride and Prejudice* co-star). Hugh Grant's real-life liaison with a prostitute figures in the novel, and Grant stars as Bridget's scandalous boss and love interest (a fact that crystallizes the film's inclusion in the cycle of British romantic comedies, or Britcoms, in which Grant often stars). All of these intertextual moments are framed by the generic intertexts of the romance novel and the romantic comedy film and are reinforced by the production personnel: Helen Fielding is credited on the screenplay, as are Andrew Davies, who wrote the script for the BBC's *Pride and Prejudice*, and Richard Curtis, who wrote *Four Weddings and a Funeral* and *Notting Hill*, both of which starred Grant.[3] The director Sharon Maguire, as was frequently noted in reviews of the film, is one of Helen Fielding's best friends (one of Bridget's best friends in the novel, Shazza, is based on her). In taking *Bridget Jones's Diary* as my subject I seek to foreground intertextuality as a key term in the study of adaptations.

In his article "The Dialogics of Adaptation," Robert Stam has theorized this relentless intertextuality of adaptation through Bakhtin's notion of dialogism—the "relation between the utterance and all other utterances" or the relation between the text and all its "others," whether texts, cultures, audiences, and more, as Stam describes in the following:

> [I]ntertextual dialogism refers to the infinite and open-ended possibilities generated by all the discursive practices of a culture, the entire matrix of communicative utterances within which the artistic text is situated, which reach the text not only through recognizable influences, but also through a subtle process of dissemination.[4]

Moving beyond a simplified intertextuality that considers only the source material, adaptation studies should take into account the dynamic cultural and discursive forces at play, such as multiple literary (and other aesthetic) influences, the cultural milieu, production factors in filmmaking, and audience reception. No longer is the film, or analysis of the film, confined to delineating a faithful translation. Within this paradigm, "an adaptation . . . is less an attempted resuscitation of an originary word than a turn in an ongoing dialogical process."[5] The "mosaic of quotations" in an adaptation appears in relief, revealing the multiplicity of intertexts that make adaptations multidimensional and multilayered. A dialogical approach to adaptations moves beyond the binary relationship of novel and film to recognizing the importance of context to intertextuality. As Stam has elaborated: "The context is already textualized, informed by the 'already said' and by 'prior speakings,' while the text is 'redolent with contexts,' at every point inflected by historical process and shaped by social events."[6] *Bridget Jones's Diary* can be understood, then, as inextricably bound up with and relating dialogically to (both informed by and informing) the postfeminism of its popular culture and historical context.[7]

As an adaptation and a franchise, *Bridget Jones's Diary* holds a privileged place in cultural debates about feminism, women, and gender relations in the current postfeminist climate. Bridget's name appears in widely varying articles on and for women, from gossipy tabloids to scholarly journals, responding to and furthering her high profile. She is often used as short-hand by her fans for their experiences as fin-de-siècle women (hence the phrase "a Bridget Jones moment" to refer to everything from a fashion mishap to getting a man) and in print and television news op-ed pieces to reference, or even critique, the current postfeminist state of (single) women.[8] Articles with titles such as "Forget Bridget Jones, single women are happier," tend to cauterize the debates about the possibilities of women's happiness around their (non-)relationship status through this identifiable figure.[9] The repeated use of Bridget to function metonymically for that group vitiates the actual difficulties and complexities of contemporary single women.[10] This understanding of Bridget as an occasion for feminine identification in cultural discourse has created a Bridget who "exists" and functions transtextually as a distinct but malleable image of contemporary womanhood, a postfeminist icon of the late twentieth century. The intertextuality of the novel, the film, and the adaptation process (especially the scriptwriting) colluded with the adaptability of postfeminist discourse to create the necessary iconic Bridget who transcends her texts, while simultaneously "authenticating" the adaptation.

THE ADAPTATION PROCESS AND GENERIC INTERTEXTUALITY

Not only did the process of adapting the novel to film fuel Bridget's cultural prominence, but her cultural status and popularity influenced the adaptation process, a fact noted by many journalists in their reviews:

> The filmmakers were never in the position of simply making an adaptation of a mere book. From the very beginning, they were adapting a phenomenon. Screenwriter Richard Curtis says this actually made it easier: "At least in *Bridget Jones* you kind of know what the big subject matter is. So it was convenient being able to say, 'Well, have we fulfilled the brief of what made it a phenomenon?'"[11]

According to Curtis, the perception that the filmmakers were in the process of adapting a "phenomenon" rather than simply a text appears to have eased the process of engaging with Bridget not only as an authentic representation of thirtysomething single women but as a character, allowing the adaptation to escape the usual emphasis on textual fidelity.

Instead, the screenwriters created an adaptation with a network of generic intertextualities that reflects the way the phenomenon depends on a network of postfeminist discursive assumptions and categories. In press releases and interviews, the contributors stressed the collaborative nature of the project and focused on the development of the script. In a press packet for the film, the director Sharon Maguire recalls the scriptwriting process as a kind of relay. Fielding's contract with her publisher required her to start the second book and leave drafts of the script to be finished. Some rumors circulated that conflict between Davies and Maguire over the development of the script caused Davies to leave and Curtis to be brought in. Maguire's account omits that version of events and suggests that only time and other commitments led to a tri-authored script:

> That's when Andrew Davies took up the reins. So I worked with Andrew for a while on the script and then he also had a certain cut-off time; but when he left, it was in better shape. It then went to Richard and he did a comic pass at it, but very much collaborating with Helen.[12]

Although film scholarship has long been aware of the collaborative nature of filmmaking as opposed to the cultural image of the solitary work of writ-

Bridget Jones (Renée Zellweger) and her diary in the film version of Bridget Jones's Diary.

ing a novel, and despite the difficulties of assigning authorship to films (and especially the weaknesses of auteur theory), adaptations often highlight the role of the director as author of the text because of the apparent parallel to the novelist's role as author. Discursively, for *Bridget Jones's Diary*, the authorial responsibility for the success of the film as an adaptation is distributed among the filmmakers and falls more on the screenwriters as a group than on the director. Collaboration as a fundamental process of filmmaking undercuts the idea of the director of the adaptation as the translator of the novel and in turn resists fidelity criticism's emphasis on a one-to-one correspondence between book and film. It also foregrounds the production context as another layer of intertextuality.

In hindsight, the producers' choice of Sharon Maguire appears self-conscious, as if they were trying to ensure an authentic adaptation with a director who had personal links to the novelist herself, as well as the story; however, Maguire's lack of feature film experience underscores the high profile of the screenwriters involved in this adaptation. *Bridget Jones's Diary* was Maguire's first feature film, and it is well known that the producers tried for many other directors first. They hired Maguire at the insistence of Fielding, who had repeatedly suggested her friend for the job. The repeated references to her personal connection to the material in place of any professional expertise in reviews of the film, despite the fact that Maguire had made television documentaries (a not uncommon career path for film directors), work to undermine her agency as the director of the film. In the popular discourse of *Bridget Jones's Diary*, Maguire, as a friend of the author's, becomes another member of the "tight-knit team" that brought Bridget Jones "to life."[13] The rest of the team consists of the scriptwriters: Helen Fielding, Andrew Davies, and Richard Curtis. As author-scriptwriter, Fielding maintains some authorial status over the adaptation that reinforces the discourse that her "genius" as an author was not in the writing of an outstanding text but rather in the creation of an outstanding character who can traverse the adaptation process—Fielding's name on the script and role as executive producer legitimize the film while simultaneously obscuring Maguire's authorial role as director. Davies and Curtis retain their own authorial function next to Fielding in a way that Maguire cannot because they were critically and popularly known for scripts written before *Bridget Jones's Diary*. Davies wrote the screenplay for the highly popular BBC adaptation of *Pride and Prejudice* and has received critical praise for many of his other screenplays of classics adapted for television. Before working on *Bridget Jones's Diary*, Curtis wrote the screenplays for *The Tall Guy* (1989), *Four Weddings and a Funeral* (1994), and *Notting Hill* (1999).[14] At the very least, discursively, Davies's name sanctions the film as a "literate" adaptation, while Curtis's name suggests the influences of British romantic comedy.

Both Davies and Curtis have prior links to the novel, and it is this intertextual and interpersonal web that invites the "phenomenon" into the adaptation process. As mentioned earlier, the Davies-scripted *Pride and Prejudice* appears in Fielding's novel, while Bridget's obsession with the serial is a self-conscious nod to the stolen plot from Austen's most popular novel. In the novel, Bridget fancies Mr. Darcy as played by Colin Firth. She compares his merits with those of Mark Darcy, the "right" man for her (and with whom she eventually falls in love). In the film version of *Bridget Jones's Diary*, Mark Darcy is also played by Colin Firth, adding to the self-consciousness of the adaptation and another layer of self-reflexivity to the script.

Richard Curtis and Helen Fielding knew each other from their days at Oxford University; apparently a couple for some time, they later worked together on Comic Relief, a British charity fundraising show.[15] His role on the script is highlighted in the film by Hugh Grant's presence as Bridget's boss and love interest Daniel Cleaver. Curtis's films *Four Weddings and a Funeral* (1994) and *Notting Hill* (1999), as well as the later *Love Actually* (2003), all starred Grant and, in effect, solidified his floppy-haired, nervously foppish but likeable persona and situated him as a signifier of this romantic comedy subgenre, the Britcom. Like Firth's casting, Grant's presence highlights the self-reflexive nature of the adaptation process because of his perceived role as Curtis's "secret weapon."[16] In addition, Working Title, the successful British film production company that produced each of Curtis's transatlantic hits, "bought the rights to the book," as Fielding says, "before it was a big success."[17] So far, Working Title has not allowed the script to be published. The differences between the shooting script and a transcript of the film are largely edits that kept the film to the ideal ninety minutes for a romantic comedy.[18] Fielding has said, "There was no on-set writer, although Richard and I wrote some voice-overs during the edit."[19] Her statement corroborates the idea that the writers have fairly equal imprints on the text.

In addition to adapting the phenomenon, the writers also had to keep in mind the novel and its attendant cultural and generic intertextualities; the novel *Bridget Jones's Diary* is quintessential chick lit. It is often said to have launched the genre, which focuses on the travails of late twenties and thirty-something "singletons." Chick lit in the 1990s and the early 2000s is generally understood to refer to popular novels (as well as short story collections and novellas) that focus on a young, often quirky and witty contemporary female protagonist who is (financially) independent but looking for the right man. In the much broader sense of popular fiction for and about (and sometimes by) women, chick lit and its textual cousin the chick flick have been consistently popular throughout the twentieth century. This popularity has been sustained alongside and in spite of the general critical disparagement of romance novels, romantic comedies, and women's melodramas. From the comic romance to the family melodrama, novels and films given the "chick" prefix may seem to have little in common. Still, the apparent "regulation elements" of "chick fiction" are generally considered to be a female main character, a main plot defined by romance, and a "female" marketing focus and consumption profile.[20] This means that chick texts can range from the deadly serious to the highly comical, and although they are mostly assigned to "low" culture, a few have attained an arguably high-culture status. It may not be all that surprising, then, that two of the most direct influences on the adaptation of *Bridget Jones's Diary* are the romance novel, via the nineteenth-century novel of manners, and late twentieth-century romantic comedy, both of which find their way into the script via Fielding's, Davies's, and Curtis's respective generic interests.

DIALOGICAL ROMANCE AND SELF-CONSCIOUS COMEDY

The "stolen" plot is the novel's most transparent intertext, a fact routinely observed in both the popular and academic discourse on *Bridget Jones's Diary*. As literary characters, both Bridget Jones and Elizabeth Bennett "need" to find a good man. However, this parallel elides the significant historical differences between a nineteenth-century husband who will provide social and economic welfare for a young woman whose only possibilities for the future are marriage or genteel poverty and a late twentieth-century boyfriend who might provide dinner and sex for a financially independent woman who is fixated on getting a date for the next family event. Many of Elizabeth's important plot points are also Bridget's: the ill-fated first meeting with Darcy, the attachment to a man of dubious character who has wronged Darcy in the past, a wayward female relative who runs off with a good-for-nothing suitor, and the dénouement, in which Darcy saves the heroine and her family from scandal by taking action and spending lots of money, winning from the heroine the love that he desired all along. This recognizable marriage plot, which requires a fairly passive heroine, is one of the main reasons that *Bridget Jones's Diary* is criticized for being a postfeminist-era text with prefeminist sensibilities. Germaine Greer states that it is "an updated version of the old Mills & Boon scenario where girl eats heart out over (not-so-rich) Mr. Wrong until (extremely-rich) Mr. Right makes his play on the second last page."[21] Before her success with Bridget Jones, Helen Fielding wrote a formula romance novel that was rejected by Mills and Boon, the U.K. equivalent of the U.S.'s Harlequin romance series.[22] Although some bookstores have separate sections for romance novels and chick lit, one of the newest publishers of "singleton" chick lit, Red Dress Ink, is owned by Harlequin Enterprises Limited.[23] With each new imitator of Bridget who makes more money, drinks more alcohol, and experiences more dramatic adventures, the latest novel from Red Dress Ink may seem to inhabit a wholly other world than *Pride and Prejudice*, especially for those Austen fans who have a "sensibility that revels in the long ago world of country dancing, chaste heroines, and polite courtships in delightful villages."[24] However, in her early book on popular romance narratives, *Loving With a Vengeance*, Tania Modleski writes, "it has not been sufficiently recognized how much Jane Austen's *Pride and Prejudice* has contributed to the development of the [Mills and Boon] formula."[25]

The two historically distinct romances of Austen and Mills and Boon have vastly differing sexual mores, influencing Fielding's novel in collusion and competition with each other and articulating the dualisms of postfeminist discourse regarding sex and romance. The BBC's television adaptation of *Pride and Prejudice* acts like another character in the novel and mirrors the narrative machinations of the "marriage plot" in *Bridget Jones's Diary*, reflecting Bridget's confused, romantic idealism:

> Just nipped out for fags prior to getting changed ready for BBC *Pride and Prejudice*. Hard to believe there are so many cars out on the roads. Shouldn't they be at home getting ready? Love the nation being so addicted. The basis of my own addiction, I know is simple human need for Darcy to get off with Elizabeth.[26]

Two languages of romance interact dialogically here. Bridget's main attraction to the BBC adaptation of an Austen novel, full of period costumes and a single tepid kiss, is to see Darcy and Elizabeth "get off." The modern slang for sexual interaction applied to the main characters of this very mannered and restrained narrative continues when she writes, "They are my chosen representatives in the field of shagging, or, rather, courtship."[27] Competing, historically specific sensibilities about romance and intimacy operate in Bridget's own language. Her experience is of a sexual freedom, and its attendant language, that is coextensive with modern "courtship"; or, rather, for Bridget, shagging *is* courtship. Initially, she does not consciously recognize any difference between her own narrative and a narrative circumscribed by the sexual morality of the time in which it was produced.[28] However, Bridget concludes, "I would hate to see Darcy and Elizabeth in bed, smoking a cigarette afterwards. That would be unnatural and wrong and I would quickly lose interest."[29] Among the competing languages of romance here, Victorian chastity seems to have won out. And yet the authorial irony, highlighted in the next section, where Bridget says that Mr. Darcy's biggest fault is that he is imaginary, suggests that Bridget has not suddenly recognized the historical specificities of nineteenth-century courtship but rather that her experience of sex as romance does not exclude an idealized (prefeminist) view of romance in which sex is reserved for marriage. The two competing ideologies are intrinsically interrelated with Bridget's status as representative of postfeminist culture because the voices combine to create a "narrative [that] insist[s] on the 'sanctity of marriage', but with an irony that suggests that 'feminism has been taken into account.'"[30] In other words, Bridget can have a healthy sex life of her own (and fret about the lack of sex when necessary), a freedom attributed to feminism's part in the sexual revolution of the 1960s, while delighting in the portrayal of a sexually restrained and restricted courtship that she herself would not abide because the ultimate goal of both—romantic partnership—is the same.

By foregrounding romantic partnership as the goal rather than legal, economic, psychological, or physical partnership, the narrative of *Bridget Jones's Diary* is a product of a postfeminist era that has denounced feminism's supposed unromantic and pragmatic approach to relationships but cannot return to an overriding culture of prefeminist morality, and so instead attempts to realign itself with a romantic idealism associated with that morality. This tenuous accommodation sometimes exposes itself in the narrative (and in culture more broadly). It is also the source of comic effect when, despite the apparent wholeness of the ideology of romance, the competing, historically specific sensibilities slip, and Bridget's mind stumbles on the image of Darcy and Elizabeth having a postcoital cigarette. This slippage in the novel parallels a characteristic of romantic comedies of the 1980s and 1990s that Frank Krutnik has delineated as generic self-consciousness:

> [T]he contemporary romantic comedy film grapples with the difficulty of speaking of love in an age when the values of heterosexual union lack the integrity they once possessed . . . [and] what distinguishes the new romances is the self-consciousness of their bid to revalidate and reconstruct heterosexual intimacy and the genre of the romantic comedy.[31]

One film that has a link with *Bridget Jones's Diary* and exemplifies the new romance's attempt to embrace love with some irony is *Four Weddings and a Funeral*. After leaving his fiancée at the altar, Hugh Grant's Charles runs after Carrie (Andie McDowell) and asks her, "Do you think, after we've dried off, after we've spent lots of more time together, you might agree not to marry me? And do you think not being married to me might maybe be something you'd consider doing for the rest of your life?" Carrie responds as if they were at the altar and emphatically says, "I do." Peter William Evans and Celestino Deleyto highlight this ending as an example of how contemporary romantic comedy deals with the dislocation of marriage in a romantic narrative: "the conceit used by Charles practically amounts to a fully-fledged proposition of marriage . . . [but] its absurd use of the negative undercuts the long-term engagement which it apparently enunciates."[32] Like the moment discussed above in *Bridget Jones's Diary*, though, the doubled language of commitment within the romance not only operates ideologically but also creates comic effect. In this way, postfeminism's adaptability allows for the signification of its ideology via the generic conventions of the comic chick lit novel as well as through the generic conventions of the romantic comedy film.

The film of *Bridget Jones's Diary* also negotiates its postfeminist milieu through the various generic intertexts brought to the film by the scriptwriters. A key scene that reflects this negotiation occurs in the first five minutes of the film, after Bridget and Mark have had their awkward first meeting. The conclusion of the scene exemplifies the intertextual "quoting" of Davies's *Pride and Prejudice*. This intertexuality then frames the dialogical relationship between feminist images of women and prefeminist ideas about love and partnership within postfeminism, which depends on a simultaneous irony about both feminism and romance for comic effect. Bridget has gone home for New Year's Day, and her mother coerces her into wearing "something nice" she has "laid out for her," an outfit Bridget deems "a carpet." Then her mother and her aunt force her to speak to Mark Darcy. Bridget fails miserably at engaging the eligible bachelor in conversation, babbling incoherently about her New Year's resolutions to quit smoking and drinking while holding a cigarette in one hand and a glass of wine in the other. Adding indignation to her shame, she overhears Mark tell his mother, "I do not need a blind date . . . particularly not with some verbally incontinent spinster who smokes like a chimney, drinks like a fish, and dresses like her mother." At this, Bridget walks past Mark with her head held high to an accompanying voice-over in which she says, "That was it . . . right there, that was the moment. I suddenly realized that unless something changed soon I was going to live a life where my major relationship was with a bottle of wine." The determined look on Bridget's face as she passes Mark and his mother combined with the initial tone of the voice-over that suggests Bridget will turn an embarrassing situation into a catalyst for positive change suggests a dramatic choice of personal determination and pride, although in the face of a brief, awkward moment of embarrassment. What from a feminist political standpoint looks like a minor personal victory gains the weight of a narrative climactic moment within the development of a romance plot and portrays a postfeminist version of the personal as political. Postfeminism's claim that the fight for legal and economic equality is over wholly displaces the ideal of female independence onto personal interactions and self-esteem, both of which are always undermined by postfeminism's inclusion of a prefeminist emphasis on chivalric romance.

The prefeminist accent on this scene can be marked out by tracing its difference from the book, in which the New Year's turkey curry buffet ends with Mark being forced, by his mother and Bridget's aunt, to offer Bridget a ride home, which she refuses, and its similarity to another intertext. The scene from the film of *Bridget Jones's Diary* closely resembles a scene in Davies's adaptation of *Pride and Prejudice*. Elizabeth Bennett, who sits through several dances at a ball, overhears Mr. Darcy tell his companion, who has suggested that he dance with Elizabeth, "She is tolerable I suppose, but not handsome enough to tempt *me*; and I am in no humor at present to give consequence to young ladies who are slighted by other men." Upon overhearing this, an ironic smile plays on Elizabeth's face and, head held high, she walks past him, making it clear that she has heard him and his arrogance only amuses her, which is signified by her standing with a group of women, whispering and giggling as she looks in Darcy's direction. The scene carries the same narrative weight as Bridget's; we might even consider that it imbues Bridget's moment with extra weight for those audience members who have seen and remember the TV adaptation. This same scene ends differently in Jane Austen's novel. At the end of his tirade against dancing, Mr. Darcy simply walks off, and Elizabeth, alone, "remain[s] with no very cordial feelings toward him."[33] The change from the Austen novel to the television serial is indicative of a noted trend in Austen adaptations to "update" the heroines through a postfeminist lens.[34] Elizabeth Bennett walking confidently and purposefully past Mr. Darcy rather than sitting and fuming appears as a self-empowering moment for her and those women who watch her, especially as the "sisterhood" image concludes the scene and invites viewers to feel a part of the laughter. It appeals to the modern woman's feeling that she need not put up with such public abuse from any man. Walking past an arrogant and offensive man can hardly be construed as political, but the imagery of the scene fits well within a postfeminist discourse that privileges the individual act over political action. The succeeding giggles and glances at Darcy act like a heritage film version of postfeminist phrases such as "you go, girl." However, in the middle of a Regency period piece in which women's social and economic stability depends on securing a good marriage, it obscures that cultural reality in favor of the postfeminist desire for the drama of feminine independence. The parallel scene in the film of *Bridget Jones's Diary* obscures the contemporary cultural reality that Bridget does not need marriage for social or economic stability in favor of postfeminism's desire for the drama of the romance.

That we recognize Davies's signature on this moment in the film owing to its resemblance to his Austen adaptation might suggest that he wrote his versions of the *Bridget Jones's Diary* script more with Austen in mind than Fielding, but Fielding has said, "a lot of the book was inspired by [Andrew Davies's] adaptation of *Pride and Prejudice*."[35] The comment almost implies that Davies will know, therefore, what Fielding would have wanted in the *Bridget Jones's Diary* script because she knowingly used his version of Austen's novel as an intertext to her own novel. However, the following journalistic anecdote suggests that Davies needed to be "updated" by Fielding as much as Austen's plot was updated in Fielding's novel: "To appreciate the fictional life of the chain-smoking, caffeine-addicted, young and always single heroine, Fielding took the screenwriter around some of her old haunts (you know the kind of thing: coffee at Coins, dinner at 192)."[36] In the shooting script of *Bridget Jones's Diary*, the scene with Darcy's overheard insult does not end with Bridget safe in a group of women, like Davies's version of her Austenian counterpart; she walks away, "smiling broadly," and her voice-over says, "Oh, God. Oh, God. Oh Jesus. Even dumped divorcee wearing reindeer sweater thinks I'm horrible. Am destined to die alone." It appears that although Davies had already read Austen through his version of an empowering postfeminism, Fielding needed to teach Davies to read Austen through Bridget's powerless, postfeminist milieu. That the finished film ends differently, with Bridget walking past, head held high, but alone, suggests that the director reinflected the scene with a sense of the ambivalence of the contemporary postfeminist culture that needs to hold on to images of feminism while rejecting its political identity.

In the film, after Bridget walks confidently past Mark Darcy at the New Year's party, instead of laughing off his remarks with friends, we next see her drunk and alone in her apartment, lip-syncing to the pop song "All By Myself." The juxtaposition immediately undercuts the fleeting moment of self-determination and imprints Bridget's story with the postfeminist image of a single woman who has her own apartment filled with nice furnishings and all the appropriate modern amenities but who suffers under her singleness, even wallows in it. As the camera zooms in on an isolated, freestanding apartment building (not attached to other buildings as is usual in London), Bridget projects a vision of her future: "I'd finally die fat and alone and be found three weeks later half-eaten by Alsatians, or I was about to turn into Glenn Close in *Fatal Attraction*." We then get an interior shot of

Bridget in her pajamas, lying forlornly on the couch in her apartment, a glass of wine in one hand and the television remote in the other. A brief shot of her TV shows the opening credits of the sitcom *Frasier*. This image of self-pity stands in contrast to Bridget's expressed fear of becoming the ultimate 1980s' postfeminist woman who has lost all humanity and become a monster. *Fatal Attraction* is a film that has often been referenced as a central image of early postfeminist culture that vilified feminism through the character of Alex Forrest as the successful, independent "career woman" driven mad by her desire for companionship and maternity. Here again is a doubled language, but this time it is the language of female independence. The feminist trope of Bridget standing tall in the face of Mark's rejection is undercut by the 1990s' postfeminist trope of Bridget fearing the social death of long-term singleness. The self-consciousness of the romance narrative has branched out into self-consciousness about femininity in a postfeminist culture. At the same time, the stark contrast between the reference to Glenn Close in *Fatal Attraction*, which immediately conjures up the image of Alex Forrest wielding a knife in her lover's house, and the image of Bridget lounging on her couch works to comic effect.

In a press packet for the film, a comment from Richard Curtis corroborates, from a production and marketing point of view, my suggestion that the comedy in romantic comedy partly functions to hold all the various languages of romance, commitment, and femininity together: "My memory is that the film kept getting better with each draft, but as it did so, it was getting better dramatically rather than necessarily getting funnier. There was a feeling that Helen's first draft had actually been the funniest, so it was my job to reconcile the drama and the comedy."[37] Later in the film, after finding a naked American girl in Daniel's apartment, Bridget watches TV in bed, and a shot of the TV shows *Fatal Attraction*. The camera pauses to let us watch Alex (Glenn Close) violently rise up from the bathtub and then got shot.[38] The "reconciliation" of drama and comedy here actually operates more as an undercutting that goes both ways. Bridget's pathos reflects and mitigates Alex's bathos, and vice versa. Considering Kathleen Rowe's comment that "[romantic comedy and melodrama] are linked by common ideologies about femininity and the limited plots they allow for narrative representations of female desire," we can understand the tragedy and the comedy in *Bridget Jones's Diary* as flip sides of the same coin of contemporary notions of femininity and the competing dialogical discourses that coexist in postfeminist tropes of singleness, femininity, and female subjectivity.[39]

Fielding calls Bridget an "ironic heroine," adding that "you can't really explain irony.... Either you think it's funny or you don't. One of my favorite parts of the book is when Bridget declares, 'There's nothing quite so unattractive to a man as a strident feminist.'"[40] This is postfeminist "speak" in its clearest form. The sense of authentic self that the diary form of the novel creates allows the dualities of postfeminism to be located in Bridget rather than in the world around her: "Sharon maintains ... men are so catastrophically unevolved that soon they will just be kept by women as pets for sex ... the men will be kept outside in kennels. Anyway, feeling v. empowered. Tremendous. Think I might read bit of Susan Faludi's *Backlash*."[41] In the diary, in her own head, she personifies the dualities of postfeminism. In an almost lucid moment, she writes, "Wise people will say Daniel should like me just as I am, but I am a child of *Cosmopolitan* culture."[42] After four hours of washing, waxing, exfoliating, and decelluliting for a date, Bridget slumps under her Sisyphean existence and declares, "[I] have been traumatized by supermodels and too many quizzes and know that neither my personality nor my body is up to it if left to its own devices. I can't take the pressure."[43] This self-focused neurotic attention to the inability to live up to the *Cosmo* standard of beauty has been trumpeted as hitting a cultural nerve based on the popularity of the novel in both the United Kingdom and the United States: despite the media saturation of feminine self-improvement narratives in everything from novels, to advertising, to advice columns in women's magazines, women are aware (another way that feminism has been "taken into account") that the "ideal" is impossible but cannot help pursuing it, even if everyone tells them that they are beautiful as they are. This is the point about Bridget being an ironic heroine: no one but Bridget herself thinks that she is fat.[44] The script does not engage Bridget's mistaken self-perception. Not even the shooting script has any dialogue that suggests she shouldn't be worried about her weight. Richard Curtis describes the script's role in moving Bridget's voice in the novel to her body in the film, "The book is her talking herself out of it, whereas in the film we found we had to show it at times ... it did change it."[45]

In the film, Bridget's sense of herself as fat becomes associated with Renée Zellweger's "chubby" (compared to her usual size) appearance on screen. Reviewers generally lauded Zellweger's choice to gain weight. Comments from Sharon Maguire capitalize on this critical success and play up Zellweger's choice to gain weight as a creative achievement; in an interview, she said, "We were very proud of her cellulite."[46] The externalization of Bridget's neuroses and the attendant postfeminist tropes display themselves through

Bridget Jones on her way to turning everything upside down.

her body. From the view of a positive strand of postfeminist discourse, its relative bigness is flaunted and made appealing compared to her rival Natasha's hyperthin body and Daniel's skinny, new American girlfriend. The contrast seemingly privileges a postfeminist confidence in female sensuality and appetite, as sometimes Bridget purposefully shows off her body. For example, when she walks past Daniel's office in a short skirt and see-through blouse, she attempts to flaunt a power of attractiveness, to get his attention at her will. However, her clumsiness and penchant for saying the wrong thing at the wrong time combine with her body to discount that kind of postfeminist power. On her first job as a television reporter, her plump body ruins an interview when she slides down a fireman's pole, her miniskirt framing and highlighting her full posterior, which fills the television screen and then lands on the camera.

The joke here is obviously Bridget's bottom: its size, its in-your-faceness, the way it takes up space and causes havoc, almost literally turning the world upside down by knocking the cameraman over. Her body and its size are as much a running joke as is her proclivity for saying the wrong thing and making a mess of public speaking moments (all of which act in the service of her comedic romantic quest). She is, if against her own will, an unruly woman. The unruly woman, a figure Kathleen Rowe takes from historian Natalie Zemon Davis, is, among other things, fat, loud, sexually loose, and someone who laughs a lot.[47] Rowe says "that the unruly woman eats too much and speaks too much is no coincidence; both involve failure to control the mouth" and "in white late-twentieth-century America [and I might add England] fatness signifies a disturbing unresponsiveness to social control."[48] Every time Bridget tries to live up to her mother's or *Cosmopolitan*'s expectations of how to get a man, either her mouth or her body (or her bottom) get in the way.

However, those around Bridget, her mother, her aunt, her married friends, ascribe her singleness to another postfeminist anxiety, her "career," which was at the center of the backlash against feminism in the 1980s and then coupled with the emphasis on singleness in the 1990s. In the opening party scene Aunt Una says in a singsong voice, "You career girls can't put it off forever, you know," in response to which Bridget takes a large gulp of her morning libation. Later, Bridget attends a dinner party full of "smug-married" couples, as she calls them, and the camera work emphasizes Bridget's singleness by giving a medium two-shot of each couple as they are introduced to her, and then she sits alone, at the end of the long table. When one male guest, shown in a medium two-shot with his pregnant wife, interrogates her about her love life, her retort is to say, "Tell me, is it one in four marriages or one in three that end in divorce these days?" Mark Darcy briefly comes to Bridget's rescue by saying, "It's one in three," but the husband continues, "Seriously though, offices full of single girls in their thirties, fine, physical specimens but just can't seem to hold down a chap." The camera cuts to a medium shot of Bridget alone at the end of the table drinking wine, and then the pregnant wife adds, "Yes, why is it there are so many unmarried women in their thirties these days?" In a long shot of the entire table from Bridget's position, we see the guests have stopped eating to listen and stare at her, and instead of making any attempt to give a real answer to an unanswerable question, Bridget makes a joke about her body by saying, "Well, it doesn't help that underneath our clothes we're covered in scales," a joke that falls horribly flat among the couples at dinner. Here the script, even as the joke's punch line plays on the trope of woman as monster, reinforces Bridget's body as problem. Bridget is constantly in an ambivalent position between desiring romance, love, and heterosexual coupledom and resisting the cultural pressure to acquire those in the "right" way because her body, almost of its own will, insists on it. She will never be the tall, thin, well-dressed, well-coifed, eloquent, and seemingly perfect Natasha. As Rowe says, "the figure of the unruly woman contains much potential for feminist appropriation."[49] Bridget's body, as manifested through the temporarily enlarged body of the star Zellweger, resists and confounds the *Cosmo* image of the sexually attractive and romantically successful woman (a parallel to the way the novel's irony can be read as a critique of the problems of postfeminism). However, Rowe is clear that "carnival and the unruly woman are not essentially radical but are ambivalent, open to conflicting appropriations."[50] Even though Bridget is a woman whose unruliness keeps her from conforming to Hollywood standards of beauty, making her a carnivalesque character who overturns typical standards of femininity and beauty for romantic comedies, she also inhabits a narrative that ultimately uprights what has been undone by successfully situating her in heterosexual coupledom.[51] As a consequence of these competing ideologies, Bridget literally embodies postfeminist ambivalence and duality.

THE AUTHENTIC ADAPTATION

Germaine Greer seemed to anticipate the postfeminist emphasis on the body in the film and the popular discourse surrounding it when the news of the adaptation increased her frustration with the character; in *The Whole Woman*, her sequel to the feminist polemic *The Female Eunuch*, she wrote, "[Bridget] will soon be baring her empty little soul in cinemas and on video."[52] Fans' concern over the adaptation (as disseminated through popular British celebrity magazines such as *Heat* and *OK*, as well as women's magazines like *Cosmopolitan* and some fan Web sites) centered on the casting of Bridget and the general feeling that "[t]he news that Texas-born Zellweger was cast to play the quintessentially British Bridget was greeted with dismay and disbelief."[53] However, what in preproduction was the film's biggest weakness became, on release, the adaptation's greatest asset. Very few reviewers comment on the adaptation of the tone of the novel or Fielding's style, but almost all comment on Zellweger as Bridget: "Thankfully, with an accent coach and a diet of hamburgers, pizza and candy, she was transformed into the perfect representation of Bridget."[54] The implications of Zellweger "putting on" Bridget's body reflect popular fiction's interaction with the issue of fidelity and adaptation. The fans' desire for an authentic representation of character depends on a popular understanding of faithfulness, but the fans' original fear that the "lifestyle" associated with Zellweger's star status (American and hyperskinny) would never translate into Bridget's "lifestyle" presented in the novel (English and full-sized) emanates from the prevailing understanding that adaptations should be "faithful." However, the fans and reviewers largely accepted Zellweger's transformation and excised the expectation of faithfulness because they accepted her performance as an authentic representation of the character, allowing for positive reviews of an adaptation that was in many ways unfaithful to the text. The script, then, becomes an inextricable part of Zellweger's authenticating of the adaptation: "The script, unlike the book, doesn't hammer [Bridget's obsession with weight and getting a boyfriend] into you like so many torturesome thumbtacks. Maybe that's partly because Zellweger is so at home in the character of Bridget that she doesn't need them."[55]

For many of the fans, Zellweger became "our little Bridget." The possessiveness of Zellweger as Bridget reflects their original possessiveness of Bridget as narrator/character; purportedly many women readers felt that "[*Bridget Jones's Diary*] is *autobiographical* for any number of single women trying to make a living while going through the process of life and dating."[56] The general sense of authentic representation that fans found in the novel did not lessen with the release of the adaptation, even though many plot, character, and even tonal changes (many of which are part and parcel of the intertextual dialogism of the texts) were made in bringing the book to the screen. In an essay in Natasha Walter's collection, *On the Move: Feminism for a New Generation*, Katharine Viner suggests that Greer may be missing the point and that "the real reason single women in their thirties have been buying *Bridget Jones's Diary* in record numbers" is because "Bridget has a good job. She has her own flat. She is young, she is single and she is attractive and she can't quite believe that she got here and there aren't any men to be a part of it."[57] The fans' love of the book adapted to the film in a metonymic way, judging Bridget the only necessary sign of authenticity. In other words, the textual faithfulness, usually required of adaptations, to narrative functions was sublimated for a Bridget they could still relate to. As one fan said after leaving the U.S. premiere, "The movie was just wonderful and very accurate. And we are real-life Bridget Joneses."[58] The very popular book became a very popular film, and many critics, like the fans, judged the film authentic because the filmmakers, especially the scriptwriters, "fulfilled the brief" of the "Bridget phenomenon," resulting in the adaptation participating in the development and extension of the phenomenon. Faithfulness, then, as an evaluative term regarding the adaptation of the original text (the novel) into film still informs the discourse around popular fiction adaptations, but it has lost its formal, aesthetic imperative, overturned by the vengeance of intertextuality. The book and the film as the beginning and end of the adaptation process remain successful postfeminist texts because Bridget's postfeminist iconicity is one size that fits all.

In this chapter, I have analyzed all of Bridget's texts—the novel, the film, the script, the cultural milieu, the generic influences—through the lens of intertextuality, in the hope of continuing the example of other scholars who have pushed the limits of adaptation studies by seeking approaches beyond fidelity criticism and pursuing noncanonical texts. Film adaptations as texts will have a much broader purview in film studies, literary studies, and cultural studies if, instead of confining our readings to the novel and the film, we engage with all their various intertexts.

NOTES

I thank Yvonne Tasker, Diane Negra, Neil Ewen, and Jack Boozer for their help and support while I was working on this chapter.

1. André Bazin argued against the simplistic assessment of faithfulness in "Adaptation, or the Cinema as Digest" (Film Adaptation, ed. James Naremore [New Brunswick, NJ: Rutgers University Press, 2000]), but the language of fidelity persists, and the most recent scholarship on adaptation (see Brian McFarlane's *Novel to Film: An Introduction to the Theory of Adaptation* [Oxford: Clarendon Press, 1996])

continues to feel obliged to address its prevalence and limitations, while ultimately often still struggling to disengage from its power.

2. Julia Kristeva, "Word, Dialogue, Novel," in *The Kristeva Reader*, ed. Toril Moi (Oxford: Basil Blackwell, 1986), 37.

3. Both were also produced by Working Title, the same British production company that made *Bridget Jones's Diary*.

4. Robert Stam, "The Dialogics of Adaptation," in *Film Adaptation*, ed. James Naremore (New Brunswick, NJ: Rutgers University Press, 2000), 64.

5. Ibid., 64.

6. Robert Stam, *Subversive Pleasures: Bakhtin, Cultural Criticism, and Film* (Baltimore: Johns Hopkins University Press, 1989), 19.

7. See Sarah Projansky, *Watching Rape: Film and Television in Postfeminist Culture* (New York: New York University Press, 2001). Projansky delineates five strands of postfeminism, all of which declare the end of feminism. Some announce feminism's collapse as a natural progression of its goals. Most proclaim feminism's demise as the predictable outcome of its negative effect on women. Those strands split into others that advance differing views as to what that effect is, be it a prevailing "victim" mentality among women or the "have-it-all" syndrome that keeps women from enjoying the traditionally feminine pleasures of marriage and family. It is important to note that "most versions of postfeminism can function as either a condemnation or a celebration of women and feminism" (86). According to postfeminist discourse, feminism has established equality for all women, and women can choose to have it all or not have it all. The relevance of class, race, and sexual identity to women's experience is elided by this emphasis on choice; therefore, despite the dualities and multiplicities of postfeminism, "the central figure of postfeminist discourse [is] a white, heterosexual, middle-class woman" (12). Its appropriation and adulteration of feminism, its varying manifestations, and its racial, sexual, and class bias combine to produce postfeminism's adaptability, making it "extremely versatile, containing appeals to multiple and contradictory audiences" (86).

8. Bridget's fans are not exclusively heterosexual women. Heterosexual men and lesbians and gay men are among the novels' readership and the film's viewership as well. However, gay men in particular have appropriated the language of Bridget's iconicity. For an example of the gay "Bridget Jones moment," see Angela McRobbie, "Feminism and the Socialist Tradition... Undone? A Response to Recent Work by Judith Butler," *Cultural Studies* 8, no. 4 (2004): 503–522. Race and class identities are not foregrounded here because they are elided by the Bridget Jones texts and in the attendant cultural discourse of her iconicity, a quality that firmly ties Bridget to popular postfeminist discourse.

9. Alexa Baracaia, "Forget Bridget Jones, single women are happier," *The Evening Standard*, London, December 22, 2003, 19.

10. The various public remarks made about Bridget by "average" women, academic feminists, and other cultural commentators create a discourse within our

postfeminist (Western) culture that situates Bridget as representative of that culture as it is articulated through the single, heterosexual, middle-class (white) female.

11. Gaby Wood, "A Bridget Just Far Enough," *The Observer*, March 4, 2001, http://film.guardian.co.uk/print/0,3858,4145710-3181,00.html (accessed June 3, 2004).

12. Sharon Maguire, interview, *Total Film*, May 2001, no. 52.

13. Meg Ryan, "'Zellweger and Co. Bring 'Bridget Jones' to Life," The Scene, *The Online Observer*, April 19, 2001, www.nd.edu/~observer/04192001/Scene/0.html (accessed November 7, 2003).

14. Curtis established his writing career in British television on the popular *Blackadder* series (1983, 1986–1999).

15. Vanessa Thorpe, "Private diarist (vg)," *The Observer*, April 8, 2001.

16. The stars operate as signifiers of the scriptwriters' authorial function whether or not Firth and Grant were cast before, during, or after Davies's and Curtis's respective tenures on the script. On Hugh Grant's role in the recent cycle of successful British romantic comedies, see Andrew Spicer, "The Rewards of Diffidence: Hugh Grant and the Revival of English Romantic Comedy," in *The Trouble With Men: Masculinities in European and Hollywood Cinema*, ed. Phil Powers, Ann Davies, and Bruce Babington (London: Wallflower Press, 2005).

17. Helen Fielding, interview by Alan Waldman, WGA.ORG Exclusive, February 2002, www.wga.org/pr/awards/2002/helen-fielding.html (accessed November 7, 2003).

18. In the director's commentary on the DVD, Sharon Maguire mentions more than once that she insisted on keeping the film to ninety minutes because she did not think romantic comedies should be any longer.

19. Fielding, interview by Waldman.

20. Of course, these are the stereotypical characteristics. It has been posited, as I have already noted, that gay men are another significant audience and readership.

21. Germaine Greer, *The Whole Woman* (London: Transworld Publishers, 1999), 314.

22. Harlequin Enterprise Limited owns Mills and Boon.

23. I do not wish to suggest that the publishing connections had any direct effect on *Bridget Jones's Diary*, as Red Dress Ink came into being in 2001, but the fact that Fielding attempted a novel for Mills and Boon and that the company has created a division to compete with the chick lit phenomenon as a way of recouping losses suggests both an industrial and an ideological relationship. For information on Harlequin Enterprises losses, see Edward Wyatt, "Chick Lit Is the Romance Novel's Newest Homewrecker." *New York Times*, August 17, 2003, www.nytimes.com/2004/08/17/books/17romance.html (accessed August 24, 2004).

24. Cecilia Salber, "Bridget Jones and Mark Darcy: Art Imitating Art . . . Imitating Art," *Persuasions On-Line* 22, no. 1 (2003), www.jasna.org/pol104/salber.html (accessed November 7, 2003).

25. Tania Modleski, *Loving With a Vengeance* (London: Routledge, 1990), 36.

26. Helen Fielding, *Bridget Jones's Diary* (London: Picador, 1996), 246.
27. Fielding, *Bridget*, 246.
28. And, of course, the class milieu in which it is set.
29. Fielding, *Bridget*, 247.
30. McRobbie, "Feminism and the Socialist Tradition," 514.
31. Frank Krutnik, "Love Lies: Romantic Fabrication in Contemporary Romantic Comedy," in *Terms of Endearment: Hollywood Romantic Comedy of the 1980s and 1990s*, ed. Peter William Evans and Celestino Deleyto (Edinburgh: Edinburgh University Press, 1998), 29.
32. Peter William Evans and Celestino Deleyto, eds., *Terms of Endearment: Hollywood Romantic Comedy of the 1980s and 1990s* (Edinburgh: Edinburgh University Press, 1998), 8.
33. Jane Austen, *Pride and Prejudice* (London: Planet Three, 2003), 16.
34. See, for example, "'Piracy Is Our Only Option': Postfeminist Intervention in *Sense and Sensibility*," in *Jane Austin in Hollywood*, ed. Linda Troost and Sayre Greenfield (Lexington: University Press of Kentucky, 1998), and "Books to Movies: Gender and Desire in Jane Austen's Adaptations," in *Jane Austin and Co.: Remaking the Past in Contemporary Culture*, ed. Suzanne R. Pucci and James Thompson (Albany: SUNY Press, 2003).
35. Fielding, interview, www.wga.org.
36. Jasper Gerard, "Double Act," *The Times*, February 6, 1999.
37. Richard Curtis, interview, *Total Film*, May 2001, no. 52.
38. It can hardly be a coincidence that Bridget finds out about Daniel's American girl while wearing the Playboy bunny suit from the Tarts and Vicars party and then goes home and takes a bath. In fact, the shooting script has Bridget watching *Fatal Attraction* while in the bathtub.
39. Kathleen Rowe, *The Unruly Woman: Gender and the Genres of Laughter* (Austin: University of Texas Press, 1995), 96.
40. Reading Guide, "*Bridget Jones's Diary* by Helen Fielding," Penguin Group USA, www.penguinputnam.com/static/rguides/us/bridget_jones_diary.html (accessed November 7, 2003).
41. Fielding, *Bridget*, 77.
42. Ibid., 59.
43. Ibid., 59.
44. After finally losing half a stone (seven pounds) Bridget attends a party where all her friends tell her she looks tired and "flat." After asking her friend Tom if he noticed how thin she is, Tom's reply is "I think you looked better before, hon" (107).
45. Wood, "Just Far Enough."
46. Bob Graham, "Zellweger put on the pounds and the accent for Bridget Jones," *San Francisco Chronicle*, April 4, 2001, http://seattlepi.nwsource.com/movies/17235_zellweger04.shtm (accessed November 7, 2003).
47. Rowe, *Unruly Woman*, 31.

48. Ibid., 37, 61.

49. Ibid., 11.

50. Ibid., 44.

51. It should also be noted that many articles suggested that Zellweger's subsequent loss of weight after filming finished (to a size apparently even thinner than her physique before playing Bridget) undermined any possible positive ramifications on women's body culture. One article on ivillage.co.uk titled "Why Kate Winslet Should Have Been Bridget" suggests that Winslet's voluptuous body would have fit the body type necessary for the film and would have sent a better body image message to women.

52. Greer, *Whole Woman*, 314. For Greer, Bridget seemingly operates as a negative image of women and feminism, in contrast to the way she performs for her fans as an authentic portrayal of their own experiences in a postfeminist culture. It is necessary to consider Projansky's work on postfeminism's versatility here because of the way Bridget exemplifies the contemporary state of (single) women, both in actuality and in media representation. Projansky says that postfeminism can "function as either a condemnation or a celebration of women and feminism." However, whether negatively or positively, Bridget functions iconically for both groups as the specific image of a certain stratum of society.

53. Evelyn Gough, "Bridget Jones's Diary," *The Northern Rivers Echo*, August 2, 2001, http://echonews.com/730/movie_reviews.html (accessed November 7, 2003).

54. Ryan, "Zellweger and Co."

55. Stephanie Zacharek, "*Bridget Jones's Diary*: A smarted up, tarted up take on a book about a girl who unapologetically enjoys sex," *Salon.com*, April 13, 2001, http://dir.salon.com/ent/movies/review/2001/04/13/bridget_jones/index.html (accessed November 7, 2003).

56. Rebecca Ekmark, "*Bridget Jones's Diary*," Desert Isle Reviews, *All About Romance*, 1999, www.likesbooks.com/becca41.html (accessed November 7, 2003), emphasis mine.

57. Katherine Viner, "The Personal Is Still Political," in *On the Move: Feminism for the Next Generation*, ed. Natasha Walter (London: Virago Press, 1999), 24.

58. Ellen Hale, "Zellweger's Bridget Is 'Bang on' Bits, if a Bit Posh," *USA Today*, April 12, 2001, www.usatoday.com/life/movies/2001-04-12-bridget-jones-lit-appeal.htm (accessed 7, 2003).

12

"WHO'S YOUR FAVORITE INDIAN?"
The Politics of Representation in Sherman Alexie's
Short Stories and Screenplay

//

Elaine Roth

WHEN SHERMAN ALEXIE ADAPTED HIS OWN SHORT STORY COLlection, *The Lone Ranger and Tonto Fistfight in Heaven* (1993), into a 1998 screenplay, he necessarily condensed a range of stories, multiple characters, and many perspectives into a single narrative arc. In the transition from the screenplay to the film *Smoke Signals* (1999), that narrative became even more focused. The screenplay and film versions of *Smoke Signals* demonstrate the streamlining required to render experimental fiction, as well as Native American storytelling, accessible to a mass audience. *Smoke Signals* made history as the first U.S. feature film about Native Americans that was both written by a Native American (Alexie) and directed by a Native American (Chris Eyre) to achieve major distribution (Miramax backed the project early on). The film effectively, at times humorously, debunks many standard Native American stereotypes, from the noble savage to the mighty warrior to the resigned martyr. Specifically, Alexie and Eyre challenge the myth of the "authentic" Native American, a favorite cliché of U.S. popular culture. If *Smoke Signals* narrows the formal and thematic sprawl of Alexie's short stories, the film proved immensely successful with mainstream audiences and thereby introduced portraits of complicated, late-twentieth-century Indian identity into the realm of popular cinema. A practitioner of both experimentation (in his short stories) and convention (in the *Smoke Signals* screenplay), Alexie has produced a varied body of work that raises the issue of the politics of representation. In this chapter I argue that Alexie's adapted screenplay reveals that accessible narratives can produce effective political interventions in the U.S. social and cultural imagination.

Native American cultural scholar and historian Vine Deloria has explained the U.S. cultural preoccupation with Native Americans in the following way: "Underneath all the conflicting images of the Indian one fundamental truth emerges—the white man *knows* that he is an alien and he *knows* that North America is Indian—and he will never let go of the Indian image because he thinks that by some clever manipulation he can achieve an authenticity that cannot ever be his."[1] While popular culture has demonstrated a longstanding investment in the idea of Native Americans, it has also evinced a deep disinterest in the specificities of Native American identity. Alexie and Eyre counteract the white quest for authenticity by depicting multifaceted Native Americans in *Smoke Signals*. By presenting offbeat, confused characters, the film invokes the quirkiness of independent cinema while also destabilizing the stereotypical figure of the earnest, natural Indian.

Alexie, a Spokane/Coeur d'Alene Indian, was already fairly well-known when he made his first foray into screenwriting with *Smoke Signals*. Although only thirty-two, Alexie was already the author of two poetry collections, *The Business of Fancydancing* (1991) and *I Would Steal Horses* (1993); the *Lone Ranger* short story collection, which won the PEN/Hemingway Award for the Best First Book of Fiction; and two novels, *Reservation Blues* (1995) and *Indian Killer* (1996). His work was both recognized—among other awards, he received a National Endowment for the Arts Poetry Fellowship in 1992—and varied—he also released a collaborative album with Jim Boyd, titled *Reservation Blues*. Director Chris Eyre, a Cheyenne/Arapho Indian, even younger than Alexie, was still in his twenties when he directed *Smoke Signals*. He had previously directed several short films.

The *Lone Ranger* collection contains twenty-two short stories, ranging from fairly straightforward, realist accounts of life on the Spokane Indian Reservation in the 1970s, 1980s, and 1990s to lyrical exercises with no fixed time period that draw from a wide array of literary styles. Although the pieces vary widely in terms of form, most feature young male protagonists in a variety of conflicts with families, lovers, and friends. Many follow a group of young male Indian characters:[2] Victor, who becomes an alcoholic over the course of the collection; Thomas Builds-the-Fire, an idiosyncratic monologist; and Junior Polatkin, who leaves the reservation to attend a primarily white high school, where he succeeds in the classroom and on the basketball court (mirroring Alexie's own biography). The subjects of basketball, alcoholism, heterosexual romance, and alienation appear frequently. In several short stories, Alexie adopts an experimental writing style, privileging creative wordplay over linear narrative and character development. Even the more realist stories that compose the majority of the collection include complex mixes of hallucinations, nightmares, and drug-induced visions.

The short story "This Is What It Means to Say Phoenix, Arizona" provides the screenplay's primary narrative. *Smoke Signals* focuses primarily on Victor Joseph, a young Coeur d'Alene Indian living with his mother on the Coeur d'Alene Indian Reservation near the Washington-Idaho border. Victor's father, Arnold, an alcoholic, abandoned the family when he was a child. Estranged from his father, Victor must reconcile himself to Arnold when he learns that Arnold has died in Phoenix, Arizona. With his geeky childhood friend Thomas, an orphan, Victor travels to Arizona to recover Arnold's ashes. The film thus invokes the conventions of the buddy picture, with a sympathetic protagonist and his more eccentric sidekick, as well as the road trip movie, depicting the spectacular terrain on the boys' journey from the Idaho reservation to Phoenix and back. During their travels, Victor encourages Thomas to conform to a more conventional version of Native American masculinity, while Thomas helps Victor view his father more sympathetically. The film primarily depicts Victor and Thomas as young adults, although it also includes regular flashbacks to their childhoods, revealing the origin of problems that haunt them later (such as Victor's father's alcoholism and abandonment, and Victor's persecution of Thomas). Often colors orchestrate these temporal transitions; Victor is associated with the volatile color red, which he wears as both child and adult.

Alexie took on an unusual project in adapting his own work into a screenplay. In an interview with Dennis and Joan West for the film magazine *Cineaste*, Alexie claimed, "I didn't have any problems with mutating my own book. I treated my book of short stories in adapting the screenplay as though I didn't write it."[3] After adapting the collection, Alexie continued to shape the film by contributing original songs, participating in the shooting of the film, and making suggestions about the editing process. In terms of formal and thematic adaptation, Alexie imported some of the lyricism of the short stories into the film's occasional episodic interludes, a characteristic of independent films. For instance, the film begins with a joke delivered by a low-tech weatherman who has neither much to report nor an extensive listening audience and whose equipment seems to consist entirely of a cell phone and a broken-down van. Similarly funny, eccentric characters who do nothing to advance the plot appear throughout the screenplay, in keeping with independent cinema's penchant for meandering, non-plot-driven films.

But what was at stake for Alexie in the adaptation from text to moving pictures? Alexie had to perform two weighty tasks simultaneously: negotiating the loaded politics of Native American representation in cinema while also presenting a coherent, entertaining story. As a result of its focus on coherence and entertainment, the transition from screenplay to final film necessitated even more streamlining. Alexie, who undertook many roles in making the movie, was acutely aware of the transformation necessary to move from screenplay to motion picture.

The book *Smoke Signals: A Screenplay* (1998) chronicles how the formal innovation and radical content of the original short stories became even more streamlined during the multiple stages of the adaptation process (from short story collection to screenplay and then from screenplay to final film). The book includes Alexie's original screenplay, which departs in significant ways from the resulting film. In a scene-by-scene commentary, Alexie unveils the process of adaptation by explaining how each scene was finally shot. He flags every change made to the original screenplay during the shooting and editing of the film, and includes as well his own response to the changes. While charting these revisions, Alexie also notes the strengths of the resulting film.

During his discussion of changes made to the original screenplay, however, hints of a struggle, or at least of tension, between Alexie and director Chris Eyre emerge as well. Alexie repeatedly describes instances in which Eyre's choices departed from Alexie's own (such as the filming of the car accident that Victor and Thomas are involved in, or the film's ending). Several times, Alexie generously notes that Eyre's version was superior to his own. For instance, he comments on a scene between Victor and Thomas: "During preproduction Chris Eyre suggested that Victor throw the water canteen off-screen and force Thomas to trot off-screen, only to come back on-screen with a humorous vengeance. I wrote it in because it was a damn good idea. Chris scored on this one."[4] More often, however, Alexie worries that Eyre's departures will undermine the film. For example, in one commentary he notes, "When I saw the dailies of this scene, I knew that Chris had shot it incorrectly. The scene was simply not funny enough. So I storyboarded the scene and then told the producers how it should be shot. They reshot it the next day. This scene now receives the biggest laughs in the film."[5] An interview with Eyre also suggests a difference of artistic vision. As part of an explanation of how Sundance funding helped the film in its early stages, Eyre comments that "Sherman's material gave me a chance to try certain things that didn't work, and I'm glad I tried them there."[6]

In addition to charting the changes made to his screenplay, Alexie notes each scene excised, explains its removal, and provides his reaction. Significantly, the cuts that most concern him are ones that carry ideological weight. For instance, in accommodating the imperative for cinematic succinctness,

Alexie called the choice to eliminate the only reference to Suzy Song's tribe "the most painful cut."[7] In another instance in which Alexie and Eyre part ways, Alexie explains that he and Eyre advocated different performance styles for filming this revelation. Alexie wrote the scene one way (earnestly), but Eyre filmed it another (comically); ultimately, Eyre's version was cut from the final film. Thus, significant information about the only major Native American woman character in the film may have been sacrificed to a power struggle between Alexie and Eyre.

Earlier in the adaptation process, the transition from the original *Lone Ranger* collection to the *Smoke Signals* screenplay offered another compelling example of adaptation. Alexie's short stories challenge a ready adaptation into cinematic form in several ways, such as their use of multiple protagonists and experimental stylization. Narrative ambiguity is a hallmark of Alexie's prose, whereas screenplays generally rely on conventions such as causality, a linear plot, and a three-act structure.

For instance, deliberately ambiguous moments occur in Alexie's stories when characters in the same story present the same event from several different perspectives. The resulting polyphony is one that Alexie resists reducing to a single account that might be deemed authentic, accurate, or real. Instead, contradictory versions of the same event remain adjacent on the page, informing each other through a paratactic proximity without subordinating one to the other. For instance, in "Because My Father Always Said," Victor provides several accounts of the dissolution of his parents' marriage (a subject that is also central to the screenplay and film):

> Because of all that, my father always remembered the second before my mother left him for good and took me with her. No. I remembered the second before my father left my mother and me. No. My mother remembered the second before my father left her to finish raising me all by herself.[8]

Validating several mutually exclusive accounts of the family history suggests that every version is in some sense "true" for its narrator. Alexie returns to this device in other short stories.

Privileging multiple voices and contradictory accounts of the same event promotes a model of storytelling well suited to the experiences of disenfranchised native peoples, whose own narratives do not generally coincide with dominant versions of history, literature, or cinema. This narrative strategy questions the accuracy of a single, privileged account, asserting instead multiple versions of events. Alexie's refusal to champion one narrative over another allows for alternative versions of both personal family histories and national history (such as the "discovery" of America).

Although it is more streamlined, Alexie's screenplay upholds his artistic and ideological investment in multiple voices. As in the short stories, both Thomas and Arnold, Victor's father, deliver exuberant monologues that resist categorization as truth, lies, or fiction. Thomas's stories work within the framework of a largely traditional screenplay because he is coded as an eccentric, embarrassing Victor with his propensity to break into long, unprompted, but skilled speeches. Arnold's single monologue occurs in a dreamy, nostalgic flashback that accommodates a departure from linear storytelling.[9] Two equally possible versions of Arnold's story occur in the screenplay and film. According to Arnold, as a child, Victor successfully defeated a team of Jesuit priests in a basketball game; as an adult, Victor instead remembers having lost the game. Such variation in accounts of the same event recalls Alexie's use of multiplicity in his short stories. The contradictory versions uphold Alexie's investment in a narrative and historical multiplicity that invoke the perspective of a colonized indigenous people.

The film's visual style achieves a balance between accessibility and innovation; it mixes the invisibility of classical Hollywood cinema with unique subject material uncharacteristic of even independent films. The poverty of the Coeur D'Alene Indian Reservation is visually apparent, but is also juxtaposed with long shots of the lush surrounding environment. As Alexie notes, "We were very conscious of photographing the reservation in beautiful ways.... Contemporary films about Indians always highlight the poverty, the ugliness of reservations. We wanted to show, exactly, the beauty of this reservation."[10] The natural beauty helps temper the protagonists' financial difficulties (as well as keep the film in the genre of comedy). Other moments are similarly reservation-specific, such as the minor characters of Thelma and Lucy, two young Indian women who give Victor and Thomas a ride to the border of the reservation, drive a car that only functions in reverse, demand to barter in exchange for the ride, and warn the two men that they are leaving the reservation for "a whole different country."[11] In what Alexie has called the "rezziest Indian performances in cinematic history,"[12] Thelma and Lucy encourage Victor and Thomas to get vaccinations before proceeding. During the women's brief interlude, they remind each other of their pledge to stay sober, trigger one of Thomas's fanciful accounts of Victor's father, and interject humor into Victor's otherwise somber quest. The scene also rewrites the reservation as safe, familiar territory, the norm for these characters as opposed to the perils found in the greater United States. Not unlike their namesakes, Thelma and Louise, the two women disrupt the otherwise male genre of the road trip (if only momentarily). Generally, however, the film visually privileges the story and contains none of the more confusing formal experimentation found in Alexie's short stories.

While the film largely upholds mainstream cinematic conventions, it also champions a handsome Indian as its protagonist. It remains so unusual for a film with a major distribution deal to have a Native American protagonist that this seemingly straightforward choice resonates as a radical innovation.[13] This radical casting choice in turn relies on mainstream techniques for its effectiveness. Victor and Thomas wear typical lower-middle-class Northwest male clothing (jeans and flannel shirts), and Victor drives a pickup truck. (Victor also wears cowboy boots, an indication of his hybrid style.) Their very familiarity belies the fact that Indians have only occasionally served as cinematic protagonists and almost never in films shaped by an Indian perspective. As Alexie has noted, "Simply having Indians as the protagonists in a contemporary film, and placing them within this familiar literary, and cinematic structure, is groundbreaking."[14] Because of the dearth of Indian protagonists in U.S. films, Alexie's choice to render that protagonist in accessible, mainstream terms may serve a purpose equally as radical as the more extensive formal experimentation of his original short stories.

The film consistently provides a uniquely Indian perspective: a scene in which two white cowboys take Victor and Thomas's seats on the bus to Phoenix exemplifies this point of view. This minor, petty moment of mean-spiritedness echoes several centuries of whites' dislocating Native Americans from their rightful locations. The screenplay and film thus acknowledge that the race of the protagonists dramatically affects the narrative. Although Victor and Thomas ultimately cede their seats to the cowboys, they resist their displacement by regaling the other passengers from the back of the bus, where they end up, significantly enough, with an impromptu song about John Wayne's teeth. Lampooning the traditional icon of cowboys and the western film genre with a mockery that also carries a trace of reverence, Victor and Thomas employ Indian song conventions to register their outrage. Not unlike the film itself, they challenge oppressive expressions of racism with humor and a hybridized mixture of popular culture, artistry, and Indian tradition.

Much of the more subversive material contained in the short stories, however, does not appear in the screenplay. Gone are the strong female characters, from the disgruntled housewife who stages a domestic revolution in

Displaced to the back of the bus in Smoke Signals, *Victor and Thomas combine popular culture and Indian tradition to fight back by singing about John Wayne's teeth.*

"The Fun House" to the powerful Norma Many Horses, who appears in several stories and who, as a young woman committed to maintaining traditional Indian narratives, provides an important link between a younger generation and a disappearing older culture. The exclusion of Norma from the screenplay limits the number of women in the film to three primary female characters, only one of whom is Victor's or Thomas's contemporary. The film includes Victor's mother, Thomas's grandmother, and Suzy Song, Arnold's young next-door neighbor in Phoenix, whose primary function is to explain Arnold's behavior to Victor. Whereas the film clearly offers new, richer representations of Native American men, the female representation remains relatively marginal.[15]

Similarly, topics raised by the short stories that might prove problematic, including diabetes, recreational drug use, and interracial relationships, do not appear in the screenplay. Although several of the short stories depict characters in interracial relationships grappling with the intersection of privilege, race, and intimacy, the screenplay does not broach this topic.[16] The short story "A Drug Called Tradition" daringly links Indian ritual with late twentieth-century hedonism when a group of Indian boys take hallucinogenic drugs and have visions of themselves as nineteenth-century warriors. The screenplay, however, eschews any reference to drugs.

Alexie was not alone in adapting a rambling short story collection to a single film format. Other 1990s films adapted from short story collections dealt with the necessity of condensing a larger and more disruptive range of material into a coherent screenplay and film, although these adaptations tackled the problem in different ways. Director Robert Altman's adaptation of Raymond Carver's short stories into the screenplay for *Short Cuts* (1993) perfectly suited Altman's directorial style, since his films tend to avoid a single protagonist, favoring instead multiple characters and an unfocused, episodic structure. The film version of *Jesus' Son* (1999), an adaptation of Denis Johnson's 1992 short story collection of the same name, benefited from the fact that the original collection featured interconnected stories about the same character, providing a single protagonist for the film adaptation. Nevertheless, director Alison Maclean chose to foreground visual style in her film, using a handheld camera and including hallucinatory fantasy sequences. The idiosyncratic narrative generally lacks causality, following a sequence of events that makes sense only to the drug-addicted main character. Maclean's stylish directorial choices thus dovetail well with the content of the short stories. In contrast to these adaptations, *Smoke Signals* registers as fairly conventional, with a single protagonist and a basically linear narrative. Not coincidentally, *Smoke Signals* was also more commercially successful than either *Short Cuts* or *Jesus' Son*. As the first feature-length film starring Native Americans to receive major distribution, *Smoke Signals* perhaps could not afford to gamble with accessibility.

In fact, *Smoke Signals* successfully reached a large audience and did so while undermining the stereotype of Native Americans as representatives of authenticity. The film contributes a unique perspective to the motion picture industry's long reliance on portraits of Indians, from the voiceless aggressors in films such as *Stagecoach* (1939) to noble warriors willing to concede defeat and disappear in films such as *Little Big Man* (1970), to countless films in which Indians were played by white actors (from Rock Hudson in *Taza, Son of Cochise* [1954] to Val Kilmer in *Thunderheart* [1992]), to the many films in which white protagonists demonstrate their authenticity by going native, as in *A Man Called Horse* (1970) and *Dances with Wolves* (1990).[17] Against such reductive portrayals, however earnestly conceived, *Smoke Signals* asserts a far more complex portrait of Native American identity.[18]

The film consistently complicates "authentic" Native American stereotypes, accommodating instead a broader range of behavior. For instance, in an invocation of matrilineal Indian heritage, Victor's mother initially explains that her recipe for traditional fry bread comes from her mother, who got it from her grandmother. But then she adds that she has also learned from gourmand Julia Child, a reference to popular culture that effectively qualifies the authentic nature of the recipe and suggests instead the hybridity of contemporary Native American culture.

Similarly, the screenplay and film locate their characters in a late twentieth-century setting replete with popular culture, thereby undermining an association with an agrarian, "authentic" Native American past. Instead of portraying romanticized, essentialized Indian characters, Alexie's screenplay depicts young Indians grappling with many aspects of their subjectivity, gleaned from family members, popular culture, and the reservation environment. While the Coeur D'Alene Indian Reservation is presented as supportive and familial, its representation is by no means romanticized, and poverty and social problems, such as domestic abuse and alcoholism, also appear in the film.

One of the film's strengths is its engagement with popular culture, the site of long-term, ongoing, even obsessive representations of Native Americans. The film's willingness to discuss directly, refute, and play with stereotypes of Native Americans challenges these reductive portrayals while not dismissing popular culture and media outright. For instance, late in the film, when Victor and Thomas heroically aid two women after a car accident, one of the women, Holly, attempts to praise them by invoking popular culture icons: "You guys were heroes, you know. Who are you, anyways? It's like you're the Lone Ranger and Tonto," to which Thomas jokes, "No, it's more like we're Tonto and Tonto."[19] Seizing on the silent sidekick to the white hero, Thomas multiplies this figure, provides him with an equal counterpart, and moves him to center-stage. In doing so, he claims heroism not only for the marginal figure of Tonto but also for himself. This moment and others like it demonstrate the film's investment in mobilizing popular culture icons humorously and strategically to undermine longstanding, limited representations of Native Americans. Because U.S. citizens of color, and particularly Native Americans, have been called on by white culture to represent the "real" and the "authentic," Alexie's embrace of popular culture opposes a fantasy of the pure, untainted, nineteenth-century Indian.

The popular culture references Alexie draws on in the screenplay and film—from John Wayne and Charles Bronson, to *Little Big Man* and *Dances with Wolves*, and the Lone Ranger and Tonto—provide familiarity for reading and viewing audiences. Alexie does not pander to his audiences by including these references, however, since he strategically mobilizes them to broaden or assert Indian identity. For instance, several times in the short stories, screenplay, and film, characters rewrite the doomed motto uttered by a Native American character in *Little Big Man*: "It's a good day to die." This solemn declaration signifies a passive reconciliation to annihilation that works to obscure the genocidal agenda of nineteenth-century whites settling the West. The film triggers guilt in its spectators about violence against Native Americans but simultaneously excuses that guilt, since the Native Americans themselves seem to embrace their abject destiny. In contrast, in *Smoke Signals*, characters announce that "It's a good day to play basketball," "a good day to be indigenous," or "a good day to have breakfast."[20] These less ponderous, more quotidian affirmations reveal the notion of Indians' collective suicidal tendencies as a white fantasy. Rejecting the tragic register, Alexie replaces it with humor, an insistently resistant presence, and active, bodily desires. Alexie has stated that the original phrase "has so little meaning in our lives that I wanted to make fun of it. It's never, ever, *ever*, a good day to die."[21]

In addition to mocking stereotypes, however, Alexie's work also acknowledges their appeal to both white and Indian audiences, suggesting the effects of a century of viewing such images. In a piece in his first published work, the collection *The Business of Fancydancing*, Alexie muses about a group of Indians in a bar: "All us stoic Indians rehearsing for parts as extras in some eternal black and white western. Shit, used to be only whites expected Skins to have monosyllabic faces, but now, we even expect it of each other."[22] In a short story in *Lone Ranger*, Alexie similarly wonders, "Does every Indian depend on Hollywood for a twentieth-century vision?"[23] And whereas Alexie does not celebrate the effect that mediated images of Indians have had on actual Indians, he recognizes their power rather than wholly rejecting them.

The performance of stoicism in the bar scene underwrites most representations of male Indians and intersects with the notion of heroism. If heroism remains a loaded index of masculinity for all U.S. men, Native American men engage with it in a particularly complicated way. Although few Indian heroes appear in U.S. history or popular culture, Indian men have consistently been portrayed in the media as natural (if necessarily doomed) heroic warriors. The many images of Indians that serve as sports teams' logos, for instance, unrealistically distort Native American culture while appropriating the stereotypical traits of strength and stoicism understood to be inherent to Native American identity.

The desire for models of male heroism informs *Smoke Signals*' screenplay and film narratives.[24] In an early flashback that draws on the first short story in the collection, young Victor searches for his besotted parents, Arnold and Arlene, at a raucous party in the 1970s. After Victor locates his father, Arnold drunkenly asks him, "Who's your favorite Indian?" When Victor refuses to respond, Arnold becomes depressed and angry.[25] The question and the lack of an answer indicate a vacancy at the heart of twentieth-century Indian identity and mythology, a vacancy that Arnold finds himself unable to fill for his son. While Crazy Horse appears as a dominant figure in Alexie's poetry and short stories, Tonto and Charles Bronson also recur in his work. Later in the film, as Victor and Thomas hike through the Arizona desert to the place where Arnold died, Thomas launches into a long riff on heroism by first bemoaning the absence of Native American representation in popular culture: "I mean, we ain't got nobody can help us at all. No Superman, no Batman, no Wonder Woman, not even Charles Bronson, man." Thomas then creates a hybridized hero of his own by immediately claiming: "Hey, did you ever notice how much your dad looks like Charles Bronson?"[26] At this Oedipal moment, poised as they are at the very site of the patriarch's death, Thomas attempts to fill the gap created by the lost father with icons of popular culture. While Victor strenuously denies this connection (and in fact, Gary Farmer, the actor playing Arnold, bears no resemblance to Charles Bronson), the suggestion clearly indicates the desire for a larger-than-life figure of male heroism. Particularly since Thomas harbors a juvenile admiration of Victor's father that borders on worship, his suggestion reveals how popular culture informs private fantasies and shapes personal histories.[27] Diane Krumrey has argued that Alexie's use of popular culture icons provides his protagonists with psychological support. She notes that the many white celebrities Victor refers to in *Lone Ranger*, from Natalie Wood to Sal Mineo, form a "popular culture family, who have been produced along with him, and have co-produced him, within this cultural formation."[28] This negotiation of mediated images of heroism and of Indians suggests a range of possible candidates to fill the void initially created by the question, "Who's your favorite Indian?"

Despite his embrace of popular culture and his willingness to form a hybridicized, popular culture family for his characters, Alexie has also regularly criticized conventional media depictions of Indians, both in interviews and in his own writing. In the *Smoke Signals* screenplay and film, Thomas, positioned in front of a television broadcasting a black and white scene of a cowboy and Indian chase, comments, "You know, the only thing dumber than Indians on television is Indians sitting in front of a television."[29] This moment attacks media representation of Native Americans as well as the Native American community's accommodation of, and even tacit participation in, this onslaught, but Alexie does more than oppose mainstream media in his work. Instead, he consistently positions his characters in contexts that acknowledge popular culture's contradictory appeal.

While literary and film critics regularly note Alexie's charges against media, too often they do so in order to promote their own reliance on a notion of Indians as innocent primeval figures, either somehow entirely removed from the melee of contemporary U.S. culture or hopelessly tainted by it. For instance, Gordon Slethaug argues that when Thomas watches television in the scene mentioned above, Alexie thereby "suggests that television programs create an unacceptable simulacra, which has the effect of defacing the authentic Native American culture."[30] However, far more often than he has criticized the media, Alexie has vehemently opposed a colonialist desire for Native American authenticity. In addition, in interviews and in his own work, Alexie has claimed popular Western culture as a "common cultural currency."[31] Rather than locating Native American identity in a remote, preindustrial environment, Alexie's own work weaves together popular culture, Native American tradition, and the contemporary Native American experience to suggest their mutual interdependence.

Alexie has in fact been criticized for privileging the arenas of popular culture and representation over a direct engagement with more specifically political dilemmas that affect the Native American community. Ernest Stromberg suggests that *Smoke Signals* is limited by the fact that "its political edge remains directed primarily at the level of representations. Not that this is insignificant, but the film provides little sense of any current political or socio-economic issues confronting Native Americans."[32] Representation remains a pressing current issue for Native Americans, however, in part because the Native American community has long endured obsessive cinematic and cultural representation while having little to no input in these characterizations. Given that unique configuration, the possibility of launching alternative representations of Native American into popular culture carries a particularly political significance. That the film also counteracts stereotypical images of Native Americans, while offering an example of self-representation is a significant contribution to Native American politics. In addition, simply testifying to the presence of the late twentieth-century Native American community in the American cultural landscape and thereby challenging that community's invisibility in so many other arenas helps broaden the range of Native American representation. Finally, the subjects of representation and popular culture are accessible to a large audience, unlike, for example, narrowly focused, poorly covered outrages such as the intimidation of Native American voters in the 2004 Nevada Senate race.[33] Popular culture thus provides a useful way to broach the notion of Native American disenfranchisement without directly addressing specifically political topics.

Alexie has defended himself ably against charges that his work is apolitical. In interviews, he has reiterated his intention to locate his fiction in his own time period and to eschew explicit discussions of politics.[34] Criticizing conventional depictions of Native Americans, Alexie has argued that "far too many deal with politics—Indian politics are incredibly narcissistic—or nostalgia."[35] Instead, Alexie intervenes in the arena of contemporary popular culture. The terms of this debate appear explicitly in his fiction. For instance, in one of the *Lone Ranger* short stories, a character muses, "But it's almost like Indians can easily survive the big stuff. Mass murder, loss of language and land rights. It's the small things that hurt the most. The white waitress who wouldn't take an order, Tonto, the Washington Redskins."[36] Shifting his focus from the broadly historical to the specific, personal and cultural, Alexie asserts the political nature of his artistic intervention.

Although the film *Smoke Signals* is not a political jeremiad, Alexie nonetheless encountered creative difficulties in making a movie with a significant budget ($2 million). Alexie chafed at the constraints that accompany major financing, stating that "[b]eing on film sets felt no different to me than visiting my friends at law firms or at Microsoft. Every decision based on money. Every decision! The whole process itself being so conservative. It was always about fear! Everything seemed to be based on some sort of negative energy."[37] In fact, early in his filmmaking experience, Alexie expressed an interest in unconventional screenplays that resist conforming to traditional film formats. In the introduction to *Smoke Signals: The Screenplay*, after noting similarities between poetry and screenplays, he wonders, "Who is writing the free verse screenplays?"[38] While experimental films continue to be made, few receive distribution deals that result in large audiences. Like other independent filmmakers, Alexie has gone on to embrace a mode of filmmaking that privileges directorial autonomy, innovation, and control but sacrifices a substantial budget and the possibility of reaching large audiences.[39] In addition, the small-budget format occasions less oversight and involves contributions from fewer people. As an inherently collaborative art form, however, filmmaking may in fact benefit from the inclusion of multiple perspectives, in contrast to the control exerted by a single vision.

After his auspicious debut, Alexie rejected traditional form and content in adapting one of his poetry collections into a screenplay for a second film, which he also directed. This film, the very low-budget *The Business of Fancydancing* (2002), did not receive theatrical distribution. Working with a small crew of friends, Alexie filmed *The Business of Fancydancing* on digital and analog video. The result is much more experimental than *Smoke Signals*. The movie follows Seymour, a gay Spokane Indian and acclaimed poet (played by Evan Adams, the same actor who played Thomas in *Smoke Signals*), as he returns from Seattle, where he lives, to the Spokane Indian reservation, where he grew up, for a childhood friend's funeral. The film's extremely unconventional style includes extensive handheld video, ghosts walking among living characters, improvised scenes, mock interviews, and staged interludes of music, dance, and recitations of Alexie's poetry. The result ultimately resembles a recording of community theater more than a feature film.[40]

The shortcomings of *The Business of Fancydancing* underscore the strength of Alexie's decision to adhere to traditional screenwriting formulas in *Smoke Signals*, which generates audience identification through its focus on a single, sympathetic protagonist. Ironically, the very accessibility of the more conventional film more effectively advances Alexie's unconventional perspective, while including independent film flourishes. According to Alexie's notes on the making of *Smoke Signals*, the film also benefited from collaborative input, a process Alexie did not employ for his second feature film, which he personally financed. While Alexie relished his excursion into low-budget experimental filmmaking, *The Business of Fancydancing* found almost no audience, in striking contrast to the commercial and critical success of *Smoke Signals*.

Late twentieth-century scholarship on films adapted from literature has promoted an understanding of adaptations as different but not inherently inferior art forms, suggesting that an investigation of the choices that shape each version yields more insights than pitting literature against film. In the introduction to *Adaptations as Imitations*, James Griffith states his purpose "to show that adaptations can do many of the things they are too commonly thought to be incapable of doing—that is, imitate, in a fashion equal to the achievement of the original novel, various narrative techniques, forms, and effects."[41] Alexie's translation of his own short stories into a feature-length screenplay, each a successful work of art in its own right, perfectly illustrates this new trend in adaptation scholarship. *Lone Ranger* and *Smoke Signals* both perform differently, from the short stories' lyrical sprawl to the screenplay's more focused thematic assertion of the complexities of late twentieth-century masculine Indian identity. The adaptation by no means represents a falling off from a more artfully expansive original. The film not only includes some of the experimental aspects of the short stories, it also presents countless moviegoers with images of Native Americans that destabilize longstanding stereotypes of Indians as figures of "natural" authenticity. In doing so, the screenplay and film testify to the complexity of contemporary Native Americans and their communities, offering a breakthrough in representational possibilities.

NOTES

I thank Rebecca Brittenham, April Lidinsky, Jeff Rhyne, and Lesley Walker, as well as Jack Boozer and Mark Gallagher, for their helpful responses to this essay.

1. Vine Deloria, "Foreword/American Fantasy," in *The Pretend Indians: Images of Native Americans in the Movies*, ed. Gretchen M. Bataille and Charles L. P. Silet (Ames: Iowa State University Press, 1980), xvi.

2. I am following Sherman Alexie's lead in using both "Native American" and "Indian" to indicate the indigenous peoples of the U.S. Alexie has stated that he prefers "Indian" because it is the term most commonly used by both whites and indigenous peoples. I use them interchangeably in this essay.

3. Dennis West and Joan West, "Sending Cinematic Smoke Signals: An Interview with Sherman Alexie." *Cineaste: America's Leading Magazine of the Art and Politics of the Cinema* 24, no. 4 (1998): 29.

4. Alexie, *Smoke Signals*, 162.

5. Ibid., 161.

6. Jacqueline Kilpatrick, *Celluloid Indians: Native Americans and Film* (Lincoln: University of Nebraska Press, 1999), 229.

7. Alexie, *Smoke Signals*, 163.

8. Sherman Alexie, *The Lone Ranger and Tonto Fistfight in Heaven* (New York: HarperCollins, 1993), 34.

9. Unfortunately, in the film itself, despite the spirited performance of Gary Farmer, the actor playing Arnold, this speech is undermined by lackluster visuals. Instead of taking place outdoors as originally planned, much of the scene had to be shot indoors because of weather constraints. Alexie acknowledges this shortcoming in his notes on the film (*Smoke Signals*, 164).

10. Alexie, *Smoke Signals*, 158.

11. Ibid., 40.

12. Ibid., 158.

13. The comedy *Harold and Kumar Go to White Castle* (2004) in fact begins by reversing the conventions of audience expectations about the protagonist's race; the film opens with a scene featuring two minor white characters and then unexpectedly turns to the main characters, who are Chinese and Indian (from the continent), respectively.

14. West and West, "Sending Cinematic Smoke Signals," 29.

15. As John Warren Gilroy has noted, however, the women are spared the fate of simply serving as heterosexual love interests for the male protagonist ("Another Fine Example of the Oral Tradition? Identification and Subversion in Sherman Alexie's *Smoke Signals*." *Studies in American Indian Literatures: The Journal of the Association for the Study of American Indian Literatures* 13, no. 1 (2001), par. 31–32).

16. Alexie has returned to this subject in short story collections published since *Lone Ranger*, such as *The Toughest Indian in the World* (2000). He may have avoided the cinematic depiction of an interracial relationship since films written and directed by whites that include Native Americans have demonstrated a consistent, even fixated interest in this topic, from *The Searchers* (1956) to *Pocahontas* (1995).

17. As Shari Huhndorf has convincingly argued, "going native comprises a cherished national ritual, a means by which European America figures and reenacts its own dominance even as it attempts to deny its violent history" (*Going Native: Indians in the American Cultural Imagination* [Ithaca: Cornell University Press, 2001], 18). This authenticity claim, then, depends in equal part on aggression and disavowal.

18. Certain twenty-first-century films have continued the portrayal of Native Americans as preindustrial and authentic. For example, describing *Spirit: Stallion of the Cimarron* (2003), an animated children's film about wild horses set during the U.S. Civil War, a friend's daughter, five-year-old Brenda O'Connor, said, "It has horses, and people, and Indians." Her description is entirely consistent with the film's racial ideology, which presents Native Americans as half-naked, natural entities wholly other than human.

19. Alexie, *Smoke Signals*, 125.

20. Ibid., 17, 32, 53.

21. West and West, "Sending Cinematic Smoke Signals," 37.

22. Sherman Alexie, *The Business of Fancydancing: The Screenplay* (Brooklyn: Hanging Loose Press, 1992), 75.

23. Sherman Alexie, *The Lone Ranger and Tonto Fistfight in Heaven* (New York: HarperCollins, 1993), 151.

24. Alexie has referenced his own youthful investment in cultural models of male heroism, from Bruce Lee to the eponymous hero of *Billy Jack* (1971) to the protagonists of blaxploitation films (*Business*, 156). Not coincidentally, all are men of color.

25. Alexie, *Smoke Signals*, 48.

26. Ibid., 68.

27. The nomination of Charles Bronson as a figure of Native American heroism deserves comment. Although he stands among the ranks of white actors who have posed as Native Americans in films, the character he portrays in *Run of the Arrow* (1957), filmed during Bronson's days as a body builder, offers a powerfully realized embodiment of masculinity and strength. Thomas, however, specifically invokes Bronson's later, more popular roles as a white vigilante, in films such as *Death Wish* (1974).

28. Diane Krumrey, "Subverting the Tonto Stereotype in Popular Fiction, Or, Why Indians say 'Ugh!' in *Simulacrum American: The USA and the Popular Media*, ed. Elisabeth Kraus and Carolin Auer (Rochester, NY: Camden House, 2000), 166.

29. Alexie, *Smoke Signals*, 73. While critics have repeatedly referenced this line of dialogue as a demonstration of Alexie's criticism of popular culture and media, Alexie states that the actor playing Thomas, Evan Adams, actually improvised it in early rehearsals of the scene. Alexie does note, however, that he wishes he could take credit for it (*Smoke Signals*, 163).

30. Gordon Slethaug, "Hurricanes and Fires: Chaotics in Sherman Alexie's *Smoke Signals* and *The Lone Ranger and Tonto Fistfight in Heaven*." *Literature Film Quarterly* 31, no. 2 (2003): 130–140, 139n8.

31. West and West, "Sending Cinematic Smoke Signals," 37.

32. Ernest Stromberg, "Out of the Cupboard and Up with the *Smoke Signals*: Cinematic Representations of American Indians in the Nineties." *Studies in Popular Culture* 24, no. 1 (2001): 33–46, http://pcasacas.org/SPC/ (accessed July 28, 2004).

33. "Federal Judge Issues Restraining Order at the Request of Senator Tom Daschle," *Morning Edition*, National Public Radio, November 2, 2004, http://www.npr.org/ (accessed November 11, 2004).

34. Stromberg ("Out of the Cupboard") has noted that *Smoke Signals* differs from most films that depict Native Americans in utilizing a late-twentieth-century rather than a historical setting.

35. Alexie has specifically targeted John Neihardt's 1932 book *Black Elk Speaks*, noting that Black Elk later repudiated the book (Julien Fielding, "Native American Religion and Film: Interviews with Chris Eyre and Sherman Alexie," *Journal of Religion and Film* 7, no. 1 [2003]: par. 5, http://avalon.unomaha.edu/jrf/Vol7No1/nativefilm.html [accessed July 28, 2004]). He has also publicly lambasted authors Barbara Kingsolver and Larry McMurty for their portrayals of Native Americans (Timothy Egan, "An Indian Without Reservations," *New York Times Magazine*, January 18, 1998, 17–19, 18; Joelle Fraser, "Sherman Alexie's *Iowa Review* Interview," *Modern American Poetry*, July 20, 2004, 2, www.english.uiuc.edu/maps/poets/). In addition, characters in *Smoke Signals* poke fun at the film *Dances with Wolves*.

36. Alexie, *Lone Ranger*, 49.

37. Alexie, *Business*, 156.

38. Alexie, *Smoke Signals*, x.

39. Director Steven Soderbergh, for example, has returned repeatedly to experimental, low-budget filmmaking in forays such as *Schizopolis* (1997) and *Full Frontal* (2002). Soderbergh stood in a unique position with *Full Frontal*, in that this experimental film starred celebrities and was partially funded by the success of his big-budget studio film, *Ocean's 11* (2001). Both of these resources, celebrity actors and big-budget studio funding, have not historically been available to Native American filmmakers. While *Full Frontal* represents a low-budget departure for Soderbergh, its budget was equivalent to that for *Smoke Signals* ($2 million). Other white direc-

tors interested in formal experimentation, such as David O. Russell (*I ♥ Huckabees*, 2004) and Paul Thomas Anderson (*Punch Drunk Love*, 2002), have also had access to sizable budgets.

40. In a *New York Times* review, Elvis Mitchell noted that the film is "occasionally sabotaged by its economy of means: the image quality is sometimes so poor that it's like watching the pixel breakup on digital cable." Mitchell, "A Poet Finds His Past Is Just Where He Left It," *New York Times*, October 18, 2002, 25, http://lexis-nexis.com (accessed July 20, 2004).

41. James Griffith, *Adaptations as Imitations: Films from Novels* (Newark: University of Delaware Press, 1997), 69.

WORKS CITED

Alexie, Sherman. *The Business of Fancydancing: The Screenplay*. Brooklyn: Hanging Loose Press, 1992.

———. *The Lone Ranger and Tonto Fistfight in Heaven*. New York: HarperCollins, 1993.

———. *Smoke Signals: A Screenplay*. New York: Hyperion, 1998.

Deloria, Vine. "Foreword/American Fantasy." *The Pretend Indians: Images of Native Americans in the Movies*, edited by Gretchen M. Bataille and Charles L. P. Silet, ix–xvi. Ames: Iowa State University Press, 1980.

Egan, Timothy. "An Indian Without Reservations." *New York Times Magazine*, January 18, 1998, 17–19.

"Federal Judge Issues Restraining Order at the Request of Senator Tom Daschle." *Morning Edition*. National Public Radio. November 2, 2004. http://www.npr.org/rundowns/rundown.php?prgId=3&prgDate=2-Nov-2004 (accessed November 11, 2004).

Fielding, Julien. "Native American Religion and Film: Interviews with Chris Eyre and Sherman Alexie." *Journal of Religion and Film* 7, no. 1 (2003). http://avalon.unomaha.edu/jrf/Vol7No1/nativefilm.html (accessed July 28, 2004).

Fraser, Joelle. "Sherman Alexie's *Iowa Review* Interview." *Modern American Poetry*, July 20, 2004. www.english.uiuc.edu/maps/poets/.

Gilroy, John Warren. "Another Fine Example of the Oral Tradition? Identification and Subversion in Sherman Alexie's *Smoke Signals*." *Studies in American Indian Literatures: The Journal of the Association for the Study of American Indian Literatures* 13, no.1 (2001): 23–42. http://oncampus.richmond.edu/faculty/ASAIL/SAIL2/131.html (accessed July 28, 2004).

Griffith, James. *Adaptations as Imitations: Films from Novels*. Newark: University of Delaware Press, 1997.

Huhndorf, Shari. *Going Native: Indians in the American Cultural Imagination*. Ithaca: Cornell University Press, 2001.

Kilpatrick, Jacquelyn. *Celluloid Indians: Native Americans and Film.* Lincoln: University of Nebraska Press, 1999.

Krumrey, Diane. "Subverting the Tonto Stereotype in Popular Fiction, Or, Why Indians say 'Ugh!' *Simulacrum American: The USA and the Popular Media.* Edited by Elisabeth Kraus and Carolin Auer, 161–168. Rochester, NY: Camden House, 2000.

Mitchell, Elvis. "A Poet Finds His Past Is Just Where He Left It." *New York Times,* October 18, 2002, 25. http://lexis-nexis.com (accessed July 20, 2004).

Slethaug, Gordon. "Hurricanes and Fires: Chaotics in Sherman Alexie's *Smoke Signals* and *The Lone Ranger and Tonto Fistfight in Heaven*." Literature Film Quarterly 31, no. 2 (2003): 130–140.

Smoke Signals. Film directed by Chris Eyre, with performances by Adam Beach, Evan Adams, Irene Bedard, and Gary Farmer. Miramax, 1998.

Stromberg, Ernest. "Out of the Cupboard and Up with the *Smoke Signals*: Cinematic Representations of American Indians in the Nineties." *Studies in Popular Culture* 24, no. 1 (2001): 33–46. http://pcasacas.org/SPC/ (accessed July 28, 2004).

West, Dennis, and Joan West. "Sending Cinematic Smoke Signals: An Interview with Sherman Alexie." *Cineaste* 24, no. 4 (1998): 28–31.

NOTES ON CONTRIBUTORS

Ernesto R. Acevedo-Muñoz is associate professor of film studies and comparative literature at the University of Colorado at Boulder. He teaches film theory, film and literature, Spanish and Latin American cinemas, classic Hollywood genres, and courses on Luis Buñuel and Pedro Almodóvar, Stanley Kubrick, and Alfred Hitchcock. His work has appeared in *Quarterly Review of Film and Video*, *Film & History*, *LIT*, and various anthologies. He is the author of *Pedro Almodóvar* (BFI, 2007) and of *Buñuel and Mexico: The Crisis of National Cinema* (University of California Press, 2003).

Rebecca Bell-Metereau teaches film studies at Texas State University and directs the Media Studies Minor Program. Her books include *Hollywood Androgyny*, *Simone Weil on Politics*, and *Religion and Society*. Shorter works have been published in anthologies, including *Cinema and Modernity*; *American Cinema of the 1950s*; *Film and Television After 9/11*; *Bad: Infamy, Darkness, Evil and Slime on Screen*; *The Family in America*; *Ladies and Gentlemen, Boys and Girls*; *Writing With*; *Cultural Conflicts in 20th Century Literature*; *Technological Imperatives*; *Women Worldwalkers*; and in scholarly journals, including *College English*, *Quarterly Review of Film and Video*, *Journal of Popular Film & Television*, and *Cinema Journal*.

Mark Berrettini is director of film studies and associate professor of English and film studies at the University of Northern Colorado. His research and publications include work on the representation of nonhuman animals, film noir, and social difference. He is currently at work on a book about Hal Hartley for the University of Illinois Press's Contemporary Film Directors series.

Jack Boozer is a professor in the Department of Communication at Georgia State University in Atlanta, where he has taught film studies, and feature screenwriting, and literature-to-film adaptation for many years. He is the author of *Career Movies: American Business and the Success Mystique* (University of Texas Press, 2002) and numerous articles and chapters in scholarly journals and anthologies. Most recently, his chapter on *To Die For* appeared in *Killing Women: The Visual Culture of Gender and Violence* (Ontario: Wilfred Laurier University Press, 2006). His essay "Movies and the Closing of the Reagan Era" appears in *American Cinema of the 1980s: Themes and Variations*, ed. Stephen Prince (Piscataway, NJ: Rutgers University Press, 2007).

Shelley Cobb is completing her doctoral thesis on the discourse of gender and authorship in fidelity criticism and adaptation studies at the University of East Anglia in Norwich, England, where she has worked as an associate tutor for both the School of Film and Television studies and the School of Literature and Creative Writing. She has presented several conference papers on adaptation, gender, and authorship and has forthcoming articles on Shekhar Kapur's *Elizabeth* (1998) and Jane Campion.

Mark Gallagher is lecturer in the Institute of Film and Television Studies at the University of Nottingham. He is the author of *Action Figures: Men, Action Films, and Contemporary Adventure Narratives* (Palgrave) and is now working on a book on the films of Steven Soderbergh. His work has appeared in *Velvet Light Trap*, *Jump Cut*, the *Quarterly Review of Film and Video*, the *Journal of Popular Film and Television*, and other journals and anthologies.

Albert J. LaValley holds a doctorate in English from Yale (1961), but he started teaching film at Rutgers and at the University of California, Santa Cruz in the late 1960s. He published an early anthology on Hitchcock (1970). He helped to establish the film studies program in the early 1970s at UC Santa Barbara, then moved to Dartmouth (1984), where he did the same, also establishing an independent department of film and television studies. While there he co-edited a book with Barry Scherr, *Eisenstein at 100*. He retired in 2000 but has since taught comparative literature courses at Dartmouth, film and television studies at Oklahoma University in Norman, and occasionally back at Santa Barbara as well.

Thomas Leitch teaches English and directs the Film Studies program at the University of Delaware. His most recent books are *Crime Films*, *Perry Mason*, and *Film Adaptation and Its Discontents: From Gone with the Wind to The Passion of the Christ*.

Cynthia Lucia is assistant professor of English and film studies at Rider University and has served on the editorial board of *Cineaste* for more than a decade. She is the author of *Framing Female Lawyers: Women on Trial in Film* (University of Texas Press, 2005), "Women and the Law: Spectatorship and Resistance in *Female Perversions* and *A Question of Silence*," in *Screen Media and Sexual Politics* (Cambridge: Scholars Press, 2006), "Teaching Nontraditional Hollywood Narrative: *Reversal of Fortune*'s Reversal of Convention," in *Creating Media-Rich Classrooms* (NCTE, 2007), and is co-editing *Blackwell's History of American Film*, a multivolume series forthcoming from Blackwell Publishing.

R. Barton Palmer is Calhoun Lemon Professor of Literature at Clemson University, where he also directs the Film Studies Program. Among his many books on film and film and literature are *Joel and Ethan Cohen* (University of Illinois Press), *Hollywood's Dark Cinema: The American Film Noir* (second revised edition, University of Illinois Press, forthcoming), (with David Boyd) *After Hitchcock: Imitation/Influence/Intertextuality* (University of Texas Press), and *19th and 20th Century American Fiction on Screen* (Cambridge University Press).

Elaine Roth is an associate professor of film studies in the English Department at Indiana University South Bend. She is currently co-editing *Motherhood Misconceived: Maternal Discourse in American Cinema*, a collection of essays on the representation of mothers in American films. Her work has appeared in *Feminist Media Studies*, the *Quarterly Review of Film and Video*, and *Genders*. She teaches courses on film adaptations, screenwriting, women in U.S. film, and U.S. black directors, among others.

Frank P. Tomasulo is professor and director of the BFA Program at the School of Motion Picture, Television, and Recording Arts at Florida State University in Tallahassee. Tomasulo has taught cinema history and theory, as well as film production and screenwriting, at Ithaca College, the University of California–Santa Cruz, Georgia State University, Southern Methodist University, and Florida State University. The author of more than sixty scholarly articles and essays and more than 150 academic papers, Tomasulo has also served as editor of *Journal of Film and Video* (1991–1996) and *Cinema Journal* (1997–2002). His co-edited anthology on screen acting, *More than a Method: Trends and Traditions in Contemporary Film Performance* (2004), was published by Wayne State University Press.

NAME AND TITLE INDEX

//

About a Boy, 257
Action in the North Atlantic, 44
Adair, Gilbert, 207
Adam, Ian, 199
Adams, Evan, 319
Adaptation, 22, 159, 161–178
Adjuster, The, 134
A. I. (Artificial Intelligence), 86
Aldiss, Brian, 104
Aldrich, Robert, 124–125
Alexie, Sherman, 256, 305–324
Allen, Allida, 78
Allen, Jay Presson, 69, 72, 73, 78, 80
Allen, Woody, 267
"Allison," 172
All the President's Men, 232
Alpert, Hollis, 206, 226
Altman, Robert, 4, 28, 126, 313
Amadeus, 17
Anchor Review, 209
Anderson, Maxwell, 78
Anderson, Paul Thomas, 323
Andrew, Dudley, 21, 29, 134, 154, 155, 161, 176, 198
Angels with Dirty Faces, 36
Annaud, Jean-Jacques, 220
Annie Hall, 267, 268
Antonioni, Michelangelo, 95
Apocalypse Now, 22
Appel, Alfred, 225, 226
Aragay, Mireia, 21, 25, 29
Arden, Eve, 54

Aristos, The, 181
Armstrong, Rod, 226
Arthur, Paul, 111, 126
Aryan Papers, The, 86
As You Like It, 187
Auiler, Dan, 77, 78, 82, 84
Austen, Jane, 26, 282, 288, 289, 292, 293, 303
Avengers, The, 229
Aventure Malgache, 64

"Baby Did a Bad, Bad Thing," 98
Bacall, Lauren, 127
Back for Christmas, 81
Backlash, 295
Backstory 4, 109
Bad Company, 26
Bakhtin, M. M., 20, 21, 194, 282
Balcon, Michael, 64
Banks, Caerthan, 137
Banks, Russell, 110, 131, 132, 134, 135, 137, 141, 142, 154, 155
Baracaia, Alexa, 301
Barr, Charles, 71, 78, 81, 82, 83, 84
Barry Lyndon, 86, 87, 104
Barth, John, 181, 184, 199
Barthes, Roland, 20, 29, 259, 274
Basic Instinct, 122
Battle of Algiers, 232
Bauer, Steven, 235
Bazin, André, 14, 15, 23, 28, 29, 134, 154, 161, 162, 168, 175, 176, 300

Beals, Jennifer, 112, 128, 129
Beauty and the Beast, 212
Beck, 172
Beethoven, Ludwig van, 105
Begley, Louis, 104
Being John Malkovich, 168
Belázs, Béla, 175, 176, 178
Belloni, Mario, 105
Benchley, Peter, 18
Bennett, Charles, 64, 67, 80, 81
Benton, Robert, 16, 26
Bergman, Ingmar, 175, 178
Bernstein, Sidney, 72
Best of Everything, The, 45
Bickford, Laura, 230, 231, 249, 250
Big Shot, The, 36
Big Sleep, The, 36, 38, 54, 55, 127
Binns, Ronald, 199
Birds, The, 72, 81, 83
Black, Jack, 262
Blackadder, 302
Black Betty, 128
Black Dahlia, The, 113
Black Elk Speaks, 322
Blackmail, 64
Black Pit, 49
Blade Runner, 126
Bloch, Robert, 34, 64, 65, 77
Blondell, Joan, 36
Blow Up, 95
Blue Dahlia, The, 113
Blues Detective, The, 118
Bluestone, George, 12, 13, 27, 178
Blyth, Ann, 54
Body and Soul, 77
Bogart, Humphrey, 36, 127
Bogle, Donald, 128
Boileau, Pierre, 65
Bolt, Robert, 186
Bonnie and Clyde, 16, 223
Bon Voyage, 64
Boorman, John, 249

Bouzereau, Laurent, 83, 84
Boxer, Barbara, 231
Boyd, Jim, 306
Boyum, Joy Gould, 26
Bramble Bush, The, 74
Brando, Marlon, 12
Brantlinger, Patrick, 199
Breaking Point, The, 39
Breen, Joseph, 27
Bride, The, 128
Bride of Frankenstein, The, 128
Brideshead Revisited, 219
Bridget Jones's Diary, 255, 281–304
Brokeback Mountain, 17
Bronson, Charles, 314, 316, 321
Brown, Dan, 2
Brown, Geoff, 82
Browning, Robert, 137, 140–142, 149–153, 155
"Bulldog Drummond's Baby," 64
Burgess, Anthony, 104
Burks, Jernard, 114
Burwell, Carter, 173
Business of Fancydancing, The, 306, 315, 318, 319
Butterfly, The, 43

Cage, Nicolas, 162, 168
Cain, James M., 33, 35, 36, 39–44, 49, 50, 55, 62
Caine, Sir Hall, 71
Calendar, 134
Camus, Albert, 181
Canby, Peter, 250
Canham, Kingsley, 62
Canning, Victor, 73
Capra, Frank, 11
Cardwell, Sarah, 25
"Career in C Major," 35
Carey, Leo, 105
Carroll, Lewis, 207
Carson, Jack, 47, 54, 59

Carson, Lisa Nicole, 113
Carter, Joelle, 271
Cartmell, Deborah, 25, 154
Carver, Raymond, 313
Casablanca, 36, 39, 46
Cash, Jim, 18
Centennial, 184
Champagne, 75, 81
Champlin, Charles, 81, 84
Chandler, Raymond, 44, 69, 70, 72, 73, 83, 113, 122
Chaplin, Charlie, 207, 208
Chatman, Seymour, 200
Chaykin, Maury, 115
Cheadle, Don, 235
Chinatown, 115, 126, 127
Chretien, Craig, 249
Christensen, Erika, 236, 238
Christie, Julie, 87
Chunguang Zhaxie, 178
Ciment, Michel, 251
Cinema Paradiso, 220
Citizen Kane, 7, 58, 77, 137, 138, 152, 154
City of Quartz, 111
Clarke, Arthur, 6
Clarke, David, 126
Clean Break, 103
Clift, Montgomery, 26
Clockwork Orange, A, 86, 87, 94, 99, 103, 104
Close, Glenn, 293, 294
Cobb, Humphrey, 103
Cocteau, Jean, 212
Coen brothers (Ethan and Joel), 9, 10, 27
Cohen, Keith, 161, 176
Cohen, Philip, 184–185, 200
Cohn, Harry, 11
Cold Mountain, 8
Cole, Lester, 56
Collector, The, 181
Collier, John, 81
Collins, Dale, 81

Connery, Sean, 75
Conrad, Joseph, 22, 178
Conradi, Peter, 197, 200, 201
Cook, David, 28
Cook, Whitfield, 80
Cooper, Chris, 166
Coppel, Alec, 73, 78
Coppola, Francis Ford, 16, 22
Corliss, Richard, 15, 16, 28, 76, 77, 83, 84, 216, 226
Corrigan, Timothy, 25
Corwin, Norman, 56
Costello, Elvis, 172
Cover, Franklin, 127
Coward, Noel, 71
Cox, Brian, 162
Crain, Jeanne, 128
Crawford, Joan, 38, 41, 43, 45, 47, 52, 54, 59–61
Crawley, Budge, 81
Crichton, Michael, 18
Crime and Punishment, 63
Criss Cross, 232, 246
Cronenberg, David, 219
Cronyn, Hume, 64, 72
Crowdus, Gary, 27
Crowther, Bosley, 226
Cruise, Tom, 89, 101
Crying Game, The, 128
Cry Wolf, 48
Curtis, Richard, 282, 284, 286–288, 294, 295, 302, 303
Curtiz, Michael, 46, 47, 52–54, 56, 58, 62
Cusack, Joan, 272
Cusack, John, 26, 255, 258, 259, 262, 269, 277, 279

Dahl, Roald, 81
Daisy Miller, 87
Damned Don't Cry, The, 45
Dances with Wolves, 313, 314
Dandridge, Dorothy, 129

332 INDEX

Dangerous Liaisons, 10, 258
Dark Mirror, The, 38
Dark Passage, 39
Dark Victory, 36
Darling, 87
Darwin, Charles, 166, 177
Davies, Andrew, 282, 284, 286, 288, 291–293, 302
Davies, J. M. Q., 104
Da Vinci Code, The, 2
Davis, Bette, 36, 38, 52
Davis, Mike, 111, 126, 130
Davis, Natalie Zemon, 297
"Dead Melodies," 172
D'entre les morts, 65
Dearden, James, 204
Death in Venice, 207
Death Wish, 321
Decker, Dianna, 215
de Laclos, Choderlos, 10
Deleyto, Celestino, 290, 303
Deloria, Vine, 305, 320
Del Toro, Benicio, 233–235, 241, 250
de Maupassant, Guy, 14
Demme, Jonathan, 8, 159
DeRosa, Steven, 66–68, 74, 78, 82–84
Derrida, Jacques, 20
Desmond, John M., 25
Desperately Seeking Susan, 210
Destination Tokyo, 44, 49
Devil in a Blue Dress, 8, 110, 111–130
DeVincentis, D. V., 255, 258, 263, 277–279
Diabolique, 65
Dial M for Murder, 66, 67
Dip in the Pool, 81
Dirks, Tim, 207, 225, 226
Dispatchers, 85
Dodge, David, 64
Doel, Marcus, 126
Donen, Stanley, 87
Donner, Richard, 122

Dörrie, Doris, 29
Double Indemnity, 33, 35, 36, 39, 40, 44, 46, 52, 114
Douglas, Kirk, 28, 203
Douglas, Michael, 17, 122, 234
Dream Story, 104
Dr. Jekyll and Mr. Hyde, 199
Dr. Strangelove, 86, 103, 104
"Drug Called Tradition, A," 312
du Maurier, Daphne, 33, 66, 71, 81
Duncan, Lindsay, 233

Eastwood, Clint, 23
Easy Virtue, 71
Ebert, Roger, 249
Eckstein, Arthur, 25
Edelstein, David, 249, 278
Egoyan, Atom, 110, 132–134, 136–138, 140, 142, 143, 145, 148–150, 152–155
Eisenstein, Sergei, 188
Ekmark, Rebecca, 304
Elliott, Andrea, 252
Elliott, Kamilla, 3, 25
Ellroy, James, 113, 125–127
Embezzler, The, 39
English Patient, The, 9, 10, 17
Epps, Jack, 18
Erin Brockovich, 232, 251
Eschwege (Lichberg), Heinz von, 208
Evans, David, 277
Evans, Peter William, 290, 303
Exotica, 134
Eyes Wide Open: A Memoir of Stanley Kubrick, 87
Eyes Wide Shut, 26, 34, 85, 88–90, 94, 103, 104
Eyre, Chris, 256, 305, 306, 308, 309

Fallen Angel, 39
Falsetto, Mario, 212, 224, 226, 227
Faludi, Susan, 295
Family Plot, 64, 73

Farewell, My Lovely, 125, 126
Far from the Madding Crowd, 87
Farmer, Gary, 316, 320
Farrell, Glenda, 36
Fatal Attraction, 204, 233, 293, 294
Faulkner, William, 33, 44, 53–56, 133, 154
Ferrer, Miguel, 235
Fever Pitch, 257, 277
Fidelio, 105
Fielding, Helen, 255, 282, 284, 286–289, 293, 295, 302, 303
Fireman's Ball, 17
Firth, Colin, 282, 287, 302
Flamingo Road, 39, 44, 45
Flashdance, 128, 129
Fontaine, Joan, 72
Ford, John, 4, 12, 13
Foreign Correspondent, 64, 81
Forman, Milos, 17
Forster, E. M., 7, 18, 207
Foster, Jodie, 8
Foucault, Michel, 20, 23, 29
Four Weddings and a Funeral, 282, 286, 287, 290
Fowles, John, 159, 179–202
Frank, Jr., Harriet, 10
Frankenheimer, John, 70
Franklin, Carl, 8, 26, 110, 111, 117, 127–130
Frasier, 294
Frazier, Charles, 8
Frears, Stephen, 10, 255, 258, 277, 278
French Connection, The, 232
French Lieutenant's Woman, The, 159, 179–202
Freud, Sigmund, 93, 94, 177
Full Frontal, 232, 322
Full Metal Jacket, 85, 86
Furthman, Jules, 15

Gaghan, Stephen, 160, 231, 232, 249–251
Gale, Steven H., 199

Gallafent, Edward, 126
Galsworthy, John, 66, 71
Georgakas, Dan, 27
George, Nelson, 129
George, Peter, 104
George Washington Slept Here, 44
Gerard, Jasper, 303
Gibson, Mel, 122
Giddings, Robert, 25
Gilda, 39, 266
Giler, David, 28
Gilliat, Sidney, 67, 68
Gilroy, John Warren, 321
Gilroy, Paul, 130
Glatzer, Richard, 27
Gledhill, Christine, 126
Glover, Danny, 122
Godard, Jean-Luc, 14, 15
Godfather, The, 16
Godfather, The: Part II, 16
Golden, Tim, 231, 234, 249
Goldman, Bo, 17
Goldman, William, 6
Gone with the Wind, 67
Good German, The, 232
Gottlieb, Carl, 18
Gough, Evelyn, 304
Grace, Topher, 236
Graham, Bob, 303
Graham, Winston, 65, 78
Grant, Cary, 80
Grant, Hugh, 282, 287, 290, 302
Grapes of Wrath, The, 12
Gray's Anatomy, 232
Greenwood, Bruce, 143
Greer, Germaine, 298, 302, 304
Griffith, D. W., 178, 188
Griffith, James, 319, 323
Grifters, The, 258
Grisham, John, 8
Grist, Leighton, 126
Gruen, Margaret, 53–55

Guzmán, Luis, 235
Gyllenhaal, Maggie, 168
Gypsy Wildcat, 40

Haggis, Paul, 23
Hale, Ellen, 304
Hall, Albert, 118
Hall, Jon, 40
Hall, Willis, 70, 73
Hampton, Christopher, 10
Hanson, Curtis, 125
"Happy Together" (song), 172–173
Happy Together (film), 178
Harder They Fall, The, 11
Hardy, Thomas, 87
Harold and Kumar Go to White Castle, 320
Harper, Phillip Brian, 130
Harris, Bob, 210
Harris, James, 203, 204, 211, 213
Harris, Leon, 127
Harrison, Joan, 71
Hart, Moss, 44
Harwood, Ronald, 18
Hasford, Gustav, 85
Haskell, Molly, 281
Hatch, Orrin, 205
Hathaway, Heather, 128
Hauben, Lawrence, 17
Hawaii, 184
Hawkes, Peter, 25
Hawks, Howard, 15, 55, 127
Hayes, Isaac, 123
Hayes, John Michael, 10, 64, 74
Hearst, William Randolph, 7
Heart of Darkness, 22
Hecht, Ben, 15, 68, 69
Hedren, Tippi, 72, 75
Hemblen, David, 147
Hemingway, Ernest, 69
Hemsley, Sherman, 127
Henley, Barry Shabaka, 130

Hepburn, Katharine, 15
Herr, Michael, 85
Herskovitz, Marshall, 230–232
Hichen, Robert, 69
High Fidelity, 26, 255–279
Highman, Charles, 62
High Sierra, 36
Highsmith, Patricia, 64, 65, 72
Highway 54, 12
Hilderbrand, Lucas, 168, 177
Hill, Rodney, 225, 226
Hill, Walter, 19, 28
Himes, Chester, 122, 129
Hirsch, Foster, 111, 126
Hitchcock, Alfred, 4, 10, 15, 22, 26, 33, 34, 63–96
Hitchcock O'Connell, Patricia, 69, 80, 81, 83, 84
Hoberman, J., 169, 178
Hogan, Michael, 71
Holliday, Judy, 15
Holm, Ian, 138, 146
Homer, 9
Hopkins, Anthony, 8
Hornby, Nick, 255–279
Horne, Lena, 129
Horne, William, 26
Horton, Andrew S., 28, 249
Hot Pants College II, 207
Howard, Ron, 3
Howard, Sidney, 67
Howard's End, 9, 10
How to Be Good, 257
Hudson, Rock, 313
Huhndorf, Shari, 321
Humoresque, 45
Hunter, Evan, 67–69, 72–74, 78, 82, 83
Hussain, Talat, 233
Huston, John, 121
Hutcheon, Linda, 184, 199

If He Hollers Let Him Go, 129

I ♥ Huckabees, 323
Independent, The, 282
Indian Killer, 306
Irons, Jeremy, 189, 191, 201, 217, 219, 220
Isaak, Chris, 98
Ivory, James, 7, 9, 18
I Would Steal Horses, 306

Jahan, Ismat Shah, 237
Jamaica Inn, 80, 81
James, Henry, 7, 87, 193
James, Joy, 128
Jameson, Fredric, 122, 130
Jaws, 18
Jeffersons, The, 127
Jenkins, Greg, 104
Jesse James, 27
Jesus' Son, 313
Jhabvala, Ruth Prawer, 7, 9, 18, 26
Johnny Belinda, 44
Johnson, Denis, 313
Johnson, Diane, 104
Johnson, Malcolm, 12
Johnson, Nunnally, 12, 27
Jones, Kent, 178
Jones, Nathaniel, 178
Jonze, Spike, 159, 161, 162, 168, 173
Joyce, James, 44
Jules and Jim, 14
Juno and the Paycock, 66, 71, 76, 80
Jurassic Park, 18

Kafka, 232
Kanin, Garson, 15
Kapsis, Robert E., 80, 84
Kar-wai, Wong, 178
Kauffmann, Stanley, 225
Kaufman, Anthony, 251
Kaufman, Charlie (and "Donald"), 159, 161–178
Kaufman, George S., 44

Kawin, Bruce, 131, 133, 135, 151, 154, 155, 177
Kazan, Elia, 12
Kelly, Grace, 80
Keon, Barbara, 73
Kesey, Ken, 17, 28
Kidman, Nicole, 89
Killing, The, 103
Kilmer, Val, 313
Kilpatrick, Jacqueline, 320
King, Rodney, 126
King, Stephen, 104
King of the Hill, 232
Kingsolver, Barbara, 322
Kinney, Terry, 112
Kiss Me Deadly, 124
Klute, 126
Knowles, Joanne, 261–263, 269, 275, 276, 278, 279
Kohner, Susan, 128
Kozloff, Sarah, 155
Kristeva, Julia, 20, 301
Krohn, Bill, 63, 79, 82, 84
Krumrey, Diane, 316, 322
Krutnik, Frank, 290, 303
Kubrick, Stanley, 6, 22, 34, 85–108, 142, 160, 203–206, 209–225
Kukura, George, 241
Kurosawa, Akira, 152, 154
Kwientiowski, Richard, 207

Lacan, Jacques, 20
L.A. Confidential, 125
Lady Vanishes, The, 67, 68, 80
Langella, Frank, 220
La Ronde, 86
Latimore, Joseph, 115
Launder, Frank, 67, 68
Laura, 36, 38
Laurents, Arthur, 82
LaValley, Albert, 27, 62
Lawrence, D. H., 44

Lazere, Arthur, 168
Lee, Ang, 10, 26
Leff, Leonard J., 72, 83
Lehman, Ernest, 64, 73, 74
Leitch, Thomas, 28
Lem, Stanislaw, 232
Lester, Richard, 249
Lethal Weapon (trilogy), 122
Lévi-Strauss, Claude, 19
Lewis, D. B. Wyndham, 81
Lifeboat, 69, 81
Limey, The, 245, 249, 251
Lion, Leon M., 66
Lippmann, Walter, 40
Little Big Man, 313, 314
Little Caesar, 36
Lodger, The, 71, 73
Lolita, 86, 94, 104, 142, 160, 203–228
Lone Ranger and Tonto Fistfight in Heaven, The, 305, 306, 309, 315, 316, 318, 319, 321
Long Goodbye, The, 126
Long Hot Summer, The, 44
Long Way Down, A, 257
Loretta Young Show, The, 213
Lorsch, Susan E., 201
Love Actually, 287
Love and Death on Long Island, 207
Lovell, Terry, 198
Lover, The, 220
Love Story, 181, 182
Lubbock, Percy, 193, 200
Lubitsch, Ernst, 15
Lucas, George, 107
Lucia, Cynthia, 26
Lumet, Sidney, 70
Lupino, Ida, 36
Lyman, Rick, 249, 250
Lyne, Adrianne, 160, 203–205, 216–225
Lyon, Sue, 206, 213, 216, 219

MacCabe, Colin, 194, 195, 196, 202
MacDonald, Philip, 71
MacDougall, Ranald, 33, 46, 47, 53–59, 61
Maclean, Alison, 313
MacPhail, Angus, 64, 66, 68, 74, 78
Madden, David, 62
Magretta, Joan, 28
Maguire, Sharon, 255, 282, 284–286, 295, 302
Mailer, Norman, 175, 178
Maltese Falcon, The, 36, 38, 121
Maltz, Albert, 47, 49, 50, 51
Mamet, David, 204
Man Behind the Gun, The, 56
Man Called Horse, A, 313
Man I Love, The, 48
Mankiewicz, Herman, 7, 26, 77
Mann, Anthony, 15
Manpower, 44
Man Who Came to Dinner, The, 44
Man Who Knew Too Much, The, 64, 66, 68, 74, 81
Manxman, The, 71
Markle, Fletcher, 81
Marnie, 72–74, 78, 80
Marr, Michael, 208, 226
Marshall, George, 113
Masculine-Feminine, 14
Mason, James, 205, 206, 213, 220
Mason, Jr., Theodore O., 129
Masterpiece Theatre, 179, 250
M. Butterfly, 219
McCamus, Tom, 140
McCarthy, Margaret, 28
McDougal, Stuart, 249
McDowell, Andie, 290
McFarlane, Brian, 25, 161, 176
McGilligan, Patrick, 19, 25, 26, 28, 69, 80, 82–84, 109
McKee, Robert, 163, 165–168, 176, 177
McMurphy, Randall P., 28
McMurray, Lillita (Lolita), 208

McMurtry, Larry, 17, 322
McRobbie, Angela, 301
Meeker, Ralph, 125
Mencken, H. L., 40
Merchant, Ismael, 7, 9
Merry-Go-Round, 50
Metz, Christian, 19
Michener, James, 184
Mildred Pierce, 27, 33, 35–62
Milian, Tomás, 234
Miller, Toby, 29
Million Dollar Baby, 23
Mineo, Sal, 316
Minghella, Anthony, 8–10, 26
Mitchell, Elvis, 323
Modleski, Tania, 288, 302
Mona Lisa, 128
Money and the Woman, 39
Montagu, Ivor, 71
Montez, Maria, 40
Moon Is Blue, The, 27
Moore, Brian, 70, 72, 73
Moral, Tony Lee, 82
Morgenstern, Stephanie, 139
Morricone, Andrea, 220
Morricone, Ennio, 220
Mosley, Walter, 110, 112, 115, 127–129
Mountain Eagle, The, 80, 81
Mr. and Mrs. Smith, 81
Mrs. Bisby and the Colonel's Coat, 81
Murder!, 80, 81
Murdoch, Iris, 87, 181
My Beautiful Laundrette, 258
Myles, Lynda, 107
My Reputation, 48, 52

Nabokov, Vladimir, 70, 104, 142, 160, 203–207, 209–227
Narcejac, Thomas, 65
Naremore, James, 25, 126, 207, 226
Neale, Stephen, 278
Neihardt, John, 322

Neill, Roy William, 67, 68
Newman, David, 16, 26
Nicholson, Jack, 28
Niemi, Robert, 135, 154, 155
Niogret, Hubert, 251
Niven, David, 213
No Bail for the Judge, 74
Nochimson, Martha, 105
North by Northwest, 64, 73, 81
Notorious, 79, 81
Notting Hill, 282, 286, 287
Now, Voyager, 36, 38, 45
Number Seventeen, 66, 80
NYPD Blue, 250

Oates, Joyce Carol, 35, 41, 61, 62
Objective Burma, 44, 56
Oboler, Arch, 56
O Brother, Where Art Thou?, 9, 10
O'Casey, Sean, 66, 71
Ocean's Eleven, 232, 244, 246, 322
Odyssey, The, 9, 10
Of Human Bondage, 48
Old Maid, The, 36
Olivier, Laurence, 213
Ondaatje, Michael, 9
One False Move, 117, 127
One Flew Over the Cuckoo's Nest, 17, 18
One More Tomorrow, 48
On the Waterfront, 12
Ophuls, Max, 86
Orchid Thief, The, 159, 161–178
Orlean, Susan, 159, 161–178
Ormond, Julia, 236
Ormonde, Czenzi, 69, 72, 73
Ossana, Diana, 17
Outer Limits, The, 68
Out of Sight, 232, 245, 251

Pabst, G. W., 104
Padilla, Marisol, 238
Pakula, Alan, 126

Paradine Case, The, 69, 70, 80
Parks, Gordon, 123
Passage to Marseille, 39
Paterson, Bill, 233
Paths of Glory, 86, 103, 203
Peace on Earth, 49–52
Pelican Brief, The, 8
Penn, Arthur, 16, 223
Peyton Place, 44
Phillips, Gene D., 104, 106, 225, 226
Pianist, The, 18
"Pied Piper of Hamelin, The," 137, 140, 149, 151–153, 155
Pierson, Louise Randall, 53, 58
Pink, Steve, 258, 277, 279
Pinter, Harold, 159, 181, 186, 188–192, 196–199, 204
Player, The, 28
Pleasure Garden, The, 80
Pocahontas, 321
Poe, Edgar Allan, 208
Polanski, Roman, 19, 126, 127
Polley, Sarah, 139, 140
Pollack, Sydney, 89, 95, 96, 101
Polonsky, Abraham, 77
Portnoy, Kenneth, 25
Possessed, 39, 45, 61
Postman Always Rings Twice, The, 35, 39, 40, 42, 125
Practice, The, 250
Pratley, Gerald, 81
Pride and Prejudice, 282, 286, 288, 289, 291–293, 303
Pride of the Marines, 44, 49
Proffer, Carl, 209
Projansky, Sarah, 301
Proulx, E. Annie, 17
Psycho, 34, 64, 65, 68, 72, 75–77
Public Enemy, The, 36
Punch Drunk Love, 323
Puzo, Mario, 16
Pye, Michael, 107

Quaid, Dennis, 235
Queen, The, 258
Queen Bee, 61

Raeburn, John, 27
Raengo, Alessandra, 25
Rafael, Fredric, 26, 34
Rafelson, Bob, 125
Raima, Sam, 18
Rainbird Pattern, The, 73
Raphael, Frederic, 87, 88–90, 94, 95, 98, 99, 103, 105, 106
Raphaelson, Samson, 15
Rashomon (and effect), 132, 137, 138, 152, 154
Ravetch, Irving, 10
Raza, Son of Cochise, 313
Read, Sir Herbert, 175, 178
Rear Window, 64, 67
Rebecca, 26, 33, 66, 71–73, 75, 80, 81
Rebello, Stephen, 77, 84
Red Alert, 104
Redelings, Lowell E., 62
Red Shoe Diaries, The, 204
Reid, Alistair, 229, 251
Reisz, Karel, 159, 180, 181, 186, 187, 189, 190, 192, 196, 197–199
Reservation Blues, 306
Reville, Alma, 69, 71, 80, 81
Rhapsody: A Dream Novel, 86
Rich, B. Ruby, 111, 127
Rich and Strange, 80, 81
Richards, Dick, 125, 126
Ring, The, 64, 81, 82
Ritt, Martin, 10
Roaring Twenties, The, 36, 44
Robbins, Tim, 265
Roberts, Julia, 8
Robertson, Peggy, 80
Roche, Henri-Pierre, 14
Rocky and Bullwinkle, 219
Rogers, Ginger, 36

Roker, Roxie, 127
Rolling Stones, The, 172
Room with a View, A, 18
Rope, 64, 72
Rose, Charlie, 134
Rose, Gabrielle, 143
Rosenberg, Scott, 277, 279
Rothblatt, Sheldon, 199
Roughly Speaking, 38, 58
Roundtree, Richard, 123
Rowe, Kathleen, 294, 297, 298, 303, 304
Run of the Arrow, 321
Russell, David O., 323
Russell, Francis, 205, 225
Russell, Rosalind, 38
Ryan, Meg, 302, 304

Sabotage, 80
Saboteur, 66, 81
Sachs, Susan, 252
Said, Edward, 246, 251
Saint, The, 230
Salamon, Julie, 250
Salber, Cecilia, 302
Salinger, J. D., 276
Sarris, Andrew, 15, 76, 77, 84
Satyricon, 205
Schatz, Thomas, 11, 27
Schiff, Stephen, 204, 207, 220, 225, 226
Schindler's List, 18, 86
Schinnerer, Otto P., 86
Schizopolis, 245, 249, 322
Schlesinger, John, 87
Schnitzler, Arthur, 85–87, 90, 93–95, 98, 99, 103–105
Scholes, Robert, 199
Schrader, Paul, 39, 61
Schulberg, Budd, 11, 12
Scott, Tony, 18
Scott, Zachary, 45, 54, 59
Searchers, The, 321
Secret Agent, 80

Segal, Erich, 181, 182
Segers, Linda, 25
Seidelman, Susan, 210
Sellers, Peter, 205, 214, 216, 220
Selznick, David, 11, 26, 33, 66, 68, 69, 71, 72, 74, 83
Sense and Sensibility, 10, 26
Sentinel, The, 6
Serenade, 42
Severed Head, A, 87
sex, lies, and videotape, 232, 245
Seymour, Cara, 167
Shadow of a Doubt, 69, 80, 81
Shaft, 123
Shah, Jamal, 230, 233
Shakespeare, William, 187
Shchyogolev, Boris Ivanovich, 209
Sheen, Erica, 25
Shelley, Mary, 207
Sheridan, Ann, 36
Sherwood, Robert, 71
Shining, The, 86, 94, 104
Shipton, Susan, 133
Short, Elizabeth, 113
Short Cuts, 313
Short-Timers, The, 85, 104
Siegel, Don, 70
Silence of the Lambs, The, 8
Simonetti, Marie-Claire, 199
Simpson, Helen, 81
Sizemore, Tom, 112
Skala, Lilia, 128
Skin Game, The, 66, 71, 80
Sklar, George, 49
Skradol, Natalia, 177
Slethaug, Gordon, 317, 322
Smoke Signals, 256, 305–324
Smoke Signals: A Screenplay, 308, 318
Snead, James, 130
Soderbergh, Steven, 109, 160, 229–232, 235, 237, 239, 241, 244–246, 248–251, 322

Soitos, Stephen, 118, 121, 129, 130
Solaris, 232, 244, 246
Sollors, Werner, 128
Sons and Lovers, 44
Sound and the Fury, The, 44, 133
Southern, Terry, 104
Spartacus, 203
Speaking Parts, 134
Spellbound, 38, 64, 68, 81
Spicer, Andrew, 302
Spider-Man, 18
Spielberg, Steven, 18, 86
Spirit: Stallion of the Cimarron, 321
Spoto, Donald, 82
Stagecoach, 313
Stage Fright, 80
Stam, Robert, 3, 20, 21, 24, 25, 29, 201, 203, 205, 206, 211, 212, 216, 223, 225, 226, 264, 278, 282, 283, 301
Stamp, Terence, 249
Stanley Kubrick: A Life in Pictures, 89
Stannard, Eliot, 64, 71
Stanwyck, Barbara, 36, 114
Starsky and Hutch, 129
Star Trek: The Motion Picture, 25
Stefano, Joseph, 34, 68, 72, 74, 78, 82
Steiger, Rod, 12
Steinbeck, John, 13, 69
Stella Dallas, 36
Stempel, Tom, 7, 12, 25–27
Stewart, Donald Ogden, 77
Stewart, Jimmy, 26
Stine, Whitney, 62
Sting, 128
Stoker, Bram, 207
Stolen Life, A, 48, 52
Stone, Marianne, 219
Story, 163, 164
Story, Jack Trevor, 64, 65
Stovin, Jerry, 215
Strangers on a Train, 64, 69, 70, 72, 80, 82

Strange Love of Martha Ivers, The, 39
Streep, Meryl, 166, 189, 201
Stringer-Hye, Suellen, 207, 225, 226
Stromberg, Ernest, 317, 322
Sturges, Preston, 10
Sullivan's Travels, 10
"Super-Toys All Summer Long," 104
Suspicion, 68, 80
Swain, Dominique, 219, 220
Sweet Hereafter, 110, 131–155
Swinton, Tilda, 163
Szpilman, Wladyslaw, 19

Tabori, George, 74
Tall Guy, The, 286
Tambling, Jeremy, 178
Tarkovsky, Andrei, 232
Tasker, Yvonne, 129
Taylor, John Russell, 74, 82
Taylor, Samuel, 64, 67, 73, 78, 82
Thackeray, 87
Thalberg, Irving, 11
They Drive by Night, 36, 44
They Made Me a Criminal, 36
39 Steps, The, 80
"This Is What It Means to Say Phoenix, Arizona," 307
Thompson, David, 62
Thompson, Emma, 10, 26
Thompson, Jim, 103
Thomson, David, 45
Thorpe, Vanessa, 302
Thunderheart, 313
Tibbetts, John C., 25
To Catch a Thief, 64, 80
To Die For, 22
To Have and Have Not, 39, 55, 127
Toland, Gregg, 12
Tomasulo, Frank P., 29
Topaz, 64, 70
Top Gun, 18
Tornatore, Giuseppe, 220

Torn Curtain, 70, 72, 73, 75, 81
Torrid Zone, 44
Toughest Indian in the World, The, 321
Towne, Robert, 157
Tracy, Spencer, 15
Traffic, 160, 229–252
Traumnovelle, 85–87, 94, 104, 105
Trouble with Harry, The, 64, 65, 82
Truffaut, François, 14, 15, 65, 71, 73–75, 82, 83
Turczyn, Coury, 225
Turney, Catherine, 46–54, 57, 58, 62
Turtles, The, 172, 173
Twain, Mark, 276–277
Two and a Half Weeks, 223
Two for the Road, 87
2001: A Space Odyssey, 94, 103

Ulysses, 44
Unbearable Lightness of Being, The, 17
Under Capricorn, 64, 72, 81
Underneath, The, 232, 244, 246
Unsuspected, The, 39

Vargas, Jacob, 237
Verhoeven, Paul, 122
Vertigo, 64, 67, 73, 78
Vincendeau, Ginette, 25
Vineberg, Steve, 250
Viner, Katharine, 299, 304

Wagner, Geoffrey, 26
Wald, Jerry, 27, 33, 35–37, 43–47, 49–54, 56, 57, 62
Walter, Natasha, 299
Waltzes from Vienna, 80
Wartime Lies, 104
Washington, Denzel, 8, 112, 119
Waterhouse, Keith, 70, 73
Waxman, Sharon, 249
Wayne, John, 314
Weinraub, Bernard, 105

Welch, James M., 25
Weld, William, 231
Welles, Orson, 7, 26, 56, 134, 152, 154
West, Dennis and Joan, 307, 320–322
West, Nathanael, 42
Wet Saturday, 81
Whall, Tony, 192, 193, 201
Wheel Spins, The, 67
Whelehan, Imelda, 25, 154, 155
White, Ethel Lina, 67
White, Lionel, 103
White Butterfly, 128
Whitmore, Edward Jay, 25
"Widower, The," 105
Wilder, Billy, 40, 44, 45
Wilder, Thornton, 69
"Wild Horses," 172
Williams, Cynda, 127
Williamson, Thames, 46, 47
Willingham, Calder, 103, 213
Winkler, Mel, 119
Winters, Shelley, 214–216
Wise, Robert, 11, 25, 27
Wizard of Oz, The, 166, 219
Wood, Gaby, 302
Wood, Natalie, 316
Wood, Robin, 270, 279
Wrong Man, The, 64, 74
Wyatt, Edward, 302

Yonay, Ehud, 18
Young and Innocent, 80

Z, 232
Zacharek, Stephanie, 261, 278, 304
Zaentz, Saul, 17
Zaillian, Steven, 18
Zanuck, Darryl, 12, 27
Zellweger, Renée, 8, 281, 285, 295, 298, 299, 304
Zeta-Jones, Catherine, 235
Zwick, Edward, 230–232, 246